P9-BID-829

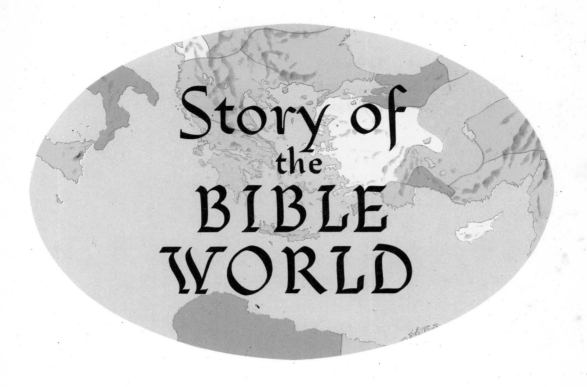

Story of the BIBLE WORLD

IN MAP, WORD and PICTURE

by

NELSON BEECHER KEYES

C. S. HAMMOND & COMPANY

MAPLEWOOD, N. J.   NEW YORK   CHICAGO   LOS ANGELES

©ENTIRE CONTENTS COPYRIGHTED MCMLIX
BY
C. S. HAMMOND & CO., INC.
PRINTED IN THE UNITED STATES OF AMERICA
Reproduction in whole or in part prohibited by the Publishers

Preface and Dedication

It is a challenge to every new generation to reassess the meaning of its great spiritual heritage. During the last five decades, our knowledge of the background of the Bible has tremendously increased. This wealth of information gathered together by historians, archaeologists and other scholars permits a reappraisal and retelling of the Bible Story with an accuracy not possible in earlier times.

These new findings may be used in various ways. The present book endeavors to increase our sense of the reality of Biblical times and peoples so that we may understand more fully the great Story. This approach seems of particular interest in this age of mechanization, when technical devices often replace our contact with reality. The attempt has therefore been made here to assemble achievements of modern research, modern map making and photography in such a way as to transmit a feeling of the vitality and strength of another age. It remains for the reader to judge how far this task has been accomplished.

Nelson Beecher Keyes has written the text with the vigor and immediacy which distinguishes his style. He has not been permitted to live to see this book in print. It represents the culmination and fulfillment of his creative effort, and the Publishers wish to dedicate it to his memory.

List of Chapters

		PAGE
	Of Peoples, Pharaohs and Prophets—Biblical Time Chart	7-13
I.	The Land of Palestine	14
II.	The Family of Nations	19
III.	Abraham, Isaac and Jacob	23
IV.	Life in Ancient Canaan	31
V.	The Route and Times of the Exodus	36
VI.	Israel Invades the Promised Land	42
VII.	The Founding of the Kingdom	47
VIII.	Israel's Golden Age	52
IX.	The Two Kingdoms	60
X.	The Syrian Invasions	65
XI.	Prosperity Turns to Disaster	70
XII.	The First Great World Crisis	75
XIII.	The Final Years of Judah	82
XIV.	A Pawn in a Pagan World	88
XV.	The Restoration of Judah	94
XVI.	The Grecian Era	99
XVII.	The Age of the Holy Warriors	105
XVIII.	The Glory That Was Rome	112
XIX.	In the Days of Herod the Great	116
XX.	Unto Us a Child is Born	122
XXI.	In the Footsteps of Jesus	129
XXII.	The First Christian Missionaries	135
XXIII.	Paul's First and Second Missionary Journeys	140
XXIV.	Paul's Latter Journey and Trip to Rome	144
XXV.	Herod, Who Persecuted the Church	148
XXVI.	The Closing Days of Bible Times	153
XXVII.	The Final Triumph of Rome over the Jews	158
XXVIII.	The Growth of Christianity	163
XXIX.	Ancient Jerusalem	170
XXX.	The Bible Lands Today	176
	Subject Index	191

List of Maps

PAGE

Physical Map of the Holy Land 16
The Nations According to Genesis 10 20
The Biblical World at the Time of the Patriarchs
     (2000-1600 B.C.) 25
Canaan Before the Conquest 32
The Route of the Exodus and the Conquest of Canaan . . 40
Canaan as Divided Among the Twelve Tribes
     (c. 1200-1020 B.C.) 44
The Kingdom of Saul (c. 1020-1000 B.C.) . . . 48
The Empire of David and Solomon (c. 1000-925 B.C.) . . 53
The Kingdoms of Israel and Judah (c. 925-842 B.C.) . . 61
Israel and Judah at the Time of the Syrian Conquests
     (c. 840-800 B.C.) 68
Israel and Judah at the Time of Jeroboam II
     (c. 785-745 B.C.) 72
The Assyrian Empire (824-625 B.C.) 77
Judah After the Fall of Israel (c. 700 B.C.) 84
Great Empires of the Sixth Century B.C. 89
The Restoration of Judah (c. 445 B.C.) 96
The Empire of Alexander the Great (323 B.C.)
     and the Kingdoms of Alexander's Successors (c. 305 B.C.) 101
Palestine Under the Maccabees (166 to 63 B.C.) . . . 109
The Roman World in the Time of Caesar (60-44 B.C.) . . 113
The Dominions of Herod the Great (37 to 4 B.C.) . . 117
Palestine in the Time of Christ 124
The Journeys of Christ
     a. Early Journeys b. Galilean Ministry c. Later Ministry 133
The Journeys of the Apostles 136
St. Paul's First and Second Journeys 140
St. Paul's Third Journey and His Journey to Rome . . 144
Dominions of Herod Agrippa I (37-44 A.D.) . . . 149
Palestine at the Time of the Jewish-Roman War (66-73 A.D.) . 156
The Roman Empire at its Greatest Extent (c. 117 A.D.) . 160
The Spread of Christianity 164
Ancient Jerusalem
     a. The City of David (c. 1000 B.C.)
     b. Temple Area of Jerusalem as Built by Solomon
     c. Jerusalem Under Nehemiah (c. 445 B.C.)
     d. Jerusalem in New Testament Times (20 B.C.-70 A.D.) 173
The Holy Land Today 177
Geographic Index 185

PICTURE CREDITS

Page No.	
11, 15	Jordan Tourist Attaché, N.Y.
17	U. S. Air Force Photo
18	Philip Gendreau
19	Davies, "Ancient Egyptian Wall Painting" Pl. LI
21	Lepsius, "Denkmaeler," Part 3, Pl. 40
22	University Museum, Philadelphia
23, 24	Oriental Inst., Univ. Chicago
26	Egyptian State Tourist Admin.
27	TWA—Trans World Airlines
28	Metropolitan Museum of Art
29	TWA—Trans World Airlines
31	Religious News Service
33	Palestine Exploration Fund Annual
35 (top)	Davies, "Ancient Egyptian Wall Paintings," Pl. X and XI
35	American Schools of Oriental Research
36, 37	Oriental Inst., Univ. Chicago
39	Egyptian State Tourist Admin.
41	Jordan Tourist Attaché, N.Y.
42	TWA—Trans World Airlines
43	Palestine Exploration Fund Annual
45	Jewish Museum, N.Y.—Frank J. Darmstaedter Photo
46	Bonfils
47	Oriental Inst., Univ. Chicago
49	Francis Jenkins Olcott
50, 51, 52	Jordan Tourist Attaché, N.Y.
54	Religious News Service
57	Jordan Tourist Attaché, N.Y.
58, 60	Oriental Inst., Univ. Chicago
62	Palestine Exploration Fund Annual
63	Frederick G. Clapp
64	Palestine Exploration Fund Annual
65	Oriental Inst., Univ. Chicago
66	Philip Gendreau
69	Metropolitan Museum of Art
70, 71, 73	Jordan Tourist Attaché, N.Y.
74, 75	Metropolitan Museum of Art
75 (top)	Oriental Inst., Univ. Chicago
76	Metropolitan Museum of Art
78, 79	Oriental Inst., Univ. Chicago
80, 81, 82, 83	Metropolitan Museum of Art
85	Frederick G. Clapp
87	Jordan Tourist Attaché, N.Y.
88, 91, 92, 93, 94	Oriental Inst., Univ. Chicago
97	New York Public Library
98	Oriental Inst., Univ. Chicago
98 (lower right)	Jewish Museum, N.Y.—Frank J. Darmstaedter Photo
99, 100	Royal Greek Embassy, Washington, D.C.
100 (lower right)	Oriental Inst., Univ. Chicago
102	Metropolitan Museum of Art
102 (lower left)	Volunteer Air Reserve Training Squadron
103	Oriental Inst., Univ. of Chicago
104	Metropolitan Museum of Art
105	Miriam Schloessinger, N.Y.— Frank J. Darmstaedter Photo
106, 107	Palestine Exploration Fund Quarterly
107 (upper right)	Jewish Museum, N.Y.—Frank J. Darmstaedter Photo
108	Oriental Inst., Univ. Chicago
110	Jewish Museum, N.Y.—Frank J. Darmstaedter Photo
111	Hebrew University, Jerusalem
116	Frederick G. Clapp, Photo
118	Harvard Theological Review
120, 121	Jordan Tourist Attaché, N.Y.
122	U.S. Air Force Photo
123, 125	Jordan Tourist Attaché, N.Y.
126	Philip Gendreau
128, 129	TWA—Trans World Airlines
130, 131, 132	Jordan Tourist Attaché, N.Y.
132 (lower right)	TWA—Trans World Airlines
134, 137	Jordan Tourist Attaché, N.Y.
138	Religious News Service
139	Arab Information Center
141	Bonfils
142	New York Public Library
143	TWA—Trans World Airlines
145	Italian State Tourist Office, N.Y.
146	U.S. Army Photo
148, 151	Jordan Tourist Attaché, N.Y.
152	Israel Government Tourist Office, N.Y.
154	Sukenik, "Ancient Synagogues in Palestine and Greece," Pl. XVI:A
155	TWA—Trans World Airlines
157	Israel Government Tourist Office, N.Y.
159	Italian State Tourist Office, N.Y.
161	Jewish Museum, N.Y.—Frank J. Darmstaedter Photo
162	U.A.R. Consulate, N.Y.
163	Metropolitan Museum of Art
165	Italian State Tourist Office
166	TWA—Trans World Airlines
167	Metropolitan Museum of Art
168	U.A.R. Consulate, N.Y.
169	American Schools of Oriental Research
170	Jordan Tourist Attaché, N.Y.
171	TWA—Trans World Airlines
172	Israel Government Tourist Office, N.Y.
174	Jordan Tourist Attaché, N.Y.
175	Bonfils
176	Israel Government Tourist Office, N.Y.
178, 179, 180	Philip Gendreau
181	U.S. Air Force Photo
182	TWA—Trans World Airlines
183	Jordan Tourist Attaché, N.Y.

Of Peoples Pharaohs and Prophets

Those of us who are familiar with the Bible probably have a vague recollection of the Philistines and their clash with Samson and David. Beyond that, what do we know of these "Peoples of the Sea"—where was their original homeland and at what time did they invade Canaan? Many may remember the episode of Israelite bondage in Egypt under a Pharaoh who "knew not Joseph," but how many know the historical background of that enslavement? Who was this Pharaoh and what was the reason for the change in the treatment of the children of Israel who dwelt in the land of the Nile? During another period of captivity, that in Babylon under the Chaldaeans, the prophet Daniel revealed the meaning of the handwriting on the wall, and that night an empire was overthrown. How was Babylon captured, and what have archaeologists and historians to add to the brief statements in the Book of Daniel? And of the Holy City of Jerusalem itself, what was the extent of the City of David, where was Solomon's Temple, and what is known of the city of Jesus' day? The answers to questions like these, even if they are sometimes incomplete, will increase our knowledge about the land and the times and will help us to understand better the dramatic events recorded in the Bible.

To this end, the reader may first broaden his viewpoint by becoming aware of the countless political and cultural upheavals that influenced both directly and indirectly much of what took place in the Holy Land. But a mere chronicling of kings and kingdoms, princes and provinces, tributes and tribunals would present a distorted picture. The peoples and the way they lived must be recorded also. Nor should the continuous flow of history, both secular and sacred, be reduced to convenient static periods or individual events isolated

from the main stream of time. With this in mind, the rich historical background has been sketched in this book with words or presented in map form with occasional glimpses at what was going on beyond the bounds of Palestine, to note the emergence of a new empire such as that of Rome or the decline of an older empire like that of Assyria.

To further aid in restoring the dimension of time, the editors have prepared a time chart of Bible history. This chart, to be found on the following pages, traces the progress of nations and peoples of the Bible from the last years of the Stone Age through to the times of the early Christian Church. The dates of important events and persons, along with helpful illustrations, are placed next to the colored column representing a specific people. The early periods of a people's history, when they have not yet achieved national status, are shown by a lighter shade of color. In times when political control passes to a conquering nation, the same lighter shade of color appears enclosed in bands of the color of the ruling power. When a nation disappears from the stage of world affairs, or more accurately, when its peoples no longer retain their separate political or cultural individualities, the column merges into that of the conquering group. Changes due to territorial expansion or decline are indicated by the varying width of the colored column. Although the widths of the columns only approximate the territory held by a nation, they do serve to give a graphic picture of each nation's importance in the ancient world.

What, then, is the historical pattern that our chart unfolds? Starting with those two centers of ancient civilization, Egypt and Babylonia, we can see the development of powerful kingdoms while the Hebrews were still a wandering pastoral people. A look at another part
(Continued on page 10)

TIME CHART OF BIBLE HISTORY

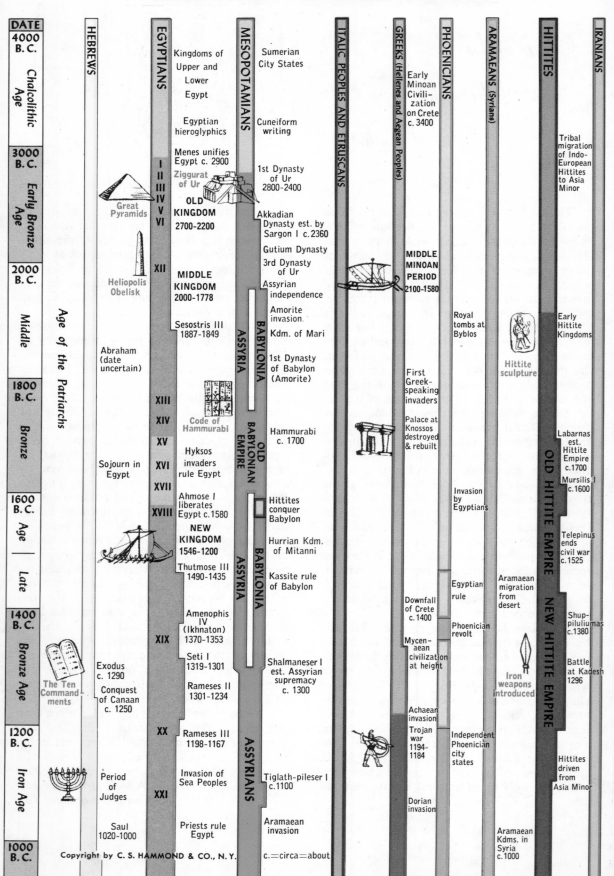

DATE	HEBREWS	EGYPTIANS	MESOPOTAMIANS	ITALIC PEOPLES AND ETRUSCANS	GREEKS (Hellenes and Aegean Peoples)	PHOENICIANS	ARAMAEANS (Syrians)	HITTITES	IRANIANS
4000 B.C. — Chalcolithic Age		Kingdoms of Upper and Lower Egypt; Egyptian hieroglyphics	Sumerian City States; Cuneiform writing		Early Minoan Civilization on Crete c. 3400			Tribal migration of Indo-European Hittites to Asia Minor	
3000 B.C. — Early Bronze Age		I II III IV V VI — Menes unifies Egypt c. 2900; Great Pyramids; Ziggurat of Ur; OLD KINGDOM 2700-2200; Heliopolis Obelisk	1st Dynasty of Ur 2800-2400; Akkadian Dynasty est. by Sargon I c. 2360; Gutium Dynasty; 3rd Dynasty of Ur		MIDDLE MINOAN PERIOD 2100-1580				
2000 B.C. — Middle	Age of the Patriarchs; Abraham (date uncertain)	XII — MIDDLE KINGDOM 2000-1778; Sesostris III 1887-1849	ASSYRIA / BABYLONIA; Assyrian independence; Amorite invasion; Kdm. of Mari; 1st Dynasty of Babylon (Amorite)			Royal tombs at Byblos	Hittite sculpture	Early Hittite Kingdoms	
1800 B.C. — Bronze	Sojourn in Egypt	XIII XIV XV — Code of Hammurabi; Hyksos invaders rule Egypt; XVI XVII	OLD BABYLONIAN EMPIRE; Hammurabi c. 1700		First Greek-speaking invaders; Palace at Knossos destroyed & rebuilt			Labarnas est. Hittite Empire c.1700; Mursilis I c.1600	
1600 B.C. — Age / Late		XVIII — Ahmose I liberates Egypt c.1580; NEW KINGDOM 1546-1200; Thutmose III 1490-1435	Hittites conquer Babylon; Hurrian Kdm. of Mitanni; BABYLONIA; Kassite rule of Babylon; ASSYRIA		Invasion by Egyptians; Downfall of Crete c. 1400	Egyptian rule; Phoenician revolt	Aramaean migration from desert; Iron weapons introduced	OLD HITTITE EMPIRE / NEW HITTITE EMPIRE; Telepinus ends civil war c.1525; Shuppiluliumas c.1380	
1400 B.C. — Bronze Age	The Ten Commandments; Exodus c. 1290; Conquest of Canaan c. 1250	XIX — Amenophis IV (Ikhnaton) 1370-1353; Seti I 1319-1301; Rameses II 1301-1234	Shalmaneser I est. Assyrian supremacy c. 1300; ASSYRIANS		Mycenaean civilization at height; Achaean invasion; Trojan war 1194-1184	Independent Phoenician city states		Battle at Kadesh 1296; Hittites driven from Asia Minor	
1200 B.C. — Iron Age	Period of Judges; Saul 1020-1000	XX — Rameses III 1198-1167; Invasion of Sea Peoples; XXI — Priests rule Egypt	Tiglath-pileser I c.1100; Aramaean invasion		Dorian invasion		Aramaean Kdms. in Syria c.1000		
1000 B.C.									

c.=circa=about

Copyright by C. S. HAMMOND & CO., N. Y.

TIME CHART OF BIBLE HISTORY, Continued

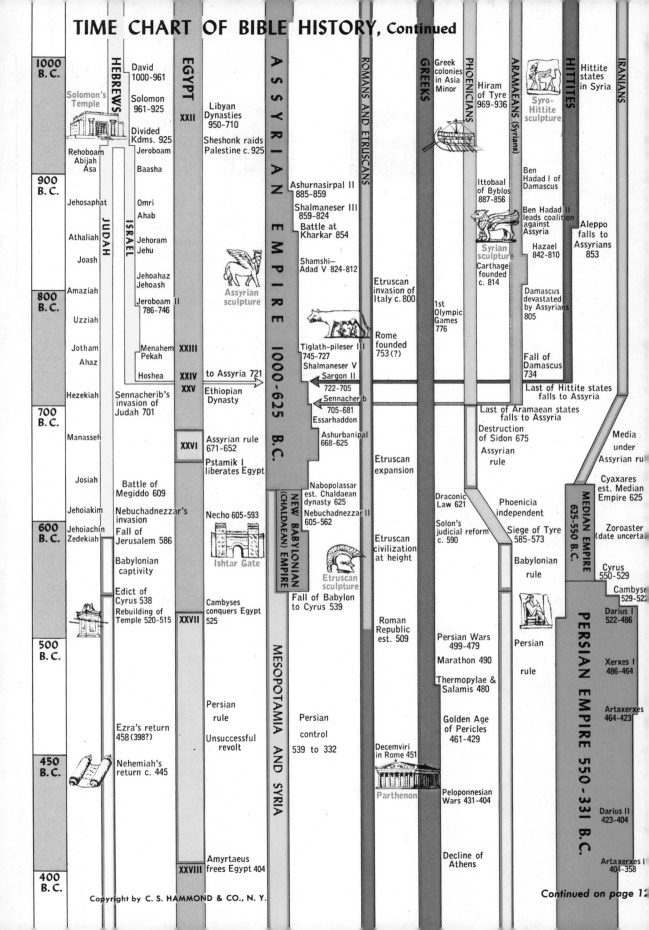

Time scale (left margin): 1000 B.C., 900 B.C., 800 B.C., 700 B.C., 600 B.C., 500 B.C., 450 B.C., 400 B.C.

HEBREWS

Solomon's Temple

David 1000-961
Solomon 961-925
Divided Kdms. 925

JUDAH
Rehoboam
Abijah
Asa
Jehosaphat
Athaliah
Joash
Amaziah
Uzziah
Jotham
Ahaz
Hezekiah
Manasseh
Josiah
Jehoiakim
Jehoiachin
Zedekiah

ISRAEL
Jeroboam
Baasha
Omri
Ahab
Jehoram
Jehu
Jehoahaz
Jehoash
Jeroboam II 786-746
Menahem
Pekah
Hoshea — to Assyria 721

Sennacherib's invasion of Judah 701
Battle of Megiddo 609
Nebuchadnezzar's invasion
Fall of Jerusalem 586
Babylonian captivity
Edict of Cyrus 538
Rebuilding of Temple 520-515
Ezra's return 458 (398?)
Nehemiah's return c. 445

EGYPT
XXII
Libyan Dynasties 950-710
Sheshonk raids Palestine c. 925
Assyrian sculpture
XXIII
XXIV
XXV
Ethiopian Dynasty
XXVI
Assyrian rule 671-652
Pstamik I liberates Egypt
Necho 605-593
Ishtar Gate
XXVII
Cambyses conquers Egypt 525
Persian rule
Unsuccessful revolt
XXVIII — Amyrtaeus frees Egypt 404

ASSYRIAN EMPIRE 1000-625 B.C.
Ashurnasirpal II 885-859
Shalmaneser III 859-824
Battle at Kharkar 854
Shamshi—Adad V 824-812
Tiglath-pileser III 745-727
Shalmaneser V
Sargon II 722-705
Sennacherib 705-681
Essarhaddon
Ashurbanipal 668-625

NEW BABYLONIAN (CHALDAEAN) EMPIRE
Nabopolassar est. Chaldaean dynasty 625
Nebuchadnezzar II 605-562
Fall of Babylon to Cyrus 539

MESOPOTAMIA AND SYRIA
Persian control 539 to 332

ROMANS AND ETRUSCANS
Etruscan invasion of Italy c. 800
Rome founded 753 (?)
Etruscan expansion
Etruscan civilization at height
Etruscan sculpture
Roman Republic est. 509
Decemviri in Rome 451

GREEKS
Greek colonies in Asia Minor
1st Olympic Games 776
Draconic Law 621
Solon's judicial reform c. 590
Persian Wars 499-479
Marathon 490
Thermopylae & Salamis 480
Golden Age of Pericles 461-429
Parthenon
Peloponnesian Wars 431-404
Decline of Athens

PHOENICIANS
Hiram of Tyre 969-936
Ittobaal of Byblos 887-856
Carthage founded c. 814
Destruction of Sidon 675
Phoenicia independent
Siege of Tyre 585-573

ARAMAEANS (Syrians)
Syro-Hittite sculpture
Ben Hadad I of Damascus 887-856
Ben Hadad II leads coalition against Assyria
Hazael 842-810
Syrian sculpture
Damascus devastated by Assyrians 805
Fall of Damascus 734
Last of Aramaean states falls to Assyria
Assyrian rule
Babylonian rule
Persian rule

HITTITES
Hittite states in Syria
Aleppo falls to Assyrians 853
Last of Hittite states falls to Assyria

IRANIANS
Media under Assyrian rule
Cyaxares est. Median Empire 625
Zoroaster (date uncertain)

MEDIAN EMPIRE 625-550 B.C.

PERSIAN EMPIRE 550-331 B.C.
Cyrus 550-529
Cambyses 529-522
Darius I 522-486
Xerxes I 486-464
Artaxerxes 464-423
Darius II 423-404
Artaxerxes II 404-358

Copyright by C. S. HAMMOND & CO., N. Y.

Continued on page 12

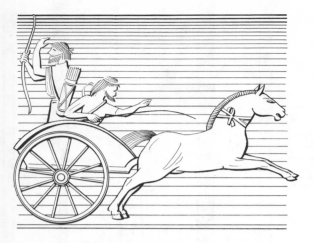

of the ancient world brings into view the emerging cultures of the Minoans of Crete and the Hittites in Asia Minor. By the time of the Exodus of the Israelites from Egypt, Babylon has yielded to the Assyrians and the Hittites had forged an empire which clashed with that of Egypt under Rameses II in the battle of Kadesh. Another, more famous encounter, the one that took place before the walls of Troy, occurs a century later while the Israelites are still trying to make a home in Canaan. The year 1000 B.C. finds a unified Hebrew kingdom of David and Solomon alongside the friendly Phoenician city state of Tyre and antagonistic Aramaean kingdoms in Syria.

Then Solomon's kingdom is divided and the two units continue until Israel is erased by the Assyrian armies. The remaining Jewish people are all but lost in the changing empires that succeed the overgrown Assyrian state. By now the Hittites are but a memory. Median and Chaldaean empires are relatively short-lived as Persia emerges as the power of the ancient world. Only the Greeks have remained free to challenge the Persian rulers of the next two centuries. Western civilization begins with the heroes found in the histories of Herodotus and Thucydides. Unfortunately, our time chart cannot record the full table of Greek accomplishments — the long list of achievements in philosophy, science, politics and art that have been our heritage. Greek thought both preceded and followed Alexander and his army into Asia and he himself was strongly influenced by it. But the untimely death of Alexander lost for the Greeks the chance to see what they could have done with a world empire. Again the east is divided into kingdoms

and a new list of monarchs appears—Seleucus, Antigonus, Ptolemy — poor imitations of the man who led them to India. By the time of the Maccabees, the Holy Warriors who restored political control of Palestine to the Jews, Rome has expanded its territory beyond Italy to embrace the lands of conquered Carthage and Greece. Roman penetration in Asia actually aided the Jews in their war with the Seleucids but the legions of Pompey did not stop at Antioch. Jerusalem was to hear more than once the clank of Roman arms and armor. The Jewish state may have had its strong-willed Herods but ultimate authority rested in Rome. The dramatic story of Christ's life and the subsequent establishment of a new faith based on His teachings unfolds against a backdrop which is dyed in imperial purple. It was in Rome that Paul had to stand trial as a Roman citizen. His missionary journeys, aside from their religious interest, read almost like a geography of the eastern half of the Roman world. The last struggles of the Jews to win their freedom from Rome were desperate attempts doomed to failure. Only the Parthians could successfully challenge the Roman legions and even these hard-riding archers of the east were humbled by Trajan, the Emperor who ruled the empire at its greatest extent.

Our chart ends at 150 A.D. During the following centuries Roman power will wane and finally disappear, but the two beliefs Rome sought to erase will grow and spread. Judaism will disperse throughout the world with its center no longer the Temple at Jerusalem. In its stead, the synagogue will gain in importance as the place of religious instruction and ceremonial. Christianity, in turn, will rise to become the dominant religion of the nations of the western world.

Text and chart help to comprehend the historical background of the Bible world, giving the sequence as well as the correlation of events—in short, the dimension of history in time. But history has yet another dimension —that of space. It unfolds in definite places, it has a geographical setting. The relief maps, photographs and purely descriptive text of this book bring into focus the geographic setting of the Bible. The varied landscape of the Holy Land and the rest of the ancient world becomes more real and familiar as we learn more about such places as the vineyard-covered hills of Galilee, the inhospitable wasteland of Sinai, the fertile alluvial plains of Babylonia, or that geologic wonder of the world, the Dead Sea. Ancient cities—some, like Ur, buried for centuries, others, such as Damascus, inhabited continuously throughout history — take their proper positions within the framework of political boundaries of tiny states and vast empires on the maps of the Bible lands.

Maps of some kind, we may assume, were used by man before he learned to write. The oldest map in existence today is one etched on a clay tablet, about 2500 B.C., in ancient Babylonia, the homeland of Abraham. Moses or Joshua probably resorted to the age-old prototype of the military and strategic map, the drawing in the sand, to instruct their helpers. Bible maps of Palestine are not a modern idea. As early as the sixth century A.D., a mosaic map of Palestine, complete with explanatory notes, was constructed on the floor of a church in the village of Madaba (Biblical Medeba). Only parts remain intact, but one can identify several important Biblical sites and read the accompanying note with Biblical text. Medieval cartographers often centered their world maps

on Jerusalem and had a fondness for locating the Garden of Eden in the unexplored margins of their maps.

The maps of this book have been prepared by using the latest information available from archaeologists, historians and Bible scholars. The fairly recent discoveries of the Hittite civilization and the even more recent unearthing of the Essene community near the Dead Sea are but two of the many new additions to the map picture of the Bible world. Some, but by no means all, of the problems of dating and accurate identification of Biblical sites have been solved by archaeologists and have been properly incorporated. With due regard to the modern scholars, we should not omit credit to the older historians and geographers, Herodotus, Strabo, Tacitus, Josephus, Ptolemy, to whose works even the modern scholar must constantly refer.

For the editors and cartographers who have worked on this volume, it has been a stimulating and informative project. It is hoped that their efforts and those of Mr. Keyes will prove equally rewarding to the reader.

Mosaic map of Madaba, oldest map of Palestine

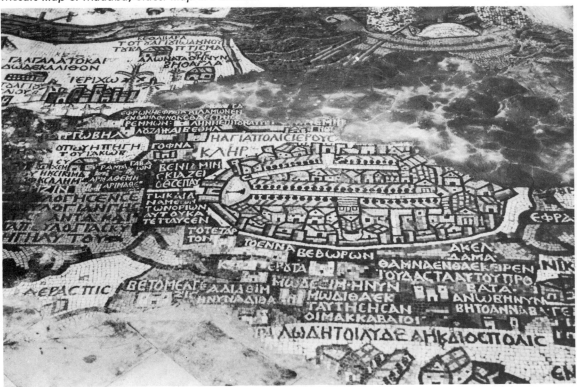

TIME CHART OF BIBLE HISTORY, Continued

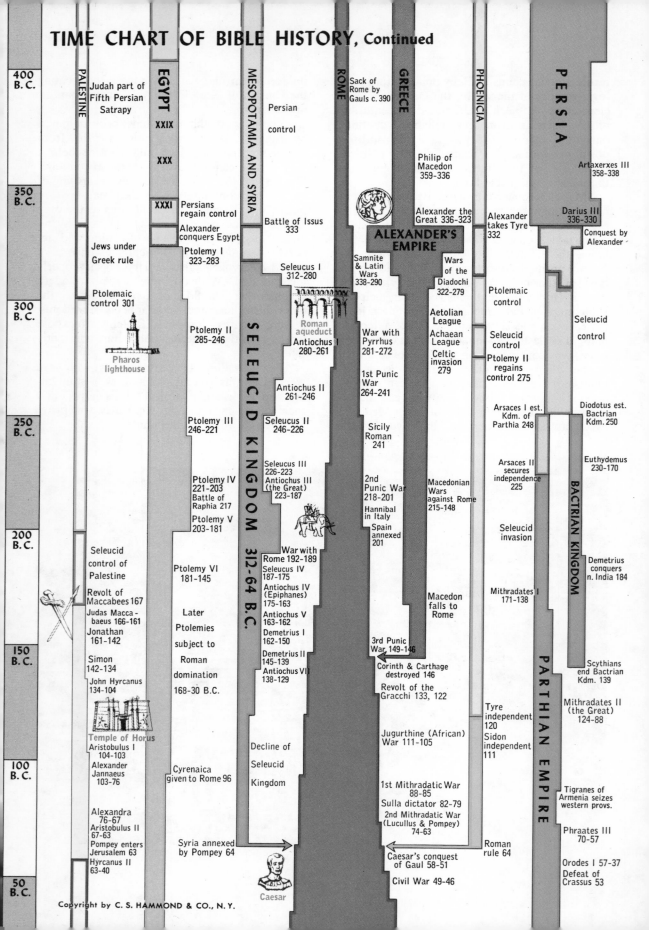

Time scale (left): 400 B.C., 350 B.C., 300 B.C., 250 B.C., 200 B.C., 150 B.C., 100 B.C., 50 B.C.

PALESTINE
- Judah part of Fifth Persian Satrapy
- Jews under Greek rule
- Ptolemaic control 301
- Seleucid control of Palestine
- Revolt of Maccabees 167
- Judas Maccabaeus 166-161
- Jonathan 161-142
- Simon 142-134
- John Hyrcanus 134-104
- Aristobulus I 104-103
- Alexander Jannaeus 103-76
- Alexandra 76-67
- Aristobulus II 67-63
- Pompey enters Jerusalem 63
- Hyrcanus II 63-40

Temple of Horus

EGYPT
- XXIX
- XXX
- XXXI
- Persians regain control
- Alexander conquers Egypt
- Ptolemy I 323-283
- Ptolemy II 285-246

Pharos lighthouse

- Ptolemy III 246-221
- Ptolemy IV 221-203
- Battle of Raphia 217
- Ptolemy V 203-181
- Ptolemy VI 181-145
- Later Ptolemies subject to Roman domination 168-30 B.C.
- Cyrenaica given to Rome 96

MESOPOTAMIA AND SYRIA
- Persian control
- Battle of Issus 333
- Seleucus I 312-280

Roman aqueduct

- Antiochus I 280-261
- Antiochus II 261-246
- Seleucus II 246-226
- Seleucus III 226-223
- Antiochus III (the Great) 223-187

SELEUCID KINGDOM 312-64 B.C.
- War with Rome 192-189
- Seleucus IV 187-175
- Antiochus IV (Epiphanes) 175-163
- Antiochus V 163-162
- Demetrius I 162-150
- Demetrius II 145-139
- Antiochus VII 138-129
- Decline of Seleucid Kingdom
- Syria annexed by Pompey 64

Caesar

ROME
- Sack of Rome by Gauls c. 390
- Samnite & Latin Wars 338-290
- War with Pyrrhus 281-272
- 1st Punic War 264-241
- Sicily Roman 241
- 2nd Punic War 218-201
- Hannibal in Italy
- Spain annexed 201
- 3rd Punic War 149-146
- Corinth & Carthage destroyed 146
- Revolt of the Gracchi 133, 122
- Jugurthine (African) War 111-105
- 1st Mithradatic War 88-85
- Sulla dictator 82-79
- 2nd Mithradatic War (Lucullus & Pompey) 74-63
- Caesar's conquest of Gaul 58-51
- Civil War 49-46

GREECE
- Philip of Macedon 359-336
- Alexander the Great 336-323

ALEXANDER'S EMPIRE
- Wars of the Diadochi 322-279
- Aetolian League
- Achaean League
- Celtic invasion 279
- Macedonian Wars against Rome 215-148
- Macedon falls to Rome

PHOENICIA
- Alexander takes Tyre 332
- Ptolemaic control
- Seleucid control
- Ptolemy II regains control 275
- Tyre independent 120
- Sidon independent 111
- Roman rule 64

PERSIA
- Artaxerxes III 358-338
- Darius III 336-330
- Conquest by Alexander
- Seleucid control
- Arsaces I est. Kdm. of Parthia 248
- Arsaces II secures independence 225
- Seleucid invasion
- Mithradates I 171-138

BACTRIAN KINGDOM
- Diodotus est. Bactrian Kdm. 250
- Euthydemus 230-170
- Demetrius conquers n. India 184
- Scythians end Bactrian Kdm. 139

PARTHIAN EMPIRE
- Mithradates II (the Great) 124-88
- Tigranes of Armenia seizes western provs.
- Phraates III 70-57
- Orodes I 57-37
- Defeat of Crassus 53

Copyright by C. S. HAMMOND & CO., N.Y.

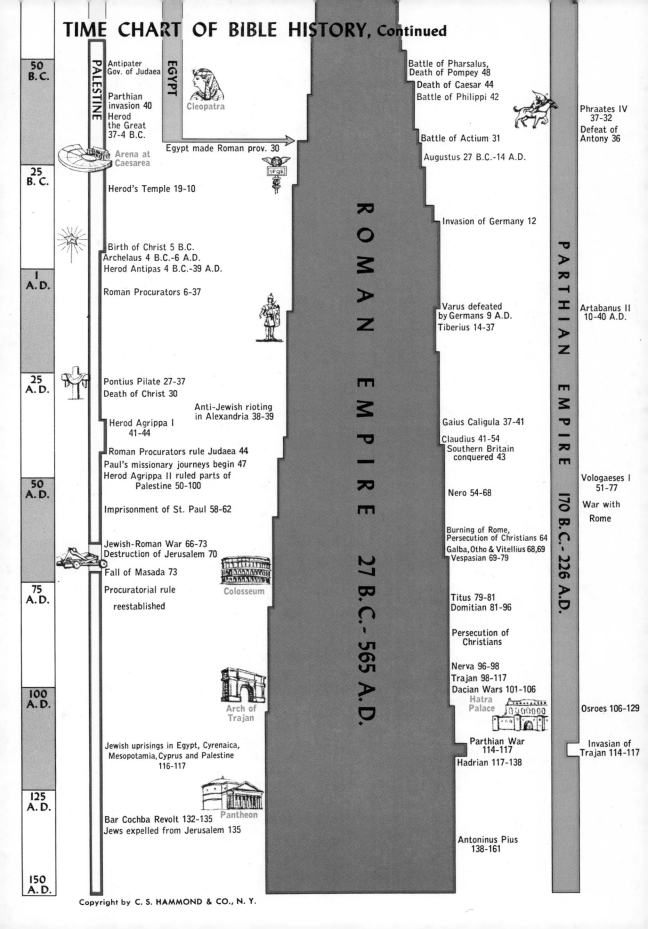

Time Scale (left)

50 B.C.
25 B.C.
1 A.D.
25 A.D.
50 A.D.
75 A.D.
100 A.D.
125 A.D.
150 A.D.

PALESTINE

Antipater Gov. of Judaea
Parthian invasion 40
Herod the Great 37-4 B.C.

Arena at Caesarea

Herod's Temple 19-10

Birth of Christ 5 B.C.
Archelaus 4 B.C.-6 A.D.
Herod Antipas 4 B.C.-39 A.D.

Roman Procurators 6-37

Pontius Pilate 27-37
Death of Christ 30

Anti-Jewish rioting in Alexandria 38-39

Herod Agrippa I 41-44

Roman Procurators rule Judaea 44
Paul's missionary journeys begin 47
Herod Agrippa II ruled parts of Palestine 50-100

Imprisonment of St. Paul 58-62

Jewish-Roman War 66-73
Destruction of Jerusalem 70

Fall of Masada 73

Procuratorial rule reestablished

Jewish uprisings in Egypt, Cyrenaica, Mesopotamia, Cyprus and Palestine 116-117

Bar Cochba Revolt 132-135
Jews expelled from Jerusalem 135

Pantheon

EGYPT

Cleopatra

Egypt made Roman prov. 30

Colosseum

Arch of Trajan

ROMAN EMPIRE 27 B.C.- 565 A.D.

Battle of Pharsalus, Death of Pompey 48
Death of Caesar 44
Battle of Philippi 42

Battle of Actium 31

Augustus 27 B.C.-14 A.D.

Invasion of Germany 12

Varus defeated by Germans 9 A.D.
Tiberius 14-37

Gaius Caligula 37-41

Claudius 41-54
Southern Britain conquered 43

Nero 54-68

Burning of Rome, Persecution of Christians 64
Galba, Otho & Vitellius 68,69
Vespasian 69-79

Titus 79-81
Domitian 81-96

Persecution of Christians

Nerva 96-98
Trajan 98-117
Dacian Wars 101-106

Hatra Palace

Parthian War 114-117
Hadrian 117-138

Antoninus Pius 138-161

PARTHIAN EMPIRE 170 B.C.- 226 A.D.

Phraates IV 37-32
Defeat of Antony 36

Artabanus II 10-40 A.D.

Vologaeses I 51-77

War with Rome

Osroes 106-129

Invasian of Trajan 114-117

Copyright by C. S. HAMMOND & CO., N. Y.

I

THE LAND OF PALESTINE

Although small in area, the Holy Land has played a large and important role in the affairs of humanity. Some like to compare it to a small stage at the center of a huge arena embracing all the world. Certainly, some of the most stirring and dominant scenes in the drama of the human race have been acted out here; they run the whole gamut of mankind's interests and range far back to days before history came to be written.

Geography played an important part in these matters, for the little land, tucked away at the southwest corner of Asia, forms a part of the "Fertile Crescent," the huge semicircle of inhabited and cultivated land which reaches from Egypt through Palestine and Syria and then along the Tigris and Euphrates to the Persian Gulf. Palestine bridges the two greatest continents, Asia and Africa. Men have been forced to cross it in search of trade and of conquest, and to many it has been either a thoroughfare or battlefield. Except for a very brief "Golden Age" in the long, long ago, it has never been the home of a martially minded people. For this reason its contributions, which are many, have been largely of a peaceful nature.

How extensive is this land which is so small in size but large in deeds? The most northerly of its towns in Bible times was Dan, which stood at the foot of mighty Mount Hermon. At the southern extremity was a sort of oasis about a series of wells, called Beer-sheba, where the central highlands drop down to the wilderness steppe known as "the south country." The distance between them is only 150 miles. Over our American highways that is but three or four hours of travel. Three thousand years ago there were a few select riding camels that could make it in a little under two days. A camel caravan might well consume five days traveling between the extreme north and south of Palestine, while the herdsman burdened with his flocks, like the patriarch Abraham, would have very well needed half a month for even a fairly hurried crossing. By comparison then, it must have seemed much roomier in Bible times.

In width, this "land of promise" varied considerably. Far to the north it was but 30 miles from the shore of the Mediterranean back

to the long, deep trench known as the Jordan Valley. In the extreme south this distance increased to about 80 miles. Palestine also took in some of the hill country to the east of the Jordan, and so embraced in all something like 11,000 square miles of intermingled plains, mountains and valleys. The land is, therefore, close in size to New Hampshire or Maryland. That means that forty of our states would be larger in area, and all but three surpass the more important portion west of the Jordan.

But closely-knit though it is, Palestine divides readily into eight well-defined districts, which deserve some consideration.

The Mediterranean, which has been called "the sea in the midst of the nations," forms the land's western border. Its beaches stretch mile after mile with hardly an interruption and with few promontories running out into the breaking waves. As a consequence there are one or two port cities, but not a single really good harbor along this entire coastline. Although one of the Psalms mentions those who make their living from and on the sea, these were apparently the people of Phoenicia to the north, for there is little indication of Palestine ever having produced many sailors.

These level lands by "the great sea" served an important purpose nonetheless. Even in the north, where they were very narrow, they were heavily planted and cultivated. There they bore the name of the Plain of Phoenicia.

Below the headland known as Mount Carmel, the coastal plain broadens out markedly until it is 8 to 12 miles wide, and the northern portion, called the Plain of Sharon, runs down the coast some 45 miles as far as Joppa. This can be beautiful country when spring has painted the earth a brilliant green with growing crops and decked it out with masses of radiant wild flowers. Hillsides are then splashed with the glowing red of scarlet anemones, called in many versions of the Bible the "lily of the valleys." In other places, the air is heavy with a rich sweetness from hundreds of white narcissus, which the Bible text speaks of as the "rose of Sharon."

But, handsome as they are, the flowers do fade and wither away, while the grains and fruits which flourish are Sharon's true bounties, and this fertile stretch has fed men and beasts for uncounted ages.

Stretching on 40 miles to the south of Joppa are more maritime lowlands designated as the Plain of Philistia. Here, in a belt from 12 to 25 miles wide, is a great grain-raising section, dominated in Old Testament times by five cities joined in a close federation. The Philistines who inhabited them were a hard-working, hard-fighting group of people. Their land was pretty flat and generally treeless. It was here that Samson with his bulging muscles managed to get into all kinds of mischief. An international trade route stretched across Philistia from north to south, and, no doubt, many a caravanman cast envious eyes upon its lush acres, wishing he might give up his roaming and settle down in this fruitful granary.

East of these Philistine prairie lands lies the Shephelah, a series of low, chalky hills separated by broad, pleasant valleys. While higher than the seacoast plain, this rolling area, with hillocks 600 to 700 feet above sea level, is called the "low country" in some versions of the Bible. This term sets it apart from the true highlands of Judaea and Ephraim which rise above it on the east.

In a generally rather thirsty country, the Shephelah's valleys are fairly well watered, and their red soil formerly supported fine grain fields along with splendid "oliveyards" and vineyards. Thus there were some prosperous cities in this rich agricultural area.

Several of the broad valleys or dales came to prominence in the Bible story. The most northerly of them, Ajalon, was the site of the battle between the children of Israel under Joshua and the forces of five local kings. It was then that the sun and moon were bidden to stand still in their courses until the task in hand could be completed (Josh. 10:12).

Later on Samson was born in another of them, the Vale of Sorek. Here, too, lived the Philistine maid who first won his stalwart heart. And in its wheat fields this stout fellow, in a moment of great anger, let loose three hundred foxes with flaming torches tied to their tails, to destroy the ripening harvest.

One of the most famous duels in all history took place in one of the drier valleys, or arroyos, farther south—the Vale of Elah. It was here, traditionally, that the youthful David slew the gigantic but slow-witted Goliath. Very likely this borderland area witnessed many other bloody clashes which the Bible does not record.

Yet it was a populous section for ages, since it is rich in ruins of cities, homes,

The Jordan River near Jericho

churches, wine and oil presses, and other facilities for living. Of much interest, too, are its caves and caverns, some of which are seemingly endless. David made the one known as Adullam famous as a hideaway for himself and his outlaw band, while long later thousands of unknowns sought refuge in these hidden lairs during religious persecution under the Roman emperors.

No one likes to make a bad bargain. Hiram of Tyre was certain that Solomon had dealt unfairly with him when he looked over the twenty cities in Galilee given in return for material and labor employed in building the Temple. This is almost the sole commentary on this northern section of Palestine appearing in the Old Testament. Yet Galilee was a thriving area when Jesus and His disciples journeyed to and fro in it many generations later.

At some time in the long, long ago the earth shuddered and, in a lengthy period of tumult, thrust up a mountain ridge which stretched from Syria south into the Sinai Peninsula. Lowered mostly by slow weathering, but also by occasional moments of violence, it now forms the central highlands of Palestine. The Galilean portion is primarily a plateau; it stretches south about 50 miles from the gorge of the Litani River to the valley called Jezreel

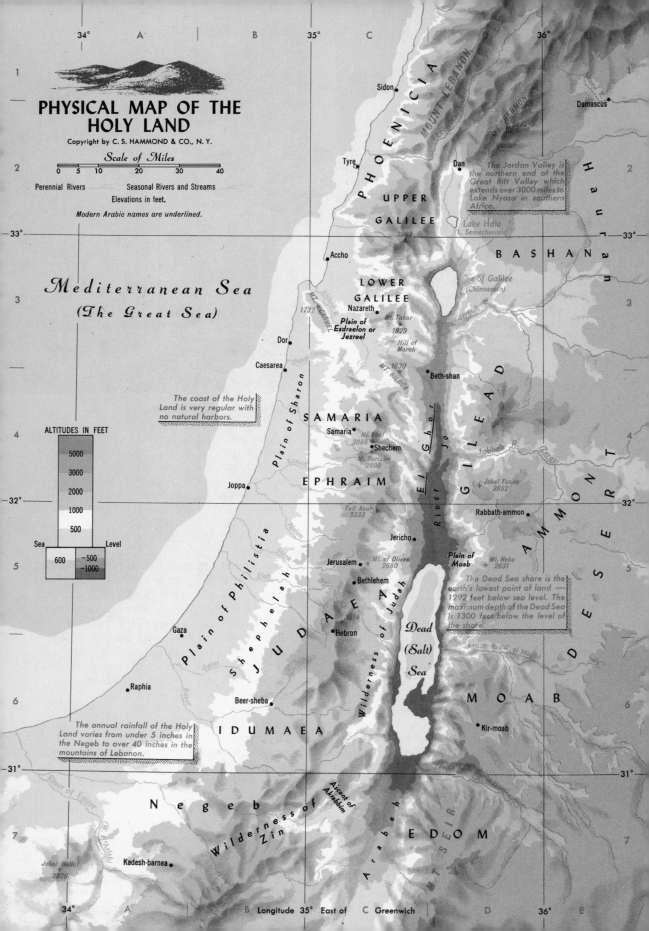

PHYSICAL MAP OF THE HOLY LAND

Copyright by C. S. HAMMOND & CO., N. Y.

Scale of Miles

0 5 10   20   30   40

Perennial Rivers   Seasonal Rivers and Streams
Elevations in feet.

Modern Arabic names are underlined.

ALTITUDES IN FEET

5000
3000
2000
1000
500

Sea   Level

600   −500
           −1000

Mediterranean Sea
(The Great Sea)

The coast of the Holy
Land is very regular with
no natural harbors.

The annual rainfall of the Holy
Land varies from under 5 inches in
the Negeb to over 40 inches in the
mountains of Lebanon.

The Jordan Valley is
the northern end of the
Great Rift Valley which
extends over 3000 miles to
Lake Nyasa in southern
Africa.

The Dead Sea shore is the
earth's lowest point of land —
1292 feet below sea level. The
maximum depth of the Dead Sea
is 1300 feet below the level of
the shore.

Sidon
Damascus
Tyre
Dan
P H O E N I C I A
MOUNT LEBANON
MT. HERMON 9232
UPPER
GALILEE
Lake Hula
L. Semechonitis
H a u r a n
Accho
B A S H A N
LOWER
GALILEE
Sea of Galilee
(Chinnereth)
Nazareth
MT. CARMEL 1732
Kishon R.
Nahr Belka
Mt. Tabor 1929
Yarmuk R.
Plain of
Esdraelon or
Jezreel
Hill of
Moreh
Dor
MT. GILBOA 1630
Beth-shan
Caesarea
Jabbok R. (Zerqa)
Plain of Sharon
S A M A R I A
Samaria
Mt. Ebal 3084
Shechem
Mt. Gerizim 2890
G I L E A D
Kanah
Jebel Yusha 3852
E P H R A I M
Joppa
Tell Asur 3333
Rabbath-ammon
A M M O N
Aijalon
Jericho
R i v e r J o r d a n
E l G h o r
Jerusalem
Mt. of Olives 2680
Bethlehem
Mt. Nebo 2631
Plain of
Moab
Sorek
Elah
3414
S H E P H E L A H
J U D A E A
Hebron
Wilderness of Judah
Dead
(Salt)
Sea
Arnon R. (W. el Mujib)
Gaza
Plain of Philistia
Gerar
D E S E R T
M O A B
Raphia
Beer-sheba
Kir-moab
I D U M A E A
Besor
N e g e b
Ascent of
Akrabbim
Wilderness of Zin
Arabah
E D O M
MT. SEIR
River of Egypt
W. el Arish
Jebel Helal 2926
Kadesh-barnea
Longitude 35° East of Greenwich

in the Old Testament and known also by its Greek name of Esdraelon. The Mount Carmel ridge south of this valley was also credited to the region, as was the upper Jordan Valley, the Sea of Galilee and certain land on the eastern shore of that lake.

The northern portion was indeed an upland, for it averages about 2000 feet above sea level and has some high points that reach to from 2500 to about 4000 feet. Lower Galilee is so called since it lies to the south and is also considerably lower in elevation. Much of it runs about 700 feet and none of its peaks exceed 1850 feet.

While rain was no more abundant here in the north, it was better retained than in Samaria and Judaea, and in the time of Jesus the countryside supported quite a dense population. In fact, passages in the Gospels give the impression the northwest shore of the Sea of Galilee was one of the garden spots of the whole land.

During one of the shudders in the earth's surface, which have been relatively frequent in Palestine, a triangular section of the high lands disappeared. The once humped-up land may have sunk back out of sight through a series of large cracks, or faults, below what is now the valley floor. One part of this plain tips gently to the west and is drained by the Kishon River. This is a lazy, almost non-existent stream in summertime, yet when swollen by winter rains it was able to swallow and destroy an army (Judges 5:21). The eastern edge sends its excess water down to the Jordan.

Along the south edge of the Plain of Jezreel the hills rise quickly again. Some of them are high and a few fairly rugged, but it is a pleasant land, because the valleys are broad and there are a number of them that are more like plains, particularly on the western slopes. Grain fields abound here; they rustle in the breeze, as does fine silk; there are orchards of olive trees to rival those in the Shephelah, and flowers to vie with those in the Plain of Sharon beyond the gentle slopes to the west. Mignonette, with its pale, greenish spikes, is common. So, too, are pink and white cyclamens and tall tufts of pale red hollyhock.

Some of the mountain tops, which rise to well over 3000 feet, command breath-taking views. Among the better known are the twin peaks Ebal and Gerizim, which towered above the ancient city of Shechem in early times, as it stood guard over the high pass which runs between these two huge sentinels. From their summits, the sapphire-colored Mediterranean shimmers in the noon sunlight as seen across ridges lowering slowly to the plains along its shores 25 miles distant. To the east there is an abrupt plunge into the violet depths of the Jordan trench and toward the deep red wall of the hills of Gilead and Moab which rises beyond. To the north are the broad green grain fields of Jezreel—or "God's sowing" as is the meaning of this Hebrew word—while 20 miles to the south rises Tell Asur, one of the highest spots in the Samaritan country.

Seven miles northwest of these sister peaks was one of the finest city sites in all of Palestine. It was the 300-foot-high "watch hill," which rose sharply from the center of the spacious valley. On this eminence was one day built the stronghold of Samaria, capital of the short-lived kingdom of Israel, a rich and handsome, albeit a most wicked city. Its luxury and the fertility of the land about it made it a target for the ambitions of the kings of Damascus, and then of the Assyrians.

The Dead Sea with the alluvial mouth of the Jordan

Caravan on its way to Jerusalem

The lower 50-mile stretch of the central highlands came to be known as the Land of Judaea. It ran from an imaginary line drawn west from a point on the Jordan some 10 miles north of the Dead Sea down to the meeting point of the caravan trails at Beer-sheba. In size it is very similar to Galilee, and so a trifle larger than Rhode Island, but somewhat smaller than Delaware.

In contrast to Samaria, it is more of a table-land, averaging about 2000 feet above sea level. There are high points about Jerusalem, and a few still higher just above Hebron. Its shallow valleys and domelike heights are heavily laced with outcroppings of limestone. The ledges are broken down into rocks which range from mere pebbles to huge boulders. Many are about the same size as the fat-tailed sheep which have grazed its hillsides since time immemorial, and sheep and rocks are easily confused.

Like the high country to the north, this area also falls away gradually toward the Shephelah and the Philistine Plain. The drop to the east is, however, very abrupt, and Bethlehem stands 3540 feet above the shore of the Dead Sea 14 air miles away. Once in the dim, distant past there were trees on these hillsides that today are mostly bare, bleak and cheerless. Yet here some of man's most sublime moments have been lived and recorded.

There is a huge scar on the face of the earth here in this corner of Asia very like the deep wound of an immense cutlass. The crust seems to have broken along two enormous parallel faults, with a downward thrust between them that left the huge rift which is the valley of the Jordan, the Dead Sea, and also the depression of the Arabah which thrusts on to the south toward the Gulf of Aqaba. This is easily Palestine's most remarkable physical feature.

The historic river, which drains its upper reaches and supplies the great sea whose waters are so salty a human body will not sink in them, rises just above the north end of this mighty trench. From springs on the shoulders of towering Mount Hermon, its waters plunge within but a few miles to tiny Lake Hula, where the shoreline is 230 feet above the level of the Mediterranean lying 25 miles over the Galilean hills to the west. Then in another 12 short miles, the Jordan drops over 900 feet, for the waters of the Sea of Galilee are 696 feet *below* sea level.

It is but 65 air miles from the point where the Jordan leaves this lake to where it empties into the Dead Sea. Yet to go down it by canoe or boat requires a trip of three times that distance, for the stream twists and turns for some 200 miles, since it falls an average of only 3 feet per mile. Still when it has been absorbed in the great briny lake at its end, the surface there is 1292 feet *below* sea level. In fact this is the lowest known point on the earth's surface. The valley, or rift, however, is actually considerably deeper, since the Dead Sea is over 1300 feet deep in the northern part. The water has increased its salinity in the course of time until its present "saltiness" is about four times that of the ocean and considerably above that of our own Great Salt Lake. Since neither its waters nor the area immediately about it are conducive to animal or plant life, it has acquired its name of "Dead" Sea.

Beyond the rocky walls which form the eastern edge of the Jordan Valley, there is a long strip of hill country. It manages to extract the last of the moisture from the clouds rolling in from the Mediterranean, so that it long has been a well-watered, fertile, satisfying land. The northern portion furnished good pasture and became noted for its "bulls of Bashan." Further south there were woods, orchards and farms in a section which gave origin to the once popular phrase "the balm of Gilead." Below it, and east of the Dead Sea, was the land of Moab. All three of these tracts in Eastern Palestine as well as the other seven divisions into which this Holy Land is separated, will have their part in the Bible Story that unfolds in the following pages.

II

THE FAMILY OF NATIONS

The first book of our Bible, Genesis, is, as the name infers, a "book of beginnings." It starts quite naturally with the beginning—the creation—of the heavens and the earth. Then we are told of the creation of the first man and the first woman, our earliest parents. Born to them are the first children, and we have the beginning of that very basic human grouping—the family. This latter, both the simple family and its extension to the clan or tribe, plays a very important part in the Bible narrative, for it is the very foundation of the brotherhood of mankind under the fatherhood of a beneficent and benevolent God.

Where Adam and Eve first trod this earth and encountered the punishment of their sin, we do not know. Neither do we know much about their children or where they made their home following their forced departure from Paradise. There were ten patriarchs recorded from Adam to Noah, but we know little concerning them other than their names and acquired age. Did they live perhaps in Mesopotamia, that land in the valleys of the Tigris and Euphrates Rivers? Was that the cradle of mankind? It very well could have been, for the spades of the archaeologists searching for evidences of man in the remote past have dug up some remarkable finds there. Not only have some of the earliest known houses and farm buildings been uncovered in this area, but well beneath the surface of the present valley floor is another indication that history, as we know it, may have begun in this area. It has to do with that remarkable experience of the son of Lamech, Noah.

It was he who built the ark at the instructions of God, loaded it with the members of his own family and with one or more pairs of each of the animals and living creatures, stocked it with provisions and then rode out upon the mounting flood the wrath of God, as he poured rain and destruction upon the earth during forty days and forty nights. And after that colossal devastation, during which the earth had been washed clean of its gross wickedness, the ark came once again to shore. The persons and creatures aboard were all that remained alive upon the earth.

Noah's three sons, Shem, Ham and Japheth, and their wives, were thus the parents of all who followed this cleansing flood. It was by means of the family of Noah, chosen by the Lord, that the earth was repeopled and the Family of Nations established (Gen. 9:19).

Where did it have its beginning? On the 17th day of Tishri, the seventh month, Noah and his craft came to rest on "the mountains of Ararat" (Gen. 8:4). But it was months later before those aboard could debark in the mountains of eastern Turkey. It is very likely they would have sought the area in which they had formerly lived and where the flood had overtaken them. Where might it have been? Where are there any evidences of a flood such as is described in these early chapters of Genesis? Quite remarkable indications have been uncovered near Ur of the Chaldees, the city in lower Mesopotamia where the great patriarch Abraham appears to have been born.

While archaeologists from the University Museum in Philadelphia and from the British Museum were investigating this ancient place, a test pit was sunk in 1928-29 outside the city. In it a heavy strata of clay was encountered and was at first thought to be the former bed of the Euphrates. Fortunately digging continued through this heavy deposit of waterborne silt, and beneath it was uncovered the remains of an early civilization, with bricks and other objects of sizes and make-up not previously known.

Harvest scene in ancient Egypt, from the tomb of Menna, 18th dynasty

THE NATIONS ACCORDING TO GENESIS 10

Copyright by C. S. HAMMOND & CO., N.Y.

Scale of Miles

0   100   200   400   600

GOMER Descendents of Japheth   OPHIR Descendents of Shem

LUBIM Descendents of Ham

Descendents of Magog later inhabited this area.

Descendents of Gomer and Javan later inhabited this area.

Isles of the Gentiles

Descendents of Ham later inhabited this area.

E U R O P E

A F R I C A

MAGOG

GOMER

ASHKENAZ

MESECH

TUBAL

TOGARMAH

ASHKENAZ

GREECE

RIPHATH

GOMER

ASIA MINOR

LYDIA

LUD

CILICIA

JAVAN

GREECE

TIRAS

THRACE

ELISHA

TARSHISH

KITTIM

CYPRUS

CRETE

CAPHTORIM

(Mediterranean Sea)

Great

Black Sea

Caspian Sea

Caucasus

PARTHIA

MADAI

MEDIA

ASSHUR

ASSYRIA

MESOPOTAMIA

Tigris

Euphrates R.

NIMROD

SHINAR

BABYLONIA

CHALDEA

ARPHAXAD

MASH

ELAM

PERSIS

Persian Gulf

S

ARAM

SYRIA

DESERT

HETH

CANAAN

PHILISTIM

PALESTINE

MIZRAIM

EGYPT

PATHRUSIM

PATHROS

Nile

LEHABIM

LUBIM

LIBYA

PHUT

HAVILAH

DEDAN

SHEBA

ARABIA

ARABIAN

DESERT

DEDAN

ARABIA

RAAMAH

OPHIR

JOKTAN

HAZARMAVETH

HAVILAH

UZAL

SHEBA

OPHIR

Arabian Gulf

(Red Sea)

CUSH

ETHIOPIA

TARSHISH

The Sea of the Gentiles

Captives making bricks in Egypt. Mural from a tomb of the time of Thutmose III

This had been no mere river flood, but something far, far greater which had brought a whole way of life to a complete stop, and had, as other tests seemed to prove, left evidence of its ravages over a very great area. Had this section been Noah's former home and did he return to it again? Life did start anew here, and it can well be from this centrally located valley that his descendants spread out over the earth. And spread out they did—into Asia, Africa and Europe.

The tenth chapter of Genesis is indeed a unique document. It is claimed that no compilation just like it has ever been found in the literature of any other ancient people. And the fundamental spirit of it is still being tested in our own land and throughout the world today. It seeks to show that the nations sprang from a common ancestry, and that all men are indeed "brothers," with a human unity like unto the Unity of God.

There is a religious purpose in it, a serious attempt to show that mankind has a common ancestry and that despite our being separate peoples and races, we are one in the sight of our Creator. The belief in, and practice of, this moral truth tends to raise western civilization high above heathenism and is our one great promise of eventually attaining worldwide peace.

But apart from its religious and moral values, this singular chapter is proving, as the years pass, also to be a most dependable table of nations, peoples and places of ancient time. The names employed are given as those of the descendants of the old patriarch's sons, the eldest of whom was Shem, followed by Ham, with Japheth the youngest. In the list the order is reversed, both since the children of Ham and Japheth receive far less direct attention in Bible pages, but especially since Abram, of the posterity of Shem, comes to the fore in the following chapters.

His sons, and thus the grandchildren of Noah, are given in Gen. 10:2 and prove to be the names of peoples inhabiting western Asia in

early Old Testament times. *Gomer* undoubtedly designates the Cimmerians, that is, the Kimmerioi of Homer, a gloomy people finally living in the Crimean peninsula.

Magog is in all likelihood the Scythians, who inhabited the area north and east of the Caspian Sea. There can be little doubt but that *Madai* means the Medes, who lived in the hill country between the Caspian Sea and the Persian Gulf. From *Javan* comes the term "Ionian," meaning the Greeks and especially that branch inhabiting the Aegean islands and western Asia Minor. *Tubal* and *Meshech* perhaps peopled the eastern and southern shore of the Black Sea, while *Tiras* was very likely the Thracians.

Gomer's eldest son, *Ashkenaz* (Ashchenaz) seems, according to Jer. 51:27, to have lived in the vicinity of Mount Ararat. Still this name came ultimately to denote the German peoples in Jewish literature, and the tribe may have pushed on into Europe. Riphath and Togarmah were peoples of Asia Minor.

Javan's four children were *Elishah* whose descendants peopled southern Italy, Greece and the neighboring islands; *Tarshish* was Spanish; *Kittim* were the ancient Cypriots, allied to the Phoenicians; while *Dodanim* probably inhabited the Rhodian Islands in the Aegean Sea.

Ham's own name may be associated with the very ancient designation of Egypt, *Shem,* which means black, and alludes to the soil of the Nile Valley. His son *Cush* designates Ethiopia; while *Mizraim* is a common name for both Upper and Lower Egypt. *Phut* signifies *Libya,* while *Canaan* was applied first to the maritime plains and then to all of Palestine west of the Jordan. The name probably came from a root word meaning "low" or perhaps is associated with the term for the purple dye made from the shellfish in Phoenicia.

The sons of Cush, as listed in Verse 7, include tribes and localities along the shores of the Persian Gulf. They also may have been located along the shores of the Red Sea. Outstanding among them was the people of *Sheba,* their queen making a well-known visit to Solomon at a later time. *Nimrod,* in Verses 8 through 12, also deserves mention, for this "mighty one" was a founder of the Babylonian civilization.

Mizraim seems to have sired or fostered the Philistine peoples; while *Canaan's* offspring populated the land which came to bear his name. *Sidon* (Zidon) stood for the whole Phoenician coast; *Heth* refers to the Hittites, who built a remarkable civilization in Syria; and the *Jebusites* held Jerusalem until dispossessed by David. The other names in Verses 16-18 were local Canaanite tribes. These various nations are mentioned here as descended from Ham because they were politically subject to Egypt at the time when this ancient list was drawn up.

The names of Shem's immediate descendants can be quite readily connected to certain eastern Semitic groups. *Elam* is unquestionably the Elamites immediately north of the Persian Gulf. *Asshur* (Assur) is surely Assyria and *Arphaxad* is generally conceded to be Chaldea. *Lud* is the Lydians of Asia Minor and *Aram* the Aramaean peoples of Syria and Mesopotamia more generally known as the Syrians.

Verses 24 and 25 of this tenth chapter of Genesis give the impression that the forebears of Abram, the *Habiru,* or Hebrew, from whom God's chosen people descended, had lived for some generations in Mesopotamia. Arphaxad, the grandson of Noah, seems to typify the inhabitants of the area about Ur. His grandson in turn was *Eber,* the ancestor of Abram and from whose name some scholars believe the term "Hebrew" was derived. Abram, the "Friend of God," was of the sixth generation, or era, following Eber—a generation which seems surely to have had Ur of the Chaldees as its place of birth (Gen. 11:27, 28).

Eber had two sons, *Peleg,* in whose days, as Gen. 10:25 explains, "the earth was divided," and his brother *Joktan.* Some scholars contend that this *division* was the one described in the following chapter, wherein the Lord showed the supremacy of His power over that of man by causing a diversity of languages, so that the work on the Tower of Babel had to stop and the nations were scattered again over "all the earth."

There is no listing of this second relocation of peoples except in this respect. The name Peleg is believed to be derived from the Assyrian *palgu,* which means "canal." Some scholars believe he may have had a prominent part in introducing the system of irrigating canals so important to life along the Tigris and Euphrates Rivers. In the 1930's French archaeologists uncovered a lost kingdom centered at Mari well up the Euphrates, and, in the wealth of records recovered, the names of Abram's forefathers listed in Gen. 11:16-28 appear as those of cities in northwestern Mesopotamia.

The thirteen sons of Peleg's brother Joktan seem to have been evicted and have moved on to another land. Down the ages this character —whose name meant "he will be made little" —has been thought to be the "father" of the Southern Arabs. One son was named *Hazarmaveth,* whose name has been preserved in that of modern Hadramaut, the territory along the southern coast of the Arabian Peninsula. Another son was *Ophir,* who, perhaps, gave his name to another area in this same vicinity and which was famous for its gold, sandalwood and ivory in Solomon's time. Seemingly, too, the remaining sons settled somewhere in this great desert country to the southeast of the Holy Land.

There would be other dispersions of peoples throughout Bible times, as one member of this Family of Nations fought against one or more of its brother nations. Many of these clashes between brothers will have to be considered in following pages, and we will find there were displaced peoples in those times also.

But next we must follow in the footsteps of one of the grandest characters, not only of the Bible, but of all time, the man Abram, whom the Lord called to do His bidding and who served His sublime purposes so well that he came to be called "The Friend of God."

Babylonian cylinder seal with mythical figures

III

ABRAHAM, ISAAC AND JACOB

Formerly it was generally felt that Abram, or Abraham, must have stemmed directly from a nomadic people who lived a distinctly pastoral type of life, far removed from large cities and concentrations of population. Still, if he was born in Ur of the Chaldees, as the Bible seems to clearly indicate, he grew up in one of the largest, most progressive and important metropolises of the ancient world. Ur was a thriving commercial and political center long before and after the days of Abraham. Scholars have long believed that Ur was much closer in those days to the open water of the Persian Gulf; research indicates, however, that the ancient coast line was much the same as that of today. The city then stood on the left, or eastern bank of the Euphrates River, high upon an artificial platform, within huge walls, teeming with a quarter million, or more, residents. Actually it lay on an island formed by the river and a huge feeder canal which supplied water through smaller canals to an irrigated area which stretched away as far as the eye could see. This planted area included grain fields, gardens and particularly date-palm groves, for there were many mouths to be fed in the closely crowded city at its center. There were also farms, hamlets and villages scattered through this agricultural section.

Behind its military outer wall Ur was a huge and continuing maze of narrow streets, most of them not above six to eight feet wide, and along which the fronts of houses—windowless for the most part—ranged on both sides without a break. They were largely brick cubes, two stories high, with flat roofs, built around a central patio into which the house opened for air and light. On the first floor were the more public rooms, sometimes used for business affairs such as weaving, metal work and other crafts. Sleeping rooms were on the second floor, while much of the family life was lived upon the flat roof, sheltered by awnings.

Terah, father of Abraham, was presumably of the middle or merchant class, and his home in the city would have contained between ten and twenty fairly spacious rooms, in which a reasonably pleasant existence could be had. His son probably went to a private school where he would have learned to read,

Cuneiform code by Hammurabi

write and figure; beyond this schooling, he would also have been taught a trade.

Consequently Abraham must have had some formal education and attained his majority in a city which was one of the most highly civilized and enterprising centers of that time. Why did his father pull up stakes and remove some 600 miles to a place that was by comparison little more than a caravan crossroads far north in the Euphrates Valley? The answer is not clear, but Sir Leonard Woolley, who found many other interesting things in Ur, thinks he may have uncovered a sound reason in the family chapels attached to almost all but the poorest homes. In them a "family god" was being worshipped, evidently a new custom in Abraham's day. The fact that this family god came to mean far more to Terah and his sons than did the worship conducted under the moon-god cult, which centered at the huge temple-tower, or *ziggurat,* that dominated the entire city, may have prompted this move. It could, of course, have been merely a matter of business advantage, or perhaps it had something to do with the death of the elder son, Haran, who passed away before they moved on. But whatever the reason, move they did.

In what period did this dramatic episode occur? The Patriarchal Age of the Bible corresponds to the Middle Bronze Age of 2000-1500 B.C., but the exact dates when Abraham lived are as yet uncertain. Modern Bible scholars place the migration from Ur to Haran in probably the 20th or perhaps the 19th century. Thus the traditional date of 1926 B.C. found in some editions of the Bible may not be far wrong.

In the northwestern part of Mesopotamia there is a prairie area called Padan-Aram, or the Plain of Aram. About at its center lay Haran, where important caravan trails met. It was far removed from Ur in distance, size

Plain of Aram is most certainly closely identified with the forebears of the Hebrew people.

But however important the stay at Haran may have been, we know little about it, and the first recorded details of Abraham's life are given us as he heeds God's call and sets out for Canaan. How did he go? Moving south down the Balikh, he would have forded the Euphrates and then crossed the Syrian desert in

Frieze from Ur showing dairy

and importance. Yet it was not, as was formerly thought, a trail village well beyond the limits of civilization. At the time when the patriarchs called it home, it must have been a flourishing city, and its frequent mention in cuneiform tablets of the 18th and 19th centuries B.C. is clear evidence that it was an important junction and trading point.

It lay on the bank of the Balikh River, which joined the Euphrates about 60 miles to the south. A similar distance to the east was famous *Tell Halaf,* from which have been dug up some of the earliest evidences of man's rise above the primitive life, and of his transition from stone to metal tools, together with the first representation of a wheeled vehicle.

About 200 miles away down the Balikh and the Euphrates was the long-forgotten city of Mari, which was uncovered beginning in 1933. In it was found perhaps the largest castle of the ancient world, containing well over 200 rooms. But far more important were the more than 20,000 tablets removed from the palace archives. It will take many more years to translate all of them, but those already deciphered have added materially to the knowledge of this whole section, ruled by peace-loving kings of Mari in the time of Abraham.

Not only is Haran mentioned in them, but frequently another place called "Nakhur." This turns out to be none other than Nahor, the home of Rebekah, who became the wife of Abraham's son, Isaac. This country in the

this same general direction, seeking Biblical Tadmor, better known under its Roman designation of "Palmyra." This huge oasis supported a most splendid city for many centuries, which was long ruled by its merchant princes.

From there he would have moved on another 150 miles to fair Damascus, which, if it was spring when he arrived, would have been most colorful with its great groves of apricot and almond trees in bloom. The city is probably the oldest continuously inhabited place of any size in the world. Many may in some respects be more inviting, yet few stand in so sightly a spot, with snow-capped Mount Hermon to the west, the desert stretching off in other directions but the town itself ringed with the greenery springing from irrigated soil made rich and lush by the waters of the Abana, or, as the river is known today, the *Barada.*

How long did Abraham pause in this city, which to the Arabs is Paradise upon earth? Long enough at least to acquire a most able bond servant, Eliezer, who became his steward and prospective heir (Gen. 15:2).

Below Damascus, Abraham had a choice of three trails. One would have skirted the base of Mount Hermon, forded the Jordan near its source, and come down along its west bank to the point where it emptied into the Sea of Galilee. A second, more direct, and probably the most traveled trail even in his day would have struck off directly southwest, crossed the river about six miles above the

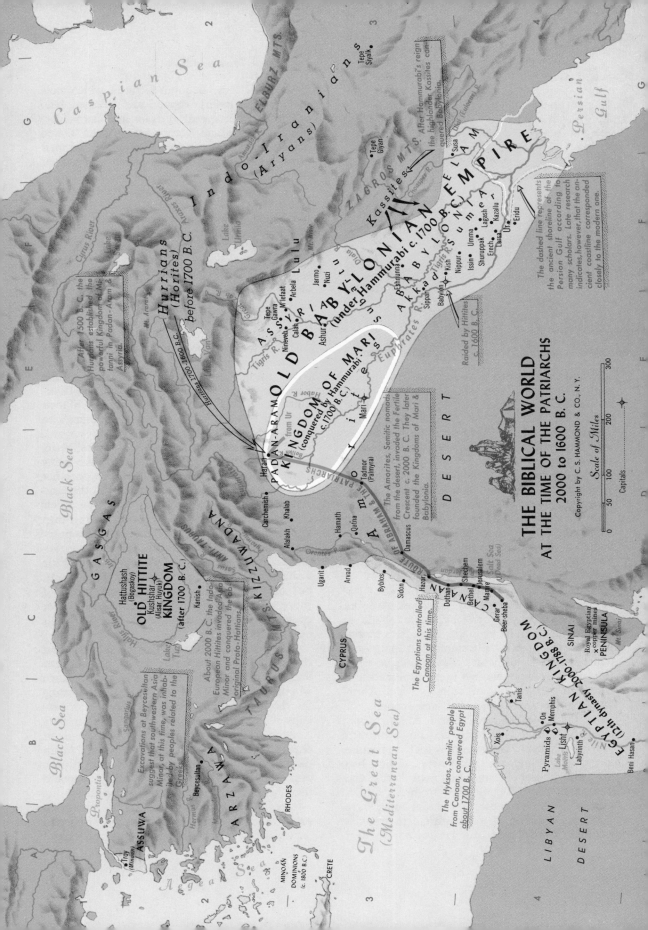

lake and there joined the first. The third route started down the very ancient "King's Highway," and then slanted over to the south shore of Galilee, crossing the Jordan where that stream left the lake. Keeping along that river's west bank for a short distance, the route then swung up into the throat of the Valley of Jezreel to the powerful fortress city of Beth-shan. Which of the three he took is not certain, for they were all in active use 4000 years ago. We do know that his first recorded campsite was in the broad valley before ancient Shechem—the name of which has several spellings—and lay well up on the highlands some 25 miles southwest of Beth-shan by trail.

Abraham's own "household," composed primarily of his bond servants, or slaves, since he and Sarah (Sarai), his wife, were childless, must even then have made up a substantial party. Presumably their numbers ran to several hundred in all, which was a sizeable clan. It was surely large enough to have herded and tended a great array of animals. Yet Abraham's possessions alone did not account for all of the large band of humans and creatures which had made its leisurely way down through northern Palestine and was now seeking pasture in the central highlands. His nephew, Lot, had his own household and his own herds and herdsmen, probably inherited from his father, Haran. Together these two sheiks must have seemed something of a dire threat to the Canaanites, whose land was subject to frequent

invasion by these Bedouin factions, which stole in from the desert, robbed and pillaged, and as promptly disappeared again into the wilderness. Abraham and Lot must have been looked upon with real foreboding as they pitched their black goathair tents on the broad valley floor before Shechem.

The people about Bethel, 20 miles to the south along the highland trail, must in turn have been equally apprehensive when this sizable horde moved on down in that area. Abraham's peaceful ways had no doubt been frequently commented upon along the caravan routes, but by and large you just could not tell about these nomads, these irresponsible "sand flies." The city of Bethel was walled, but a little small; and the neighboring place known as Ai, there is now reason to believe, was at that time merely a heap of ruins, as these towns frequently were after attack. Also there was a drought in progress, water was scarce and the pastures were already over-grazed. The Bethelites were very evidently relieved when their uninvited guests moved on down the trail to the south.

The combined flocks and herds were taking heavy toll of the grazing areas; and, like many other shepherds of that age, Abraham, together with his nephew, had to seek refuge in the land watered by the mighty Nile. What was their course? Most likely they continued on down the highland trail through the plateau country that would later on come to be known as Judaea. They would have passed a stout little walled city of Jebus at a crossing of the trails, but only small villages and camps south of there until they descended from the higher country to another trail junction at the wells of Beer-sheba.

Here the trail they probably followed started its 200 mile thrust across the desolate Wilderness of Shur. It must have been slow, worrisome going, with hungry beasts contesting for the lean supply of fodder. So it was perhaps with strongly mixed emotions that they arrived at the border of Egypt and came to one of the string of stout forts that made up the "Princes' Wall" by which the border was policed. Beyond lay good pastures, but would they be permitted to pass through to them?

Pass they did, however, and Abraham seems to have been a sufficiently important personage so that the Egyptian Pharaoh sought to make an alliance with him by marriage. Then occurred that unhappy mix-up over whether Sarah was actually his wife or his sister. And since she was both, and Abraham's deception caused much havoc, the monarch had the desert sheik banished. But in the meanwhile both husband and wife must have had an opportunity to see many of the wonders of this remarkable land.

In this fabulous country an outstanding civilization had been in the making for many, many centuries. As he made his way to and from his audience with the Pharaoh in Memphis, he would have seen the pyramids, the temples and priestly college at On, or Heliopolis, some of the clean, remarkable fine cities and other notable features of this country that rivaled the one in which he had been born. But while his progeny would live in this lush land for many generations, he was soon thrust back over the border, richer in cattle and goods, but heading once again for Canaan and its more rigorous austere way of life.

Working their way up into the highlands, it was not long before the uncle and nephew were once again hard pressed for pasturage and forced to part. From the high hills at Bethel, a dozen or so miles north of Jerusalem, the country was surveyed. Lot was given his choice, which fell upon the torrid, promising, but exceedingly wicked area in the lower Jordan Valley. There he soon came to grief and was captured by an invading army sent to collect tribute for Mesopotamian kings. While this valley has long seemed to be virtually uninhabitable, except just below the Sea of Galilee and in the oasis about Jericho, it now yields evidence of once having been fairly well peopled. There must have been some wealth there 4000 years ago to attract these marauding kings from far to the east.

Abraham not only rescued Lot and drove away the oppressors, but in doing so made his position in the hill country, and particularly in southern Palestine, most secure. Although Lot came to ruin and dispossession in the destruction of evil Sodom and Gomorrah, his uncle became a factor in this land which the Lord God had promised to him and to his seed "forever." Yet this man, destined to be father of both the Jews and the Arabs, considered Canaan a heathen place. He did bury his wife in the cave at Hebron, but rather than ally his descendants with any of the local princes, he preferred to send his steward far to the north to his former homeland in the Plain of Aram, there to choose a wife for his son Isaac from among the daughters of his kindred still inhabiting that area.

And Isaac and his Rebekah continued on in this Promised Land, spending their lives mostly in the "south country" along the edge

Pyramids at Gizeh

of the wilderness stretching inland from the Philistine towns on the coastal plains, about the wells at Beer-sheba, and in the higher valleys about Hebron. Their twin sons were surely not an unmixed blessing. The willful, lusty elder son, Esau, insisted upon uniting with the local people, married their daughters, and became the "father" of the Edomites who, in generations to come, would make much trouble for the "chosen people"—descendants of the wily, artful younger son, Jacob.

In the contest over the birthright, Jacob was forced to flee to his mother's home in Padan-Aram. There he served a stern apprenticeship as a shepherd and herdsman, but finally broke away and headed back toward his former home in Canaan. This was the distinct break between the developing Hebrew race and the Aramaean land and peoples which had fostered their development.

Jacob, as he set out for his home in Canaan, no doubt at the start followed the trail taken by his grandfather years before. But below Damascus he seems to have kept east of the Jordan, perhaps seeking the better pasturage in the hills of Bashan and Gilead. There, on the bank of the twisting, brawling Jabbok River, he wrestled with the angel and the following day made peace with his brother Esau.

He seems to have forded the Jordan at the mouth of the Jabbok, where a trail from the east pressed up the steep grade out of the deep valley to Shechem and on to the coast. In the

plain to the east of the city, he set up his own tents in this land of promise, near or at the very spot where Grandfather Abraham had camped nearly two centuries before.

For the next thirty odd years he and his growing family would pitch their tents and feed their flocks at many familiar points in the highlands of Samaria and Judaea and in the lower "south country." He was the husband of several wives, a not unusual arrangement in a time when many children died in infancy, and those who grew to an age when they could work added materially to the parents' wealth.

But his favorite wife was the lovely Rachel, for whom he had served the crafty Laban 14 long years. Her elder son, Joseph, had become the father's especial favorite. The youngster's half-brothers were much older than he, and his boyish imprudence, plus the father's partiality, made him much hated by his ten grown brethren. The tents were perhaps still pitched at Hebron the year Joseph was 17, and the ten inflicted their vengeance upon him. He seems to have been a sort of messenger between his now elderly father in the main camp and the sons seeking better outlying pastures, sometimes at quite a distance.

It was on one of these missions that the important young man, clad in his very distinctive cloak, hurried north to Shechem. Not finding his father's sons and cattle there, he continued another 20 miles to Dothan and at that place ran into dire trouble. He was saved from death but sold into what might have been a sort of living death—slavery.

His immediate purchasers were a group of traders who had forded the Jordan and were heading for the main trail into Egypt running down through the seacoast plains. The transaction which they had just completed was, perhaps, not an unusual one in those times, particularly in this rather lawless, thinly populated land. Although the Bible story is pretty much withdrawn from this region for the next ten or twelve generations, it will be well to revisit it in the next section. However, before doing that it can be interesting to follow the apparently unfortunate Joseph into a land where he will be unwittingly preparing a home for a people that will one day possess Palestine—the Children of Israel—his own, and his brother Benjamin's descendants.

What were the times like in the lengthy, narrow land stretched along the Nile? Joseph presumably arrived there during the 15th and 16th dynasties in the period between the Middle and New Kingdoms during the rule of the Hyksos, or Shepherd Kings. The Jewish historian Josephus (Against Apion, 1, 14), quoting from the Egyptian scholar Manetho, explains how the land of the Pharaohs fell under the control of these "barbarians." According to him: "There was a king of ours whose name was *Timaus*. Under him it came to pass, I know not how, that God was opposed to us, and there came in most surprising manner, men of ignoble birth out of the East, who were bold enough to make an expedition into our country, and with ease subdue it by force, yet without our hazarding a battle with them. So, when they had those that governed us under their power, they burned down our cities, demolished the temples of the gods, and treated the people most barbarously . . . At length they made one of their number king, whose name was *Salatis*. He also lived at Memphis, and put both Upper and Lower Egypt under tribute, and left garrisons at all strategic places."

For the first time in its already long history, Egypt was in the hands of foreign conquerors; they continued to possess this land for about a century and a half, and it could well be that they held power at the time Joseph arrived there. That would mean that both the rulers and their more important officers were of the same Semitic racial stock as this able young man, especially befriended by God.

But this must needs be mere conjecture and nothing more. For thirteen centuries, or from about the year 3000 B.C., no nation had been more careful about preserving a record of its history than Egypt. Then, as the Hyksos took over, the recovered records promptly cease, and during the term these foreigners sat upon the throne our knowledge of affairs in the land is a virtual blank. When control was returned to native hands again after these interlopers had been driven out, such records as they had left seem to have been completely erased. This all tends to make more understandable the passage in the 1st chapter of Exodus (Ver. 8), in which it is claimed that the king, who had recently ascended the throne, had no knowledge of any previous prime minis-

ter named Joseph ben Israel. Joseph had served during that unhappy period which every native Egyptian forever after was supposed completely to forget.

However, Joseph did rise to a position of great power under one of these shepherd Pharaohs. Also he managed to bring his clan down into this land and settle them in the rich delta area known in the Bible as Goshen. This he did, too, despite the fact that, as is admitted in the text of this account, shepherds as a class were repugnant and a virtual abomination to the Egyptians (Gen. 46:34). Evidently the way was smoothed because of the understanding and connivance of the foreigners in power.

While the entry of Jacob and his family into Egypt can hardly be thought to picture the seizure of the country by the Hyksos, as Josephus infers, still the departure of the tribes under Moses may suggest to some extent the freeing of the land from the final remnants of its oppressors.

Thus we are entirely dependent upon the Bible for the story of the long Israelite sojourn in the country along the Nile, and that story seems to emphasize certain features of Egyptian history. One such point is brought out by the reference to the elevated Joseph riding in "the second chariot." There were chariots there in those days, that presumably had been very recently introduced by these Hyksos intruders, along with the horses to pull them. In fact the wheel was in use in Babylonia at the other end of the "Fertile Crescent" fully 1500 years before it was adopted in Egypt, and there were four-wheel carts in use in Ur when Abraham

Native craft on Nile at Luxor

was a boy there. Extensive confiscation of property by the throne seems to have taken place during the Hyksos regime (Gen. 47:20). Actually many important changes in life, culture and customs came about through the intimate contacts with these foreign peoples. They were warlike it is true, but they had many peaceful accomplishments as well, for they were competent smiths and metal workers, expert potters and were skilled in masonry and fortifications.

In the earlier years in which they held Egypt, the local peoples seem to have accepted them without marked resistance. Then there came a time when the native princes began to make trouble. One of the first to resist was the Theban prince, Sekenenre. But he came to a violent end, for his mummy shows five major skull wounds, any of which might have been fatal. His elder son, Kamose, was far more successful, while the younger one, Ahmose, put the Hyksos to rout, and then spent a number of years ferreting them out in the cities in Palestine where they had taken refuge.

But these happenings came long after the days of that last of the patriarchs, Jacob, whose name was extended to *Israel* during his night encounter with heavenly powers at Mahanaim. He finished his years in peace in the delta country, but on his deathbed exacted a promise of his next to youngest son, now risen to power in a foreign country, that he would take the parent's remains back to the land of promise and place them in the sepulcher at Machpelah. And when the body had been embalmed and the days of mourning were past, Joseph set out dutifully upon his somber journey. Many, however, after reading the account in the final chapter of Genesis, have wondered why he made a roundabout trip that would have taken him into the country east of the Jordan.

Egypt had long had important interests in the Sinai Peninsula. There were copper and turquoise mines there, and there were also important commercial relations with the far larger Arabian Peninsula beyond. Consequently there was a busy trail leaving Memphis that skirted the north end of the Gulf of Suez and ran across the Wilderness of Paran to the upper end of the Gulf of Aqaba. Here, at the townside known as "Ezion-geber," began the famous "King's Highway" leading north toward Damascus.

About 200 miles to the north, after this latter route had traversed Edom and Moab, it intersected an east-west trail at the town of Heshbon, which plunged down into the valley of the Jordan. After fording the river at Jericho, it climbed steeply to Jerusalem, where it met the highland trail that not only Jacob, but Isaac and Abraham before him had traveled and known so intimately. Not far south of the tight-walled little city then known as Salem was Hebron and the massive crypt that held the "parents" of the Hebrew race. Here Jacob-Israel was laid to rest.

Could it be that his son had mixed in a little official business along the way? Or had he chosen to make this longer journey because it was at that time a safer one? This much is certain, however, the Palestinian land bridge was well supplied with trade routes and highways even 4000 years ago.

Joseph returned to Egypt to further honors and to a long and useful life. The land of which he was the premier had slipped from its former greatness; it was in the hands of usurpers at the moment, but would in the years ahead drive out the foreign elements, as has been indicated above. And, after this greatest of Jacob's sons had passed on, such a day of reckoning did come to pass.

To accomplish his purposes in this respect, the hard-hitting Prince Ahmose raised and trained a sizable army. Not content with having bundled the Hyksos and their supporters over the border, he harried them all up and down the length of Palestine, sacking their cities and carrying home much booty. This plunder, the recollection of the years of humiliation, and an available army bred and fostered a far more militant and aggressive attitude throughout the land. In the years ahead Egypt would be a power to reckon with.

Ahmose I, already an able soldier, also became a competent ruler and the founder of the 18th dynasty in the year 1580 B.C. For a long time now the land was far more fortunate in its rulers, and its power extended over ever increasing areas. Before the death of his great-great-grandson, Thutmosis III, this new Egypt was mistress of the immense area running north from the Fourth Cataract of the Nile to the upper shore of the far away Euphrates.

This of course included the whole land of Palestine, which it might be prudent to revisit at this point.

IV

LIFE IN ANCIENT CANAAN

The years between the two World Wars, and on until the upsurge of Arab nationalism, was a most fortunate period for the archaeologists working in Palestine. More stable conditions and easier access to rights to dig permitted the uncovering of a more extended and detailed picture of human evolution, especially in prehistoric times, than has been completed in any other area the world around.

The caves, with which the Holy Land is liberally and widely supplied, began to be searched in the early 1920s, and the floors and terraces in front of many of them proved most happy hunting grounds. The stone tools their inhabitants made and used, their bones and the bones of the animals they either consumed as food or fought against, even the ashes of their fires, have been subjected to the closest study and scrutiny. They permit a pretty good idea of what life and living were like on this land bridge during the long span from the time the glaciers had much of the northern hemisphere in their icy grasp, until man became an agriculturist and began to live in a house and behind protecting city walls.

Arrow and spear points tell of the countless ages during which these very early men and women subsisted through hunting. Yes, there were fishhooks, and possibly some of the tiniest of their flints were fish "points," as they were among certain of the Indians in our own Southwest. But the impression is that fish were not important as an item of diet.

Toward the latter end of this prehistoric period, sickles began to appear, skillfully made of deer ribs and other long, and preferably curved, bones. These were slotted on the concave side, and in this recess a series of short, sharp flints were cemented to form a blade. With them man perhaps reaped at first the wild grain, as he moved slowly from hunting into agriculture, learning later to till and seed the earth, and also to domesticate animals.

Over the centuries the climate varied widely. In ages when certain animal bones predominate, such as those of the gazelle, it

Jacob's Well near Shechem

is safe to believe that the rainfall was light and the area quite dry. But by contrast there were periods when not only the elephant, but the rhinoceros, hippopotamus and crocodile were plentiful. In such times the rivers and marshes must have contained much water throughout the year.

At long last, when man did begin to gather his grain and bray it into coarse flour with a crude mortar and pestle, and to tame the animals, he also began to move out of his caves, into tents or other types of shelter, and finally into permanent houses. As he learned husbandry and could obtain greater sustenance from it than by hunting, his numbers began to increase. Then, where he had had to protect his hunting rights against others of his kind, he now had to protect his fields, creatures and home. Life began to grow more complicated, as many bits of evidence left behind tend to show, including pins of bone which began to appear and clearly meant he had begun to clothe his nakedness with some sort of garments.

Actually, about 7000 years ago, man began to take some giant steps. One of them was the assembling of his houses into communities—the building of cities—which activity is at the base of our term, *civilization*. Others were the development of religious forms and observances, attempts at civil government and the extension of trade and commerce.

Stone tools gave place to those of copper, later to bronze, and, after the Israelite conquest, to more effective iron. Woven goods and garments replaced those of animal hide, and the permanent home shelters of more tempor-

CANAAN BEFORE THE CONQUEST

Copyright by C. S. HAMMOND & CO., N. Y.

Scale of Miles

0 5 10   20   30   40

Perennial Rivers
Seasonal Rivers & Streams
Capitals ....

Phoenicians from the cities of Sidon and Tyre traded throughout the Mediterranean.

HITTITE EMPIRE
Ubi

Sidon
Damascus

Zarephath

Tyre
Kanah

Kedesh

Misrephoth-maim

Achzib

Laish (Dan)

BASHAN (KINGDOM OF OG)

Hazor
Merom

Accho

Achshaph

Chinnereth

Karnaim

Ashtaroth

Madon

Sea of Chinnereth

Yarmuk R.

Shimron

Mt. Tabor

Edrei

Jokneam

Dor

Megiddo

Ham

Ramoth-gilead

Taanach

Beth-shan
Pella
Jabesh-gilead

Ibleam

Dothan

Mahanaim

The 13th and 12th century kingdoms of Bashan, Ammon, Moab and Edom displaced the Rephaim, Zuzim, Emim and Horites respectively.

Sochoh

Tirzah

Mt. Ebal

Shechem
Mt. Gerizim
Jacob's Well

Succoth

Jabbok R.

Penuel (Peniel)

The Great Sea

(Mediterranean Sea)

Aphek

Tappuah

Adam

Joppa

Ono

Jazer

Rabbath-ammon

Lod

Bethel
Ai

Gezer

Beeroth
Gibeon

Jericho

AMMON

Ekron

Chephirah

Gilgal

Kirjath-jearim

Jerusalem (Jebus, Salem)

Plains of Moab

Heshbon

Ashdod

Beth-shemesh

Jarmuth

Bethlehem

Mt. Nebo (Pisgah)

Canaan at this time was an Egyptian province organized on a city-state system. The local kings were only required to pay tribute and to furnish labor for Egyptian royal projects.

Makkedah

Libnah

Adullam

Medeba

Ashkelon

Gath

Lachish

Mamre

Kirjath-arba (Hebron)

Jahaz

Eglon

Gaza (Azzah)

Kirjath-sepher (Debir)

Hazeon-tamar (En-gedi)

Kiriathaim

Dibon

Gerar

Aroer

Arnon R.

Raphia

Sharuhen

Beer-sheba

Arad

Ar

Kir-moab (Kir-haresheth)

MOAB

Hormah

Rehoboth

Ascent of Akrabbim

Zoar

The destroyed cities of Sodom and Gomorrah are believed to be beneath the shallow waters of the Dead Sea which now cover the Vale of Siddim (shaded portion).

River of Egypt

Wilderness of Zin

Bozrah

Oboth

EDOM

Kadesh-barnea (En-mishpat)

Punon

MT. CARMEL

Canaanites

Sidonians (Phoenicians)

MOUNT LEBANON

MT. HERMON

Plain of Sharon

Canaanites

Hivites

Jebusites

Hittites

Amorites

KINGDOM OF SIHON

Salt Sea (Dead Sea)

Amalekites

Kenites

Arabah

MT. SEIR

River Jordan

ary sort. However, the fringe of the population in Palestine has continued to live in tents and even in caves down into modern times.

Much progress was made in pottery; improvement in kind, form, size, decoration, and particularly in baking, gave it wider use and greater permanence. Of the various artifacts which have come down through the ages, pottery has proven to be the most frequent and most useful means of locating man in the scale of time and progress. Since life came to be concentrated in the cities, they have been the most rewarding spots in which the archaeologists could work as they sought to learn more about man as he moved more rapidly toward the beginning of written history.

Fortunately Palestine has some very early city sites, and the most ancient of those that have been investigated is one whose name is quite widely known—Jericho. But knowledge of it has to do principally with its recorded destruction, rather than with its long and highly interesting period of occupancy.

Early Palestinian city builders usually sought a knoll or hill convenient to a spring and to a clay pit or limestone outcropping. With water from the former, they molded bricks of the clay and also mud mortar with which to lay them, or the stone broken from the ledge, into walls. Jericho was just such a site, lying about nine miles northwest of the point where the Jordan River empties into the Dead Sea. Very primitive men had lived on the spot during the Stone Age and were among the earliest groups that organized for city life. Their first efforts were pitiably crude in many respects, but they did make progress, although the city was destroyed a number of times during its long life, perhaps by earthquakes, which have been severe in this trenchlike valley down the ages.

This city of early Bible times is quite separate and distinct from one which later took its place and has continued down to the present. These cities grew higher, level by level, through the ages, and, when abandoned, formed into a mound, or *tell*. Some of them had acquired considerable height, yet surface indications were pretty well obliterated. In fact Jericho was long thought to be merely an 80-foot-deep pile of worthless refuse, and simply not worthy

of investigation. Even some of those who first delved into it came to this same conclusion and so nearly ruined it for systematic examination before ceasing their burrowing. But when it began to be properly opened up in 1929, it yielded one of the most complete and valuable records of life in early Palestine yet uncovered.

In its lowest strata there is ample evidence of the long apprenticeship man served in the school of experience while learning to bake lasting pottery. There are the remains, too, of some of his earliest shrines and of figurines used in his rituals, which were, perhaps, not too unlike the "images" which Rachel hid in the saddle of her camel centuries later (Gen. 31:19, 34). Some of the layers of occupancy just above bedrock reach back as much as 7000 years.

Well over 5000 years ago the city began to increase in size and importance, for the walls were expanded to enclose as much as 4 acres, and houses and appointments within it were more ample. Influences began to appear also which are thought to have been Babylonian, evidence of interchange with that land nearly a thousand miles away. The grain silos grew larger and more numerous, and for a period of 500 years or more Jericho seems to have enjoyed peace and a measure of prosperity and progress.

Then, about 2500 B.C., the city was completely destroyed, but by what means is uncertain, although fire was an accompaniment. Some think it the result of a violent earthquake, while to others it perhaps spells conquest. This much is certain, the city was begun anew, and while the walls and houses were more soundly built, the latter were much smaller and more crowded. Evidently the population had increased materially, possibly because those who had lived without the walls previously, had experienced the ravages of an invading army and now demanded the protection of the thick, double ramparts.

Other major cities were growing up in other sections. Notable among them was Beth-shan, in the *wadi* where the Harod River hurries down out of the Valley of Jezreel into that of the Jordan. Its eighteen distinct periods reach far back to primitive conditions in the times of the Painted Pottery People. It was a strategic military center, dominating that whole area long before history was written, for it controlled both east-west and north-south caravan routes that ran close to it.

Another of these more important ancient cities standing beside a main thoroughfare of trade was Megiddo, in the vale that cleaves the rear end of the Carmel ridge and through which flowed the principal traffic between Mesopotamia and Egypt. While probably not quite as old as Jericho as a city, it and Beth-shan became organized communities as early as 3500 B.C. It will be dealt with in connection with the period in which it achieved its greatest development—the "Golden Age" of Solomon.

These three were major cities, in size, strength, population and general importance. Others were Taanach, fortified with huge walls built of so-called cyclopean masonry, or giant stones with smaller rocks filled in between them. It seems to have been the headquarters of a famous oracle of the goddess Astarte. Another was Bethel, a much larger but not nearly so strategically located city as Salem (Jebus, Jerusalem), a few miles to the south. A third was Beth-shemesh in the Shephelah between Philistia and Judah. It was a rich city, as its fine pottery, jewelry and weapons testify, and was the site of a conflict in ancient times between cultures—between East and West—the same antagonism that still plagues the area today.

One of the largest of the ancient cities that has been opened up must go nameless, for nothing unearthed there indicates what it was called in the long ago, and it presumably missed mention in Bible text. It is the *Tell el-'Ajjul*, or "mound of the little calf," and one of three city sites in the long *wadi* which empties into the ocean just below modern Gaza. Despite the fact it cannot be recognized, it was a thriving place—just possibly an ancient former site of Gaza—and covered about 30 acres. This was really a huge town, for it would have been three times the size of David's Jerusalem and at least twice that of Megiddo. Ancient Canaan had an abundance of cities.

Some of these places were relatively small and little more than fortresses, where, perhaps, the "king" and his officers and courtiers lived within the walls, while the common folk existed in squalor in wattle huts built outside the parapets. And some quite frankly were fortresses, not only for protection of pioneer areas, but in many instances for the collection of toll from passing caravans. Such was Gerar near which Abraham had lived, and with whose king he had a serious misunderstanding (Gen. 20). It evidently controlled a well-traveled route, and the men and animals that paused beneath its walls while the impost was collected must have been legion, for the trench worn by their feet over the years is a deep one indeed.

Not all the people lived within city walls, although perhaps the bulk of the native Canaanites did make their homes in protected communities by the 17th or 16th century before the beginning of Christian times. Since they were by then agriculturists, the Canaanites had become vegetarians rather than primarily meat eaters as they had been as hunters. In the storage bins at Jericho there have been found some remnants of their cereal crops, a few grains each of millet and barley, a few pea-like lentils, together with the residue of grapes. There were stone wine presses, too, scattered through the hill country. Surely there was familiarity with figs, dates, olives and a variety of fruits which man first gathered in the wild and had slowly brought under cultivation. Flax seems to have become quite a staple crop, as in Egypt, and was used for clothing, as was the wool of the sheep. Certainly, shearing must have been a far easier task as hard bronze knives, which could be ground to a reasonably keen edge, came into rather general use. Goat's hair was a much-used textile fiber, and later camel's hair. However, it should be pointed out, it now appears that this creature was not common in Palestine until toward the time of the

Egyptian wall painting from the time of Abraham showing a caravan of semitic people

exodus of the Israelites from Egypt. But since cloth tended to decay and disappear, it is necessary to travel to the tomb paintings in Egypt to get some glimpse of what the peoples in Palestine might have looked like. There, in the crypt at Beni-Hassan, is the now internationally famous sketch of a Semitic family of about the time of the Patriarchs, which probably gives a fair impression of clothing, arms, gear, and pack-bearing animals in the second millenium before the Christian era.

Life, however, was not completely humdrum. Man had his lighter moments. He wrestled for sport in Egypt, he ran races there, and almost certainly did so, too, in Palestine. He had time for music, even from very early days, for deep down in the *tell* at Jericho there were bone flutes on which he could play a tune. That he danced is very probable, expressing rhythm not only with his feet, but also with his hands, as he clapped them together.

Also he found time for expression in various art forms. In the Middle Bronze period his efforts were still rather crude; he leaned heavily upon Egypt for ideas, and many of his attempts were rather sketchy copies of the exquisite productions from the land to the south. Also, as a craftsman, he was far less dextrous and skilled than the Syrians and Phoenicians to the north. But then, he was a husbandman, a grain grower, the tender of small herds and flocks, and not much of an industrialist. Toward the end of the Bronze Age he became familiar with writing—not with just one single system, but with four, and perhaps five, separate schemes. They were the wedge-shaped cuneiform writing used in Mesopotamia; the pictorial Egyptian hieroglyphs; a modified cunei-

Early Canaanite scarabs from Debir

form alphabet perfected in Ugarit far to the north; a rather transient syllabic script used for a time in Byblos in Phoenicia, the city from which comes our word *Bible;* and also the linear alphabet (one which is written, rather than drawn, or impressed) from which, via Hebrew, come our own Greek and Roman characters.

Thus Palestine was by the year 1300 B.C. a fairly "civilized" section, which had come very much under the control of its neighbor to the south, Egypt. The Hyksos, who had passed through Palestine en route to the conquest of the land by the Nile and who had sought refuge in the cities on the land bridge when at last they had been routed out, had taught the Egyptians a lesson. To avoid another surprise sortie like this last one, the Theban princes who had returned to the throne felt need of a buffer state; and that precisely is what Palestine became.

This was of course not strictly a one-sided affair. Canaan had been ravaged countless times in the past, and after the Egyptian bridle was affixed some degree of protection was given the lines of little city-states which crisscrossed the country from Dan to Beer-sheba. There was perhaps greater stability, for these cities were not leveled and rebuilt with such great frequency. Yet Palestine, as the remains of its ancient centers of population indicate, paid for this overlordship, and paid heavily. Prosperity lessened slowly there, and by the time the Israelites were fording the Jordan and heading for Jericho, much of the area's former vitality was pretty well spent.

V
THE ROUTE AND TIMES
OF THE EXODUS

Much misunderstanding, unfortunately, has come about because of Bible "chronology." Today time is of the very essence of much that we do, both as individuals and also collectively. Its careful, accurate computation seems both most natural and necessary to us. We tend to be much interested in seeing that exact dates of all occurrences be given and that they be arranged in the precise order in which they happened.

fore by Archbishop Ussher of Armagh. While his efforts were careful, they were based upon the limited knowledge of that time; and, although having served well for two and a half centuries, his datings have proved inaccurate and obsolete at many points.

One of them in particular which is subject to serious question is the time of the Exodus. Students have long doubted the year 1491 B.C. set by Ussher, but it was not until archaeologists had uncovered ancient sites in the Nile delta mentioned in the first chapter of the Book of Exodus that a more accurate date could be computed. Competent authorities today set

Tell el-Judeideh in Syria with "step-trench" showing layers of occupation. Cultural levels are indicated by typical objects. Earliest occupation c. 5000 B.C., latest c. 600 A.D.

But the interest in such matters in Bible times was either deficient or lacked the precision we expect today. Methods of recording elapsed times were quite different, and totals arrived at by employment of different processes varied markedly. Thus the dating of Bible episodes was long delayed and first appeared in the pages of Bibles in English in the year 1701, having been worked out nearly a half century be-

the withdrawal *about* the year 1290 B.C., in the reign of the Pharaoh Rameses II, or approximately 200 years later than Ussher's computation.

The fact that Egypt tended to become a more warlike nation following the expulsion of the Hyksos has already been pointed out. For the better control of the border and the buffer state in Palestine, the capital had been moved down the Nile into the eastern delta country. This happened while Rameses, "This Beloved of Amun," occupied the throne. The Pharaoh appears to have been every inch a king and, while perhaps a greater builder than a warrior, he did tend zealously to his country's safety.

He seems to have rebuilt or strengthened the "Prince's Wall" of forts stretching from the shore of the Mediterranean to Lake Timsah. And then, for their better servicing as well as that of the soldiery in Palestine, he erected store cities nearby. For these he used forced labor, recruited largely, it would seem, from among the Israelites in the neighboring land of Goshen. The two places mentioned by name are Pithom and Rameses.

The first is *Tell er-Retaba* in the *Wadi Tumilat,* and which seems to have been christened Pi-Tum, or "house of the god Tum." The other is almost certainly Tanis, the Delta place of residence of the Rameside Pharaohs. It was formerly thought to be the *Tell el-Maskhuta,* about 8 miles east of Pithom, but this mound is now considered to be Biblical Succoth, the first campsite (Ex. 12:37).

Since excavation at these sites leaves little doubt but that they were built by Rameses II, it becomes evident that to him falls the dubious honor of being the "Pharaoh of the Exodus."

Opposed to him was one of the great characters of all literature—Moses. Born into the serfdom his kinsmen had been brought to suffer, fate made him a foster son of "the Pharaoh's daughter," so that he was reared in a luxury he would one day be forced to renounce

and schooled in wisdom he would have to put behind him.

But his loyalty to his own people was unshakeable; when he sought to protect one of his blood brethren, he suddenly found himself an enemy of Egypt and forced to flee the land. In which direction did he go? To the south and east, thus missing the border patrol, and heading toward the Land of Midian, which lay along the shores of the Gulf of Aqaba, the northern arm of the Red Sea. Here, among descendants of "father" Abraham, he lived the life of a shepherd and was trained for his task of leading the Israelites in their years of wandering in the neighboring wilderness.

It was at the foot of a rugged, colorful, but rather forbidding mountain in the midst of this wilderness that God called Moses to his herculean task. The traditional spot in the shadow of Mount Sinai has been marked by a church and then a monastery during the past fourteen centuries. With the assistance of his elder brother, Aaron, and backed by miraculous power from on high, he finally won permission from an unwilling Pharaoh to lead his country-

Egyptian potter at work, beside him 3 finished jars. Gizeh, 2500-2100 B.C.

men from Egypt where they had been enslaved.

Their objective was the "Promised Land" (Gen. 12:7) and the party—in numbers the greatest migration in all history (Ex. 12:37)—was assembled at the royal city of Tanis, or Rameses. What would be their route? The shortest would be by way of the coastal highway, "The Way of the Land of the Philistines," but it was guarded by forts at the outset and, as implied in Bible text, perhaps too risky an avenue of exit.

So they headed for Succoth, 32 miles to the southeast, and perhaps a two-day journey, but more likely three, for somewhat less than half that distance would be an average day's march for these novices burdened with creatures which must graze beside the trail. They went on to Etham on the edge of the wilderness and then, perhaps as a deceptive measure to confuse the authorities, backtracked to Baal-zephon near the so-called "Reed" Sea.

The exact spot where the waters were parted and the crossing of the sea was made may never be positively established. There are a number of possible places. However, it should be pointed out that the Hebrew name for the body of water which the Israelites crossed in leaving Egypt means "the Sea of Reeds" or "the Reed Sea." This would seem to refer to the region of marshland and shallow water through which the Suez Canal was later cut. The Greek version of the Old Testament (the Septuagint), made a couple of centuries before Christ, was apparently the first to confuse this body of water with the Red Sea, some miles to the south. Hence the Greek New Testament also speaks of the Israelites crossing "the Red Sea."

But a crossing into the Sinai Peninsula was effected, and with Pharaoh no longer a threat, the Israelites set off along the route leading to the copper and turquoise mines toward the tip of this harsh spearpoint of land. In recent times the whole area has never managed to support more than about 7000 underfed wanderers. What a wilderness it must have seemed then to almost a hundred times that many tenderfeet, completely inexperienced in the rigors of this arid steppe! There still are long waterless stretches, and there are also brackish wells, any one of which can have been Marah, while a tempting oasis of palm trees and sweetwater still exists which is undoubtedly Biblical Elim.

The easterly flight of migrating quail heading from Africa to Central Europe still drop down each spring to feed after their crossing of the Gulf of Suez, and are pounced upon by hungry Bedouin wanderers. And if you journey near this area you will probably be offered honey-sweet *manna*, drippings from tamarisk trees whose bark is attacked by a minute insect found only in Sinai (Ex. 16:4-35).

The Israelites spent many months at the foot of Mount Sinai where Moses received the Ten Commandments. Then, with another spring season at hand, they moved to the north, paralleling the shore of the Gulf of Aqaba whose waters have come to our attention again today because of their importance for the countries in that area. To locate *all* their campsites listed in the 33rd chapter of the Book of Numbers would be impossible and largely fruitless. Some of their stopping places, however, do have special significance.

One of them, Ezion-geber, at the head of the Gulf, came to prominence in Solomon's time, for he had a copper smelter and navy yard there. It is again most important as an eastern seaport of modern Israel.

Swinging to the northwest, the Israelites headed for the "South Country," and, as Moses hoped, an armed entry into the land of promise. They seem to have found sufficient water and pasture in the vicinity of Kadesh-barnea, where a permanent camp was set up while a spying party sought information on which the strategy of invasion might be planned. This body seems to have gone only to a point some 20 odd miles south of Hebron, at the southern edge of the settled area.

There ten out of the twelve became so timorous that they quickly returned to headquarters, bearing indisputable evidence of the richness of the land, but babbling their fear in words which sounded like silly caravan gossip. Moses was appalled and very angry. But Egypt had made these people soft and fainthearted, therefore nothing could be done but return to the wilderness and allow the rigors of life there to build up sufficient stamina in the next generation, so that it would be bold enough to fulfill God's purposes. This considerable period evidently was spent largely in hunting grass and water in this heartless steppe country southwest of the Dead Sea.

At long last these years of stern disciplining

The traditional Mt. Sinai

and the weeding out of the fearful were accomplished, and once again Israel was on the move. They cannot have been years of indifference to conditions in both Egypt and in Canaan, where changes seem to have been going on. The land along the Nile had grown less warlike, but had succeeded in bleeding the city-states in Palestine pretty white. The land bridge had been measurably weakened and the time for the Israelites to strike was at hand; but for reasons not too clear, it seemed more promising to attack from the east than from the south, which faced toward Egypt.

As they swung over toward the land of Edom, they suffered the loss of their first chief priest, Aaron. A grave was found for him on Mount Hor. Its location is not definitely known; the traditional spot is marked by a tomb on an eminence now called Jebel Harun.

For a time they were once again at Eziongeber, the plan being to move up along the "King's Highway," which ran directly north from that port through the lands of Edom, Moab, Sihon the Amorite, Ammon, Gilead and Bashan toward Damascus. Many people in those days lived along this active trade route, and it would be but natural that the passage of so great a horde through their lands would be resisted. The years past had been fairly free of hostilities; now there was to come a decided change. Active resistance began with the refusal by the Edomites of right of passage through their country.

So an attempt to bypass it had to be made, and a route was chosen through the Arabah, the great depression leading north to the lower end of the Dead Sea. One campsite mentioned in this valley, Punon, is the copper town which the local Injadat Arabs today call Feinan. Pressing on to the Brook Zered, which empties into the great Salt Sea near its southern extremity, the Israelites swung east up this dry valley, which formed the boundary of Moab. And, since they had been forbidden right of way through that land, too, they bypassed it by a swing out over the desert along its eastern edge.

Coming to the Arnon River, they turned west along it, since it marked the southern border of the Amorite kingdom. Sihon, the Amorite king, offered the third refusal, and the new generation of Israelites had their baptism of

blood and, with the Lord's help, were victorious. The armed seizure of a homeland had begun here well to the east of the Jordan. Quickly following up their first success, they pushed hurriedly north and were soon masters of the whole area on this side of the deep valley running down to the Sea of Galilee.

This swift conquest quite naturally brought terror to the people of Moab and to their king. Most Bedouin peoples have long prided themselves on their fighting abilities, and these younger Israelites seemed to be true sons of the waste spaces and very able fighters. Balak the Moabite king dared not pit his people against such masterful warriors; instead he resorted to trickery and magic. Moab joined with the neighboring Midianites in hiring the arch diviner Balaam.

But Balaam failed, and so did the attempts of the women of Moab and of Midian to encourage idolatry among the people of Israel. The Midianites were slaughtered in great numbers, while the Moabites, whom God refused Moses the right to attack—they were descendants of Lot, Abraham's nephew — were excluded from the congregation of Israel to the tenth generation.

And what of Moses, old by now in years and experience, but still young in spirit and ability? Having been denied the right, as was Aaron, to enter the Promised Land, his task was virtually ended. The country east of the river, beyond which he could not go, was secure and open to settlement by a portion of his charges; but one duty still remained. It was essential he give an account of his great stewardship and review the laws ordained by God for His people's guidance. So, calling the leaders and the people together at the base of Mount Nebo, he addressed them in three great ora-

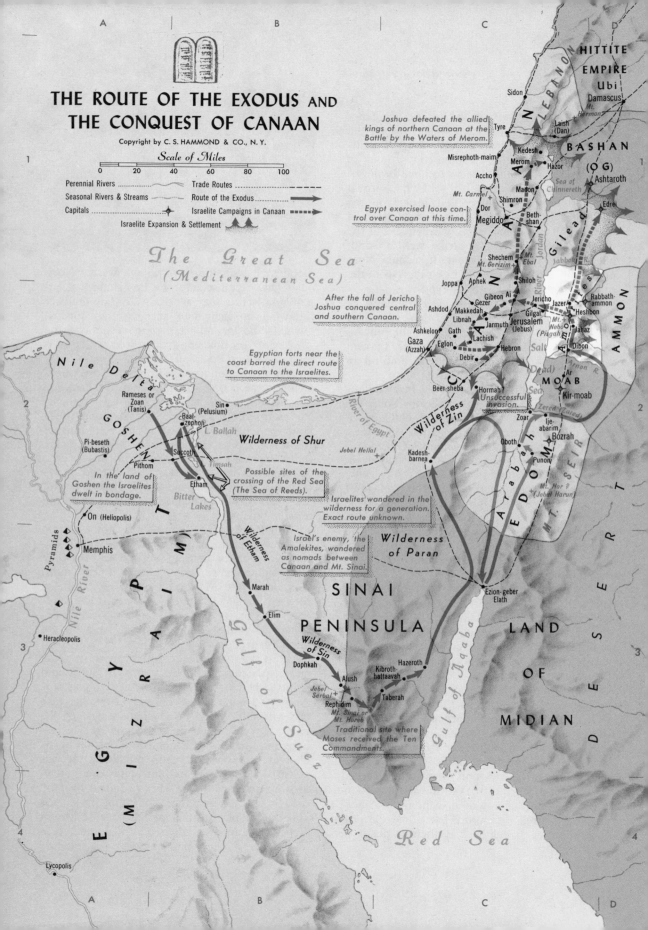

THE ROUTE OF THE EXODUS AND THE CONQUEST OF CANAAN

Copyright by C. S. HAMMOND & CO., N.Y.

Scale of Miles

0   20   40   60   80   100

Perennial Rivers ....
Seasonal Rivers & Streams ....
Capitals ....
Trade Routes ....
Route of the Exodus ....
Israelite Campaigns in Canaan ....
Israelite Expansion & Settlement

The Great Sea
(Mediterranean Sea)

Joshua defeated the allied kings of northern Canaan at the Battle by the Waters of Merom.

Egypt exercised loose control over Canaan at this time.

After the fall of Jericho Joshua conquered central and southern Canaan.

Egyptian forts near the coast barred the direct route to Canaan to the Israelites.

Possible sites of the crossing of the Red Sea (The Sea of Reeds).

In the land of Goshen the Israelites dwelt in bondage.

Israelites wandered in the wilderness for a generation. Exact route unknown.

Israel's enemy, the Amalekites, wandered as nomads between Canaan and Mt. Sinai.

Traditional site where Moses received the Ten Commandments.

HITTITE EMPIRE
Ubi
Damascus
Sidon
Tyre
Laish (Dan)
Kedesh
BASHAN
Merom
Hazor
(OG)
Ashtaroth
Misrephoth-maim
Accho
Edrei
Mt. Carmel
Shimron
Madon
Sea of Chinnereth
Dor
Bethshan
Megiddo
Gilead
Shechem
Mt. Gerizim
Mt. Ebal
Jabbok R.
Joppa
Aphek
Shiloh
AMMON
Gibeon Ai
Rabbath-ammon
Ashdod
Gezer
Jericho
Jazer
Makkedah
Gilgal
Heshbon
Libnah
Jarmuth
Jerusalem (Jebus)
Mt. Nebo (Pisgah)
Ashkelon
Gath
Lachish
Jahaz
Gaza (Azzah)
Eglon
Hebron
Dibon
Debir
MOAB
Salt (Dead) Sea
Ar
Kir-moab
Beer-sheba
Hormah
Unsuccessful invasion.
Zoar
Wilderness of Zin
Ije-abarim
Bozrah
Kadesh-barnea
Oboth
Punon
Arnon R.
Zered (Zared)
EDOM
Mt. Hor ? (Jebel Harun)

CANAAN

River of Egypt

Nile Delta

Rameses or Zoan (Tanis)
Sin (Pelusium)
GOSHEN
Baal-zephon
L. Ballah
Wilderness of Shur
Jebel Helal
Pi-beseth (Bubastis)
Succoth
Pithom
Timsah
Etham
Bitter Lakes
On (Heliopolis)
Wilderness of Etham
Memphis
Pyramids
Wilderness of Paran
Ezion-geber Elath
Arabah
Mt. SEIR
Heracleopolis
Marah
Elim
SINAI
PENINSULA
LAND
OF
MIDIAN
Wilderness of Sin
Dophkah
Alush
Hazeroth
Gulf of Aqaba
DESERT
Jebel Serbal
Kibroth-hattaavah
Rephidim
Taberah
Mt. Sinai or Mt. Horeb
Gulf of Suez
Nile River
Lycopolis

Red Sea

tions which make up the major part of the Book of Deuteronomy, the Greek name of which means the *Second Law*.

Having completed his instruction of them, this grand old man added his farewell song and his parting benediction. Then, turning up the slope behind him, he made his way along to the summit of this peak which lies about 10 miles due east of the mouth of the Jordan. From its top there is a breath-taking view of the Land of Israel, and his eyes feasted upon the scene, as he communed with his Lord, whom he had served so well. And his heart, like his life, now being full, he died there on the heights of Pisgah in the land of Moab. Later he was secretly buried in a sheltered valley close by, where his remains would be safe from marauding hands.

Not far to the north of this mountain lay the trail which dropped down from Heshbon, the former capital of the Amorites, to the ford of the Jordan, about 6 miles east of Jericho. The trail then climbed up to Jerusalem and pushed on west through the city of Gezer to Joppa on the Mediterranean. Presumably the camp stood near this highway in the flatlands known as the Plains of Moab.

Israel had acquired a new leader, Joshua, a prince of the tribe of Ephraim, a brave soldier and a clever strategist. He, and Caleb, prince of Judah, had been the only two of the twelve spies sent into Canaan 39 years before who had favored making an attack at that time. Now that Moses had passed on, the moment in which to strike was at hand. The Lord had but to speak to Joshua's heart and he would quickly be on his way. Instructions were thus given the people to be in readiness for the march.

Arrangements had been completed between Moses and the tribes of Reuben and Gad and the half-tribe of Manasseh, that they were to find homes in the land already conquered in this Trans-Jordan area. So they parted with their brethren and went off in search of pastures and living space. The interest of the remainder was concentrated in the west. Jericho stood in their way, so spies were dispatched to search it out; and, pending their return, the new leader bided his time.

The report of these scouts, not only in regard to this first large city along the way, but with respect to fear engendered throughout the land, was so favorable that Joshua acted immediately. The camp on the high tableland was promptly struck; the tribes formed into their accustomed marching order (Num. 2:34) and started off. The trail drops rapidly to the valley floor, and the east bank of the river would have been reached easily before nightfall. There camp was pitched again; the people rested while Joshua and his officers and other leaders were, no doubt, busy preparing to ford the stream and to set up a base camp beyond it from which the attack on Jericho might be launched.

These preparations appear to have consumed three days, and on the afternoon of the third the officers passed through the camp giving instructions for the morrow. The crossing of the Jordan, like the crossing of the "Red Sea," would be a most memorable day in Israel's history—and here it was upon them. The following morning they would enter the Promised Land!

On site of ancient Moabite town lies El Karak with Crusader castle

VI

ISRAEL INVADES
THE PROMISED LAND

It was early April, for the Passover season was at hand as the Israelites paused on the eastern bank of the Jordan. What year was it? There is still disagreement as to the time of the destruction and the beginning of the long abandonment of the older city of Jericho, but a date not far from 1250 B.C. is probable.

There was of course the river to ford, and the stream was normally running with its banks overflowing with melting snow water at this particular season. But a miraculous crossing was made, even though the miracle of the dry river bed may well have been the result of a landslide upstream, touched off by an earthquake. There are a number of recorded phenomena of this same kind resulting from earth tremors and bringing about a temporary damming of the stream, one of them as late as 1927.

Once across, the tents were pitched at Gilgal, which seems to have been about halfway between the river and Jericho, their first military objective. There were solemn religious observances at this base camp, which was consecrated as holy ground and remained a sacred center until at least the early years of the kingdom. Troops from the tribes of Reuben, Gad and Manasseh assembled there, too, for they had agreed to aid with the conquest of the remainder of the land (Josh. 4:12).

Jericho, as the well-known Bible account relates, fell quickly, utterly and also miraculously, even though another trembler may have shaken the valley and hurled its double walls to the earth. The manner in which their remains were scattered make it seem that a 'quake may have been the means selected by the Lord to aid His chosen people. Also it could have touched off the holocaust that consumed this oldest Palestinian city. What now lay ahead?

Able strategist that he was, it hardly seems that Joshua merely attempted to smash his way into and through Canaan. His fighting men had gained experience in the encounters in the Trans-Jordan, but in number and ability they could not hope to sweep all before them. Spies such as those that visited Jericho were very probably already busy elsewhere. There were the opinions of sharp-eyed caravan men to be sought and weighed. And over the longer period there must have been evidence of the slow weakening of Egypt and the loss of strength of some Canaanite cities. No doubt Joshua's intelligence department worked overtime gathering data on which his campaign was based.

The first move beyond Jericho could have been by way of the trail used by Lot as he parted from Abraham and sought a home in the valley. But of course the Israelites were moving in the opposite direction and climbing up the steep path toward Bethel and Ai (Hai), 13 miles west of (and 3200 feet higher than) Jericho. By the Bible account, there was first a defeat and then a victory at this latter place. However, the sites of both Ai and Bethel have been very carefully unearthed. There is evidence that the former was destroyed about 2200, or even as early as 2400 B.C., and never became a city again. Its very name, *ha-'Ai*, means "the Ruin." Nearby Bethel—about 1½ miles from *et-Tell*, which had once been Ai— was reduced to burnt rubble about the time of the Israelite invasion. Its overthrow very likely provided their first foothold in the central highlands. The Canaanites now knew they were in for trouble, and the tactics of the crafty Gibeonites clearly indicate as much (Josh. 9).

The mound of ancient Jericho

The mound of Lachish

At this point it is well to recall that Jacob's sons were shepherds when they entered Egypt. Their children presumably followed this same way of life during the long period of "bondage," and it had surely been their occupation throughout the years of wandering. Consequently they would have been most interested in those sections of Palestine which were best adapted to the pasturing of their flocks, or the highland areas. Two and a half tribes had already elected to make their home in the grazing lands to the east of Jordan, but about three quarters of the people were still to be cared for.

After subduing the strong point at the center of the highlands, Joshua seems to have next turned his attention to the confederacy of the five Amorite kings. Israelite forces had returned to the base camp at Gilgal, and from there a forced march was made to Gibeon, present day el-Jib, about 5½ miles north of Jerusalem. There, in the Vale of Ajalon, "the sun stood still and the moon stayed" long enough for a decisive battle to be won with heavenly aid.

Moving southwest through the rolling Shephelah, the next encounter was the ancient, wealthy city of Lachish. This place seems to have fallen to the invaders about the year 1230 B.C., according to the remains of tax records dug up at the city site in *Tell ed-Duweir*.

Debir, formerly known as Kiriath-sepher, was the next objective, and there are two separate accounts of its taking (Josh. 10:38, 39; and 15:15-17 with Judg. 1:11-13). Now known as *Tell Beit Mirsim,* or "the mound of the house of the fast camel driver," it has yielded a wealth of evidence, both of the life lived in olden times and as to the dating of its capture a number of years previous to 1200 B.C.

Other places in this same section, such as Beth-zur, give evidence of having also changed hands at the close of the Late Bronze Age, and so indicate that some important Canaanite towns did fall to these trespassers from the wastelands. Hebron, by the Bible account, was another. Israel had also gained a footing in the southern highlands, although the campaign may not have been the whirlwind affair one of the accounts in the Book of Joshua intimates.

A second and somewhat larger league of Canaanite kings then sought to stop the inroads of these marauders from the wilderness. They assembled their forces in the upper Jordan Valley under the command of a King Jabin. There, by the "waters of Merom," which was either Lake Hula or, more probably, a spring a few miles southwest of it, a battle took place in which the Israelites were eminently successful.

But perhaps as important as this decisive engagement was Joshua's siege and taking of the capital of this northern confederacy, the city called Hazor which lay hard by. When a careful archaeologist, writing about its current excavation, speaks of it as a "big city," he is far from exaggerating. Its built-up area of some 200 acres made it by far the largest center of population in Palestine in Canaanite times, and as much as ten, twenty or more, times as large as some of its fortified contemporaries. The invaders seem to have achieved a strong, well-trained striking force.

While the list of Joshua's conquests is imposing, it is frankly admitted that all of Canaan was not immediately subdued. Yet sufficient cities had been destroyed so that it seemed safe for the remaining nine tribes to divide the land west of the Jordan between them. It was necessary, too, to find additional territory for the half-tribe of Manasseh, the area in Gilead and Bashan not being sufficient for this sixth largest of the thirteen groupings of the Israelites. It would now be safe to remove the women, children, old people and herds and flocks from Gilgal, and the camp there could be abandoned.

In the section west of the Jordan, the areas assigned by the drawing of lots and ranging from north to south, were roughly as follows: Asher received a coastal strip about 12 miles wide, stretching from the Leontes River above Tyre to the upper edge of the Plain of Sharon below Mount Carmel. Beside it was the land of the tribe of Naphtali, running south from the Leontes to Mount Tabor and east to the Jordan

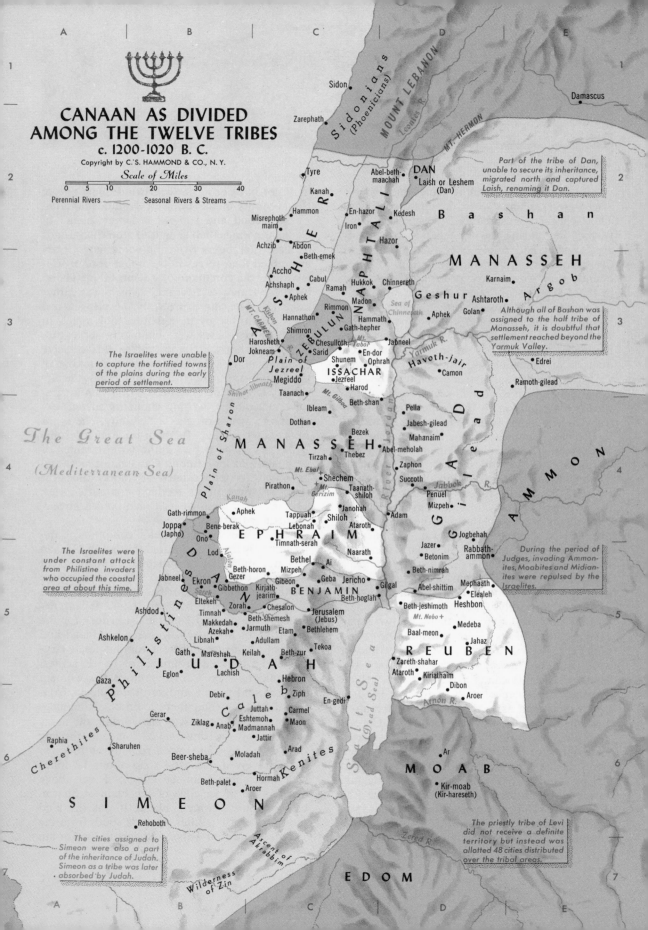

and the Sea of Galilee. Below these two was the small tract of Zebulun and next east of it the area, about equal in size, which had fallen to Issachar.

Below them and Asher was the large, very irregular-shaped block stretching from the seacoast to the Jordan, which had also been given to Manasseh. Immediately below it were the three far smaller parcels to provide homes for Ephraim, Benjamin and Dan. It should be pointed out perhaps that this latter tribe was unable to take over the coastal plains which which were located in the lands of Judah, Simeon and Benjamin.

In return for his wonderful leadership, Joshua was assigned a town of his own, Timnath-serah in the hills of Ephraim. There he died, aged 110 years, but not until he had established a new religious center at Shiloh, about 10 miles to the northeast, in the same tribal area. Here a new sanctuary was erected to house the venerated Ark of the Covenant; and Shiloh is supposed to have been the first city the Israelites ever constructed for themselves.

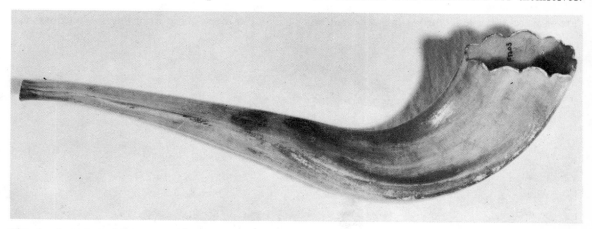

The shophar or ram's horn, Jewish ceremonial instrument used at Jericho

made up the bulk of its allotment. The portion in the hills was inadequate, so a number of its members went to the headwaters of the Jordan, there seized the city of Laish (Leshem), changed its name to Dan and so peopled this northern outpost.

The lot which fell to Judah was bounded on the north by the Vale of Sorek and a curving line from Kirjath-jearim swinging just south of Jerusalem and reaching the northern end of the Dead Sea. It bordered the lower edge of the highlands on the south, and stretched through from the Mediterranean to the Dead Sea. Below it, in the Negeb, or "south country," the tiny tribe of Simeon shared with its larger neighbor, Judah, the cities in the extreme south of Canaan.

One other group still remained to be cared for, the Levites, or descendants of Levi. This whole tribe had been set aside and charged with the care of the sanctuary. Consequently it was given rights in a total of 48 towns scattered through all the tribes, while those Levites who were priests lived in other towns all of For many years pilgrimages would be made there by devout members of all the tribes.

But if Shiloh was the first city which these invaders built from the very lowest foundations, there were many which they rebuilt after assailing and demolishing them. Unhappily they were shepherds, not mechanics or artisans, and the remains of this early reconstruction work is pretty shabby and inferior, by comparison, to what they had destroyed. This warrants a few comparisons between life as it had been and as it now began to develop.

Canaan was a land of city-states, whose kings squabbled among themselves, even during the period when Egypt had kept a firm hand on the land. While the Israelites were formed into families, clans and tribes, and tended to keep this type of social organization, the situation in the Canaanite cities was quite different. In them there was a ruling class, an aristocracy, as in Egypt, and a lower class who were serfs and so virtually slaves. Thus the labor of the majority was at the beck and call of their masters, and their cities could be built by forced labor to whatever standards were demanded.

By contrast, the Israelite was a relatively independent person. He had, and respected, his tribal and family loyalties. But in Israel there was no *corvée,* no conscription of labor until after the beginning of the kingdom. And so it was that when the Israelites of a city went to work as a group to rebuild its walls, they worked together just long enough to construct their minimum requirements. Once these were completed, each man went about his own affairs again, with the result that the Palestinian towns were much less sturdy and well built af-

period the Moabites, under their King Eglon, harassed Israel until he was dispatched by the brave, left-handed Ehud. Then at a little later time there had been the threat by the Canaanite federation, in which its general, Sisera, was slain and his chariot corps hacked to pieces by an Israelite army recruited from the northern tribes. This exploit had not only made a hero of Barak, the leader of these victorious troops, but also a heroine of the prophetess Deborah, then judging Israel, who had prevailed upon Barak to raise the forces to overcome the enemy host.

However, there were internal tensions also.

Mt. Tabor in Lower Galilee

ter the invasion. It took these shepherds several generations to advance from being "tenters" and wanderers to becoming city-dwellers. Also, they were not able to spend all their time cultivating the gentler arts of peace. There was war, from within as well as from without. During the period of the Judges there were invasions from the east by the Ammonites, the Moabites and the Midianites. It was these latter pillagers that brought the able Gideon to fame, when he crushed their power and in return was offered the kingship in Israel.

For eighteen years the Ammonites held Israel east of the Jordan in subjugation, until dislodged by another "judge" or national leader and hero, Jephthah. During another 18-year

There had been threats against the tribe of Reuben when its members erected a memorial altar within its own territory. But the serious outbreak came toward the end of the period of of the Judges, when the Benjamites were nearly blotted out for having offered protection to wicked folk of the city of Gibeah (Judg. 19;20).

This strife all came about during that period regarding which the Bible tells us distinctly there was no king in Israel, and everyone did as he thought best (Judg. 21:25). Yet the Samson escapades bring to light a new threat which soon became so great that Israel was forced to draw closer together and in but a few years select a king. It appears that another invasion of Canaan had come.

VII

THE FOUNDING OF THE KINGDOM

There are a goodly number of earnest Christians today who like to feel that the first five books of the Bible—the Books of Moses—are little altered from the form in which it is presumed he composed them. There is, none-theless, unmistakable evidence that through extensive editing the form in which we now know them was not achieved until long after the great leader had passed from this life on the summit of Mount Nebo. In recent years it has been shown beyond doubt that the people known as the Philistines did not secure a foot-hold in the Holy Land before the 12th century before Christ. Thus when we find mention of them in Genesis (Gen. 21:32) or Exodus (Ex. 15:14), their inclusion should be looked upon as the expression of a later viewpoint, and as referring rather to the Canaanitish people occupying these seacoast plains which were later taken over by the invading Philistines.

The "Sea Peoples," as the Egyptians called them, apparently originated in Caphtor, which is the island of Crete. From this mountain fastness they attacked Greece and also the eastern shores of the Mediterranean Sea. A horde of them seems to have swarmed down along that coast, supported by a fleet of ships off-shore, conquering and gaining strength as they went, their final objective being Egypt and its abounding wealth. But the Egyptians made effective preparations and, under Rameses III, defeated and turned back these bold raiders in the year 1188 B.C. Those who escaped slaughter retreated up the coast and established a five-city confederacy—Ekron, Ashdod (Azotus), Ashkelon, Gaza and Gath—in the plains along the seacoast between Joppa and the Egyptian border. The episodes involving Samson the strong man are thus a forecast of the strife to come between these well organized,

hard-fighting Philistines and the loosely knit and highly independent Israelites. God's chosen people would be subjected to far more severe tests from within and without during the next several generations, for their new neighbors would prove to be archenemies.

The theocracy formed at Sinai was proving too ideal a government for imperfect men. Also the priestly house of Eli was doomed, so God called Samuel as a seer, or prophet, and the last of the competent judges, so he might hold these chosen people together. And his ministrations came none too soon, for the Philistines thrust their way into Israel and gave the Israelites a severe beating in two sharp battles. In addition, they seized the venerated Ark of the Covenant and carried it off with them as a battle prize. However, this revered trophy proved the source of much trouble and, after keeping it for seven months, they willingly returned it.

Almost with one accord the elders of Israel began to plead with their new leader, Samuel, to form them into a kingdom, so they might compete more successfully with neighbors provided with such leadership. While an arrangement of this kind had long been the divine intention (Gen. 17:6, 16; Deut. 17:14-20), the king was to have been a direct representative of the Lord, and neither a political symbol nor an absolute worldly monarch. But what the people were now proposing looked very much like a transfer of faith from an almighty invisible god to a visible, if imperfect, king. And while Samuel patiently warned what might happen to the peoples' freedoms if a ruler was placed in power, they continued their clamor, and the Lord finally consented to their faulty wishes. The heavenly choice fell to a personable, youngish man of the tribe of Benjamin, Saul, the son of Kish, and this preference was made known to the prophet.

Shortly thereafter he met this chosen of the Lord at the little city of Ramah (Rama), 15 miles east of Joppa, and honored and anointed him. A short while later Samuel called the people of Israel together at Mizpeh (Mizpah),

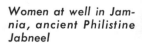

Women at well in Jamnia, ancient Philistine Jabneel

THE KINGDOM OF SAUL
c. 1020-1000 B.C.

Copyright by C. S. Hammond & Co., N.Y.

Scale of Miles

0 5 10   20   30   40

Perennial Rivers

Seasonal Rivers & Streams

Capitals ....

Israelite Forces ....

Enemies of the Israelites

Kingdom of Saul at its greatest extent

The Philistines invaded Israel through the Plain of Jezreel. The Israelites were defeated and Saul slain at Mt. Gilboa.

Saul defeated the Ammonites besieging Jabesh-gilead. For his triumph Saul was proclaimed King of all Israel.

Jonathan's exploits at Michmash routed the Philistines.

Home of Samuel. Saul anointed here.

Encounter of David and Goliath.

David, driven into exile by Saul, finally took refuge among the Philistines and settled in Ziklag.

Saul secured the southern border of Judah by defeating the Amalekites.

The Great Sea
(Mediterranean Sea)

Place names

Sidon
Zarephath
Damascus
ZOBAH
MOUNT LEBANON
Leontes R.
MT. HERMON
SYRIAN
Tyre
Kanah
Abel-beth-maachah
Dan
Ijon
MAACHAH
STATES
Kedesh
Aramaeans
Achzib
Hazor
GESHUR
Bashan
Accho
Karnaim
Cabul
Chinnereth
Ashtaroth
Aphek
Rimmon
Sea of Chinnereth
TOB
Shimron
Hammath
Mt. Tabor
Plain of Jezreel
En-dor
Havoth-jair
Edrei
Dor
Shunem
Camon
Ramoth-gilead
MT. CARMEL
Kishon R.
Megiddo
Jezreel
MT. GILBOA
Beth-shan
Taanach
Jabesh-gilead
Mahanaim
Ibleam
Dothan
Bezek
GILEAD
Plain of Sharon
Thebez
Mt. Ebal
Shechem
Succoth
Penuel
Jabbok R.
Mt. Gerizim
Jordan River
AMMON
Canaanites
Aphek
Shiloh
Adamah
Joppa
Ramathaim
Ophrah
Rabbath-ammon
Lod
Bethel
Beth-horon
Michmash
Mizpeh
Geba
Jabneel
Gezer
Gibeon
Ramah
Gilgal
Heshbon
Ekron
Kirjath-jearim
Gibeah
Nob
Ashdod
Timnah
Beth-shemesh
Jerusalem (Jebusite city)
Mt. Nebo
Elah
Azekah
Socoh
Bethlehem
Medeba
Ashkelon
Adullam
Tekoa
Keilah
PHILISTIA
Gath
Lachish
Hebron
Gaza
Eglon
Ziph
En-gedi
Dibon
Aroer
Carmel
Maon
MOAB
Gerar
Ziklag
JUDAH
Jattir
Wilderness of Judah
Salt Sea (Dead Sea)
Ar
Raphia
Beer-sheba
Cherethites
Hormah
Kenites
Besor
Aroer
Kir-moab (Kir-hareseth)
Amalekites
EDOM
Phoenicians

Ruins of Beth Shan, ancient strong point in Canaan

about 8 miles northwest of Jerusalem. There, by casting lots, they agreed upon Saul the Benjamite as their king. While some were anything but pleased by this choice (1 Sam. [1 Kings] 10:26, 27), enough of them did follow him to beleagured Jabesh-gilead beyond the Jordan, so that they drove off the besieging Ammonites. Soon after this victory, Saul was formally proclaimed their ruler at Gilgal.

The new king took up his residence in tiny Gibeah, whose name means "height." The little town stood on an eminence some 3 miles north of Jerusalem. The remains of Saul's royal city were unearthed in the *Tell el-Ful,* which in turn means "hill of beans" and is an indication that the soil, unsuited to grains, still raises most excellent legumes. Even the pots and bowls from the kitchen of the modest little palace have come again to light, and it is now known that the throne room was only about 15 by 24 feet. But then the double walls of the palace fortress enclosed a space less than 40 by 60 yards, and in this Gibeah of Saul, life tended to be rather crude and primitive. The kingdom of Israel had most humble beginnings.

Whatever his personal ambitions may have been, necessity demanded that Saul be a king indeed. One of his first official acts was to institute conscription for military service and to establish a standing army, said to have totaled 3000 men. Soon a routine action involving a part of this force under the leadership of Saul's eldest son, Jonathan, touched off another war with their foes to the west. A sizable Philistine force promptly invaded the hill country and pitched its camp at Michmash. Whereupon Israel promptly fled, some to the Jordan Valley, a few even taking refuge beyond that river.

In rallying forces at Gilgal and preparing to march against these invaders, deeply worried Saul committed the first of two serious and costly errors, this first one depriving him of the right to establish a dynasty. Samuel had firmly promised to appear and entreat the Lord in behalf of His people. But the wily priest, having some doubts evidently of Saul's dependability, purposely delayed his arrival and so allowed the volunteers to grow restless and begin to desert the cause in alarming numbers. In this crisis the king usurped the priestly prerogative and himself conducted the sacrifice. Thereupon Samuel suddenly appeared, berated the king for

his disobedience and presumption, and threatened that the throne would pass from both him and his family.

Finally his son, Jonathan, defeated the invading forces, whose weapons of iron may, in those very early years of the use of this new metal, have made their equipment far superior to that of the Israelites. The Philistine smiths had a monopoly for many years in the production and working of iron, which knowledge was withheld from the Israelites (1 Sam. [1 Kings] 13:19-22). One of their ancient smelters has been discovered in the *Wadi Ghazzeh* to the south of Gaza.

Saul's second grave error, his failure to obey God, was not long delayed. After securing the southern border of the Promised Land by defeating the Amalekites, he failed to completely destroy them and their possessions as had been his instructions. After upbraiding the king for this disobedience, Samuel departed for his home in Ramah and broke off all further contact with the man he had anointed as ruler.

But after a number of years Samuel was instructed to go to Bethlehem and there select a youthful shepherd lad, David ben Jesse, and anoint him as the one chosen by the Lord to succeed Saul as sovereign. Thus begins a most dramatic period, related in greater detail than any other similar span of years in all of the Old Testament. It ultimately climaxed in the "Golden Age" of Solomon, but there were many exciting years at the outset before this shepherd boy managed to ascend first the throne of Judah, and a little later that of all Israel.

Saul, who had grown neurotic—"an evil spirit from the Lord troubled him" (1 Sam. [1 Kings] 16:14)—first met his successor when this lad became his armor-bearer and court harper. David's skillful playing and singing were sufficient to rouse the king from his attacks of deep despair. There was a period during which he returned home from life in the palace, and then, as a slightly older David, he suddenly came back into contact with the king when he slew the Philistine giant, Goliath. His great popularity following this heroic act soon touched off Saul's violent jealousy, and David, although by then the king's son-in-law, was in a short while forced to flee for his life.

Quite naturally he sought refuge in the southern highlands, the land of Judah, which he knew so well. There he was destined to live, sometimes with as many as 400 followers, as a sort of Hebrew "Robin Hood." On his flight, he stopped and secured food and the iron-bladed sword of his victim Goliath in the little priestly city of Nob beside the north-south trail and within sight of the walls about "Canaanite" Jerusalem. And Saul at Gibeah soon knew of the direction he had taken.

From there he hurried on to the Philistine city of Gath, some 25 miles west and a little south of his native Bethlehem. He went there

seeking an alliance with Israel's enemies. But in the midst of his audience with King Achish, he decided against it, pretended to be crazy and was allowed to depart. It was then that he gathered his supporters about him and went to live in one of the numerous caves in these limestone hills. His choice among them was Adullam, about a dozen miles from both Bethlehem and Hebron. And since Saul appeared ready to attempt his capture and his aged father and mother would thus be in much danger, he took his parents to Moab–where his family had roots, as is told in the Book of Ruth–and put them under protection of its king. Actually he was coming to be known as a "king" himself, even by Israel's enemies (1 Sam. [1 Kings] 21:10, 11).

And Saul did make strenuous attempts to seize this younger man who was due to one day become his successor. He would willingly have wiped him and his whole family out. Yet David was quite the contrary. Twice Saul was completely in his power and he could have slain him easily. On one occasion the king sought a few minutes of rest in a cave in the wilderness west of the Dead Sea, into which David and several companions had fled to escape Saul's soldiers. As the weary ruler paused, his quarry sliced a piece of cloth from the hem of the kingly garment, as evidence that he could, just as easily, have slit the royal throat. The second time, David and his cousin Abishai stole into Saul's camp in the hills below Hebron in the dead of night and made off with the king's own spear. Consequently it should be emphasized that when David finally came to the throne it was not as an assassin.

For a time he did have to take refuge among the Philistines and, as their vassal, was assigned little Ziklag as his own city. It lay well to the south, probably in the vicinity of Gerar. Would he now be forced to take up arms in the great new contest between these able farmers, artisans and soldiers of the seacoast plains and the Israelites, which was then in the making?

Jealousy on the part of certain of the Philistine princes perhaps kept David from being thrust into a highly embarrassing spot. As the host of Philistia marched off to the north to engage Saul, the one-time shepherd boy and his Hebrew band were attached to and accompanied King Achish. When the army paused

Shepherd boy with flute

Shepherd with flock near Bethlehem

at Aphek, the suspicious lords of the Philistines put sufficient pressure upon their king so that David and his party were hurriedly ordered back to Ziklag in the "south country."

Saul had also been assembling the fighting men of Israel and seems this time to have been forced to accept battle in the northern Plain of Jezreel, rather than in the central highlands. The king's confidence was by now evidently pretty badly shaken. He had totally lost contact with God. And he also had a feeling that he was about to suffer serious defeat and part with his throne and his life. Could he perhaps get in touch with the long-dead Samuel?

There was at En-dor, a settlement on the shoulders of the Hill of Moreh, a hillock to the north of Jezreel, a female soothsayer and spiritualistic medium. At Saul's orders, he was taken to visit this "woman of En-dor," who conducted a seance for him at which the spirit of Samuel appeared. A voice which Saul took to be that of the former prophet and judge spoke most frightening words. Israel, it said, would be badly defeated by the Philistines on the following day—and—the king and his sons would be slain. Promptly Saul fell in a faint.

Yet, whatever the source of these prophetic words, they proved to be only too true.

The battle was joined on Gilboa, a northeastern spur of the highlands as they drop away into the south rim of the Valley of Jezreel. There the Philistine archers raised havoc with the Israelites, who fled the field, so that these mighty bowmen were able to easily pick off the three royal princes one after another. Then a final deadly shaft lodged in the body of the king himself. Poor man! He had lost his Lord. He was definitely losing his kingdom. And he was ready, if his armor-bearer would kindly take it, to lose his faltering life, rather than fall prisoner to his foes.

But his youthful aide refused to strike him down, so the pathetic first king of Israel had to fall upon his own sword and end his sufferings. The following day his head was hacked off and taken away as a somber memento of victory, while his body and the bodies of his sons were fastened to the walls of nearby Beth-shan, now a Philistine stronghold.

These bloody cadavers were removed secretly and given decent burial by the men of Jabesh-gilead, in return for Saul's aid to their city years before. Also David, the outcast, wrote a most moving lamentation for his dead king and father-in-law, for whom he still maintained considerable admiration and affection (2 Sam. [2 Kings] 1:17-27). But the affairs of Israel seemed at that moment to be at a very, very low ebb.

VIII

ISRAEL'S GOLDEN AGE

While contemporary Old Testament records are lacking, the Apostle Paul, who lived about ten centuries later, tells us that Saul reigned for 40 years (Acts 13:21). Record keeping in Palestine in New Testament times seems to have embraced "writing" by means of a pen and ink, with papyrus or prepared animal skins as the recording material. Unlike Egypt, where in a dry climate papyrus was extensively used as a durable recording material, the Holy Land was relatively damp so that both papyrus and leather slowly broke down even in storage. Both materials burned quite readily, too, and since Jerusalem was twice totally destroyed, and probably thoroughly sacked and pillaged on several occasions, early records, other than the closely guarded text of the Holy Scriptures, have largely disappeared.

As a consequence, accurate dating during this era of the combined kingdom is almost impossible. Paul's notations of 40 years for Saul's reign may be taken in the broad sense of "one generation," which would make it considerably less than 40 years. Modern chronology places Saul's reign at c. 1020-1000 B.C.

The chronology of Ussher with which so many are familiar, lags some 50 years behind at this point in Bible history.

So let it be assumed that Saul was anointed at Gilgal about 1020 B.C. About this time a drastic change in affairs in Egypt occurred. There the high priests of Amun seized the reins of government and held power almost a century and a half. Egyptian might and prestige quickly crumbled, and during that period this land of the Pharaohs was in no manner a threat to its neighbors, including Israel.

By the time David came to the throne in 1000 B.C., international affairs were relatively tranquil. A few of the smaller countries nearby were willing to challenge the badly weakened nation the slain Saul had left behind him. But that was because they were not at first aware of the caliber of the leader with whom they must deal from then on.

David was in little Ziklag, far to the south, when word came of the disaster in the Valley of Jezreel. What ought he to do? His response was characteristic of many of his acts from that point on. He sought the will of the Lord and was told to betake himself to Hebron, the Hittite settlement which had become quite a substantial city since Abraham first camped beside it hundreds of years before. So he took his two wives, and his 600 fighting men and their fam-

The Dome of the Rock stands upon the site of Solomon's temple

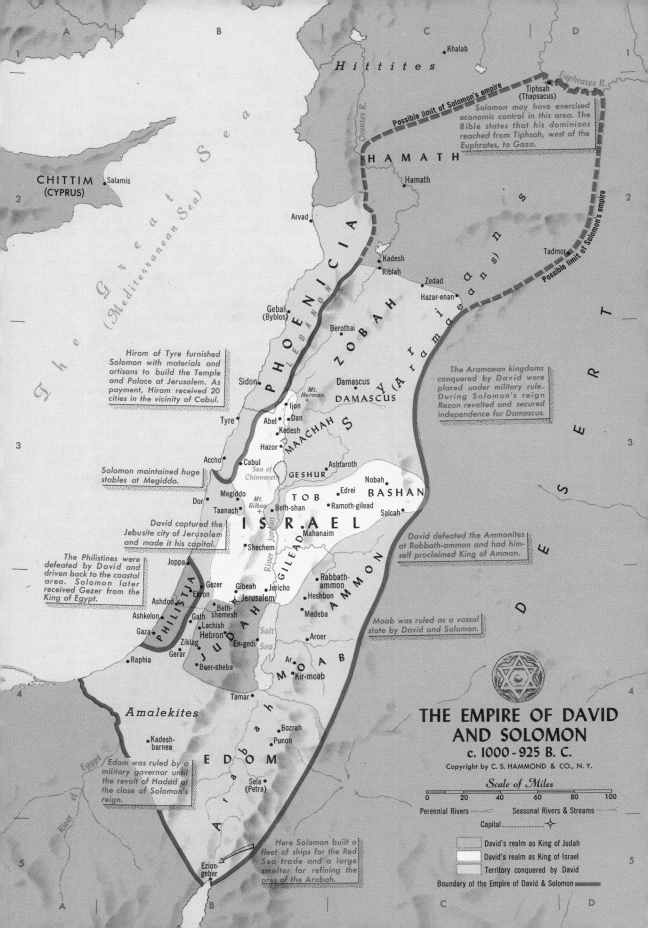

THE EMPIRE OF DAVID AND SOLOMON
c. 1000-925 B.C.

Copyright by C. S. HAMMOND & CO., N.Y.

Scale of Miles

0   20   40   60   80   100

Perennial Rivers —— Seasonal Rivers & Streams ---

Capital ——————◇

▢ David's realm as King of Judah
▢ David's realm as King of Israel
▢ Territory conquered by David
━━ Boundary of the Empire of David & Solomon

Khalab

Hittites

Tiphsah (Thapsacus)   Euphrates R.

Possible limit of Solomon's empire

Solomon may have exercised economic control in this area. The Bible states that his dominions reached from Tiphsah, west of the Euphrates, to Gaza.

HAMATH

Hamath

CHITTIM (CYPRUS)   Salamis

The Great Sea (Mediterranean Sea)

Arvad

Kadesh
Riblah
Zedad
Hazar-enan

Possible limit of Solomon's empire

Tadmor

Gebal (Byblos)

Berothai

ZOBAH

DAMASCUS

Damascus

The Aramaean kingdoms conquered by David were placed under military rule. During Solomon's reign Rezon revolted and secured independence for Damascus.

Hiram of Tyre furnished Solomon with materials and artisans to build the Temple and Palace at Jerusalem. As payment, Hiram received 20 cities in the vicinity of Cabul.

PHOENICIA

Sidon

Mt. Hermon

Ijon
Abel   Dan
Kedesh
Hazor

Tyre

Accho

Cabul

Sea of Chinnereth

MAACHAH

S Y R I A (Aramaeans) DESERT

Solomon maintained huge stables at Megiddo.

GESHUR
Ashtaroth

Nobah

Dor   Megiddo

Mt. Gilboa

TOB

Edrei

BASHAN

Taanach   Beth-shan
Ramoth-gilead
Salcah

ISRAEL

David captured the Jebusite city of Jerusalem and made it his capital.

Shechem

GILEAD

Mahanaim

David defeated the Ammonites at Rabbath-ammon and had himself proclaimed King of Ammon.

The Philistines were defeated by David and driven back to the coastal area. Solomon later received Gezer from the King of Egypt.

Joppa

Gezer   Gibeah   Jericho
Ekron

PHILISTIA

Ashdod
Beth-shemesh
Ashkelon
Gath   Lachish
Gaza   Hebron   En-gedi
Ziklag
Gerar

JUDAH

Jerusalem

Rabbath-ammon
Heshbon

AMMON

Medeba

Moab was ruled as a vassal state by David and Solomon.

Salt Sea

Aroer

MOAB

Beer-sheba

Ar
Kir-moab

Amalekites

Tamar

River of Egypt

Edom was ruled by a military governor until the revolt of Hadad at the close of Solomon's reign.

Kadesh-barnea

EDOM

Bozrah
Punon

Sela (Petra)

Arabah

Here Solomon built a fleet of ships for the Red Sea trade and a large smelter for refining the ores of the Arabah.

Ezion-geber

ilies, and moved about 20 miles northeast into the higher country. There, in sight of the Cave of Machpelah, in which the bodies of the founders of the Hebrew nation lay, David was anointed King of Judah.

What sort of person was this thirty-year-old man? He has been called a "genius" and is without doubt fully entitled to that designation. On the gentler side, he was a poet, and a most able one, as shown by the magnificent eulogy he wrote at the death of Jonathan (2 Sam. 1:17-27), and seventy-three of the psalms are traditionally ascribed to him. He was a competent musician as well, for he was able with his eight-string lyre (harp) to bring his badly confused king and master back to moments of reasonableness. There is little doubt, too, but that he was a composer, and that some at least of the tunes mentioned in the titles of his psalms were of his own production.

On the sterner side, he proved himself a real statesman, for he found Israel but little more than a loose federation of tribes and made it a much more stable nation, well on its way to becoming an empire. But sterner still were his soldierly qualities, which so soiled his hands with blood that the Lord finally forbade him to build the Temple which had long been his great ambition. Yet the tremendous store of material which he gathered for this sacred structure indicates great ability in still another direction— the businessman. Ruddy, handsome and born to command, this former shepherd boy was indeed the chosen of the Lord (Ps. 78 [77]:70).

But there were tasks ahead to try his mettle, such as the refusal of the northern tribes to swear allegiance to him. Instead they proclaimed Ish-bosheth (Ish-baal, "Man of Baal"), one of Saul's younger sons, king of Israel, with his capital at Mahanaim east of the Jordan. There he ruled for two fruitless years. But he sought to wage war against David, whereupon he and his commander-in-chief, Abner, were both soon dead. At that point, Saul's dynasty came to an abrupt end.

It was in the year 993 B.C. that the tribes traveled down to Hebron and anointed David king over all Israel. These northern clans were, in part at least, vassals of the Philistines, and one of the first tasks of the combined monarchy was to break this strangle hold. Because of its strategic location, and the fact that it shut off Judah from the north and from the better highway to the east, the king wished to gain possession of Jebus, or Jerusalem. So he organized his forces, stormed its stout walls, but apparently captured it by craft. The word rendered "gutter" in some English versions (2 Sam. [2 Kings] 5:8) probably referred to a shaft cut through solid rock, which then led down from inside the old city to the never-failing spring, Gihon. David's forces very likely made their breach through into this corridor, which permitted them to make their way about within the walls, and Jerusalem was quickly theirs. In that manner the former Jebusite stronghold began its long history as the "Holy City," venerated to this day by the three great living religions that worship but one God.

It now became David's stronghold, the capital of Israel, and a threat to ambitious neighboring nations. The walls were strengthened, and other fortresses were erected in Judah, apparently with the Philistines in mind. But the king's acts were not all of a military nature. One great forward step was the organization of the government which was put upon an orderly basis. It is probable that regular records were first kept during this reign.

Another move which had profound effects was the making of a league with the Phoenicians, and principally with Hiram, king of the fabulous trading city of Tyre. Among other things, the Israelites still lacked mechanical skills, craftsmanship and dexterity. The Tyrians, by contrast, were talented artisans, and David invited them into his new city to build him a palace—modestly spoken of as "a house of cedar." Their ability with tools could help offset the proficiency possessed by the Philistines. So David saw to it that the people of Tyre continued to be allies.

These Phoenicians were the great traders of the ancient world, and they stood in need of David's cooperation just as certainly as he needed theirs. Soon they would be getting together, but just at the moment another matter demanded his immediate attention. The annoying Philistines had marched an army almost into his back yard—at least into the Valley of Rephaim, 2 or 3 miles northwest of the city walls. Promptly driven out, they returned a second time, only to be badly beaten and the remnant of them chased back into their own land. Their hostile power was decidedly on the wane.

The Ark of the Covenant was brought to Jerusalem, where a tabernacle had been built to receive it. From then on worship would center in the city. And hardly had that been done, when the Philistines, growing desperate, took one final fling. This time David trounced them thoroughly and, it is assumed, took possession of one of their royal cities, Gath. They gave but little trouble from then on.

Yet the subduing of the Philistines raised a disturbance in other directions. Neighboring nations, worried by the growing strength of Israel, grew tense. The Ammonites joined forces with the Syrians, but their combined armies were defeated. Moab had had to be crushed. Soon afterward difficulty arose with the land to the south of it, Edom, which lay largely south of the Dead Sea. It was made a vassal state, with garrisons of Israelite soldiers scattered across it. And then David suddenly discovered a way to great wealth—through the mines of Edom. Its iron was vital to any nation with a sizable army, while its copper, the basis of brass and bronze, was a most valuable commodity.

Edom, too, lay athwart trade routes coming up out of the huge Arabian Peninsula, in those days, as now, a storied region, and then a storehouse of spices and other valuables. The aggressive Phoenicians would surely have wished to have clear access to trade with the East and no doubt shared its profits with David in return for permission to cross through Israelite territory in search of it. While his son Solomon would bring these business affairs to full fruit during his own reign, his father very likely did far more than merely lay the foundation. The

gifts which he made to the Temple building fund represent an enormous fortune for those days, and the king had assembled it rather than having inherited it from his sheep-raising forebears. Beside being an able soldier and the sweet singer of Israel, he was also a keen business tycoon. Several important caravan routes crossed Israelite territory at one or more points and very probably paid substantial fees into David's coffers.

Certainly the royal establishment, which came to center about his "house" in Jerusalem (2 Sam. [2 Kings] 7:2), was in strong contrast to the simple court Saul maintained at Gibeah. It began to take on the intrigue and low morality which were typical in the palaces of other eastern sovereigns, and David unhappily made his own contributions to these failings. His family had grown to a wide assortment of wives and concubines, plus quite an array of children. With great power and wealth accumulating, it was perhaps only human that there should be strife and contention among his offspring. Their father seems to have been rather an indulgent parent and perhaps just a trace too easygoing.

Also, David was growing older. The years of hardship as an outcast and outlaw were perhaps reflecting on his health. And as his grasp on family and empire affairs lost some of its former firmness, a contest with the favorite among his sons began to build up. The handsome, tactful, glad-handing Absalom, who was quite the apple of his father's eye, decided to try his wings. Other princelings of that age quite frequently shared the throne with their aging parents, so why not he? Perhaps he may have surprised himself with the popular support he obtained. But in any event, by the time his father awoke to what was afoot, Absalom and his followers were in a position to seize the government. Sixty-two-year-old David had to hurriedly flee Jerusalem and, to escape assassination, take refuge in the hill country east of the Jordan.

He seems to have been badly caught off guard, and with life and throne at stake, he called forth his former sagacity and dispatch, rallied his forces, and prepared to meet those seeking his capture, his much-loved son at their head. There was a sharp encounter in the forest in Gilead in which the king, at the request of his generals, took no part. In it Absalom, caught by his long hair in the low-hanging branches of an oak as his frightened mule plunged beneath it, was slain by three well-placed darts flung by Joab, David's flint-hard commander-in-chief. The rebellion from that moment was at an end, but it took rather stern words from ruthless Joab to steady the king, brokenhearted over the loss of his unstable son, so there might be a triumphant return to Jerusalem.

Yet as generally popular as the able monarch continued to be, he did have enemies and there were still factions that opposed him. The following year there was another short-lived rebellion, led by the Benjamite, Sheba. This uprising which was crushed at Abel-beth-maachah, was one of those early expressions of the mutinous tendencies of the ten northern tribes which, a half century later, burst into open revolt and permanently divided Israel.

David's martial spirit seems to have come again to the fore. His bodyguard, made up of valiant and mighty men of many nationalities, was probably strengthened. Also he very willfully and in opposition to his chief officers took a military census of all the tribes. Some consider this to have been a first step in the old soldier's device of starting a war with other nations in the hope of patching up strife at home. But the Lord punished him, and the nation along with him, for his imprudence. The consequence was that the king gave his last years to more peaceful pursuits, especially the preparation for the Temple he was prohibited from building.

Illness seized the once robust man, old far beyond his years, and the impression is given that he became a semi-invalid confined to the palace. Once again, as in the period when Absalom was seeking power eight years before, David's grip on national affairs slackened. And soon there was trouble, for he had at least two more ambitious sons.

The old king's final months were spent as an invalid, for he probably never left the royal quarters. But then Abishag, the fairest young woman in all the kingdom, had been chosen as his nurse. Perhaps she was as patient as she was beautiful and listened attentively as the elderly man prattled on hour after hour, reliving what had been an active, full and intensively useful life. Certainly he was in some way very much preoccupied. Once again the castle, and probably the capital city too, could have been alive with intrigue and rumors, yet David appeared to be totally unaware of what was going on.

This time it was Adonijah who "exalted himself" and was secretly planning to seize the throne. Part of the court circle favored him, while another portion of it, headed by the prophet Nathan and the king's favorite wife, Bath-sheba, supported the latter's son, Solomon. David, it seems, had made a firm promise that this younger prince should succeed him. And by skillful maneuvering he was anointed to be king while the older half-brother and his supporters were celebrating an accession to the throne which never took place. There was quite naturally a disturbed period which followed this coup, during which David passed on. Almost at once came days and weeks of intense violence in which Solomon slew the leaders who opposed him, along with his aspiring half-brother. Then, for the next forty years, the throne was his without further contest.

When he came into undisputed possession about 961 B.C., the international situation was in much the same relaxed state as when David had begun his reign years before. He was, however, called upon to subdue Hamath, far to the north, but otherwise his long term on the throne was free from war. He was forced to take a firm stand with Damascus and with Edom, but upon the whole it was a period of uninterrupted peace.

The empire continued to be slightly indefinite in extent but ran quite certainly from a point well to the northeast of Damascus down along the edge of the Arabian Desert to Ezion-geber. From Kadesh on the Orontes River in Syria, its borders skirted Phoenicia as far south as Mount Carmel, then ran along the shore to Joppa, swung behind Philistia as far as Gaza and, returning to the coast again, continued on to the *wadi* known as "the River of Egypt." A line from the point where this latter emptied into the Mediterranean back across to Ezion-geber completed the circuit of Solomon's realm.

Since he, too, needed Phoenician skills and trade ability, he renewed the league with Hiram begun by his father. While there seemed to be no special threat to his security from out of the land of Egypt, yet if the taking of a wife from among its princesses would help, why not? So the reigning Pharaoh became the young king's father-in-law. Over the years he would make "affinity" with many lands, sealing the compact with a wife taken from among the

Solomon's Pools which bring water to Jerusalem even today

damsels of its ruling family. During his term on the throne, he is claimed to have accumulated, in round numbers, no less than 700 wives and 300 concubines (1 [3] Kings 11:3). If that total is accurate, his was a stupendous harem, undoubtedly the largest in all history.

But his first consuming interest was to erect the Temple which his parent had been denied permission to build. The site, the former threshing floor of a Jebusite farmer, was already available. So, too, was the great store of precious metals accumulated by David, and, with Tyrian assistance, Solomon began the great task. Also he made a move which ultimately helped to bring about the lasting breach in the Israelite nation. Needing an abundance of labor, he established the *corvee,* or impressment of the common people. They had been conscripted in time of war and had surrendered their freedom then in the face of the general alarm. But to be dragged from their farms and homes in time of peace and led away for one out of each three months was rather a bitter pill. The day of reckoning might be delayed, but it eventually came.

The Temple alone was seven long years in construction. Then its furnishings had to be made and the impressive dedication ceremony is supposed to have taken place in October of 950 B.C. (1 [3] Kings 8:2). It is presumed to have remained in continual use for about four centuries, or until its destruction by Nebuchadnezzar in 586 B.C.

The "House of God" being finished, Solomon now turned his efforts to more personal needs. The nation had become strongly aristocratic, with an extensive ruling coterie attached to the court. His own immediate household was large, and with these hangers-on, many of whom evidently lived in the palace, his housing needs were most substantial. This makes it easier to understand why he found it necessary to spend 13 years erecting the complex of structures that made up "his own house." Also of a peaceful nature, there was the planting of gardens and vineyards (Eccl. 2:4-6), some perhaps at a rural retreat at Etam, 7 miles south of the city, as Josephus relates *(Antiq. VIII 7, 3),* while some may have been in the high country far to the north.

He seems to have, at least in the earlier years of his reign, taken considerable interest in religious matters over and above the effort expended in the creation of the Temple. Certainly he took a most prominent part in its dedication exercises, leading the nation in prayer and also invoking divine blessing upon the assembled multitude. Both these were primarily priestly roles.

At the opposite pole, and despite the manifold promises of peace, he gave much attention to military preparedness. The army was maintained at full strength and kept in training and the walls of the capital city enlarged and strengthened. The breach in them effected by David's troops during its capture had been only temporarily filled in. It is now thought that a substantial tower fortress, probably the Millo of Solomon, was erected at this spot. Also there is the probability that he may have walled in the western hill, since remains of ancient stone work there have the characteristics of other construction definitely of his time.

an invading army and quite as favorably situated to exact heavy toll from the stream of trade flowing by.

Few ancient sites have had a more thorough going-over than this one, which fortunately proved quite fruitful. As it was rebuilt by Solomon, it became a most effective fortress city and the headquarters of twenty or more squadrons of his extensive chariot corps. The most interesting find was the huge stables, laid out in systematic order along a broad, paved, central street. The stalls were arranged on either side of paved runways which gave access to them. Each cubicle had a stone manger and a stone column, a roof support, with a hole through it for a tie-rope. Usually the stalls were in groups of 24, which is taken to mean

Model of the Stables of Solomon at Megiddo

Whether the division of the land into twelve districts, which cut across old tribal boundaries, may have been military as well as political, is not certain. That they were "supply" divisions seems to favor the view that they were part of a preparedness plan. But the great contribution to defense were the several fortified towns which were pretty much army posts. Best known among them was Megiddo, at the gap in the Mount Carmel ridge, where the international caravan trail cut through from the Plain of Esdraelon, or Jezreel, to the coastal flatlands of Sharon and Philistia, on its way to Egypt. It was thus well located to give pause to

that, with two horses to a chariot, the corps was based upon squadrons of 12 chariots each. No less than 450 such stalls have so far been unearthed at this one site. While it may be doubtful that the remains of Gezer, Hazor and the other fortified towns will ever yield anywhere near the number of stalls needed to stable the horses for King Solomon's corps of 12,000 horsemen mentioned in the Bible; yet these ruins at Megiddo substantiate reports of a lively trade in horses (1 [3] Kings 10:26-29).

And Solomon, either directly or through his associates, was soon very active in a whole array of business enterprises. While alluded to, and hinted at, they are not treated in detail in Bible text. For several reasons, these activities focused in the east. This was partly because of the wealth of minerals which could be mined in the Edomite dependency between the Dead Sea and the Gulf of Aqaba. The port of Ezion-geber, at the northern end of this latter body of water, eventually became the center of these undertakings.

There, possibly as a joint enterprise with Hiram of Tyre, a copper smelter, a manufacturing plant and a shipyard were erected. The smelter, most ingeniously designed and built, is indeed one of the industrial wonders of the ancient world. Metal refined in it from ores partly "roasted" in the neighborhood of the mines was shipped, either as ingots, or after being processed locally into weapons, tools, fishhooks, nails and other products. Vessels launched there traded down the shores of the Red Sea and possibly as far away as India, Ceylon and the eastern coast of Africa. The products brought home give a fair indication of how far away they may well have journeyed.

There is still evidence today of somewhat more limited operations of this same sort having been carried on in the Jordan Valley, in the area about *Tell Deir 'Alla* and the ancient Succoth. Wood from Bashan and Gilead, burned to charcoal, fed the fires in many smelteries where copper was refined and fused into alloys. Molds for casting were made from the abundant native clay. It was here that Tyrian craftsmen turned out the building trim and ceremonial objects for the Temple.

These Tyrians, or Phoenicians, had ships roaming the Mediterranean, possibly venturing out into the Atlantic and up as far as the tin mines of Cornwall in the south of England. Solomon seems to have had a fleet of vessels accompanying them in trading operations in these western waters. The port of Tarshish (1 [3] Kings 10:22) may have been the most westerly port of call and is thought to have been on the island of Sardinia or in southwestern Spain outside the Strait of Gibraltar. Overland transport of goods between Tyrian ports on the Mediterranean and the port of Ezion-geber serving the eastern ocean was in all probability fairly heavy.

This latter place, which was perhaps one with the town of Elath, was a station on the "King's Highway," and also the objective of the many camel caravans heading up out of that huge spice chest, the Arabian Peninsula. The Land of Sheba, or present-day Yemen, lay at the southwestern corner of this immense chunk of land, and the visit of its queen to the court of Solomon may have been for business purposes quite as well as for political and intellectual concerns. Some of her "hard questions" can have been aimed at smoothing trade relations (1 [3]Kings 10:1-11). But where the gold-rich land of Ophir may have been is still a moot question.

The splendor of the king's court, the bounties of his table and the sense of pomp and circumstance which evidently attended him, pictures the true oriental potentate. Yet "Solomon in all his glory" developed two major defects.

One stemmed from the women he took as wives, who were principally the pledges of other monarchs held as hostages that these rulers would keep the peace. In Hebrew eyes, these women were idolatrous heathen. But political necessity forced Solomon to erect shrines to their gods and to give the appearance of taking part in certain ceremonies at them when visiting dignitaries were at his court. For this apostasy and crass disloyalty "the Lord was angry with Solomon," and the bulk of the kingdom was rent from the hands of his family (1 [3] Kings 11:9-13). In comparison to David, the son's religious spirit was pretty shallow, casual and even opportune.

His second point of weakness resulted from his excessive, sensual worldliness, which expressed itself particularly in his immoderate luxury. This imposed an onerous burden upon his subjects, the bulk of whom had but indifferent loyalty to him, to his family and so to the throne of the combined kingdom. Yet the ruling clique which he had organized and placed in power were too potent and firmly entrenched for his enemies—and he had them—to hope to seize the throne during his lifetime.

So the "Golden Age" continued throughout his forty-year reign and probably brought reasonably wide-spread prosperity despite heavy imposts and levies. But taxes, especially heavy ones, are certain poison politically, and the king was far from being immortal. In fact, Solomon was an even younger man than his father when he finally died—possibly in his sixtieth year. And he had hardly been laid away "in the city of David his father" when the vengeance of the Lord, and of the outraged northern tribes, crashed down.

IX

THE TWO KINGDOMS

Because of his organizing ability and his position at a highly focal point in world affairs, Solomon was quite a factor in his own times. Also, he was Israel's first real dictator, and his death could well bring some dramatic happenings. And if his closing days came within our own times, we might expect that the cables would fairly crackle with rumors and tips and that the event would be noted in the press, over the radio and on television. For, as a host of hangers-on at the court were quite likely well aware, the passing of this ornate king might signal the end of an era.

The diplomatic circle in Jerusalem of that day had in all probability mulled over all attendant facts in its disillusioned way, and had coldly assessed each of the personalities involved. What, then, of the heir presumptive, the Prince Rehoboam, whose mother had been an Ammonitess? Although then in his early forties, he seemed still to be very much the sophomoric type, an arrogant coxcomb and the facade and toast of the younger set. And were there no other royal princes, no younger brothers with ambitions, who might give their elder kinsman a contest? Apparently not.

And what about outside opposition, that is, beyond Israel? There was none to be con-

cerned about at the moment evidently, but there was strong possibility of serious disturbance much closer to home. It centered principally in Jeroboam, the Ephraimite who had at one time been Solomon's superintendent of forced labor. A prophet had forecast that this protégé of the monarch would one day be crowned king over ten of the twelve tribes. When it was known by Solomon, he immediately sought to have this contender for honors slain. Thus Jeroboam, like David in the days of Saul, became an outcast and fled to Egypt.

That land was experiencing a strong, if short-lived, revival. Its throne had been seized by a character known in the Bible as Shishak and to world history as Sheshonk. He had formerly been a Lybian soldier, and it was he who managed to give refuge to Solomon's enemy without causing a breach with that king. The area on the land bridge had once paid substantial revenues into Egyptian coffers, and this new Pharaoh surely had ambitions in that direction.

The funeral was barely over, and Rehoboam little more than hastily and perhaps secretly anointed king, than a call went out for all Israel to meet in solemn conclave at Shechem—yes, Shechem, not in Jerusalem. This location near the tribal center of the nation held a strong note of foreboding. So, too, did the speed with which Jeroboam had raced home from his place of sanctuary, to become spokesman for the northern tribes. Facing Rehoboam, insecure occupant of the throne, he demanded to know whether those who lived beyond Judah's borders might expect a more just, equitable and lenient reign at his hands than had been received at his father's.

The scion of the house of David stalled and begged three days for soul-searching and consultation. The elders of Judah recommended that he promise far greater tolerance. His own age group, however, told him to be adamant. So on the third day he very foolishly informed the tribal leaders that, if they thought his father had been rigorous, they better be on their guard. He was their lawful ruler, and he intended to handle them just as vigorously as he knew how!

This statement was all the dissatisfied Ten Tribes needed to proceed with plans of their own. It was quite true that the decision had been made long since at the foot of Sinai to form

Carved plaque with winged sphinx from Megiddo

60

THE KINGDOMS OF ISRAEL AND JUDAH
c. 925-842 B.C.

Copyright by C. S. HAMMOND & CO., N.Y.

Scale of Miles

0 5 10 20 30 40

Perennial Rivers ....
Seasonal Rivers & Streams ....
Capitals .... ✦
Egyptian & Syrian Attacks ➞

Elijah took refuge in Zarephath and brought back to life the widow's son.

In the reign of Baasha the cities of northern Israel were raided by the King of Damascus in league with Asa, King of Judah.

Aram waged almost constant war against Israel. The Syrians were held in check by Ahab until his death in battle at Ramoth-gilead.

Elijah challenged the prophets of Baal at Mt. Carmel.

The introduction of Phoenician cults following the marriage of Ahab with Jezebel caused violent reactions in Israel that eventually wiped out the house of Omri.

Samaria, fortress capital of Israel was built by Omri c. 870 B.C.

Moab was ruled as a vassal kingdom during the Omri dynasty. The Dibon stele commemorates the victory of Mesha, King of Moab, over Israel and the return of Moabite independence.

Shishak (Sheshonk), Egyptian Pharaoh, raided the divided kingdoms, plundering Jerusalem c. 925 B.C.

During the reign of Jehosophat Judah regained control over Edom.

The Great Sea

(Mediterranean Sea)

PHOENICIA

MOUNT LEBANON

Leontes R.

MT. HERMON

Damascus

Abana R.

Sidon

Zarephath

Tyre

Ijon

Abel-beth-maachah

Dan

Kedesh

Hazor

Accho

Cabul

Chinnereth

GESHUR

Karnaim

Ashtaroth

Sea of Chinnereth

Aphek

Yarmuk

Bashan

Dor

MT. CARMEL

Kishon

Hammath

Mt. Tabor

Plain of Jezreel

Shunem

Jezreel

Havoth-jair

Edrei

Megiddo

Taanach

Beth-shan

Ramoth-gilead

Dothan

Ibleam

Jabesh-gilead

Sochoh

Abel-meholah

Tishbe

Mahanaim

Samaria

Mt. Ebal

Tirzah

ISRAEL

Plain of Sharon

Shechem

Mt. Gerizim

Janohah

Jordan River

GILEAD

Jabbok R.

AMMON

Aphek

Shiloh

Penuel

Joppa

Jeshanah

Lod

Zemaraim

Bethel

Beth-horon

Mizpeh

Jericho

Rabbath-ammon

Jabneel

Gezer

Aijalon

Ramah

Geba

Gilgal

Ekron

Gibbethon

Elealeh

Heshbon

Ashdod

Timnah

Zorah

Jerusalem

Mt. Nebo

Medeba

Azekah

Beth-shemesh

Baal-meon

Jahaz

Ashkelon

Shoco

Etam

Bethlehem

Libnah

Adullam

Gath

Mareshah

Tekoa

Lachish

Beth-zur

PHILISTIA

Adoraim

Hebron

Ataroth

Gaza

Debir

Ziph

Dibon

Aroer

Gerar

En-gedi

Arnon R.

MOAB

Ziklag

Salt Sea (Dead Sea)

Raphia

Beer-sheba

JUDAH

Wilderness of Judah

Ar

Kir-moab (Kir-hareseth)

Valley of Salt

Zered R.

EDOM

A   B   C   D   E

one indissoluble nation. But neither this Rehoboam, nor his father before him, measured up to the high standards of royalty which had been set forth by the Lord (Deut. 17:14-20). Let these people of Judah go their own way. The real kingdom must needs be built from the Josephite tribes. Was it not Joseph who had been Jacob's favorite son?

As Rehoboam announced his fatal decision, Jeroboam and his followers cried out: "What further interest have we in this house of David? Our heritage is in no way dependent upon any descendant of Jesse's! To your own tents, men of Israel! And as for you, you sons of David, attend to your own affairs!"

Rehoboam, faced with the immediate loss of four-fifths of his kingdom, sought to put up a bold front and a show of strength. Choosing his tax collector Adoram, probably a belligerent type, he hurried him off to tell these mutinous folk what might very well happen to them. It was only after the Israelites stoned this hated emissary to death that the pretentious, undesirable king began to come to his senses. These people made it very evident they wanted no part of him. So he had his chariot wheeled out and, jumping aboard, hurried off down the highland trail to the stout walls of Jerusalem. There the men of his own tribe, and of Benjamin, accepted him as head of the dominion his worthy grandparent had at first occupied— the Kingdom of Judah.

The ten other tribes promptly made Jeroboam King of Israel. And he in turn chose their place of meeting, Shechem, as his capital. The fact that he strengthened its fortifications indicates that he felt there could be trouble ahead. This division of Israelite power would quickly be evident to all surrounding nations, too, and in some cases might serve as an invitation to them to take the offensive. Even Rehoboam quickly regained his courage, or, perhaps, his audacity, for he began to plan a war to force his former subjects back into the fold. But the Lord, through one of His prophets, ordered him to cease and desist. This arrangement had been ordained on high and was the penalty for the father's shortcomings, so there was no call for an attempt at national suicide through civil war.

Jeroboam, it appears, had not been entirely a unanimous choice, and sensitive to the attitudes of many of his people, and possibly in part to flatter the groups living east of the Jordan, he established a second, or alternate, capital at Penuel. It was here in the long, long ago that "father" Jacob had wrestled with the angel. It could be, too, that this move was in part to dissuade Syrian forces, then gathering strength in Damascus, from casting covetous eyes on the area east of the river.

Geography also managed to exert considerable influence on religious concerns. The Temple built at Jerusalem acted as a magnet and would continue to attract some members of the northern tribes on down the ages until its final destruction toward the end of Bible times. And because he needed religious as well as political loyalty, Jeroboam took a drastic step. He set up shrines at two old sanctuaries at the extreme limits of the land. The first was at Bethel, about 12 miles up the trail above Jerusalem, and the other at far-off Dan, at the foot of Mount Hermon. As a counterattraction to the Temple, he reached far back to those ancient traditions which had once deceived Aaron

Carved Ivories from Samaria

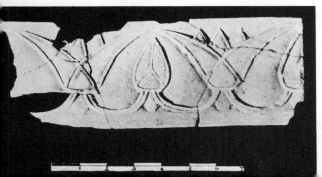

and set up at each shrine a golden calf. While he had recently dwelt in Egypt, where the sacred bull Apis was worshipped, it is doubtful that Jeroboam sought to jettison the worship of Yahweh, for he repeated Aaron's very words when the calves were put in place (1 [3] Kings 12:28 and Ex. 32:4). Heathen influences, nevertheless, led the Israelites into worship of false gods. Also, since the Levites without exception had taken refuge in Judah, laymen had to be impressed into priestly duties. This new throne which he had helped to set up posed many problems indeed.

During the sickness of his son, Abijah, his queen had sought word of the prince's possible recovery from a prophet at Shiloh. Much to her consternation, and that of the king as the word was relayed to him, not only was the prince to die, but Jeroboam's line would be extinguished and the people of Israel would one day be carried into exile and bondage. While the king's way was most evil in the sight of the Lord and his ailing son died as had been foretold, he did finish out his twenty-two year reign and was succeeded by his son, Nadab. Much that was baneful and corrupt, and little that was good and noble, would transpire in this newer Kingdom of Israel before it passed away.

Back in his restricted realm of Judah, Rehoboam was compounding difficulties of his own. Even despite the glorious Temple in the midst of his handsome capital city, he and many of his subjects turned apostate and began setting up temple-towers, idols and pagan groves throughout the land. And in the fifth year of his reign the Egyptians attacked Jerusalem and carried off a huge amount of treasure. Finally, after 17 fruitless years, he gave place to his son Abijam, who sat on the throne but 3 years and was succeeded in turn by a son of his, Asa. This resolute man would rule for no less than 40 years.

The first ten of them were peaceful, and he rid the land of much of its idolatry and despicable practices. He even had the queen mother deposed for having erected an idol. Then, suddenly, an Ethiopian host out of Africa stormed into Judah, and by dint of great effort, and with the Lord's aid, he drove it away.

Soon Baasha, King of Israel, started to fortify Ramah, almost within sight of Jerusalem's walls. Too greatly weakened by the contest with the Africans, Asa was incapable of seizing this Israelite outpost and had to go hurriedly in search of allies. In return for a wealth of the remaining temple treasures, Ben-hadad, Syrian king of Damascus, was prevailed upon to attack northern Israel. This immediately stopped work at Ramah and opened the trail to the north to traffic again. However, this was in the nature of an invitation to the Syrians to consider carefully what might be won in the area to the west of the Jordan, and the time would come when their visits needed no stimulation. Asa, once approved in the sight of the Lord, found far less favor in the closing years of his long occupancy of the throne.

During this extensive period, conditions in the northern kingdom were far from tranquil. Nadab, Jeroboam's son, had hardly gotten accustomed to his task before he was in dire distress. As he led his forces against a town at the edge of the Philistine country, an aspirant to the throne out of the tribe of Issachar assassinated him. The house of Jeroboam had come to an end, as the "man of God" had foretold, but the kingdom of Israel would continue for a time. The assassin was the already mentioned Baasha with whom Asa of Judah had contested for Ramah. While he was no improvement over his predecessors and was threatened by the prophet Jehu, yet he managed to retain his throne for 24 years.

His son, the confirmed drunkard Elah, did

Beneath these Herodian ruins at Samaria archaeologists uncovered the palaces of Omri and Ahab

Ivory plaque from Samaria showing the infant Horus, Egyptian sun-god

Phoenician artisans, which was an indication of a close alliance then in force with these people of the upper seacoast. This league would yield strange and pernicious fruit during the reign of Omri's son, Ahab. Perhaps the best descriptive term for this northern metropolis is "luxurious," and it left a lasting impression even upon its Assyrian despoilers.

There was a league, too, with the Syrians, but whether it was voluntary or compulsory is a little uncertain, since the spirit behind the remark made later by Ben-hadad II (1 [3] Kings 20:34) is hard to determine. At least we do know that the Damascus merchants had their own trading quarter within Samaria's walls. Yet it is quite probable this was a concession granted under pressure, for it now appears that the city was hardly completed when Ben-hadad I, with his Syrian cohorts, was again in the land. He had taken three towns in the extreme north on a previous visit, and on this second invasion he may have worked his will upon Omri.

What Damascus seems to have been especially interested in at first was control of the important trading cities and the farming areas in the Trans-Jordan between the river valley and the "King's Highway" to the east. These Biblical Syrians, more generally known as *Aramaeans,* had been filtering into the area in recent years and settling down there following a nomadic life. This region had also been the first of the allotments made to the tribes of Israel some centuries before. And before them had been earlier occupants. Consequently this important portion of Omri's realm was a tinder box, and the hazards there and elsewhere had prompted a strong alliance between him and the Phoenicians. This affinity would, in the reign of that monarch's son, Ahab, produce one of the most dramatic tales in all the wondrous Bible Story.

While this fifth among the kingdom of Israel's rulers was adjudged by religious standards probably the most wicked of them all, he did manage to imprint his name indelibly upon the records of some of the other nations. His vassals, the Moabites, remembered him all too well, while the Assyrians, looming like an immense threat off to the northeast, still called Israel "The House of Omri" a century after his decease.

not last nearly as long. While carousing in the home of his steward, the commander of one of the two wings of his chariot corps, Zimri, slew him, wiped out Baasha's line, and sought to take the crown. But the army proclaimed Omri, its commander-in-chief, their king, called off a siege then in progress and hurried back to the capital at Tirzah. There was a sharp tussle, and when the palace in which he was hiding was threatened, Zimri set it afire and perished in the flames. He had ruled Israel in all for only one short week. Four of the new nation's kings in succession seem to have met violent deaths.

Omri, who now ascended the throne, had already proven his military capabilities, for he had apparently subjugated Moab during Baasha's reign. But he occupied an insecure throne during his first five years. Another aspirant, backed by about half the people, was to him a continuing threat up to the very day of this contender's death. As soon as Omri came to feel a greater sense of security, he went to work to give Israel a completely new capital city, which was named Samaria.

Excavations at its site have turned up many interesting facts. First, it was probably the most splendidly located town in all the land. It was destined to have long use, for it served until destroyed by the Maccabees, was soon rebuilt by Herod the Great and continued as an important place well down into the Crusader period. The work upon the early town was of most excellent quality and probably done by

X

THE SYRIAN INVASIONS

Just how many kings of Damascus called Ben-hadad appear in the Bible is a trifle uncertain, but surely there were four. The name means "son of Hadad," a deity closely akin to the Assyrian Rimmon, the god of rain and storm, of thunder and lightning. These Syrian, or Aramaean, monarchs were the scions of wanderers from the Syrian desert who had, several generations previously, eased their way into the plains and hill country running south from the base of Mount Hermon as far as the valley of the Yarmuk. There they had sunk their roots, ceased from their roving and grown ambitious and envious of their neighbors. The number of peoples with similar characteristics and tendencies which the land bridge has harbored since the beginning of recorded history is considerable.

The first of this line to find mention in the Bible, was the contemporary of Baasha of Israel, and of Asa of Judah. He harried the first, when rewarded by the latter, and since he seized the towns of Ijon and Abel-beth-maachah, and the shrine at Dan and ravaged the area of Galilee west of the Jordan defile, the Syrian invasions technically begin with this Ben-hadad I.

He, too, seems to have given deep concern to Omri and made Israel's league with Phoenicia highly essential. This alliance was arranged and consummated by the marriage of a Sidonian princess, the strong-willed, somewhat masculine Jezebel and the Israelite heir presumptive, Prince Ahab. Such was the nature of her contributions to the affairs of the northern kingdom during her wavering husband's twenty-two-year reign, that her name even today is the proverbial synonym for a shameless, immoral woman.

Since her father had first been a priest of Astarte (Ashtoreth), the voluptuous Phoenician goddess, she had grown up in a ritualistic atmosphere and became a devoted worshiper of Baal. This pagan "lord of the earth" was also a weather god, whose right arm hurled the lightning bolts, whose voice was thunder, and who, when he tore open the clouds, let life-giving rain pour upon a thirsty land. The myth concerning his death and resurrection made strong appeal to a still fairly primitive and largely agricultural people. He supposedly died with the close of spring's "latter rains," when a torrid thirsty sun began to bake and scorch the earth. Then, with the onset of the "former rains" in the fall, he came alive again and gave fertility to another growing period.

Baal-worship had a colorful, impressive ritual, conducted in elaborate temples adorned with Phoenician art and with Phoenician ingenuity, and also apparently garnished with what, in that day, passed for very stirring music. This deity, together with such companionate female symbols of sex and fertility as Anath, Asherah and Astarte, touched a mystic chord deep within the being of many an Israelite of both the northern and the southern kingdoms. Even in this present day and age, our religious interests are strong or weak pretty much in accord with our attachment to a community or parish church. And in these other times, the nearby "high place," or local temple of Baal (2 [4] Kings 10:21), in contrast to a Temple far removed from all but residents of Jerusalem, gave heathen ways a strong competitive pull in both Israel and Judah.

To please his queen who swayed him so readily, Ahab built a sanctuary for Baal at

The Moabite Stone commemorating the successful rebellion of King Mesha

Samaria, while somewhere hard by he laid out an "Asherah," or sacred grove. These desecrations did more "to provoke the Lord God of Israel" than the acts of all his five predecessors on the throne. But, in addition, Jezebel took the law into her own custody and declared an open season on the priests of Yahweh, and this indomitable creature slew every one of them she could hunt out and seize.

Another incident in which she was a principal, and which is intended to show how Israelite religious and moral thinking was suffering at her ruthless hands, was the dastardly affair which cost the life of Naboth and his sons. Ancestral property had almost a religious significance to God's people and could not be lightly parted with. Yet to the Phoenician it was as fluid and transferable as trade goods themselves.

Such perversion certainly could not be allowed to go unchallenged, and suddenly Ahab and his Jezebel were confronted by that most formidable of all the men of God, Elijah the Tishbite. He was a gritty, unflinching character and could even, when the hand of the Lord was upon him, outrun the king's best chariot horses (1 [3] Kings 18:46).

There was strife at once between the royal pair and this hairy prophet, clad in a leathern girdle, and it finally came to a conspicuous climax in the contest atop Mount Carmel. There, fire from heaven vindicated Elijah's offering by consuming it; and, under the influence of this miracle, the people turned upon the heathen priests of Baal and Asherah and dispatched in all some 850 of them. When this stunning setback led Jezebel to take a solemn oath to slay the Tishbite before the next day dawned, Elijah fled the land. But the Lord sent him to Syria, there to anoint a king who might become a scourge to Ahab and his headstrong wife.

And the kings of Damascus during quite a long period seem to have been thorns in the sides of both Israel and Judah. Ahab was harassed by them for a number of years, and then, suddenly, a victory was his. Yet he dared not

take full advantage of it and slay his chief adversary and cut his army to pieces. There was just then the threat of trouble from beyond Damascus, and from a foe so much more potent that discretion outweighed any desire to take complete advantage of victory. His army and people took strong exception to their king's next act, and even one of the prophets berated him harshly. Yet it was among his sanest moves. He made a quick, earnest peace with his opponent, entered a covenant with him, and started him off toward home. Then word came, probably rushed down over the caravan trail, of dismaying happenings well to the north. The Assyrians under Shalmaneser III had attacked Carchemish, the capital of a Hittite kingdom on the west bank of the Euphrates River. The appalling corollary was the news that this colossus was headed next for Palestine. The "Syrian League" formed to oppose him included Damascus, Hamath, twelve coastal cities, and certain other lands as well as "Ahab the Israelite."

Eleven members of this confederacy hurriedly mobilized their forces and met this onslaught at Karkar, well up the Orontes River 200 air miles north of Samaria. There, in 854 B.C., an inconclusive battle was fought, although the Assyrians' progress was stayed and Shalmaneser led his host all the way back to his home base at Nineveh. Ben-hadad of Damascus and Ahab of Israel had both taken part as allies, the latter leading some 10,000 men and 2000 chariots.

In the third, and again in the eleventh year following, the Assyrians would make other, but unsuccessful, attempts to overrun Palestine. Ahab would not be called upon to face them again, but his son's assassin, Jehu, would be among those who would later pay tribute to this same Shalmaneser.

Peaceful relations with Damascus, however, were fairly short-lived, and unsettled conditions in the Trans-Jordan again bred war. This time Judah managed to get involved. The sound, able ruler from the kingdom to the south, Jehoshaphat, happened to be on a state visit in Samaria, and Ahab, anxious to regain the lost city of Ramoth-gilead well to the east on the "King's Highway," prevailed upon his counterpart from Jerusalem to accompany him on a raid against this valuable and strategic town.

View of modern Damascus

Jehoshaphat, however, insisted that the will of the Lord be consulted before they set forth, and so Ahab assembled some 400 prophets of Baal. Parrot-like, this huge assemblage gave wholehearted approval and unqualified assurance of success. But the king of Judah wanted no part of these fraudulent seers. Ahab knew of only one man of God still in the land, but he hated him fervently because he prophesied no good at all concerning the king. Since the visitor from the south was determined to hear the truth, Micaiah, this sole representative of the Living God, was called. When pressed by Ahab to tell him nothing but the very words of the Lord, the man promptly prophesied his impending doom.

And that is precisely what happened. Ahab rode into battle disguised so he would not furnish a ready target. But a Syrian bowman, by merest chance, lodged an arrow in the cleft between the shoulder joints in the king's armor. There had been twenty-two evil years in his reign, and now Israel had a new and seventh king, the ineffectual Ahaziah.

Moab had been a vassal state, probably from the days of Baasha. Now, when war had weakened this northern kingdom, and Ahab was no more, the Moabites revolted. One of the interesting heritages from antiquity is the Moabite Stone, discovered nearly a century ago. On it was engraved the record of that land's shepherd king, Mesha, who had proudly led his people to freedom. It no doubt delighted this little monarch to hear that dogs had actually licked up the slain Ahab's blood by the pool in Samaria, just as Elijah had prophesied. And then, a few years later, he might have been further edified when he learned that the depraved Queen Jezebel, who had outlived her husband, had met the revolting end forecast for her. Things were easier at the moment in Moab, but there were more troubles still to come a little later on.

Jehoshaphat, who managed to get home to Jerusalem safely, finally completed his very commendable twenty-five-year reign. During it he is credited with having done that which was right in the sight of the Lord, and his chief deficiency worthy of being recorded was a commercial venture. Like his great-great-grandfather, Solomon, he, too, sought to build a trading fleet to bring home gold from elusive Ophir. Possibly it was to come from trade of copper goods made from ore mined in Edom,

ISRAEL AND JUDAH
AT THE TIME OF
THE SYRIAN CONQUESTS
c. 840-800 B.C.

Copyright by C. S. HAMMOND & CO., N. Y.

Scale of Miles

0 5 10   20   30

Perennial Rivers ....
Seasonal Rivers & Streams ......
Capitals .... ✦
Syrian Attacks .... ➔

THE
SYRIAN
KINGDOM
OF
DAMASCUS

• Damascus

MOUNT LEBANON

Abana R.

MT. HERMON

Pharpar R.

Sidon •

Zarephath •

Ijon •

Tyre •

Abel-beth-maachah •

Dan •

Kedesh •

Hazor •

PHOENICIA

Accho •

Cabul •

Chinnereth •

Sea of Chinnereth

Ashtaroth •

Bashan

The Great Sea
(Mediterranean Sea)

Hammath •

Aphek •

Edrei •

MT. CARMEL

Kishon R.

Dor •

Plain of Jezreel

Mt. Tabor

Shunem •

Havoth-jair

Ramoth-gilead •

Megiddo •

Jezreel •

Taanach •

Beth-shan •

Israel under the dynasty
of Jehu was in a weakened
state without allies and thus
unable to prevent the armies
of Hazael from plundering
and ravaging the land.

Ibleam
(Gur) •

Dothan •

Jabesh-gilead •

Mahanaim •

A lull in the campaigns
of Assyria against the
Syrians enabled Hazael,
King of Damascus, to an-
nex Gilead and overrun
Israel and Judah.

Plain of Sharon

Samaria ✦

Tirzah •

Abel-meholah •

ISRAEL

Mt. Ebal

Shechem •

Mt. Gerizim

Penuel •

GILEAD

AMMON

Aphek •

Shiloh •

Joppa •

Jordan R.

Lod •

Bethel •

Gezer •

Mizpah •

Jericho •

Jabneel •

Ekron •

Aijalon •

Gilgal •

Rabbath-ammon ✦

Eltekah •

Jerusalem ✦

Heshbon •

Jerusalem was spared
destruction by Hazael
through the payment
of tribute by Jehoash.

Ashdod •

Timnah •

Beth-shemesh •

Mt. Nebo

Medeba •

PHILISTIA

Ashkelon •

Libnah •

Bethlehem •

Gath •

Adullam •

JUDAH

Gaza •

Lachish •

Mareshah •

Beth-zur •

MOAB

Adoraim •

Hebron •

Dibon •

Debir •

En-gedi •

Aroer •

Gerar •

Salt Sea (Dead Sea)

Arnon R.

Ziklag •

Wilderness of Judah

Ar •

Beer-sheba •

Kir-moab
(Kir-haresheth) ✦

Valley of
Salt

Zered R.

EDOM

which was a dependency of Judah during this period. But evidently the little fleet suffered shipwreck before it ever got out of its home port of Ezion-geber (1 [3] Kings 22:48).

While Elijah, greatest of the non-writing prophets, outlived Ahab, he was carried on high in the fiery chariot before Jezebel was hurled to her fate. His mantle fell to another steadfast person, also a non-writing phophet, Elisha. The narratives of the miraculous acts of this remarkable character fill four and a half of the early chapters of the last of the books dealing with the rulers of the two kingdoms. Two of the incidents involve Syrian matters, evidence that the affairs of Damascus and Samaria had much in common.

While fear of the sudden reappearance of the Assyrians probably discouraged full-scale hostilities, the kings of Damascus did keep up predatory operations rather continually. Raids for the taking of booty or slaves were evidently fairly common. They were annoying and perhaps repaid in kind but did not break off relations between the two kingdoms, at least not for long.

The little maid stolen out of Israel, who turned up among the slaves in the home of the commandant of the armed forces in Damascus, is a case in point. Her new master was a leper in a society where that frightful disease did not make one an outcast. Yet to be freed of its loathsome burden was worth almost any effort or price. This Israelite child was so convincing regarding the curative powers of the man of God at Samaria, that the Syrian general—he was the well-known Naaman—started off in search of healing. He bore a letter from his king to the king of Israel. He was not turned back at the border. He quite evidently was not kept under watch of any kind. It is true, there were a few uncertain moments at the palace, for the letter the visitor bore seemed so strange to the king of Israel that he thought it a hoax, perhaps a means of fomenting real trouble. But Elisha quickly straightened the matter out, arranged for the miraculous cure of this foreigner, and the whole affair passed off peaceably. And in deep appreciation, Naaman renounced idolatry and became a worshiper of the True God.

Bloodshed between these two lands was stayed for a time, too, by the fact that Elisha, through his wonderful powers, was able to foretell all the Syrian king's secret plans. That outraged monarch finally sought to seize the prophet, but his raiding party was smitten with blindness and so returned the man of God to Samaria rather than taking him to Damascus.

Yet Ben-hadad did manage, at a time when there were no immediate threats of attack by the Assyrians, to march his troops to Samaria and lay siege to it. So tight was the cordon

Hittite hunting scene (9th cent. B.C.) from Tell Halaf

thrown about the place that there was no access to it from the outside at all. Rather promptly food supplies began to give out, and surrender seemed fairly close. Then a miracle took place. The Lord made the enemy host hear a noise like the clatter of chariots and their horses, and the tread of marching feet. The one thought among the Syrian besiegers was that the Hittites had been hired to attack them from the rear. Fear seized them and lent speed to their limbs, and they went hurrying off home to Damascus.

These insistent Syrians would continue to make trouble for Samaria and for other areas in the kingdom of the Ten Tribes, forcing them to suffer much from their oppressions. Ultimately they would receive three sharp defeats at the hands of Joash, king of Judah. He even managed to recover the cities lost to the kings of Damascus by Israel. Yet this was all pretty much petty squabbling and carried on, in many instances, by rather petty kings. Soon a far more puissant foe would descend upon the land and strike part of it a permanently crippling blow.

XI

PROSPERITY TURNS TO DISASTER

What were these ancient kingdoms like— Judah, Israel, Damascus, and even the larger states? They were what is known as "absolute monarchies," where the king had supreme power and the members of a ruling family sought to retain the throne for generation after generation, and by the use of force and violence whenever necessary. This was especially true in Israel where a number of dynasties, such as those formed by Jeroboam, Baasha, Omri and Jehu, were finally uprooted by bold men thirsting for power.

It is possible in a world where the great majority of people were very backward, and war was so frequent, that no other type of government would prove practical. Actually it was just another form by which authority similar to that possessed by the patriarchs, or the headman of a clan or tribe, was meted out. At least it was the prevailing sort of government in the Orient in ancient times, and it has continued down through the ages in most primitive communities. Yet there were ambitious men in those far-off days, and the Bible pages dealing

with the period between David's accession to the throne and the carrying away of the Jews to captivity in Babylon are sprinkled with assassinations and other acts of ferocity and brute force.

Most of these instances are much alike, although one in particular is rather unique, since it involves the only woman ever to actually rule as queen in either Israel or Judah. She was Athaliah, princess royal of the northern kingdom and a daughter of the wicked Jezebel, whose masculine courage she inherited in abundance. She was married to King Jehoram of Judah, and her son Ahaziah succeeded his father on the throne in that land. But he was slain by Jehu of Israel, since he might also have had some claim upon the throne in the northern kingdom through his mother.

Immediately upon his death, the unscrupulous Athaliah had all of her dead son's male children slain, save one infant son, Joash, who had been hidden by an aunt. Then, seizing the throne, the doughty woman reigned for six years. In attempting at the end of that time to put down a rebellion of the priests in favor of young Joash, she was slain at the chariot entrance to the palace.

Joash was crowned when but seven and appears to have been married and the father of a son when but fourteen or fifteen. He reigned in Judah for forty years, only ultimately to be slain in bed by his own servants while suffering a severe illness.

Amaziah, son of the murdered Joash, perhaps deserves recognition. He had conducted the government during his parent's illness and managed to seize the throne after his assassination. The murderers were summarily put to death but their children spared in conformity with Mosaic law (Deut. 24:16). His Edomite vassals in the area to the southeast had revolted, however, and he hired 100,000 fighting men of Israel and set forth to put down this uprising. On the advice of one of the prophets he dismissed these Israelite mercenaries along the way and marched on with merely his own troops and captured the Edomite capital, Sela.

He foolishly, though, brought away Edom's idols and set them up for his gods. The hired troops, homeward bound to Israel, had plun-

Old Samaritan with Scrolls of the Law

dered several cities of Judah; and Amaziah, flushed with his recent victory in Edom, started a war with Jehoash, their king. But he was roundly defeated at Beth-shemesh, taken prisoner there and dragged home to Jerusalem. A portion of that city's wall was broken down and much treasure and many hostages carried off to Samaria.

Amaziah had reigned about seventeen years when a conspiracy took form in the capital and drove him from Jerusalem. He sought refuge in Lachish; and while this first intrigue seems to have failed, a later one some twelve years afterward did snuff out his life. His twenty-nine years on the throne had evidently been uneasy ones, yet very much of the kind which many an oriental potentate might look forward to in those days. It was indeed a ruthless day and age.

Still the two little kingdoms on the land bridge knew a few years of great prosperity during the 9th century before the Christian Era. Once again, as in the time of David and Solomon, there was an untroubled period free from major wars. Egypt was occupied within her own borders, while the Assyrians far to the northeast were involved with neighboring peoples and domestic concerns. Even the Syrians immediately to the north stayed at home. The times were actually secure enough so that Phoenician Tyre could give time and effort to the founding of one of the great cities of antiquity, Carthage, on the northwest coast of Africa.

This boom period was some years in getting under way and finally came to fruition during the reign of two able kings, Jeroboam II of Israel and Uzziah of Judah. The former was third in descent from that furious charioteer, Jehu, who forced his way to the throne of the kingdom of the Ten Tribes by wiping out the house and dynasty of Ahab. The other was the grandson of Joash. Uzziah is sometimes called Azariah.

Jeroboam II had been king of Israel for several years when sixteen-year-old Uzziah took over the rule of Judah. Both kingdoms now knew a plenteous period, and Israel in particular really flourished. However, the religious life of Jeroboam fell so far short of the standards recognized by the scribes who compiled the Books of the Kings, that they paid only the scantest attention to his forty-one-year reign. Yet his true moral worth may actually be less than the seven verses of text given him. Despite the fact that his father, Joash of Israel, had been able to defeat Judah, the northern kingdom was in rather a sorry state when he ascended the throne sometime about the year 786 B.C.

He did manage to subdue the persistent Syrians, eventually capturing Damascus. This was rendered possible through the repeated Assyrian attacks on this Aramaean state east of the Jordan. Jeroboam was further credited with restoring the border of Israel "from the entering of Hamath unto the sea of the plain," meaning from the upper reaches of the Orontes River to the Dead Sea. Thus the area possessed by the Kingdom of Israel was at its greatest extent and knew more prosperity than it had found since the death of Solomon.

Still, there is some reasonable question as to whether any particular advantages flowed to the small farmers and shepherds who composed the bulk of the people, or if the upswing merely lined the pockets of a class which some scholars believe is best termed a "gangster-nobility." Such a caste had been developing, particularly in Samaria, for a number of generations. Certainly the remains of the royal palace which have been dug up show this to have been a most luxurious period. Clay invoices covering shipments of wine and oil to the court indicate

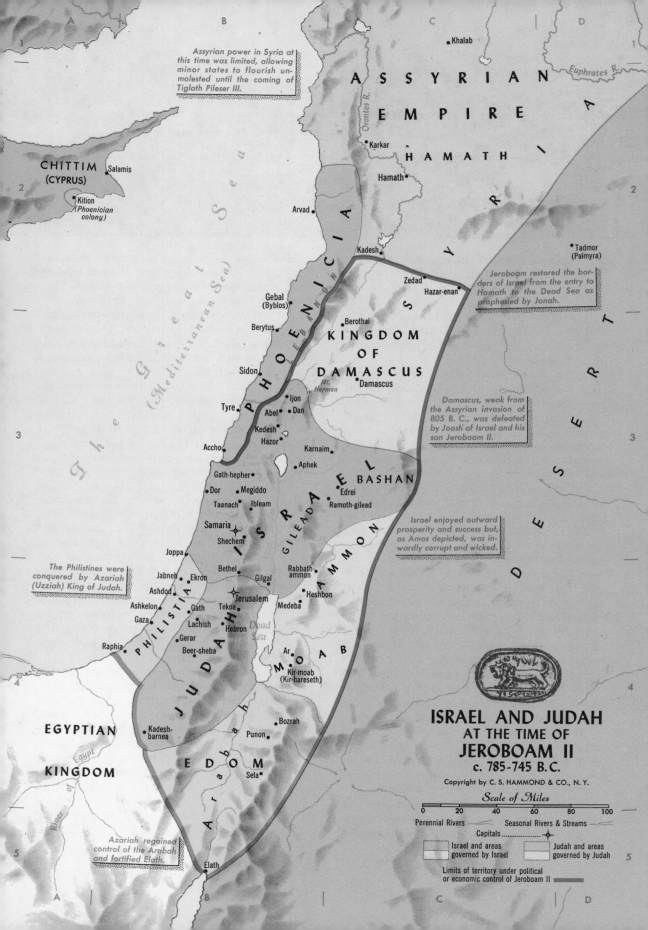

1

Khalab

A S S Y R I A N

E M P I R E

Euphrates R.

Assyrian power in Syria at
this time was limited, allowing
minor states to flourish un-
molested until the coming of
Tiglath Pileser III.

Orontes R.

Karkar

H A M A T H

CHITTIM
(CYPRUS)

Salamis

2

Hamath

S Y R I A

Kition
(Phoenician
colony)

Arvad

Tadmor
(Palmyra)

Kadesh

Zedad

Hazar-enan

Jeroboam restored the borders of Israel from the entry to
Hamath to the Dead Sea as
prophesied by Jonah.

Gebal
(Byblos)

Berothai

Berytus

KINGDOM
OF
DAMASCUS

P H O E N I C I A

Sidon

Mt.
Hermon

Damascus

T h e   G r e a t   S e a

(Mediterranean Sea)

Tyre

Ijon

Abel   Dan

Kedesh

Hazor

Karnaim

Damascus, weak from
the Assyrian invasion of
805 B.C., was defeated
by Joash of Israel and his
son Jeroboam II.

3

Accho

Aphek

D E S E R T

Gath-hepher

I S R A E L

BASHAN

Dor

Megiddo

Edrei

Taanach

Ibleam

Ramoth-gilead

G I L E A D

Samaria

Israel enjoyed outward
prosperity and success but,
as Amos depicted, was in-
wardly corrupt and wicked.

Shechem

A M M O N

Joppa

The Philistines were
conquered by Azariah
(Uzziah) King of Judah.

Jabneh

Bethel

Rabbath-
ammon

Ekron

Gilgal

Ashdod

Jerusalem

Heshbon

Ashkelon

Gath

Tekoa

Medeba

Gaza

Lachish

Hebron

Dead
Sea

4

Raphia

Gerar

Beer-sheba

Ar

M O A B

Kir-moab
(Kir-hareseth)

EGYPTIAN

Kadesh-
barnea

Bozrah

ISRAEL AND JUDAH
AT THE TIME OF
JEROBOAM II
c. 785-745 B.C.

KINGDOM

Punon

E D O M

Copyright by C. S. HAMMOND & CO., N. Y.

Sela

Scale of Miles

0   20   40   60   80   100

Perennial Rivers   Seasonal Rivers & Streams

Azariah regained
control of the Arabah
and fortified Elath.

Capitals

Israel and areas
governed by Israel

Judah and areas
governed by Judah

5

Elath

Limits of territory under political
or economic control of Jeroboam II

Port of Aqaba on Red Sea near Biblical Eziongeber

high living, while beautiful objects carved from ivory and embellished with gold and fine jewels, are among other evidences of great wealth. Tribute from conquered areas and from burgeoning commerce, together with taxes in kind levied on the produce of fields and flocks, advanced the well-being of at least some of the Israelites.

The expanded domain had been forecast by the prophet Jonah, the Galilean whose home was at Gath-hepher near Nazareth. And a second prophet, Amos, humble farm laborer from the hill country south of Bethlehem, pictures Jeroboam as a strong and wealthy king, ruling over prosperous people.

Yet to men with a strong moral and ethical sense, such as this fiery Amos, these were evil times. Leaving his rural home in Tekoa, he made his way north, beyond the confines of his own land, and started to preach near the shrine of the golden calf at Bethel. Bitter indeed are his sermons condensed in the nine chapters of the Bible book bearing his name. In them he bluntly attacked members of the court clique at Samaria. Their wives he likens to "cows" and he berates them because of their demands upon their husbands, which forced the latter to oppress the poor and crush the needy.

Amos points out the number of *gibborim*— or strong men—the king keeps by him to tyrannize the freedom-loving shepherds and farmers. The small landholders, burdened with taxes, were ruthlessly exploited by the city's moneylenders; and the picture of society which can be read between the lines in Amos' prophecy is in many respects much like that which prevailed among the Canaanite cities when Israel first entered the land five centuries or more earlier.

The desert *mishpat*—that is the customs and the sense of justice which had obtained among God's people as tribesmen—was breaking down. Their concept of morality was going into decay; and they were forsaking Yahweh, the One, the Only True God, for a whole host of pagan deities, idols and cults. The cities were dominating the rural areas, and a whole way of life was altering and growing sinful, with the poor and lowly the greatest sufferers. And here was this foreigner, this dauntless Amos, thundering his denunciations at the ruling classes of Israel. Small wonder he was accused of treason and threatened with expulsion.

Still, his was not the only voice speaking in

protest at conditions in the booming land of the Ten Tribes. The other was a native of this northern kingdom, the fine-fibered, sensitive, poetic Hosea. While he did not emphasize so strongly the economic upheaval which had taken place, he was conscious of the nation's sinful ways and made a series of impassioned pleas for national repentance and uprightness.

But what of conditions in Judah, where Uzziah's fifty-two-year reign was under way? Although his time on the throne is given far more space in the Books of the Kings than is Jeroboam's, some of the best impressions of real conditions within the kingdom come, in this case too, from the writings of two prophets, Isaiah and Micah. Here in Judah there was new-found wealth, and once again it was evidently not benefiting the many nearly as much as it was corrupting the few. There was a time, not too long ago, in our own land when many of our people were strongly criticized for their supposed worship of the "Almighty Dollar." And in Judah, as in Israel, too, in that long calm which preceded a most disastrous storm, there was much worship of the "Almighty Shekel."

However, geography seems to have had a marked influence upon conditions in the two little kingdoms. It should be remembered that of the old Canaanite cities which were not immediately taken over, the greater number were so located that their landed aristocracy had a most pronounced influence upon Israel. Also this northern area was either astride of, or very close to, the great trade routes and had many more commercial interests and activities than did even the capital of the southern kingdom. Some believe there was a shepherd aristocracy in Judah before the reign of Saul and that David was a product of it. But even Jerusalem, heavily adorned by Solomon, was a country town by comparison with Jeroboam's very metropolitan Samaria. Things, social, economic and moral were in a ferment, but the pressures upon men and women in the northern kingdom seem to have been more direct and more potent than was the case in Judah.

If there was apathy to the moral decay at home, there was surely crass indifference to threats to national security building up beyond the limits of these two monarchies on the little land bridge. Assyria, which had finally dealt Damascus so severe a blow that it and its surrounding territory had fallen into the hands of Israel, was busy at home at the moment but was not permanently removed as a serious threat. Yet so full was the present of luxury and splendor that it seemed to be the pattern for all the foreseeable future. Even Amos, the country boy turned prophet, appears to have had an infinitely better appreciation of what was going on in the world at large than did the Hebrew princes,

whether of Israel or of Judah. A life and death struggle was building up ahead, and in the northern kingdom especially there was a sharp falling off in the stamina and fortitude needed to meet it.

When Jeroboam II died, a son, Zachariah, held the throne for only a few months and was then slain by a hopeful aspirant, Shallum. But after one single insecure month, he in turn was assassinated by Menahem, who, whatever his other qualifications, did manage to rule for ten years. By contrast, though, they were lean bitter years; and while of considerable significance, they rate but eight verses in the opinion of the compilers of Bible text (2 [4] Kings 15:14, 16-22). For the inevitable happened, and as described in Byron's classic words, "The Assyrian came down like the wolf on the fold."

The Biblical Pul, who was no doubt Tiglathpileser III, led a gigantic host to the south, confronted Samaria and exacted a crippling tribute of 1000 talents of silver, or just under two million dollars. In our own time when we talk glibly in thousands of millions, this may seem almost a paltry sum. But 2700 years ago it was sufficient to start Israel quite definitely on a downward course. This first visitation by the "wolf" from the north was a bitter experience, but merely a taste of what lay ahead.

Judah, fortunately, was not molested on this incursion; yet her turn would come. It would perhaps be well to scrutinize these Assyrians rather closely, for their influence upon the ancient world was fearsome and formidable.

King Ashurnasirpal II attacking a city. (885-859 B.C.)

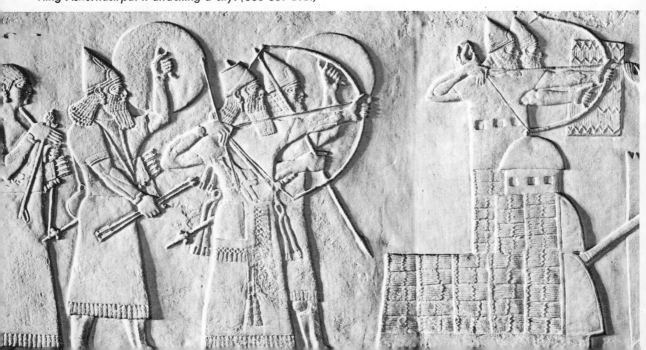

XII

THE FIRST GREAT WORLD CRISIS

The highly interesting tenth chapter of Genesis contains a description of the make-up of a prehistoric "empire," ruled by a great-grandson of Noah. At the head of the list, and no doubt its principal city, was Babel, or Babylon, one of the most ancient towns in Bible text. This chief seat of Nimrod's power was apparently a very early center of the Semitic peoples. Asshur, the son of Noah's first-born son Shem, came from here and with his descendents moved to the north along the Tigris River. There they made their home in an area on its right bank between the tributary streams *Great Zab* and *Little Zab*. Here a kingdom seems to have grown up, dominated by the town of Ashur, the remains of which have been found at *Qal'at Sherqat,* about 60 miles downstream from the more famous Nineveh.

This was the traditional origin of Assyria and of a people destined to make their name a synonym for ruthlessness, who built the first great war machine, created the first extensive international empire, and perished through exhaustion brought on by military excesses. Yet in its early years this country was evidently subject to Babylon and under the control of governors appointed by the kings of this latter city-state, which lay about 275 miles to the south on the Euphrates River. Actually scholars have found it exceedingly difficult to separate the two

Winged bull from palace of Sargon II

great empires which ultimately grew up about Assyria and Babylon, for, both geographically and historically, their relationships were closely interwoven.

While Babylon may have been dominant in early historical times, there came a period when the northern kingdom began to gather strength. This was in the 14th century B.C., at about the time the children of Israel were in bondage in Egypt. Authority was extended first over lands to the north, northeast and northwest, and finally, about 1290 B.C., or close to the same time as the exodus from Egypt, Babylon succumbed to the authority of Assyria. During the next seven centuries, with but relatively brief interruptions, Assyria would be the leading power in the east.

At the end of the twelfth pre-Christian century, King Tiglath-pileser I greatly extended his empire by his conquests over the Hittites who occupied the upper Euphrates Valley to the west, and also over the Aramaeans, or Syrians, to the southwest. He pushed his influence as far as the shores of the Mediterranean; he even forced Egypt to acknowledge his independence and to send gifts to Asshur as that land had done during the reign of two previous Pharaohs. Yet this second period of ascendancy was rather short-lived and crumbled rapidly with Tiglath-pileser's death. Then, for two centuries, this ambitious land was compelled to attend to concerns within her own distinct and fairly limited boundaries. It was during this untroubled term that Israel experienced its "Golden Age" in the reigns of David and Solomon.

Assyrian affairs began to look up again with the accession of Ashurnasirpal II in 885 B.C. His campaigns were well planned and executed

Assyrian winged figure (9th century B.C.)

of clay which were practically indestructible.

It took a number of years for the key to this writing to be discovered. But when at last it was possible to translate the wealth of these earthy documents which had been recovered, light was thrown upon the history of Assyria and Babylon and many points in Bible text were verified. One great objective of the Assyrians down the years was the conquest of Egypt, the cornerstone at the southwestern end of the "Fertile Crescent." In order to achieve it, it was necessary to clear away opposition along the great pathway to trade and to empire that ran down the land bridge through Syria and Israel. While the forays recorded in the Books of the Kings were in part for plunder, they were also to open up the pathway to the ultimate objective, the fabled cities by the waters of the Nile. And these incidents mentioned in the Bible are confirmed among the exploits of the Assyrian kings. In the records of the military accomplishments of Ashurnasirpal, that monarch says, "From Aleppo (in north Syria) I launched the attack and crossed the Orontes . . . I marched from the Orontes . . . I conquered the cities . . . I caused much slaughter, I destroyed, I devastated, I burned. I took their fighting men prisoners and impaled them on sharpened stakes in full view of their cities. I settled Assyrians in place of them . . . I bathed my weapons in the Great Sea."

On this assault the enemy did collect huge plunder, especially of gold and silver, and also of the more serviceable metals lead and copper. They exacted heavy tribute of the coastal cities of Tyre, Sidon and Byblos, and what they did there had a profound effect further south. Even that hard-bitten soldier, King Omri, realized that discretion was indeed the better part of valor. So he drew two talents of silver, the equivalent of about $3900, from the royal treasury, bought the most readily defended hillock in the northern kingdom from its owner, Shemer, and set about building the new and heavily fortified capital, Samaria. Omri's wise move so impressed the Assyrians that in their faithfully kept records the Kingdom of Israel bore the designation "the House of Omri" for many years after his passing.

But again, as in a previous period of dominance, Assyria demonstrated its major weak-

and waged more relentlessly than those of any previous Assyrian monarch. As a consequence, the lands to the northeast and also the northwest were burned, pillaged, ravaged for all removable booty and placed under heavy annual tribute. But he was a builder as well as a soldier, and during his 25 years on the throne magnificent palaces, temples and other structures were erected. The then ancient and ruined city of Calah was chosen as his capital; it was rebuilt and greatly beautified. Its remains, hidden beneath the mound of Nimrod, were uncovered by the young Englishman, A. H. Layard, in 1845. At that time, Assyria, of which all traces had been completely buried for centuries, began to come to light again. Fortunately some of the ancient palaces had remarkable libraries, filled with carefully-kept records, inscribed in cuneiform characters on small pats

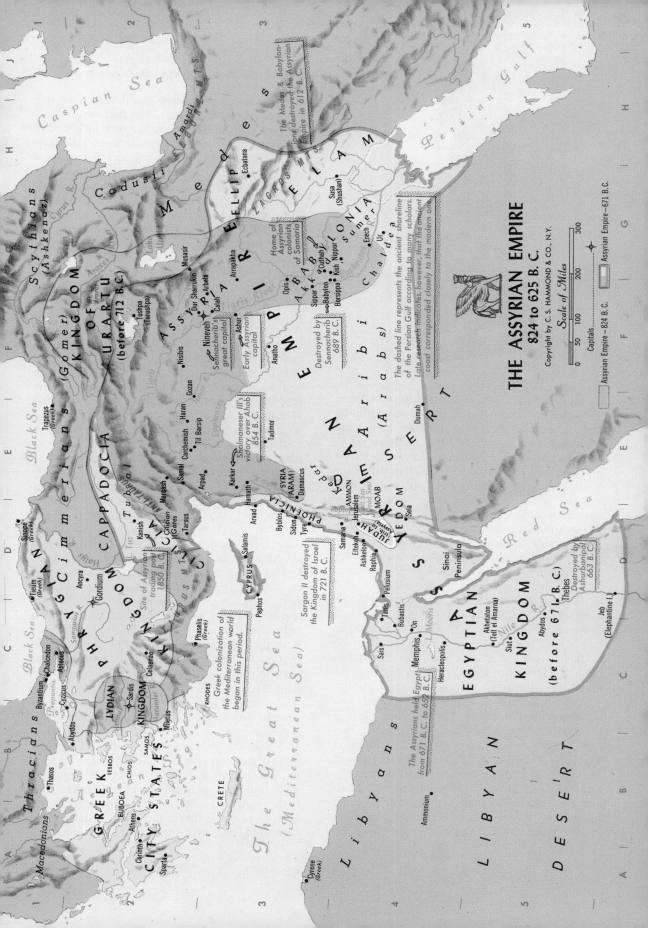

THE ASSYRIAN EMPIRE
824 to 625 B.C.

Copyright by C. S. Hammond & Co., N.Y.

Scale of Miles

0 50 100 200 300

Capitals: ⭐

Assyrian Empire—824 B.C.   Assyrian Empire—671 B.C.

The dashed line represents the ancient shoreline
of the Persian Gulf according to many scholars.
Late research indicates, however, that the ancient
coast corresponded closely to the modern one.

The Medas & Babylon-
ians destroyed the Assyrian
Empire in 612 B.C.

Home of Assyrian
colonists of Samaria

Destroyed by
Sennacherib
689 B.C.

Sennacherib's
great capital

Early Assyrian
capital

Shalmaneser III's
victory over Ahab
854 B.C.

Sargon II destroyed
the Kingdom of Israel
in 721 B.C.

Site of Assyrian
trading post
1850 B.C.

Greek colonization of
the Mediterranean world
began in this period.

The Assyrians held Egypt
from 671 B.C. to 652 B.C.

Destroyed by
Ashurbanipal
663 B.C.

Place names and regions

Caspian Sea

Scythians
(Ashkenaz)

Cadusii

M e d e s

KINGDOM
OF
URARTU
(before 712 B.C.)

Cimmerians
(Gomer)

ELLIP

ELAM

BABYLONIA

A S S Y R I A

E M P I R E

 Sumer

Chaldea

A r i b i
(A r a b s)

D E S E R T

Thracians

PHRYGIAN
KINGDOM

CAPPADOCIA

CILICIA

LYDIAN
KINGDOM

GREEK
CITY STATES

Black Sea

The Great Sea
(Mediterranean Sea)

PHOENICIA

SYRIA
(ARAM)

JUDAH

AMMON

MOAB

EDOM

ASSYRIA

Red Sea

EGYPTIAN
KINGDOM
(before 671 B.C.)

LIBYAN
KINGDOM

LIBYANS

D E S E R T

Sinai
Peninsula

City labels
Ecbatana, Susa (Shushan), Musasir, Arrapakha, Arbela, Calah, Dur Sharrukin, Nineveh, Ashur, Anatho, Erech, Sippar, Babylon, Cuthah, Kish, Nippur, Borsippa, Opis, Nisibis, Gozan, Haran, Carchemish, Til Barsip, Samal, Arpad, Karkar, Hamath, Tadmor, Arvad, Byblos, Sidon, Tyre, Damascus, Samaria, Jerusalem, Eltekeh, Ashkelon, Raphia, Pelusium, Tanis, Bubastis, On, Memphis, Sais, Heracleopolis, Akhetaton (Tell el Amarna), Siut, Abydos, Thebes, Jeb (Elephantine I.), Ammonium, Dumah, Sela, Arbela, Tushpa (Turushpa), Kanish, Maqash, Tarsus, Cilician Gates, Ancyra, Gordium, Celaenae, Sardis, Miletus, Samos, Chios, Lesbos, Euboea, Athens, Corinth, Sparta, Thasos, Teium, Chalcedon, Byzantium, Cyzicus, Astacus, Sinope (Greek), Trapezus (Greek), Abydos, Phaselis (Greek), Paphos, Salamis, Cyrene (Greek)

Geographic features
Zagros Mts., Amardi (Zagros Mts.), Araxes River, Cyrus River, Lake Van, Lake Urmia, Tigris River, Euphrates River, Halys R., Sangarius R., Taurus Mts., Anti-Taurus Mts., L. Tuz, Maeander R., Hermus R., Dead Sea, Red Sea, Nile R., L. Moeris, Aegean Sea

RHODES, CRETE, CYPRUS, EUBOEA, LESBOS, CHIOS, SAMOS

gris. Assyrian ambitions would very definitely have to be reckoned with from here on.

Not only did these conquerors lack ability in maintaining order and submission in the conquered lands, but another inherent weakness was their tendency toward frequent and very disturbing internal rebellions. This same Shalmaneser, who had fought his way well toward the southern border of Syria, must have been as humiliated as he was incensed when, only a few years before his death, he had to put down an uprising lead from the very palace itself in the person of his son, Ashurdaninapal. This upheaval was sufficient to give the firmly held provinces, even Babylon, an opportunity to mutiny, and the next monarch, Shamshi-Adad V, spent his twelve years on the throne in one campaign after another attempting to reconquer the formerly subjugated lands.

In fact the following century was filled with just such uncertain efforts. Assyria's rulers fought and struggled merely to hold their kingdom together. Yet the ambition to dominate remained intact, and when a usurper came to the throne in 745 B.C., he ushered in an era filled with famous rulers, and a "Golden Age" for these soldierly potentates.

The first king in this remarkable galaxy was Tiglath-pileser III, called in the Bible Pul, and by the Babylonians *Pulu*. Five months after he had seized the throne he was off to the wars. His first objective was Babylon, and shortly that land was brought under direct control of the Assyrian throne. Both there, and in other restless dependencies to the east, deportation on a large scale was put to work. Native populations were strongly adulterated with foreigners driven sometimes great distances from their home countries. The purpose in back of this brutal device was to temper national consciousness — to break up special groups and with them the will to resist.

Lands and provinces to the north and northwest next demanded Tiglath-pileser's attention. Yet he needed income, and since the tributaries in Syria and Palestine were withholding their annual payments, the mailed fist was needed in that quarter too. One noticeable improvement had been made and quickly began to bear fruit. With a wealth of past experience — and errors — to draw upon, the army had been reorganized, and with the help of this improved

ness as a hopeful world power. Although its people proved to be effective soldiers, they very surely lacked political sagacity and ability. The governors appointed to rule conquered territories must have been either inept, or weak, or both. Surely they were in decided contrast to governors mustered by the Romans centuries later, who in many cases were quite able to keep whole nations subjected. The consequence was that Assyria bled herself white through military campaigns directed time after time at very much the same regions, in which she should have been undisputed mistress for long, peaceful and prosperous periods.

This condition seems to be well illustrated in the experiences during the reign of Shalmaneser III, who followed Ashurnasirpal and came to the throne in 859 B.C. Although he had a long reign of 35 years, no less than 26 of them were filled with virtually continuous fighting. This must have proved a heavy drain upon the country's manpower and resources. The spoil claimed to have been captured during these martial enterprises was huge, but in the belief of most scholars the quantity was very heavily exaggerated. He made a lunge at Syria and Palestine in 854 B.C. and was stayed in his advance at the battle at Karkar near the Orontes River in Syria. It was there that Ahab and the Israelites joined with members of the Syrian and Phoenician confederacy formed to oppose this monster from the banks of the Ti-

tool, Assyria now began a century and a half of virulent warfare. In a purely military sense, their achievements have been admired by the best strategists, ever since their extensive records were re-discovered in the last century.

It was a few years before Tiglath-pileser came to the throne and some 1800 miles to the west, that, according to venerable legend, a city was founded by the twins Romulus and Remus, sons of the god Mars. This was Rome, which one day would rule the western world. Seven centuries later its ability to govern would be far superior to that of the Assyrians. Yet its legions were probably never any better or more audacious soldiers than the well-trained horde that finally set out with Pul in command, seeking to right matters on the little land bridge. The prosperous period which Israel and Judah had both known had ended, for Jeroboam II had been dead for a number of years, and old Uzziah, who ruled in all for 52 years as king of Judah, had been struck with leprosy and had died two years before Tiglath-pileser had come to power.

After Pul's successes in the north of Syria, the move on to the south met with no serious resistance, and one city and country after another became vassals of the invincible host. Even the stout walls whose foundations Omri had laid over a century before did not seem nearly adequate, and Israel gave up voluntarily. Its king, Menahem, bought peace and the retention of his throne for 1000 talents of silver, or about $1,950,000, a tremendous amount for those days. This impost is recorded in 2 (4) Kings 15:19,20, and also in the annals of Pul's reign, in which it is admitted very briefly that: "I received tribute from Menahem of Samaria . . . Like a bird, alone he fled and submitted to me."

The levy seems to have been collected from some 60,000 of his subjects, assessed 50 shekels each. This would have been about the going price of a good pair of oxen or donkeys, or a male slave, or a small house and a bit of surrounding land, and so a burdensome tax. And since taxes are never popular, these bred an uprising in Israel. Their king had taken the easy way, which had been profitable perhaps to him but ruinous to many of his subjects. The turmoil soon headed up in the person of an army

Inscribed prism of Sennacherib records his campaign against Hezekiah

officer, Pekah, who slew Menahem's son and took possession of the throne. The Assyrian grip on Samaria began to falter at once. It would appear that Tiglath-pileser had improved his army but apparently not his governmental control over captive nations.

There was trouble, too, in Damascus, where Rezin, king of the Syrians, began to plot organized resistance through a defensive league; it was in reality a renewal of the same confederation which had on another occasion stemmed the Assyrian advance. All the little countries hurried to join, all, that is, except Judah, which was paying tribute as a vassal of the common enemy, preferring that way to one of violence. But Rezin was determined that Assyria would have no potential allies in the whole area, and either by persuasion, or pressure, encouraged Pekah to accompany him to Jerusalem where they put that city under siege. But King Ahaz could not be forced to yield.

His position, however, was now most unfortunate, and emissaries were sent galloping off to the north begging for Assyrian aid, the plea being accompanied by lavish gifts of silver and gold stripped from the Temple and the palace. The Bible record of this transaction has its brief counterpart in Assyrian chronicles which reads: "I received tribute from Jauhazi (Ahaz) of Judah."

In 734 B.C. the cohorts from the north were again at the gates of Damascus. Just how

long that city withstood siege is not certain, but it seems to have been but a brief one. Rezin the king was slain, the noblemen were impaled upon stakes, the city itself was surely ransacked, if not burned, and towns and villages in sixteen surrounding Syrian districts were leveled. Some 800 citizens, probably of leading, influential families, were led away to servitude elsewhere.

It was only about 100 miles by trail down to Samaria; and either later that same year, or early in the following one, Tiglath-pileser moved over this roadway, or possibly along two of them, conquering and reducing to impotence the countryside through which he passed. Hazor, Gilead, Galilee and the land of Naphtali felt the grinding heel of Assyrian might. Governors were put over the remnants of the people left behind, while great numbers were marched away to the north and east.

Then it was the turn of "Bet-Omri," or Israel. The outlying districts fell easily. The Assyrian records of this particular campaign state very briefly: "All its people I took away to Assyria." Actually the "all" did not include Samaria itself, but meant that every other city and town in the northern kingdom had been taken over and combined into several Assyrian provinces. The area had been subjected to utter disruption and heavily depopulated through deportation. It was rather a ghost country in comparison with the land which had risen to such

plenty and luxury under the second Jeroboam.

In the capital city, too, there had been grave trouble. Another conspiracy had flared up, and the usurper Pekah was now removed by assassination at the hands of one Hoshea, a puppet of the conquerors. Samaria, although not completely subdued, was shorn of its former power and thus was an easy target at any time when it would seem essential that it be disposed of. Judah, too, was also free of complete domination, but still under a certain degree of vassalage. At that moment Assyria was mistress from the Persian Gulf around the great "Crescent" to the very borders of Egypt. And this latter land, bereft of the shield afforded by the cities of Syria and Palestine, had its diplomats and representatives busy exploring means of rebuilding this protective curtain. Its turn would come in a few years.

Conditions seem to have gone on with little change during the remaining six or seven years of Tiglath-pileser's reign. But there was the customary stir and test of strength at his death. Despite the fact that spy systems were probably as well organized then as today, Hoshea withheld his annual tribute and hastily entered into an agreement with the Egyptian Pharaoh, So, or Sewe. It was a bold move and a desperate one, which was almost certain to prove fatal. The new Assyrian sovereign, Shalmaneser V, who took the throne in 727 B.C., did not temporize with such disloyalty, so it was

not too long before his forces were assaulting the walls of Samaria. To the great credit of its people, the city did manage to hold out stubbornly through three long years. Actually it seems to have withstood the siege better than did the Assyrian king, for before the city capitulated, he was dead; one of his generals had usurped the throne and taken the illustrious name of Sargon II.

At one time this monarch was something of a mythical character, since his name was unknown except in the Bible text. Then, in the year 1843, a French consular agent and scholar, Paul Emile Botta, uncovered his palace at Khorsabad. This proved a most remarkable find, especially since high spots in the history of the king's reign appeared as legends inscribed on the palace walls. In one of these inscriptions is this very illuminating bit: "At the beginning of my rule, in the very first year I reigned . . . I set siege to and conquered Samaria . . . I carried away into captivity 27,290 persons who lived there; I took 50 fine chariots for my royal equipment." Other recovered records add that he later rebuilt the city, making it even greater than before. Deported people from other lands were then brought in and settled there, so that the population might be strongly mixed. A governor was placed over the people of this new province and tribute and taxes "imposed upon them as upon the Assyrians."

These facts closely parallel those found in the Bible passage of 2 (4) Kings 17:3-6. In the 24th verse of this same chapter it is explained how those who had been led away were replaced by other unfortunates uprooted in distant lands and herded in from as far away as Babylon. The members of the Ten Tribes who had been hurried off to Mesopotamia became indeed the "Lost Tribes," for they have never again definitely emerged in world history. It is interesting to note in passing, though, that certain faiths, basing their contention on various Bible verses, believe that remnants of them formed the early inhabitants of America.

The mixture of people in and about Samaria came to be known as the *Samaritans*. One gets the impression that their numbers were far less than those who had peopled this highland area in more prosperous times. In fact they were so few that wild beasts began to multiply, and God used them for a scourge. Finally the poor, discouraged folk asked the Assyrian king for aid and guidance, and he sent them a priest from among the captives taken from Israel. The latter established a shrine at Bethel and sought to instruct his charges in the worship of Yahweh. But their idolatry was too ingrained; they began to set up graven images, and combined the worship of God with that of idols.

The dates during the reigns of David and Solomon are still far from certain, so that the exact period during which the ill-fated Kingdom of Israel existed is a little uncertain. Even by the most liberal figuring it was not much over two and a half centuries; indeed, it appears probable that it was somewhat less. The stupendous ruin and wretchedness spread by the Assyrians reached even distant lands, and Israel received its full share.

Many of the victims came back to life, and some, like Damascus, Babylon, Sidon, Memphis and one or two others went on to still greater fame. But while Samaria continued to exist, its glory had permanently dimmed, and its wickedness, which was great in the sight of the Lord, seems to have lastingly sapped its vitality. For years the greatest of Palestinian cities, it was from now on just another hill town in the central highlands. The Lord's will had been worked upon it at the hands of the first real empire builders, the malicious, barbarous Assyrians.

Assyrian banqueting scene (7th century B.C.)

XIII

THE FINAL YEARS OF JUDAH

What havoc time had wrought in this land of promise! How hopefully its conquest had begun, as a new and sternly disciplined generation had moved in out of the wilderness and sought its subjugation under the capable direction of Joshua. There was great promise after it had been welded into a combined kingdom by the firm hands of David. Then prosperity had showered down during the days of Solomon, despite the fact the seeds of discord were sprouting and had made a lush growth before he laid down the scepter. At once the kingdom had split in two, and finally, now, the greater portion of the domain promised as a homeland for God's elect had passed back into heathen hands.

Of this realm, only tiny Judah remained, a little oval block running from a few miles above Jerusalem south to Kadesh, and from the Dead Sea to just west of Lachish. It now embraced little more than half the area of present day Connecticut, and far less territory than lies within the bounds of hundreds of American counties. In fact it was only a mere trace of the kingdom passed along by David to Solomon; and what was worse, even this remnant was heavily entailed and virtually a possession of the Assyrians.

Hezekiah, its king, had continued the role of vassal assumed by his father, Ahaz, and

records of his annual payments of tribute may still be seen on the numerous clay tablets unearthed in Assyria. Yet he and his people found the burden unbearable, and he was a sufficiently resolute ruler so that he hoped to be able in some way to lighten this load. The first world empire extended down to the west of Judah; it included certain of the Philistine cities, and when rioting broke out in Ashdod, Hezekiah was greatly encouraged. But when a number of the neighboring cities and peoples formed a confederacy to combat their powerful oppressor, he carefully avoided direct involvement, although he did connive and secretly lend encouragement behind the scenes.

Egypt, at that time ruled by an Ethiopian dynasty of kings, was very apprehensive, and was making many worthless promises in the hope of stimulating sufficient resistance on the part of her northern neighbors, so the Assyrians would keep their distance. The ruling Pharaoh at the moment may well have been Shabaka, next to the last of these Ethiopians, and it is likely that he had a large diplomatic force at the court in Jerusalem trying to win over Hezekiah.

But the Assyrian intelligence system seems to have had its full complement of spies and informers, and word of the defections in Palestine was rushed back to headquarters on the Tigris as fast as the camel post could make the long journey. Since there could be no weak points or danger spots on the road to Egypt, another series of invasions began, which ultimately were to end disastrously for Assyria.

There were apparently three waves, the first coming while Sargon was still upon the throne, but led by a tartan, *turtanu,* or a commander-in-chief, and which may even have been his own son, Sennacherib. This perhaps involved but one army corps while the main forces were busy to the north and east of the homeland. The visitation very likely lasted three or four years, and is the one recorded at four points in Bible text (2 [4] Kings 18:13; Is. 20:1; 36:1; 2 Chron. [2 Par] 32:1-8).

An even larger campaign got under way about ten years later. But in the interim several notable occurrences had taken place. One was the assassination of Sargon, which resulted in a rash of restlessness from one end of the empire to the other. But his son quickly took

Assyrian relief from the Royal Palace at Nineveh

A Mede bringing horses as tribute to King Sargon II (722-705 B.C.)

over the throne, and no major revolt seems to have occurred.

In faraway Judah, the life of King Hezekiah was threatened, not by a conspiracy, but by a "boil." While there is little enough on which to base a diagnosis, some doctors believe this fiery *shekheen,* as it is called in Hebrew, to have been the deadly *bubo* of bubonic plague, a not uncommon and often fatal disease in the East. But his competence in handling the kingdom was sorely needed, and God disclosed a cure through His prophet, Isaiah. Hezekiah was granted fifteen added years of life (Is. 38).

The "sign" which the Lord had manifested in this healing of His servant was immediately employed to shelter a little intrigue. An embassy arrived in Jerusalem from Merodach-baladan, then king of Babylon. After congratulating Hezekiah on his recovery, the group hurriedly disclosed its true purpose, to invite him to take an active part in a confederacy made up of the rulers of Babylon, Edom, Egypt, Moab, Philistia and Phoenicia. The Judaean king was much elated, and even a little foolishly took the ambassadors on a tour of his treasuries; he showed them such resources as were as yet untapped.

Hezekiah's act very definitely aroused heavenly displeasure, for Isaiah quickly sought out his king and prophesied to him the word of the Lord—how the people and the remaining treasure of Judah would some day be carried off to captivity in Babylon, the very city from which these conspirators had come. Hezekiah, however, joined this hostile alliance.

Well aware of all that was going on, the Assyrians started their main campaign against the Philistines, subduing the Phoenicians en route to the land to the south. Quickly there was a rush of ambassadors to the Assyrian king's tent, including representatives from Ammon, Ashdod, Edom and Moab. Yet some of the coastal towns, such as Joppa and Ashkelon, held out and required attention and punishment. At last Sennacherib was able to turn east into Judah, where he threw his siege troops against Lachish. Thinking perhaps to save Jerusalem from similar treatment, Hezekiah sent word to Sennacherib there, confessing his faults and defections and asking the invaders to name the price of peace and amity. The Assyrians quickly appointed it, and since it amounted to about $1,500,000, even the gold leaf had to be stripped from the Temple doors to make up the sum (2 [4] Kings 18:14-16).

After Lachish had been reduced, and possibly fresh troops had arrived, the main stage of this second invasion got under way. There seemed to be suitable provocation, so Jerusalem was now marked for immediate attention. Suddenly the Assyrian multitude was before its gates, and a *rab-saris,* or court officer of Sennacherib, bawled out a dire warning to the representatives of Hezekiah, who stood upon the wall to hear his words. What would, or could, the king now do?

His remarkable cure, plus the exhortations of the man of God, Isaiah, seem to have restored Hezekiah's faith in Yahweh, and he stoutly refused to admit these Assyrian troops set to garrison the city. The main army was just then embroiled at Libnah (Lobna), and when Sennacherib heard of the changed attitude of his vassal, he dispatched messengers with letters threatening later vengeance. But his situation at the moment was highly critical. With a major battle with the Egyptians threat-

JUDAH AFTER THE FALL OF ISRAEL
c. 700 B.C.

Copyright by C. S. HAMMOND & CO., N.Y.

Scale of Miles

0   5   10   20   30

Perennial Rivers ....
Seasonal Rivers & Streams ....
Capitals ....✦

The Great Sea

(Mediterranean Sea)

Sennacherib conquered Phoenicia, with the exception of Tyre, in 701 B.C.

With the conquest of Samaria in 721 B.C. by Sargon II, the Kingdom of Israel came to an end.

After Samaria fell, Sargon II exiled most of the influential people. The Ten Tribes were moved to various parts of Mesopotamia and disappeared forever from the pages of history.

In 701 B.C. Sennacherib captured 46 cities of Judah as he pushed down toward the Egyptians, defeating them at Eltekeh.

In 701 B.C. Jerusalem was besieged, though not taken, by Sennacherib.

Ammon, Moab and Edom fell to the Assyrian Esarhaddon in 690 B.C., but they were never held long enough to be organized as regular provinces of the empire.

Here Sargon II defeated the Egyptian army in 720 B.C.

Judah was never a province of Assyria. Throughout Assyrian domination, it preserved a nominal independence under its own king, though paying tribute regularly and homage when it was required.

PHOENICIA
MOUNT LEBANON
Leontes R.
MT. HERMON
DAMASCUS
QARNINI
A S S Y R I A N
Bashan
HAURAN
GALILEE
MT. CARMEL
Kishon R.
Plain of MEGIDDO
Jezreel
Mt. Tabor
Plain of Sharon
DU-RU
S A M A R I A
Sea of Galilee
Yarmuk R.
Jordan River
GILEAD
Jabbok R.
AMMON
PHILISTIA
J U D A H
Salt Sea (Dead Sea)
MOAB
EGYPTIAN KINGDOM
EDOM
Zered R.
Arnon R.
Arabia

Sidon
Zarephath
Tyre
Ijon
Abel-beth-maachah
Dan
Damascus
Kedesh
Achzib
Hazor
Karnaim
Accho
Ramah
Ashtaroth
Chinnereth
Aphek
Jotbah
Gath-hepher
Hammath
Edrei
Jokneam
Dor
Shunem
Ramoth-gilead
Megiddo
Jezreel
Beth-shan
Taanach
Pella
Dothan
Mahanaim
Samaria
Mt. Ebal
Shechem
Mt. Gerizim
Aphek
Shiloh
Joppa
Lod
Rabbath-ammon
Jabneh (Jabneel)
Ekron
Gezer
Bethel
Ai
Michmash
Jericho
Gederoth
Gibbethon
Beth-horon
Mizpah
Gibeon
Geba
Gilgal
Elealeh
Ajalon
Ramah
Anathoth
Heshbon
Ashdod
Eltekeh
Gibeah
Nob
Mt. Nebo
Saphir
Beth-shemesh
Timnah
Jerusalem
Medeba
Ashkelon
Libnah
Adullam
Jahaz
Gath
Moresheth-gath
Tekoa
Mareshah
Dibon
Gaza
Lachish
Hebron
Aroer
Adoraim
Debir
En-gedi
Gerar
Dumah
Raphia
Beer-sheba
Ar
Zoar
Kir-moab (Kir-haresheth)

ening, Jerusalem would have to wait. Yet with it and Ekron as strong points at his rear, the Assyrian king promptly fell back to Eltekeh, a town whose location has not been exactly determined, but which was probably about 15 miles northwest of Jerusalem.

There he met the combined forces of Egypt and Ethiopia and defeated them. Then, turning upon nearby Ekron, he added it to his list of conquests. While this inventory, like other lists of similar kind, may be heavily overdone, he does claim to have taken a total of 46 fortified cities and towns in Judah alone, from

His reign was to prove as evil and revolting as his father's had been just and good. He continued as a vassal, for two Assyrian kings, Esarhaddon and Ashurbanipal, have left records of tribute payments made by him. It was probably the latter who caused the brash young man to be led captive to Babylon. There he repented of his gross wickedness and was eventually restored to his kingdom. He did cease somewhat from idolatry, and it is interesting to note that he ruled for the incredible period of 55 years, the longest term any king of Judah held that throne. He was succeeded by his young

Looking from ruins at Mosul (Iraq) across the Tigris toward Nineveh

which he led away into bondage a reported 200,150 persons. He also plundered the countryside of countless horses, camels, donkeys, mules and sheep.

And he would most certainly have gone on and leveled Jerusalem, had not disaster just then struck him a paralyzing blow. A plague broke out in the ranks of his army and killed, according to the Bible account, 185,000 of his warriors in a single horrible night (2 [4] Kings 19:35). He had no choice but to gather his few remaining men and beat a hurried retreat. No mention of this gigantic debacle has yet been discovered in Assyrian records. But this was not all, and troubles in Babylon soon took the king there.

Hezekiah outlasted this respite by only a few years and died peacefully; he was succeeded by his twelve-year-old son, Manasseh.

son, Amon who followed the bad habits of his parent's younger years. His servants had had quite enough of him after two years and slew him. But the people of the land dispatched these assassins in turn and placed the dead king's eight-year-old son, Josiah, on the throne.

His was to prove one of the finest reigns in the history of the little land. In his immature years he was virtually a ward of the great high priest Hilkiah, who seems to have had great influence upon the formation of his religious attitudes. Even as still a young man he sought to conform his own life and that of the members of the court to the law of God, and he set about suppressing idolatry not only in Judah, but in neighboring Israel also.

He was about 24 years old when he gave orders for the repair and refurnishing of the Temple, during which an ancient copy of the

Law was discovered in the walls. Its reading profoundly impressed not only the young king, but his subjects as well. A second campaign for the elimination of every conceivable form or vestige of idolatry was set in motion, and the passover celebration at its termination is said to have had greater religious fervor than any like festival since the time of Samuel.

Although he had reigned 31 years, Josiah was but 39 when the Egyptian armies began to move north over the great caravan route on their way to attack the Assyrians. His father briefly, and his grandfather and great-grandfather over a much longer period, had paid tribute to the king of Assyria, and it had become so customary that Josiah had long considered himself a vassal and thus bound to resist Assyria's enemies. So he gathered his small army and set off in pursuit, finally catching up with the far larger body of Egyptian troops at Megiddo. There he gave battle to the Pharaoh Necho, in the midst of which a well-placed arrow dealt him a mortal wound. Hastily transferred from his own chariot to another, his attendants raced back toward Jerusalem 60 miles away, but he had no more than arrived there when he died. He was a great loss to his faltering kingdom, and the choristers under the famous Jeremiah's direction made heartfelt lamentations for him. Stern days of reckoning for Judah were once again at hand.

They would occur, however, on a changed world stage. Assyria was by 609 B.C. no longer in the unquestioned position of power it had held earlier in this same century. At that time it had extended its empire widely, and Esarhaddon had been able to seize Memphis in Egypt in 671. Then eight years later Ashurbanipal had pushed the conquest on up the Nile as far as Thebes. This latter ruler, however, seems to have been a somewhat less vigorous soldier than his forebears, and while his reign was a long one, it was during it that several weakening influences began to take hold in empire affairs.

With his death in 626, resistance began to mount in volume and strength. Finally in 612 a combination made up of Medes, a recently formed nation in the mountains of Iran, together with the Babylonians and their allies, fell upon Nineveh. While it was under siege, a flood in the Tigris carried away parts of the walls and made it indefensible. The city was then laid waste with such thoroughness that for ages it was completely lost sight of and became something of a myth. From the vantage point of today it is quite evident that this first world empire had come to an inglorious end. Yet the continued loyalty on Josiah's part tends to make it appear that even the wreck of the Assyrian capital had not that soon calmed all fears that this military goliath was truly dead and not about to rise suddenly from the carnage.

Egypt, which through the centuries had an extensive foreign service, was no doubt better informed, and for some years that country entertained extravagant ambitions. But after the Pharaoh Necho's army was cut to ribbons in a battle at Carchemish on the upper reaches of the Euphrates, that land was far less of a factor in world affairs. It was the two conquerors of Assyria which were destined to play major parts on the world stage in the years ahead, and they began to take over their new roles.

The Assyrian empire had been split between them, the Medes taking over lands to the north and northwest, while to the Babylonians fell the territory to the south and southwest. Thus Syria and Palestine were claimed by the latter whose king was Nabopolassar. But he was already advanced in age and in no mood for the long journey necessary to make a personal inspection of his greatly enlarged domain. However, he had a two-fisted son who bore a name that was the despair first of Hebrew chroniclers and later of their English translators and which is perhaps most commonly rendered as Nebuchadnezzar. His aged parent placed him at the head of a vast army and started him toward the provinces far to the west and south. In fact it was he that so rudely dashed Egyptian hopes in the engagement by the great ford on the Euphrates.

But in the very midst of this contest with the Egyptians, word came that his father had died. So Nebuchadnezzar hurried back to Babylon, leaving his army in the hands of his able generals. Affairs at the capital claimed his attention for a time, and Judah and some of the other vassals were left to their own deserts. Jerusalem quite faithfully forwarded its tribute during three years and then revolted.

Money proved as distinct a consideration with this new overlord as it had with his predecessors. So he was soon in Palestine, where he set about ending all further resistance. The sons and grandson of Josiah were to experience most overwhelming calamities. Jehoiakim had ascended the throne when Nebuchadnezzar first spread his troops about the walls of the Holy City. They were finally breached; the king was seized and bound, but eventually released; the Temple was plundered of certain of its sacred vessels, and a levy was made of youths from among the families of the nobility. With these young men as hostages, the Babylonians moved on with their other loot.

It was not too long, though, before the host returned and this time emptied the Temple and the palace of all objects of value. Jehoiachin, Jehoiakim's son, had by now succeeded to the throne; he was seized, together with the remainder of the nobility, the artisans and soldiers, and this sizeable contingent of prisoners was marched away to Babylon. A puppet king, Mattaniah, a son of Josiah, was popped upon the vacant throne. His name was changed to Zedekiah by his captors, and he was left to reign over the tiny remnant of the people remaining behind.

For eight years his loyalty went unquestioned. But in the ninth he revolted, and quickly the Babylonians were again ringing the city walls. Yet the city was too strong to be taken by open assault, so a series of fortifications were erected in a ring about it, and a withering siege began. In the previous destruction of neighboring Lachish these fiendish Babylonians had employed what might be termed the "inferno technique." From the great quantity of ashes and charred stone in the city's ruins, the archaeologists now believe that the besiegers had hewed down the forests and orchards for miles around. This mass of firewood had been dragged to and heaped against the walls of Lachish until it reached to their very tops. Then this vast stack of tinder was set afire. The heat within the little city must have been virtually unbearable and was sufficiently intense that the stonework crumbled away, so that when the fires cooled the fortifications could be easily breached.

But about Jerusalem there was no such supply of fuel, and the attackers had to depend upon their heaviest battering rams and siege equipment. With it they went to work with a will. But the efforts dragged on for months. The appearance of an Egyptian army in the vicinity drew the Babylonians away for a time. The food supply had long been exceedingly low,

Pool of Siloe at Jerusalem dug by Hezekiah

but the people had held on, hoping the Egyptians might raise the siege. But when the stores were finally exhausted, Zedekiah and his fighting men managed to slip out of the beleagured city during the night. Picking their way gingerly through the line of surrounding forts, they hurried off to the east toward the Jordan Valley.

Word of their escape soon came to the Babylonians, and a detachment was sent hurrying in pursuit. On the plain of Jericho, Zedekiah was captured, having been almost completely forsaken by his officers and men. Nebuchadnezzar had taken up residence in the town of Riblah, north of Damascus, and this last king of Judah was dragged there in fetters, tried and condemned. One by one his sons were brought in and slain in his presence. Then his own eyes were blinded, he was again put in fetters, led off to Babylon, and there thrown into prison for the remainder of his days. Liberal evidence was rapidly accumulating that these new rulers of the world were just about as brutish as the Assyrians had ever been. In one respect, albeit not a humane one, the Assyrians were in some measure more commendable. They did leave very excellent and complete records of all their military exploits, while the Babylonians left practically none.

However, the Bible tells us that Jerusalem had held out for two years. But it was now virtually defenseless, and the people still left, excepting only the very poorest of them, were promptly marched off into captivity. Then the Temple and all important buildings were put to the torch, and the walls were leveled. The Kingdom of Judah was at an end—and Zion, the Holy City, lay in ruin for the next fifty years.

XIV

A PAWN IN A PAGAN WORLD

The Temple of the Lord had been plundered and destroyed. Jerusalem lay devastated. Thousands of its leading citizens had been marched away into captivity, and more would follow. Like Israel a century and a half previously, the last of the chosen people had now become quite decisively merely a pawn in a pagan world and equally liable to lose their identity and be completely forgotten.

When the Israelites had moved in out of the desert wastes at the end of the great exodus centuries before, they were a disciplined and quite different people. Their family and tribal loyalties were strong, and their sense of *misphat,* or justice, well developed. Also they were individuals with an innate sense of freedom. Even the winning of the land had been more difficult because their leaders lacked power to draft them for military service or for labor. They were bent, however, upon conquering a pagan land where the pagan philosophy of life, which controlled so much of the ancient world, then prevailed.

In very early times when two peoples fell out and war ensued, the victors customarily exterminated the vanquished. Death proved to be the most certain manner in which to imprison the losers. Then, as the material arts advanced and the need of workers increased, the destiny of the vanquished altered. Instead of wiping out the defeated, the lives of all the able-bodied were spared, and they were en-

slaved. The economic surplus which their enforced labor puchased, spelled wealth and power to the conqueror for even further expansion.

The overall results were much the same throughout the ancient world: the more powerful segment in any group began to dominate and control the far larger numbers that made up the bottom and most of the heap. A thin top stratum was made up of aristocratic free families, while all below were serfs or outright slaves. There were, of course, variations. The communities of Canaan, for example, were tiny, not-too-effective city-states with very little adhesion between them. By strong contrast, the ruling classes in Mesopotamia and Egypt were able to centralize their efforts and build dominant nations and eventual empires, bent upon conquest not only of land, but of the productive capacity of the subject people. These were expressions of a pagan manner of life, which the world still finds hard to shake off.

One of the first recorded attempts at widespread control over others, especially for the collection of tribute, is the coalition of eastern monarchs bested by Abraham as he freed their hostage Lot from their clutches in the night battle far to the north of Damascus (Gen. 14:1-16). In the years when the children of Israel had been in bondage in Egypt, that country had controlled the coastal area in Palestine and Syria as far north as the Euphrates River. The cities in Mesopotamia had held each other in subjugation at times, and for several generations the Israelites, who had fought their way into the land of Canaan, had been under a

Plaque from a corner-stone deposit of the palace of the Persian Kings Darius and Xerxes, dated 516-15 B.C. and giving the boundaries of the Persian Empire

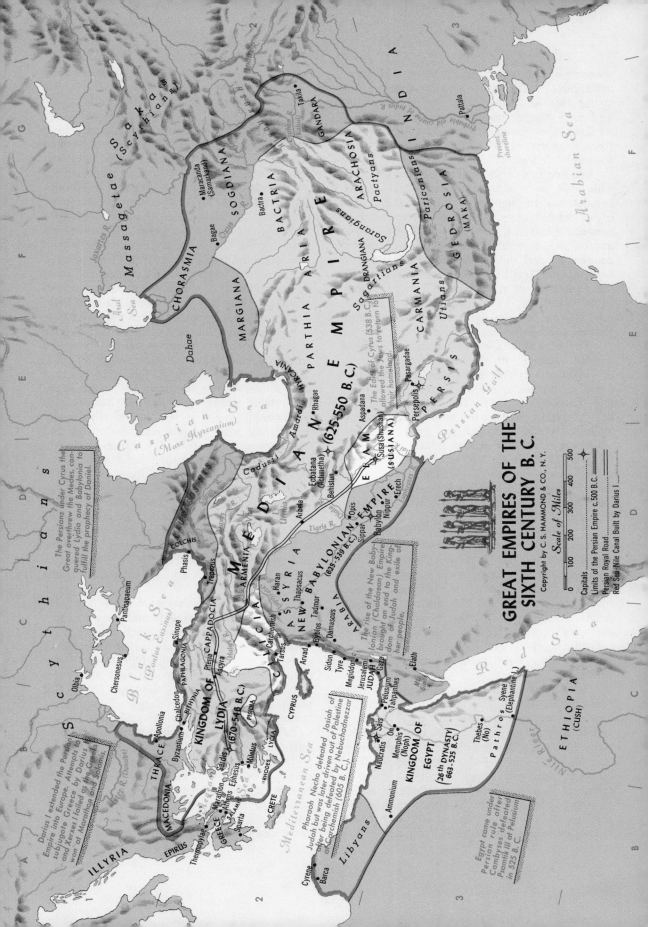

GREAT EMPIRES OF THE SIXTH CENTURY B.C.

Copyright by C. S. HAMMOND & CO., N.Y.

Scale of Miles

0 100 200 300 400 500

Capitals .... ✦
Limits of the Persian Empire c. 500 B.C.
Persian Royal Road
Red Sea Nile Canal Built by Darius I ....

The Persians under Cyrus the Great overthrew the Medes, conquered Lydia and Babylonia to fulfill the prophecy of Daniel.

Darius I extended the Persian Empire into Europe. Attempts to subjugate Greece by Darius and Xerxes failed as the Greeks won at Marathon and Salamis.

The rise of the New Babylonian (Chaldean) Empire brought an end to the Kingdom of Judah and the exile of her people.

The Edict of Cyrus (538 B.C.) allowed the Jews to return to their homeland.

Pharaoh Necho defeated Josiah of Judah but was later driven out out of Palestine after being defeated by Nebuchadnezzar at Carchemish (605 B.C.).

Egypt came under Persian rule after Cambyses defeated Psamtik III at Pelusium in 525 B.C.

Regions and places

INDIA
Arabian Sea
Massagetae (Saka) (Scythians)
Aral Sea
CHORASMIA
SOGDIANA
Maracanda (Samarkand)
Bagae
Oxus R.
Bactra
BACTRIA
Taxila
GANDARA
Kabul R.
Hindu Kush
ARACHOSIA
Pactyans
Paricanians
Probable old course of Indus R.
Pattala
Present shoreline
GEDROSIA (MAKA)
Sarangians
DRANGIANA
Sagartians
Utians
CARMANIA
ARIA
PARTHIA
MARGIANA
Dahae
HYRCANIA
Rhagae
Amardii
Cadusii
EMPIRE (625-550 B.C.)
MEDIAN
Caspian Sea (Mare Hyrcanium)
PERSIS
Pasargadae
Persepolis
Aspadana
ELAM (SUSIANA)
Susa (Shushan)
Ecbatana (Achmetha)
Behistun
Arbela
Urmia
Opis
NEW BABYLONIAN EMPIRE (625-539 B.C.)
Nippur
Babylon
Sippar
Erech
Tigris R.
ARMENIA
ASSYRIA
Haran
Harmozia
Thapsacus
SYRIA
Tadmor
ARABIA
Carchemish
Arvad
Byblos
Damascus
Sidon
Tyre
Megiddo
Jerusalem
JUDAH
Gaza
Elath
Pelusium
Tahpanhes
Red Sea
Sinai
Sais
On
Memphis (Noph)
Naucratis
KINGDOM OF EGYPT
26th DYNASTY 663-525 B.C.
Thebes (No)
Syene (Elephantine I.)
Pathros
ETHIOPIA (CUSH)
Nile River
Ammonium
Libyans
Cyrene
Barca
Mediterranean Sea
CRETE
RHODES
LYCIA
PISIDIA
Sparta
Salamis
Athens
Marathon
Thermopylae
GREECE
EPIRUS
MACEDONIA
ILLYRIA
Ister R. (Danube)
THRACE
Apollonia
Byzantium
Chalcedon
BITHYNIA
PAPHLAGONIA
Sinope
Pteria
Ancyra
CAPPADOCIA
CILICIA
Tarsus
Halys R.
KINGDOM OF LYDIA (670-546 B.C.)
Sardis
Ephesus
Miletus
Black Sea (Pontus Euxinus)
Obbia
Panticapaeum
Chersonesus
Scythians
COLCHIS
Phasis
Trapezus
CYPRUS

measure of control by the Philistines. History, unhappily, is filled with these instances of the strong and the daring seeking to rise to power and easy wealth on the shoulders of their weaker, more peaceable neighbors. Said the Roman dramatist, Plautus, "Man is a wolf toward his fellow man."

The first real crisis on anything like a world-wide scale, even in ancient times, came, as has been shown, through the well-organized savagery of the Assyrians. During the seven centuries between 1350 B.C. and 625 B.C. they conquered and dominated areas ranging from the country around the north end of the Persian Gulf, up the Tigris and Euphrates valleys into the mountains of what is now Turkey almost to the Black Sea. From there they swung south into Cilicia, through Syria and Palestine, and well up the Nile Valley in Egypt.

The Chaldeans, or Babylonians, finally banded together with the Medes from the eastern highlands to defeat the Assyrians and became joint heirs to the lands over which they had claimed suzerainty. The bulk of what had been Assyrian territory fell to the Babylonians, while the Medes took over the mountain country to the north and extended their sway until they ringed the lower end of the Caspian Sea, swung west along the Caucasus and reached the south shore of the Black Sea. From here their empire followed the Halys River in Asia Minor to the borders of Cilicia.

It was to Babylon, capital of the Chaldean empire, that the captives from Jerusalem and Judah were led into bondage. It was at this time, too, that they began to be known as Jews, at first the designation of one belonging to the tribe or to the now fallen Kingdom of Judah. Afterward this term would be applied to all members of the Hebrew race who returned from the captivity, and later to any of that race wherever they were dispersed throughout the world.

How many of them were led away? Sennacherib the Assyrian claimed that at an earlier time he deported a total of 200,150 from Judah, which is probably a gross overstatement. Nebuchadnezzar and his officers and governors sent off over a twenty-three-year period, four different contingents of which but one group is estimated as to numbers and totalled only about 11,000. Scholars have estimated that in all perhaps 50,000 were removed, although there may have been many more, for numerous Ju-

daean cities ceased to exist from this time.

How did these dislodged people fare? Many left their homes no doubt in the expectation that they would suffer annihilation, much as had their "cousins," the people of Israel, nearly a century and a half before. It is true that the prophet Jeremiah had foretold that this bondage would be for a period of but seventy years, yet it is questionable how many on being torn from their homes took great comfort in his words. In Is. 47:6 there is a hint that perhaps a few suffered harsh treatment, but by and large the Jews were in no sense mistreated and seem in most cases to have enjoyed a wide variety of privileges. Not only were they allowed to build houses and to have servants, but they were permitted to enter business. There is an open question as to how many in Jerusalem or the other Judaean cities had had any part in trade and commerce previously, but it is believed their numbers were relatively few. Just where the bulk of the refugees lived in Babylonia is not definite, but if it was in the capital city itself, they were in the great industrial and trading center of that day. It is also believed that many tried their hand at business, and some of them grew wealthy.

But beyond commercial activities other careers were open to them. They were not denied even the highest places in the state, as the story of Daniel clearly indicates. This Jewish lad was put through the royal training school for government service and eventually became one of the three "presidents," or rulers, in all the land.

Fortunately, too, they were allowed to have their priests, their prophets and their teachers with them. Many might very well have been seduced by the great pantheon of Babylonian gods and goddesses and the colorful rituals and exciting magic which accompanied mass worship in the country where they now lived. But under the leadership of the great Ezekiel, and perhaps others of similar caliber, there appears to have been a religious awakening of large proportions. Also their worship and interest was given a new direction and apparently a much more personal touch. There was now no Temple as a national center, but relatively small groups seemed to have gathered for instruction and devotions. Thus the synagogue, or assembly, came into being. It was an institution that was

to have a profound and very beneficial influence in keeping Jewish identity inviolate down the ages to the present time. When the opportunity came for some of the deportees to return to Jerusalem, they took back with them a heightened religious sense which was to serve them well.

Under the teaching of their religious leaders they began to understand that their captivity was truly to last but seventy years and an attempt was made to focus attention, particularly of the young, upon the hoped-for return. Ezekiel strongly emphasized this return to the fatherland, and much of his book is apparently a compilation of the highlights from a multitude of sermons preached in the hope that a new, a disciplined and a better prepared generation might one day leave the spiritual wilderness of Babylon, recapture the Promised Land and make Jerusalem a Holy City indeed. Many scholars believe that another unnamed priest and prophet wrote what are now chapters 40 through 55 of the book of Isaiah at this same time and for the same purpose. Some believe in fact that he took the place of the deceased Ezekiel, who is presumed to have died about the year 565 B.C. This writer it was who first pointed out and named the man who would make the return to Jerusalem possible.

The name of this "shepherd" of the lost sheep of Israel was Cyrus, the son of Cambyses. About 558 B.C., he ascended the throne of the little desert principality of Ansan, or Anshan, beyond the Elamite country on the eastern edge of the Babylonian empire. Destiny was to smile broadly upon him and had granted him intelligence and competence equal to the great tasks assigned him. The remote area where he was born and had risen to an unimportant throne, had played but a small part in world affairs previously. But to it he brought a consuming ambition and an organizing genius which was to make it mistress of a greater part of the world than any land had previously been able to control.

His first move was somewhat within family bounds, for he forcibly annexed the kingdom of Media, ruled by his grandfather, Astyages. Then, in 550 B.C., he seized Achmetha, or Ecbatana, the Median capital. This would become the summer residence of the Persian kings, a treasure city, and also the place where, at a critical moment, the decree permitting the rebuilding of the Temple at Jerusalem was found filed away (Ezra [1 Esd.] 5:6-6:2). At the end of four years, he moved far to the northwest, and at Pteria conquered Croesus, last ruler of the Lydian empire, who was noted for his wealth. The capital of Lydia, Sardis, was seized later that same year. It was another seven years before he was ready to attempt to gain the kingdom of the Chaldeans, but finally, in 539 B.C., he marched upon Babylon.

Nebuchadnezzar had then been dead for 22 years, and the throne had come into the hands of a scholar and connoisseur, Nabonidus. The government and defense of the great capital had perhaps decayed somewhat under his rule. Yet the fear of invasion by the Medes and Persians was very real and had dictated the design of the city's fortifications. One of these was the "Median Wall," which ran from near Opis on the Tigris above modern Baghdad to the outpost town of Sippar on the Euphrates. Another defensive wall ran just below the city, which in its heyday stood on the eastern bank of the Euphrates and, with its inner and outer ramparts, formed a huge right-angled triangle. A somewhat more limited space along the riverbank was surrounded by still a third wall, which formed a *tempelburg,* or citadel, about the temples, palaces and government structures.

So great is the area of all of Babylon that excavation there to date has been limited to this more important official section. It was excellently laid out and executed, with broad streets intersecting at right-angles, and must

have been fairly astounding to the men and women transported from compact, jumbled Jerusalem. Some of these avenues paralleled the continuous quay, or dock, along the river front, while others ran to great gateways in the walls which could be closed by heavy bronze gates.

Chief among these broad thoroughfares was that which has aptly been given the name of "Procession Street," for this was one of its chief purposes. It began at the famous Ishtar Gate in the north wall, and down it the images of the gods were either borne or trundled on huge floats during the festival of the new year. Near the Ishtar Gate, several vast palaces faced on this avenue. The second of these embodied one of the seven wonders of the ancient world, the famous Hanging Gardens. As the main artery passed on toward the south, it crossed over a small canal which flowed through the very center of the city, and then came to the principal temple, a towering *ziggurat,* visible for great distances in this flat, river-bottom land. After passing this imposing structure, it swung sharply to the west toward the Euphrates, which it crossed on a fine bridge supported by stone piers.

Babylon was a beautiful, imposing and unforgettable city. The river was highly important to its welfare and was ever busy with whole fleets of circular coracles, or crafts built of framework like a canoe, yet perfectly round, and covered with greased animal hides. They were not unlike the *gufas* which ply the waters of this same river today. Herodotus tells of many other peculiarities of its people, especially their carved walking sticks, and of men of importance carrying, suspended on a cord worn about their necks, the cylinder-seal with which they affixed their official signatures to legal documents.

This was the chief city in the world at the time, and also the one which Cyrus must conquer so that he might greatly enlarge his growing empire. How he succeeded in taking it was recorded by the famous Grecian general and historian of the next century, Xenophon. This able military man claims that the Babylonians had ample time to prepare for his attack, since the ordinarily well-balanced Cyrus had spent most of the summer of the year 539 B.C. rather foolishly revenging himself upon the river Di-

A reconstruction of the city of Babylon showing the Ishtar Gate

ala, or Diyala, which flows down from the Kurdistan highlands into the Tigris just below Baghdad. It had drowned one of his favorite horses, and in rebuke the emperor-in-the-making had had the stream divided into no less than 365 channels. But the Babylonians, fortunately for him, had grown soft and were entirely too ready and willing to rely solely upon their strong fortifications.

It is claimed they merely laughed when Cyrus had a deep trench excavated about the city, presumably in some way to starve them out. This was ridiculous! Had they not a full 20 years of provisions on hand? But they were too easily deceived; the Persians were not now whiling away their time; they merely waited patiently for a night most vividly described in the Book of Daniel, when the leaders of the city were busy with their feasting and a terrifying finger wrote a most disturbing message in glowing letters on a palace wall. From it the prince and co-regent Belshazzar learned the destiny of his land from the hand of fate. That was the night the besiegers drained the Euphrates into their trench and entered the city through the dry bed of the river. They then threw down the gates, and the city's defenses were worthless. Also, the diverted river did much havoc, traces of which are visible in the ruins of the inner walls. Babylon was thus readily subdued. But other remarkable things also accompanied this quick transfer of Chaldean power to the mighty Persian.

To the astonishment of the conquered, there was no mass slaughter of the inhabitants, no herd of unfortunate people marched away into captivity. Even the gods of Babylon were not disturbed; with great tolerance, Cyrus allowed life to proceed without violent alteration, quite in contrast to the practices of the Assyrians, and then the Babylonians themselves. His vision of empire was in clear distinction to these others, for he seems to have hoped for a commonwealth of self-governing nations, or dominions, under the beneficent control of a clement emperor, whereby trade and the advantages of peace throughout the world might be similarly enjoyed by all.

His prompt decree that all nationals captive in the city and surrounding country might return to their homelands extended of course to the Jews. Their captivity thus came to an end early in the year 538 B.C., and the event for which they had long been prepared was about to take place. The chosen of God, the remainder of Israel's children, were not headed for obscurity as in the case of the Ten Lost Tribes. Instead they were to go on and on, building a long, full history, hardly exceeded by that of any other people.

But although the monarch, who now ruled the empire he had recently assembled, was enlightened, liberal, tolerant and considerate, the inhabitants of restored Judah were still fated to be a pawn in a pagan world during the greater part of the ages ahead. After about two hundred years, the Persian empire would be replaced by one thrown together by the Greeks. It in turn fell prey to another with considerable persistence organized by the Romans. When this passed into decay long after the close of Bible times, the Arabs would seize control of Palestine for an extended period, only to be supplanted for a time by the Turks. Finally Israel, in fairly recent times, would experience another restoration. Yet even today it must continue to struggle to maintain its territory and identity, as it has been forced to do during much of the thirty-two centuries since this land of promise was first possessed by the Jews.

XV

THE RESTORATION OF JUDAH

The way was now clear for a return to the homeland. Such a move was even being encouraged, for Sheshbazzar a prince of Judah, had been appointed by Cyrus as the *satrap,* or civil leader. His task was to oversee the organization of the trek to Judah and to get it under way, an effort which, according to Persian methods and customs, called for tact and diplomacy. Actually he would be but the political head of this new colony, or province, and for actual leaders of the Jews he chose two men. One was a prince of the house of David, whose name was Zerubbabel, and Jeshua, the grandson of probably the last of the high priests to serve in the Temple. The details of assembling the party that would make the journey, and the accomplishment of this long trip itself, were left in their hands.

Now that the way was opened, how many would choose to go? How different this much shorter period of bondage had been from the one suffered by their forebears centuries before in the land of Egypt. Leaving the country in that former experience had meant fleeing from virtual slavery. In the present case, many had no doubt found enlarged opportunities and a fuller life here in Babylonia. The great majority, too, had never known Judah at first hand, for only a very few of those who had been deported were still alive and longed to return to the home country. A second and even a third generation had come into being in the meanwhile, and it would be from among these that candidates for a return must come.

The Bible account leaves the impression that there was hardly a stampede to find places among this first party to leave. At two points in the text a total is given of about 50,000 (Ezra 2:64, 65; Neh. 7:66, 67). Yet many of them must have perished or deserted on the way, for descriptions of happenings in Jerusalem during the next century and more seem hardly to embrace that many people altogether.

How far was it from Babylon to Jerusalem? The airline distance across the blistering, waterless desert of Arabia is 530 miles. By way of the caravan trails, the only practical course for so substantial a party, it was about 900 miles. With the best of luck and management it was easily a six-months trip for so great a number. Ezra made the same pilgrimage many years later, at the head of a far, far smaller caravan and consumed four months en route. It was indeed no "Sabbath day's journey." Many possessions must have been left behind, and all of the people walked, for the 8,136 pack animals would have been heavily burdened with food, goods and the great quantity of Temple implements reclaimed from Babylonian treasuries.

It is to be hoped these travelers reached their destination before the onset of the fall rains. For that is still the time of plowing and planting in Palestine, and, unless a grain crop had been sown then for spring harvesting, there would have been certain famine during the coming year. But they seem to have arrived in ample time, since one of their first common efforts was to erect an altar. This was placed upon the very site on which David had constructed one at the angel's command, and where countless sacrifices had been made through the years when Solomon's Temple had stood upon this spot. Tradition even claimed it to be the very place where in the long, long ago Father Abraham had sought to offer young Isaac. The new altar was perhaps a rather

Relief from Persepolis showing King Darius seated and his son Xerxes standing behind him

crude affair, but once again the worship of the Lord was centered on Zion, His "holy mountain," and it was dedicated in October of this year of 536 B.C.

In the enthusiastic plans made at a distance and out of touch with conditions on the spot, this altar was to have been but a first step in the prompt rebuilding of the whole Temple. But these people born in the warmer climate of Babylon needed houses. Their tents were not sufficient, for the winter season was now upon them. Also they must wring a living from this lean and reluctant land. Whatever religious enthusiasm they brought with them evaporated quickly in the face of the grim realities with which they were confronted. The comforts and plenty of the land of "captivity" had had a softening effect, too. No doubt there was friction with the Jews who had lived on in Jerusalem and the surrounding country; and the people of Samaria and Edom were, if anything, antagonistic rather than helpful. Thus it was two years before any further work on the Temple was undertaken.

But before it was hardly under way, there was more trouble. The Samaritans, who had lived on continuously in the Promised Land, felt they should have a part in the building and use of this Temple. But Zerubbabel and Jeshua overruled them. Cyrus, so they insisted, had commanded the Jews to rebuild the edifice, and it would be contrary to orders to extend the privilege to others. Promptly the Samaritan leaders began to exert political pressure, and the work was brought to a halt.

While this opposition continued, the great Cyrus died. Another king came upon the throne, and there was a period of unrest and uncertainty throughout the whole empire. After he died, power was seized by Darius, scion of one of the noble houses of Media, and this able ruler promptly brought order out of beginning chaos. An appeal was made to him for the right to continue with the work at Jerusalem, and he ordered a search made in the vaults at the Median capital at Achmetha (Ecbatana) for its original authorization. There the edict of Cyrus was found, and in the second year of Darius' reign the work got under way again.

The structure, which came to be known as Zerubbabel's Temple, was perhaps a trifle larger than Solomon's, but far less magnificent and well built. In fact some of the very few who were old enough to recall the first Temple were rather blunt and bitter in their criticisms. But after four years and a great deal of curt persuasion by the prophet Haggai, this second "House of the Lord" was completed. The year is now generally believed to have been 515 B.C.

There is an inventory of some 5400 gold and silver utensils from among those pilfered from Solomon's Temple which had been brought back from Babylon and were now put again in use. Although somewhat less pretentious, the walls of the new shrine had been gilded, and a considerable volume of treasure was involved in this sanctuary. Yet it, like the citizens themselves, had to exist in an unprotected city. The walls were still in very much the same condition in which they were left when the place was devastated seven decades before. Moreover, it would be another seventy years until Jerusalem was suitably fortified. Yet the worship of Yahweh in a "House" of His own had been restored, and that was a real achievement.

However, the "dispersion," which had been threatened in the time of Moses for all who departed from the law of the Lord (Lev. 26:33-37; Deut. 4:27, 28; 28:64-68), was now well under way. The captivity of the Ten Tribes, and then of Judah and of Benjamin, had gone a long way toward the fulfillment of these prophecies. Many, even of the latter, had remained in the region to which they or their forebears had been taken, and there was perhaps emigration from Judah into other lands, particularly Egypt, after the restoration was in progress.

Some of the Jews in foreign places achieved considerable prominence; one maiden whose Hebrew name was *Hadassah,* or Myrtle, became the favored wife of the Persian King Xerxes. Bible readers know this famous couple as Ahasuerus and Esther. This brave woman managed to frustrate a plot to slay countless Jews throughout the empire. Her great contribution in behalf of her people is celebrated even today during the month of February in the festival *Purim,* which terminates in a day of light-hearted rejoicing and is perhaps the most colorful of Jewish holidays. If Xerxes and Ahasuerus are actually one, as scholars now rather generally agree, then the lovely Esther became queen about the year 479 B.C.

This king died in 464 B.C. and was succeeded on the Persian throne by his third son, Artaxerxes Longimanus, or "the long-handed."

THE RESTORATION OF JUDAH
c. 445 B.C.

Copyright by C. S. HAMMOND & CO., N. Y.

Scale of Miles

0   5   10   20   30   40

Perennial Rivers

Seasonal Rivers & Streams

Route of the Returning Exiles

After Cyrus the Persian issued a decree permitting the exiles to return to their homeland in 538 B.C., many exiles took the long journey back to Judah.

In 458 B.C. (398 B.C.?) Ezra led a group of the exiles back to Judah to reform conditions there according to the laws of God.

Judah was a small province in the Fifth Persian Satrapy which extended from the borders of Syria and Cilicia to the borders of Egypt, including all Phoenicia, Palestine, Syria and Cyprus.

In 445 B.C. Nehemiah led a group of exiles back to Judah to rebuild the walls and gates of Jerusalem.

The Great Sea
(Mediterranean Sea)

Lod, Ono and Hadid were Jewish cities outside the province of Judah.

After the reformation in Judah, the priests became the dominating power and influence among the Jews. They kept the Jews a distinct race by forbidding marriage with other tribes and peoples.

Sheshbazzar, who brought with him from Babylon the sacred vessels carried away by Nebuchadnezzar, started the rebuilding of the Temple in Jerusalem. The Temple was completed by Zerubbabel in 515 B.C.

The Edomites were driven north from their land into the southern half of the old territory of Judah by the Arabs.

Sidon
Damascus
MOUNT LEBANON
Leontes R.
Tyre
MT. HERMON
From Babylonia
Dan
Aramaeans
Kedesh
Hazor
B a s h a n
KARNAIM
Accho
GALILEE
Karnaim
Sea of Galilee
MT. CARMEL
Kishon R.
Mt. Tabor
Edrei
Dor
Megiddo
Megiddo
Yarmuk R.
Ramoth-gilead
Jezreel
Beth-shan
Pella
DOR
SAMARIA
GILEAD
River Jordan
Samaria
Shechem
Mt. Gerizim
Jabbok R.
Plain of Sharon
Joppa
Ono
Rabbath-ammon
Lod
Neballat
Hadid
Bethel
Mizpeh
Ai
Michmash
Jericho
AMMON
Beth-horon
Gibeon
Geba
Gilgal
Ekron
Gezer
Ramah
Anathoth
Emmaus
Chephirah
Nob
Heshbon
Zareah
Kirjath-jearim
Jerusalem
Beth-haccherem
Medeba
Ashdod
Zanoah
JUDAH
Azekah
Jarmuth
Bethlehem
ASHDOD
Adullam
Tekoa
Ashkelon
Keilah
Beth-zur
Lachish
Hebron
Gaza
Dibon
En-gedi
Arnon R.
Philistines
Gerar
Ziklag
En-rimmon
Jeshua
Raphia
Moladah
MOAB
Beer-sheba
Kir-moab
(Kir-haresheth)
IDUMAEA
Edomites
Beth-phelet
Salt Sea (Dead Sea)
A r a b a
A r a b

There was perhaps that period of uneasiness and expected rebellion which often came with a change of ruler. It is for this reason, at least in part, that he at first refused requests made of him for the rebuilding and strengthening of the city of Jerusalem.

But a priest of the colony of Jews still resident in Babylonia, Ezra, the descendant of both Zadok and Phinehas, seems to have promoted quite an "awakening" among those to whom he ministered. Finally, in Artaxerxes' seventh year of reign, this Ezra was commissioned to go to Jerusalem on an inspection tour, during which he was to inquire into the civil and religious conditions among the people there and see if they were abiding by the teachings of God's law. He was also permitted to lead a new and sizable company of Jewish exiles numbering more than 1700 men back to Judah.

After four months on the trail, this party arrived safely at Jerusalem. New utensils for use in the Temple were turned over, sacrifice was offered, and Ezra delivered the king's orders to the governors of neighboring provinces. Then he began an examination of local affairs.

He was highly disturbed over one prevailing condition. The men, including numerous priests, had in many cases married foreign women. This was in direct opposition to the law of Moses. Ezra vigorously attacked this situation and slowly induced most of those who had taken them to put away their "strange" wives.

If there has been no alteration in the sequence of events in the material making up the books of Ezra and Nehemiah, formerly reckoned by the Jews as but a single book, there is now one of the "quiet" periods which occur at several points in the text. The impression is given that about thirteen years intervened between the arrival in Jerusalem of Ezra and that of another conscientious Jew, hopeful of vast improvements in conditions in this tiny Judaean homeland.

He, too, had risen to an elevated and responsible position in the Persian court, where he was the cup bearer to King Artaxerxes. His name was Nehemiah, and his duties consisted of pouring the drink into the royal cup and offering it to the king. Since he was in a position to either poison the sovereign or withhold lethal drafts from him, it was truly a post demanding the utmost trustworthiness. That it was invested in a foreigner is one of the strongest possible recommendations for Nehemiah and his complete reliability.

Stationed at court, he saw any and all responsible people visiting there from Judah and

Persepolis, begun by Darius I around 522 B.C., was destroyed by Alexander the Great in 331 B.C.

Relief from Darius' palace showing envoys of subject nations bearing New Year's gifts

was deeply grieved to hear of the continuing state of ruin which prevailed at Jerusalem. He finally asked and received permission to go there and give the city a measure of protection through the restoration of its wall. So great was the king's trust in him that he appointed his competent servant the governor of Judah, giving him letters to the various other Persian satraps along the way and a cavalry escort. It was in the year 445 B.C. that Nehemiah started off for the west.

As our Bible now stands, he would have found Ezra ministering in Jerusalem upon his arrival there. By the older, traditional opinion the priest had been there for thirteen years. But scholars who have given much time to the study of this situation now believe that a fairly late editing resulted in a change in the original order of the text, and that Nehemiah actually preceded Ezra. The date for the latter's mission to Jerusalem may have been 398 B.C.

However, when he did get to the city, he managed to keep his main purpose secret for several days and spent the dark hours carefully examining the shattered and demolished walls. After a third night of inspection, the new governor called his people together and disclosed his plan. Aid was willingly given, and some of the leading citizens made themselves accountable for the repairs of particular sections.

Neighboring Gentile tribes were much disturbed and did their best to hamper the work. But Nehemiah quickly showed these disturbing elements that he could not be frightened or turned from his purpose. While the work had to be carried on with weapons close at hand, this hostility spurred the men forward, and in 52 working days the fortifications had been restored.

Enthusiasm had mounted again, and a religious revival followed. During it Ezra read the law of Moses to the people of the colony. Many of them had never heard it before in its

18th century copy of the Scrolls of the Law (Torah)

entirety, and it had a particularly profound effect upon them. Very sagaciously Nehemiah then prevailed upon the chief men to join him in a most solemn compact to worship Yahweh, and Him alone.

After governing at Jerusalem for a dozen years, he journeyed back to the court of the king. Asking to be allowed to return once again to Judah, he seems to have had his commission as governor extended, and was back in the city in the highlands that same year of 433 B.C. It is probable that he continued to govern there during the remainder of his life, which, according to the historian Josephus, was a very long one. It is also believed he had died previous to 407 B.C., for there is a letter that was discovered some years ago in Egypt, which is dated for that year and addressed to the new governor of Judah, a man whose name was Bagoas.

Zerubbabel, Jeshua, Ezra and Nehemiah. These four men labored manfully to the end that Judah, and Jerusalem especially, might recapture its place in the affairs of men and in religious spirit. As the fifth pre-Christian century drew to an end, the prospects had brightened materially.

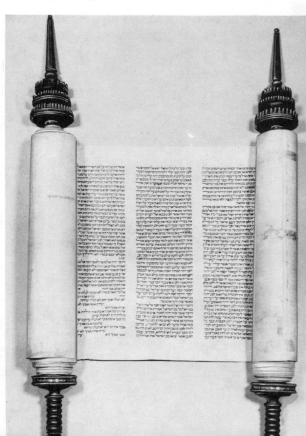

XVI

THE GRECIAN ERA

Up until the fourth pre-Christian century, the influences which had helped to shape conditions in Palestine had had their origin for the most part within the great "Fertile Crescent," or in the highlands immediately beyond its eastern point. It was in this latter area that Persian power had its beginnings, and from which it had extended its domination not only far around into Egypt, but across the Bosporus and the Hellespont into Thrace. At the time during which the Bible pictures Esther as his favorite wife, Xerxes threw two pontoon bridges across this latter narrow stretch of water and, in 480 B.C., gained a foothold in Europe.

It is claimed his army totaled a million men, but it probably numbered about 180,000. He moved on west to Thermopylae, where he defeated Leonidas and his mere handful of Spartans and their allies. He then burned Athens and seemed to be about to take possession of all of Greece. But the Athenians, who fled to the island of Salamis just east of the city, forced their attackers into a naval battle. In it the Persian ships were so utterly defeated that most of the land forces had to flee back into Asia. Persia's attempt upon Europe was dramatic, but short and exceedingly costly.

One of the European states that had been under Xerxes' domination was Macedon, the mountainous country to the north of Greece. During the next century this little land had its ups and downs, its throne was seized in 359 B.C. by an able, crafty young man named Philip. After reorganizing his army and perfecting the celebrated infantry formation known as the "Macedonian phalanx," he managed during the next 20 years to bring the Greek states pretty much under his domination. At a congress held in Corinth in 337 B.C., he was elected the commander of the allied Grecian forces that were being gathered to invade Persia and seek vengeance for the crimes which Xerxes had committed in the century before against the Greek sanctuaries.

In the spring of the following year, he sent a vanguard of 10,000 men over the Hellespont to prepare for the liberation of the Persian-held cities in Asia Minor. But by midsummer of 336 B.C., Philip had been assassinated and was succeeded by his twenty-year-old son, who came to be known as Alexander the Great. He had been educated by the famous Aristotle, and his father had made him, at 16, regent of Greece. He was both an accomplished ruler and general by the time he ascended the throne.

Secure at home by 334 B.C., he crossed over into Asia in that year with some 30,000 foot soldiers and about 5000 cavalry. At the outset, his position was somewhat uncertain and critical but was much strengthened after a decisive victory over the Persian forces near Zelea, along the banks of the Granicus, a mountain stream emptying into the Propontis. The following year at Issus, about 35 miles north of Antioch in Syria, Alexander met the army of Darius III and overthrew it so completely that the Persian king took to his heels, leaving his harem of many wives behind him.

Moving on toward the south, Alexander subdued Damascus, was resisted at Tyre, which he took by siege, and had to use force with the inhabitants of the Philistine city of Gaza. It was perhaps in the interim between these last two actions that a deputation of the leading citizens of Jerusalem, headed by the high priest,

Modern view of the Acropolis with the Parthenon at Athens

Alexander the Great as he appears on a mosaic from Pompei

appeared before the conqueror and arranged for their city to be spared.

Alexander's next objective was Egypt, in which land he was welcomed as the vanquisher of the now hated Persians. This new liberator who had many of the fine characteristics of the Persian conqueror, Cyrus, was rapidly annexing the empire which this latter warrior had founded. One of his great achievements in the land along the Nile was the founding of the city of Alexandria. It was destined to be for centuries a very great center of art, science and learning, a refuge for many Jews, and also one of the early centers of Christianity.

With Egypt now his vassal, Alexander was ready to proceed with his chief objective, to complete the conquest of the Persian Empire. For several years he was busy with this project, conquering as far as the Indus River. At last his troops would proceed no further, and he returned to Babylon in 323 B.C. There, while busily engaged in far-reaching plans, he fell sick of a fever and died, aged but 33 years.

What was to be expected of the empire he had conquered? Having no bond to tie it together beyond the personality and will of the now dead king, it was readily broken apart. The Diadochi, or army commanders of the late monarch, took the situation into their bloody and brutal hands. To clear the ground of family interference, they quickly dispatched Alexander's mother, half-brother, wife and the infant son born shortly after his father's death. The struggle for succession to Alexander's realm was resolved by partitioning the empire among the army commanders, as shown on the map.

The first to declare himself king of his portion, namely that of Asia Minor and Syria, was Antigonus Cyclops, the one-eyed Macedonian general. Antigonus hoped to become lord of all Asia and was well on his way to that goal before a coalition of the other generals defeated and slew him in the battle of Ipsus in 301 B.C. Following this battle, a new division of the spoils was made. Cassander retained control of Macedonia, and Lysimachus received western and central Asia Minor. The latter did not remain long on the scene, however, for another empire was taking shape under a line of kings which would last until 64 B.C.

This empire eventually embraced a great tract reaching from Thrace through Asia Minor, Syria, Babylon and Media on to India. Its founder was Seleucus Nicator, one who

(a) 4th century B.C. coin commemorating defeat of the Persians at Marathon. (b) Coin of Alexander minted after his death

proved to be quite a beneficent king and a patron of the arts and sciences. He founded the Syrian city of Antioch and made it his capital. The first year of this reign, 312 B.C., marks the beginning of the "Seleucid Era."

The last piece to fit into the jigsaw puzzle of the new kingdoms was the realm which fell to Ptolemy I. He founded a dynasty which, during the next three centuries, would have twelve other kings bearing his name. His was the Kingdom of Egypt, with Alexandria for its capital, and which would, during ensuing years, be principally a Grecian city. While he was still a general, Ptolemy had attempted to seize Palestine, entering Jerusalem in 320 B.C., by taking advantage of the Sabbath rest. But he did not secure definite possession until after the removal of Antigonus from the arena in 301 B.C. And even then Ptolemaic rule of the Holy Land was to be strongly contested by the Seleucids in the century to come.

In this time many of the Jews migrated to Cyrene, in North Africa, and especially to Alexandria. Here they dropped the use of Hebrew and also the international Semitic tongue, Aramaic, which they had brought back from Babylon, and spoke only Greek. After losing knowledge of Hebrew, they could no longer follow the readings from the scriptures in the synagogue services.

Ptolemy II, known as Philadelphus, was most proud of his excellent library at Alexandria and attempted to bring together there the finest selections from the writings of all the nations. According to legend he was much interested when he was told of the Jews' sacred literature. Getting in touch with the high priest in Jerusalem, arrangements were made to send

scholars to Egypt, where they were to make a translation of the Torah into Greek. It is reported that 72 learned scribes did assemble on the Island of Pharos, just off shore from the capital city, where, in 72 days, they transcribed and interpreted the Law.

This was of great service to the Jewish people, who were already widely scattered through a world in which Greek was becoming the common tongue. It was also to have a

Coins of Ptolemy II with wife and Antiochus III

profound effect upon the New Testament of our Bible. Jesus and His apostles quoted from this so-called *Septuagint* version frequently, and of the 350 quotes from the Old Testament found in the four Gospels, the Acts and the Epistles, six out of every seven of them are taken from this first Greek rendering without any variation. As evidence of its extensive use in early Christian times, there is the report of the chance encounter between Philip and the Ethiopian eunuch (Acts 8:27-30), wherein the latter, as he drove along in his chariot toward his home far away in Africa, was reading from the *Septuagint*.

Modern Arbel stands on the mound of ancient Mesopotamian Arbela. At nearby Gaugamela Alexander vanquished the Persians

The "Cilician Gates," a series of narrow passes through the Taurus Mountains near Tarsus

In 223 B.C., about 50 years after this translation was made, Antiochus III, surnamed the Great, became king in Syria; and, being ambitious, he overran the lands to the south, seeking to wrest Lower Syria, Phoenicia and Palestine from the Ptolemies. The reigning monarch in Alexandria at that moment was Ptolemy IV, called Philopator, a most debased creature. Suspected of killing his father to gain the throne, his first act after ascending it was to murder his own mother and younger brother. His whole reign was made up of a series of such horrible acts, and Antiochus had thought that one so depraved might be easy prey. But rather surprisingly his Syrian forces were roundly defeated by Ptolemy's troops at the battle of Raphia, 20 miles below Gaza, in 217 B.C.

Philopator had recovered Palestine, and, being in the vicinity, he visited Jerusalem and there insisted on offering sacrifice for his victory. But when he was prevented from further profaning of the Temple by entering the Holy of Holies, he was highly indignant, and an apocryphal book, known as 3rd Maccabees (Machabees), gives a somewhat fanciful story of his supernatural removal. On his return home to Egypt, he started a pogrom in which an attempt was made to assassinate every Jew in the city of Alexandria.

After Ptolemy's death in 203 B.C., Antiochus again invaded the southland and ultimately, in 198 B. C., was victorious in the battle of Panias. With a greater sense of security at his back, he now turned his ambitions upon Europe. He made a successful invasion of that continent and got as far as the famous pass at Thermopylae, only to meet with a sorry defeat. Hurrying back into Asia, his army was most decisively vanquished at Magnesia, near Ephesus.

This major setback in 190 B.C. brought one of the first fairly direct contacts between affairs in the Bible Lands and a people who in a few years would dominate them thoroughly during the remainder of Bible times. They were the Romans, who dictated a most disastrous peace following the battle at Magnesia. In addition to the payment of an enormous tribute, Antiochus was forced to send 20 hostages to Rome as a tender of his good will toward his conquerors, and one of these men given as security was the king's own son. His name was Antiochus Epiphanes, and he was due to spend 15 years in the Eternal City as a pledge, first for his father, and then for his brother. At last, in 175 B.C., he returned to Syria and assumed the throne, but distinctly as a vassal of his recent captors. In fact it was very much the policy of the Romans from then on to harass and weaken this eastern kingdom in every way.

Still he was active and venturesome and sought to extend and build up his domain so far as possible. Yet he was most unfortunate, having a great ability seriously to antagonize his subject peoples. This was especially true as regards the Jews. They had put all political ambitions behind them at the time of their return from Babylon and were willing to be vassals providing the overlord did not attempt to dictate or interfere in their religious matters. But Antiochus' needs were so great that he was driven to desperate means.

Before he dared think of attempting to throw off the Roman yoke, it was necessary that the various groups within his domain be much more closely welded together. In his opinion, the greatest possible unifying force was Grecian thought and way of life. It was particularly necessary that all, no matter of what their nationalities or beliefs, adopt a common faith.

Being an absolute monarch, the first step in that direction was to issue an edict to that effect. Little did he realize the intense loyalty to Yahweh and his worship which had been bred into the Jerusalem Jews, in particular since the days of Ezra and Nehemiah. Immediately he was in conflict with them for they would not give up their faith.

Hard-fisted Syrian emissaries were quickly dispatched to Judaea—as Judah was now called—with explicit orders they were to stamp

was commanded. The horrors of religious persecution enveloped the city and all other Jewish communities.

As though this were not enough, the Syrian king sent his chief tax collector into Judaea, accompanied by an armed force which could not safely be resisted. This Apollonius, due one day to meet death at the hands of an avenger of his deeds, stripped all possible spoil from the city, then set it afire, ruined houses and buildings and sought to render it completely

Greek marble relief, "Battle of Gods and Giants," 600 B.C.

out Judaism and in its place establish the worship of the greatest of the deities of the Greeks, the supreme sovereign of the universe, Olympian Zeus. These strong-arm men or "hoods," as they might be termed today, sought to do a thorough job. The Temple was robbed, and then a statue of Zeus, or Jupiter as he was known to the Romans, was set up in the Holy of Holies. All the sacred books that could be found were burned. Circumcision, the rite of initiation into the covenant privileges of the family of God and the token of the sacred covenant, was forbidden on pain of death. So, too, were any and all attempts to sanctify the Sabbath or celebrate the arrival of the New Moon. The sacrifice of swine, a most abhorrent act to any Jew,

defenseless by tearing down its walls. He treacherously ordered a massacre of its inhabitants; he then drove many women and children off into slavery and herded away the animals as food for his soldiery.

Not only had Antiochus Epiphanes profaned the Temple of God, but he had antagonized the Jews for ever and a day. It was a heavier blow than had been dealt them by either the Assyrians or the Babylonians, so heavy in fact, that for a time they were dazed and able for no better show than one of passive resistance. But within a year resistance was growing up in the little, devastated land, and one of the most spectacular periods of Jewish history lay just ahead.

XVII

THE AGE OF THE HOLY WARRIORS

Let there be no mistake about it, "the abomination of desolation" may have hovered over the Temple of Jerusalem, but Antiochus Epiphanes' indignities and enmity reached to every town and hamlet throughout Judaea. Idols of the pagan Zeus, or Jupiter, were set up in all public places. Altars were built before the doors of houses, and those who valued their lives offered prescribed sacrifices upon them regularly. For those who did not obey the decree of the king and make an open display of their zeal were seized, publicly whipped and then summarily slain.

For some this new order was more than displeasing—it was outright intolerable. Insurrection was building up, and one of the first to give it frank and open expression was an aged priest called Mattathias. His name meant "gift of Yahweh," and such indeed he proved to be. He belonged to a family of distinction, prominent in the affairs in the small town of Modin, about 17 miles northwest of Jerusalem. Suddenly a Syrian official appeared in that community and called upon Mattathias to use his influence in getting idolatrous worship started there. The old man not only resisted this officer, but, when the Syrian made preparations for offering a heathen sacrifice, he promptly slew this intruder.

Knowing that there would be a violent reaction and savage redress, Mattathias and his sons fled hastily to hideaways in the hills. The caves with which the area abounded now came in very handy, for other devout Jews began to catch the spirit of revolt and join with them. While the old priest died in the following year, 166 B.C., he did bequeath the cause his five stout sons. Quickly the increasing band of rebels chose the third son, Judas, as the new leader.

While the late father and his offspring bore the family designation of *Hasmonaeans,* this newer head of the clan received the surname of *Maccabaeus,* which was soon transferred to other members of the group. Although its meaning is not wholly certain, it is thought to have come from *makkabah,* a hammer.

Unique bronze lamp from Syria decorated with Jewish religious symbols

Under the younger man's leadership the revolt spread rapidly, and in a short time he had assembled a sufficient number of armed men to meet and defeat the Syrians in open encounter at Emmaus. Actually Roman pressure —the indirect cause of the conditions which had forced the Jewish rebellion—now helped to foster the fight for freedom. The magnitude of the tribute demanded of Antiochus by Rome compelled him to take the bulk of his army and march off to the east on a money-raising campaign. This left Syria with but a few soldiers on hand for use in an emergency. The government at home in Antioch had been turned over to a functionary and general of the army named Lysias, and one of his specific duties was to quell any and all Jewish uprisings.

Trusting the direction of the troops at first to others, he finally decided to take command himself, only to be defeated with heavy losses (1 Mc 4:27-34). Judas now retook Jerusalem, the Temple was purified and the daily sacrifice restored. This was the occasion for a joyous celebration, which became an annual affair known as the Feast of Dedication (John 10:22).

Word of the disaster which had befallen Lysias was hurriedly borne to Antiochus, who started for home. But death caught up with him and removed one of the Jews' most somber enemies. At once there was turmoil in the Syrian capital; Lysias seized the government and ruled in the name of Antiochus' nine-year-old son, Antiochus Eupator. But the late king had appointed a courtier named Philip to act as regent during the son's minority. This situation was definitely to the advantage of the Jews, since Lysias now had to give considerable attention to the absent Philip's claims.

According to the statement in 2 Mac. 11:34, another piece of good fortune favoring the Jews now came to pass. Two Roman en-

View of the valley where the Dead Sea Scrolls were found

voys, probably on their way from Alexandria to the Syrian capital at Antioch, offered to use their influence there in behalf of the people of Judaea. And evidently they kept their word, for peace seems to have resulted from their efforts.

But the Syrians were most determined with respect to the complete subjugation of their Jewish subjects, and in the very next year, 163 B.C., another army appeared out of the north. Judas Maccabaeus did his best, but the Syrians pressed on and put Jerusalem under siege. Conditions within the city quickly became critical, and it would soon have been forced to surrender, had not affairs taken a more favorable turn. News reached the besiegers that Philip the regent was hurrying home from Persia at the head of an army, prepared to obtain his rights. This brought an immediate crisis for the attackers. So the siege was called off, and the young Antiochus Eupator, on the advice of Lysias, granted the Jews complete religious liberty if they would keep the peace. Conditions now returned to about what they had been previous to the insurrection.

There was one very disturbing factor left, however. This centered about the high priest Alcimus, appointed to that post by the youthful Antiochus. This man was entirely Greek in thought and sympathies and thus fairly loathed by the pious Jews. A plea to remove him might have been made to the child-king, but he was soon afterward dethroned and slain by his cousin, who took the crown as Demetrius Soter. He, like his uncle Antiochus, had been a hostage in Rome. But when he heard of the uncle's death, he promptly made his escape and headed for Antioch. Arriving there at last, he was able to seize the kingdom; and, in addition to disposing of the younger Antiochus, he did away with Lysias, too.

As the new king, he approved of the hated high priest Alcimus. While he did grant other religious liberties to the Jews, his insistence on controlling the top priestly office fanned the still smoldering fires of revolt. Those who abhorred strife and were willing to employ diplomacy, including Judas Maccabaeus, formed a party which somewhat later became the well-known Sadducees. As the struggle blazed up, Alcimus was forced to flee the Holy City. Quickly Syrian forces appeared, and, although Judas defeated them at Adasa just north of Jerusalem, he realized outside aid was most essential. His people were too few in number to constantly withstand the might of the far larger kingdom of the Seleucids. But to whom should they apply?

His choice was clear. The Romans for some years now had not missed an opportunity to do what they could to enfeeble and cripple the Syrian rulers. Surely they would lend a sympathetic ear. So two envoys, Eupolemos and Jason, were chosen and started on their way to Italy in search of an alliance. There they received a cordial reception; and the Senate acknowledged the independence of Judaea and began to toy with the idea of making it a buffer state, to separate the Syrian and Egyptian realms.

But while the envoys were busy in Rome, the Syrians busied themselves at home. Demetrius gathered an army and hurled it at the rebellious land to the south. Judas rallied his forces and hastily met this surprise invasion but was defeated and slain at Elasa, north of Jerusalem. The year was 160 B.C.

When Alcimus had fled, the youngest of old Mattathias' sons, Jonathan, had taken over the high priesthood. Now that Judas had

Jewish coin of the period of Simon Maccabaeus,
142-134 B.C.

been killed, he took over command of the army as well. This latter choice had, in a sense, been thrust upon him. John, the eldest of the five brothers, had been taken prisoner a short time before, and dispatched. About this same time, too, Eleazar, next older than Jonathan, had been crushed to death beneath an elephant which he had wounded in battle.

Happily for the Jews, Syria was in the throes of civil war. This meant that for a number of years under Jonathan's leadership Judaea was able to enjoy a refreshing peace. Actually the favor of the Jews came to be sufficiently desirable so that their leader's position was decidedly strengthened. Rome and Sparta made treaties of alliance with him, and the new King of Syria, Demetrius II, named him civil and military governor of Judaea.

Rome, which had been heavily involved in wars in the west, had at last completely vanquished an old and powerful foe, Carthage. Also she had made vassals of the Greeks and Macedonians and was now sufficiently secure to give more direct attention to things in the east. Jonathan, a sagacious statesman, thought he saw an opportunity for enlisting Roman aid

and dispatched envoys to the capital city on the Tiber. But affairs in Syria, unstable as ever, proved to be his undoing. Another pretender to its throne, Trypho, basely murdered the able Jewish leader at Ptolemaïs. In 142 B.C. the remaining son of Mattathias, Simon, took over direction of Judaean affairs.

Under his wise guidance the little land knew continuing peace and a considerable measure of prosperity. Another remarkable transition took place during his seven years at the head of affairs. What had been no more than a religious community once again became a nation. In return for assistance in resisting the pretender, Trypho, King Demetrius II renounced all claim to tribute and granted Jewish independence. The delighted people, at a solemn assembly called for the purpose, proclaimed Simon Maccabaeus and his descendants high priests and ethnarchs "until a faithful prophet should arise" (1 Mc 14:41).

Considering it a more prudent course, he chose to trust the Romans rather than the Syrians and was much gratified when the former issued a decree circulated to the peoples of the east, proclaiming a league of friendship with the Jews. However, this gesture, which cost Rome nothing, had to be rather dearly paid for shortly by little Judaea. There was another of the frequent changes of Syrian kings, and Antiochus VII, who took the throne in 138 B. C., laid a heavy hand upon these former subject peoples.

Rights and privileges were promptly withdrawn, and finally an army appeared to collect back tribute. It was luckily defeated by Simon's two sons, John and Judas, for the leader was now too old to take the field himself. Also his days were definitely numbered; shortly his son-in-law, Ptolemy, plotting to obtain power, slew this the last of old Mattathias' five sons.

It was in 134 B.C. that Simon's son, John Hyrcanus, came to full power, for he had by then already commanded the army for seven years. Yet he had no more than disposed of his

Entrance to the cave (upper hole in the picture)
where the Dead Sea Scrolls were discovered

ambitious brother-in-law, Ptolemy, when the determined Antiochus led yet another Syrian army into Judaea in person. The only thing which could be done at that moment was to take refuge within Jerusalem's walls, and there hunger soon forced the besieged to sue for peace on any terms. They proved to be unusually harsh ones, including heavy tribute and the leveling of the city's fortifications. Burdened with them, Hyrcanus, although still determined, dared make no moves until conditions eased.

This happened with the death of Antiochus in 129 B.C. Promptly three ambassadors were dispatched to Rome begging aid. While the Romans made their customary resounding promises, it was actually the disorders in the Syrian court that gave the Jews their opportunity. While his uncle and his father had not shrunk from being vassals, Hyrcanus was far more resolute and fully resolved to stand alone if possible. So he set about perfecting the means by which he might do just that.

A primary need was a striking force which deserved the name of an "army." His nimble shepherds, fighting for their homes and pas-

tures, did remarkably well in their native hills, but they were no match for well-armed and trained troops in formal encounters on level battlefields. Actually his "men from the hills" looked pretty primitive in contrast to the professional soldiery of neighboring monarchs. What could he do? He finally decided upon very much the same course David had taken; he hired mercenaries and built up an honor guard, the prince's own, which would be responsible to him alone.

This move tended to be unpopular in itself, and the means he took to finance it was fully sufficient to tip the scales against him. He burrowed into the tomb of David and extracted treasures sufficient to his needs. The Maccabees had enjoyed wide popularity previous to these two undertakings. But from that time on, about 130 B.C., general approval of what had become a Judaean reigning house tended to diminish.

But Hyrcanus continued to raise Judaea's military power as that of Syria was decaying. A good soldier, he used his new fighting force effectively and began to extend his dominions. Samaria to the north was conquered, and the Temple which had been built upon Mount Gerizim after the Samaritans had been refused a share in the Temple of Zerubbabel was destroyed. Idumaea was also conquered, while later on Galilee became a princedom.

These conquests provoked a contest with the Syrians. But that kingdom was slipping rapidly, and its armies which sought to attack were finally and permanently recalled from Palestine. There had been more than a half century of conflict, but, after the start against heavy odds, Syria's internal troubles, plus Roman intervention, had turned the tables, and the "holy warriors" of the house of the Maccabees had at last won out. During the latter portion of Hyrcanus' thirty-year reign, Judaea knew better days than any which had been experienced since the "Golden Age" in the time of Solomon.

Finally, when this grandson of Mattathias died in 104 B.C., full of years and accomplishments, he was able to leave his son, Judas Aristobulus, a considerable kingdom. But this young man, who seems to have been the first to assume the title of king, held the throne for

One of the jars which contained the Dead Sea Scrolls

PALESTINE UNDER THE MACCABEES
166 TO 63 B.C.

Copyright by C. S. HAMMOND & CO., N.Y.

Scale of Miles

0 5 10   20   30   40

Perennial Rivers
Seasonal Rivers & Streams
Capitals ....

GROWTH OF MACCABEAN JUDAEA

Judaea at the start of the revolt, 166 B.C.
Acquisitions under Jonathan, 161-142 B.C.
Acquisitions under Simon, 142-134 B.C.
Acquisitions under John Hyrcanus, 134-104 B.C.
Acquisitions under Aristobulus I, 104-103 B.C.
Acquisitions under Alexander Jannaeus, 103-76 B.C.
Maximum extent of the Maccabaean dominions

The Maccabaean revolt arose from the attempt of the Seleucid monarch, Antiochus IV (Epiphanes) to force Hellenization upon the Jews.

Besieged and razed by John Hyrcanus.

John Hyrcanus destroyed the Samaritan Temple on Mt. Gerizim.

Site of Tryphon's treacherous seizure of Jonathan.

Original home of the Maccabees or "Hasmonaeans"

Death place of Alexander Jannaeus.

In 63 B.C. Jerusalem fell before the forces of Pompey and Judaea came under Roman control.

Feast of Hanukkah is celebrated by the Jews in memory of the cleansing of the Temple by Judas Maccabeus.

SELEUCID EMPIRE

PHOENICIA
MOUNT LEBANON
COELE SYRIA
Mt. Hermon
ITURAEA
SYRIA

Sidon
Damascus
Tyre
Leontes R.
Panias
Cades (Kedesh)
Mageth
Raphon
Hazor
Bosor
Ladder of Tyre
Carnaim
Ptolemaïs (Accho)
Magdala
Arbela
Water of Genesar
(Sea of Galilee)
Gamala
GALILEE
Hippos
GILEAD
Mt. Tabor
Philoteria
Abila
Dion
Mt. Carmel
Yarmuk R.
Gadara
Edrei
Plain of Esdraelon
Ephron
Dora (Dor)
Ephron
Strato's Tower
Scythopolis (Beth-shan)
Pella
SAMARIA
River Jordan
Mizpeh
Gerasa
Samaria
Asophon
Ragaba
Jabbok R.
Apollonia
Capharsaba
Shechem
Amathus
Pharathon
Mt. Gerizim
Alexandrium
GALAAD
Joppa
Ramathaim
AMMON
Jazer
Philadelphia (Rabbath-ammon)
Beth-dagon
Adida (Hadid)
Mt. Azotus
Gophna
Ephraim
Lydda (Lod)
Modin
Beeroth
Dok
Gazara (Gezer)
Bethel
Elasa
Michmash
Jericho
Jamnia (Jabneh)
Ekron
Beth-horon
Mizpeh
Ramathaim
Cedron
Capharsalama
Adasa
Heshbon
Samaga
Emmaus (Nicopolis)
Jerusalem
Khirbet Qumrân
JUDAEA
Medeba
Azotus (Ashdod)
Timnah
Bethlehem
Beth-zacharias
Ascalon (Ashkelon)
Free City State
Adullam
Tekoa
Machaerus
Marisa (Mareshah)
Beth-zur
Dibon
Anthedon
Adora
Hebron
Gaza
En-gedi
Arnon R.
Gerar
IDUMAEA
Masada
Raphia
Arad
Kir-moab (Kir-hareseth)
The Great Sea (Mediterranean Sea)
Plain of Sharon
PHILISTIA
Salt Sea (Dead Sea)
MOAB
ACRABATHANE

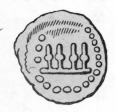

Jewish coin, struck by Antigonus, 40-37 B.C., showing earliest representation of seven-branched candlestick

only about a year. He was then succeeded by his younger brother, Alexander Jannaeus. While he bore a Grecian name and is judged to have had strong leanings toward Grecian interests, he still was a fighter like his Maccabaean forebears. Much of his twenty-seven-year reign was given to warfare directed against neighboring cities and kings. He pushed his conquests into Trans-Jordan, and at his death in 76 B.C. he had restored the "Promised Land" to about its original dimensions.

However, during much of his time upon the throne, that land had been racked by what was virtually civil war, but of a religious character. This was a struggle between the Pharisees and the Sadducees, in which it is claimed the former attempted to make over the people of the kingdom in their own image. This sect had striven to gain control over the lives of all in the previous reign, and Hyrcanus had for a time favored them. He later turned away from them, and they, capable of the most intense hatred, turned upon him and his sons.

Jannaeus' military adventures had not all terminated in success. About the year 90 B.C. he appears to have met a severe defeat east of the Jordan at the hands of the Arabs, which forced him to flee to Jerusalem. This military reverse provided his enemies the opportunity they needed, and for the next six years they gave their ruler virtually no peace. At one point he decided to compromise with them and asked them exactly what it was they wished. To his amazement they promptly informed him what they wished for most was his death.

They even went to the nation's long-time enemy, the Syrians, and sought the intervention of one of the last monarchs of that defunct kingdom, Demetrius III. There was a brief rebellion, in which Jannaeus came out the victor. His own hatred could be violent, and also calculated, as he soon proved. By way of celebration he or-

ganized a revel involving his many concubines. In the midst of it, and in their presence, some 800 crosses were erected. To them were nailed an equal number of captive rebels, while the dying men's wives and children were slaughtered before their pain-numbed eyes.

Upon his death, the reins of government passed into the hands of his wife, Salome Alexandra. She appointed her son, Hyrcanus II, as the high priest, and seems to have turned over the government itself to the Pharisees, for they appear to have seized full control and allowed Salome little beyond the title of queen.

When she died in 67 B.C., there was a contest over the throne, in which the queen's second son, Aristobulus, eventually came out the winner. Surprisingly enough, his defeated brother Hyrcanus was not slain and was soon intriguing with the Arabs, to whom he promised restoration of the lands taken from them in return for his elevation to the throne, which he had occupied but three months. The go-between in this plot deserves a trifle more than casual mention, for he and his descendants were to play a role in the affairs of the next two centuries. His name was Antipater; he was an Idumaean, who would become not only an important Roman puppet, but also the father of that warped and ruthless character, Herod the Great.

Another civil war began, this one a family affair, and of very little consequence in contrast to happenings at that moment elsewhere. Rome, which had kept an interested, and perhaps a covetous, eye on the area east of the Mediterranean for a century and a half, was now prepared to take a decisive part in affairs there. In the year 66 B.C. Pompey, the great Roman general, conquered the King of Pontus, a country on the shore of the Black Sea, and drove him into exile in the Caucasus. Then, turning his legions toward the south, he finished off the Syrian Kingdom founded by Seleucus Nicator.

This conquering hero had a legate, one Scaurus, working ahead of him, and when the latter came to Damascus he was told of the silly war between brothers still in progress at that very moment in Jerusalem. Hurrying on there, he was gratified to find that both sides were prepared to offer him sizable tribute for the aid of his master. The matter was carefully reviewed, and the more likely of the two aspirants seemed to be the younger, Aristobulus. Immediately when he received the nod of approval, the Arabs raised the siege of the city and departed for the desert.

Now the two warring sons of Jannaeus and Salome presented their respective claims to Pompey himself when he came to Damascus to see the sights. While the great man was making up his mind, a move on the part of Aristobulus encouraged the Roman commander to order the occupation of the Jewish capital. When resistance developed there, the city was quickly put under siege. Thus, in the fall of 63 B.C., Jerusalem was finally subdued. By then the Maccabaean period was over. Judaea had become a vassal principality of Rome, with all the non-Jewish portions of its territory stripped away. Hyrcanus II was removed as king, although he was allowed to continue as high priest.

From then until the close of Bible times, the Holy Land would be firmly under the heel of men from the city on the Tiber, far away across the Mediterranean to the northwest. But before considering what transpired in that period ahead, it could be well to cite a situation which has created widespread interest in the past few years.

Mention has already been made of two important religious sects which came into being and prominence during the Maccabaean period, the Pharisees and the Sadducees. There was still another group called the Essenes, which presumably got under way during this same era and by the time of Christ is thought to have embodied about 4000 members.

While not mentioned in Bible text, they perhaps exerted quite a bit of influence in their far quieter way. They were an ascetic order, living a simple, plain, highly disciplined life, with monasteries in the barren wilderness of Judaea. Some believe John the Baptist was a member of this early monastic order, which probably attracted many able men, but about which far too little has been known.

Suddenly, several years ago, their religious efforts of a literary order burst upon the world, as writing prepared by their scribes in the centuries immediately before Christ came to light. They were the already famous Dead Sea Scrolls, found in the numerous caves about Khirbet Qumran on the northwest shore of the Dead Sea.

While much scholarship has already been expended upon these unique documents, some of them in fragments, it still promises to be several years before their entire contents can be sufficiently known so that their proper relation to the Bible Story can be more satisfactorily established.

From the Dead Sea Scrolls: Sectarian Manual of Discipline

XVIII

THE GLORY THAT WAS ROME

Who were the Romans who were to play so dominant a role during the remainder of Bible times, as well as in the early days of the Christian Church? Their beginnings are clouded by a haze of novel but hardly trustworthy legends. When they first appear clearly, it is as one of several tribes living in that broad plain in west central Italy through which flows the Tiber River. The level area to the southeast of this stream was known as *Latium,* and at a point on it about 20 miles from where the Tiber empties into the Tyrrhenian Sea, tradition says the city of Rome was founded in 753 B.C.

The site selected was a group of low, easily defended hills, for the little settlement had to protect itself against some very aggressive neighbors, among them the Etruscans. To the south there were certain mountain tribes, known as Samnites, and yet another group, called the Umbrians to the north. Thus at the outset the Romans comprised but one small city in a land filled with other enterprising peoples.

Some time during the sixth century B.C. the Etruscans managed to capture Rome. But they did not hold it too long, for in 509 B.C. the Roman nobles rebelled and drove out their captors. The king, Tarquin, who had also been expelled, sought to regain the throne with the help of the Etruscan army.

But this attempt was successfully withstood; the kingdom was done away with and the Romans set up a republic. In place of a hereditary monarch, the growing city was from then on governed by two consuls, each of whom was elected to hold office for but a single year. So effective was this form of government that it was retained for nearly five centuries.

The various cities of Latium eventually formed a league to promote trade, peace and intermarriage. Slowly Rome became the chief city in this confederation, much to the envy and ill will of the remainder. In fact they were so jealous of its increasing power that when the Gauls, a people from far to the north, attacked Rome in 390 B.C., the other members refused to aid in its defense.

However, the Romans not only defeated this enemy from outside of Italy but also began to definitely dominate the affairs of the Latium

league. In addition, the city had become important enough to make an alliance with Carthage, the powerful Phoenician trading city in North Africa. It was at this time, too, that she began building the first of her famous military roads and constructing fortresses at various points of military importance.

In this period the growing city unhappily suffered a sharp setback at the hands of the Samnites, who forced a whole Roman army to surrender. But although these victors joined with the Etruscans and the Umbrians in an attempt to break the mounting power of Rome, the city on the Tiber managed to prevail.

This war had taken Roman troops far to the south and to the borders of *Magna Graecia,* a portion of the lower end of Italy having many settlements which had been made by colonists from across the Adriatic Sea in Greece. Chief among these colonies was a place called Tarentum, and there was soon the promise of a contest between this city and Rome. Seeking to gain the initiative, the people of Tarentum made an alliance with Pyrrhus, king of Epirus, a city-state in northwestern Greece. This vigorous sovereign, determined to be another Alexander the Great, attacked the Romans with such vigor that they lost several battles to him.

Nonetheless, they were "Pyrrhic" victories indeed, for the king's losses were so great that he had to sail home and leave the Greek colonists to their own deserts. Promptly Rome seized their cities, and by 270 B.C. she was in control of all Italy south of the Apennines.

But this rapid increase in power brought opposition from another quarter, this time from Carthage. It proved to be the most demanding challenge Rome ever encountered, resulting in a long costly struggle and a fight to the death. Finally, in 146 B.C., the powerful trading city on the south shore of the Mediterranean was completely destroyed. Rome also had increased its hold on Greece. In this same year Corinth had rebelled, whereupon a Roman army seized the city and reduced it to ashes.

The Eternal City was now very definitely mistress of the whole western Mediterranean and had gained wealth and strength sufficient to start her on the road to a great overseas empire. Yet conditions in the capital city itself continued sufficiently unstable to preclude any major conquests. This trouble stemmed from the very unequal distribution of wealth, which resulted in threats by the "Roman mob," a situ-

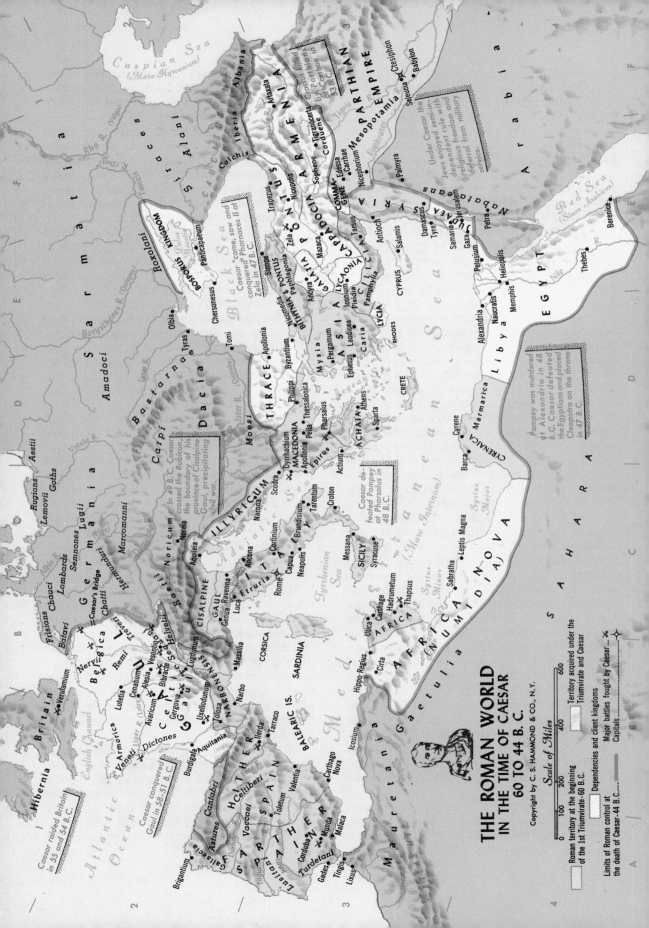

THE ROMAN WORLD
IN THE TIME OF CAESAR
60 TO 44 B.C.

Copyright by C. S. HAMMOND & CO., N.Y.

Scale of Miles

0   100   200   400   600

Roman territory at the beginning
of the 1st Triumvirate-60 B.C.

Dependencies and client kingdoms

Limits of Roman control at
the death of Caesar-44 B.C. ......

Territory acquired under the
Triumvirate and Caesar

Major battles fought by Caesar ... ⚔

Capitals ......●

Caspian Sea
(Mare Hyrcanium)

Sarmatia

Alani

Siraces

Amadoci

Aestii

Rugians
Lemovii
Goths
Lombards

Chauci
Frisians
Batavi

Britain

Hibernia

Atlantic
Ocean

English Channel
Verulamium

Caesar raided Britain
in 55 and 54 B.C.

Veneti
Armorica
Dictones

CELTIC GAUL
Lutetia
Cenabum
Avaricum
Gergovia
Alesia
Uxellodunum
Burdigala
Aquitania

Nervii
Belgica
Remi
Treveri

Germania

Semnones
Lugii
Marcomanni
Hermunduri
Chatti

Bastarnae

Carpi

Dacia

Moesi

Roxolani

BOSPORUS
KINGDOM

Panticapaeum

Chersonesus

Black Sea

Tomi

Apollonia

THRACE

Byzantium

Olbia

Tyras

Albania

Iberia

Colchis

ARMENIA

Artaxata

Tigranocerta
Sophene
Corduene

PARTHIAN
EMPIRE

Crassus killed
by Parthians in
53 B.C.

Ctesiphon
Babylon
Seleucia

MESOPOTAMIA

Edessa
Carrhae
Nicephorium

Arabia

Palmyra

SYRIA
Antioch

Damascus
Tyre

JUDAEA
Samaria
Jerusalem
Gaza
Pelusium

Nabataeans
Petra

Red Sea
(Sinus Arabicus)

Berenice

EGYPT

Nile

Thebes

Memphis
Heliopolis
Naucratis
Alexandria

Libya

Marmarica

CYRENAICA
Cyrene
Barca

SAHARA

Sabratha
Leptis Magna

AFRICA
Carthage
Utica
Hadrumetum
Thapsus

NUMIDIA
Cirta
Hippo Regius

Gaetulia

Mauretania

Tingis
Lixus

HITHER SPAIN
Cantabri
Astures
Gallaecia
Brigantium
Vaccaei
Celtiberi
Toletum

FARTHER SPAIN
Lusitani
Turdetani
Corduba
Munda
Malaca
Gades

Carthago Nova
Tarraco
Ilerda
Valentia

BALEARIC IS.

Icosium

Mediterranean Sea
(Mare Internum)

CRETE
RHODES
CYPRUS

Salamis

Tarsus
CILICIA
PAMPHYLIA
LYCIA
Caria
Ephesus
Laodicea
Pergamum
ASIA
Mysia

LYCAONIA
Iconium
Pisidia
Mazaca
CAPPADOCIA
GALATIA
Ancyra
PONTUS
Zela
Sinope
BITHYNIA & PONTUS
Nicomedia
Paphlagonia

COMM.
GENE.

Trapezus

Nicopolis

CORSICA

SARDINIA

SICILY
Messana
Syracuse
Panormus

Tyrrhenian Sea

ITALY
Rome
Capua
Neapolis
Croton
Tarentum
Brundisium

CISALPINE GAUL
Genua
Ravenna
Luca
Etruria

NARBONENSIS
Narbo
Tolosa
Massilia

Lugdunum
Vesontio
Bibracte
Helvetii
Raeti
Noricum
Norela
Aquileia

ILLYRICUM

Adriatic Sea

Corfinium
Ancona
Narona
Scodra
Dyrrhachium
Apollonia

MACEDONIA
Pella
Thessalonica
Philippi

Epirus
Actium

ACHAIA
Athens
Sparta
Pharsalus

Caesar defeated Pompey
at Pharsalus in
48 B.C.

Aegean Sea

In 49 B.C. Caesar
crossed the Rubicon,
the boundary of his
province of Cisalpine
Gaul, precipitating
civil war.

Caesar conquered
Gaul in 58-51 B.C.

Caesar's Bridge

Under Caesar the
Jews enjoyed semi-in-
dependent rule with
religious freedom and
freedom from military
service.

Pompey was murdered
at Alexandria in 48
B.C. Caesar defeated
the Egyptians and placed
Cleopatra on the throne
in 47 B.C.

Caesar "came, saw and
conquered" Pharnaces II at
Zela in 47 B.C.

Syrtus
Major
Syrtus
Minor

ation which the brothers Tiberius and Gaius Gracchus sought to correct. Both, however, were murdered for their pains, and the unsettled period which followed permitted the Roman army to seize power. Two generals now came rapidly to the fore. The first was Marius, and the second the even more potent Sulla.

This latter, who sought to quell the insurrection of the Asiatic provinces led by Mithridates, King of Pontus, had a lieutenant who completed that task and then went on to extend the domain of Rome in the eastern Mediterranean area. His name should have a somewhat familiar ring, for it was none other than Pompey. His great successes in the East made him for a time the most powerful man in the Roman world.

Soon he would be forced to bow to another ambitious Roman commander, the famous Julius Caesar. While the former had been busy annexing territory that had previously belonged to the Ptolemies and the Seleucids, the latter had been conquering a huge domain north of the Alps. He would continue to be busy about such matters for several years following his agreement to share the rule of Rome with two others, Pompey and Crassus. This so-called *Triumvirate* was established in 60 B.C. Yet each of its three members had a consuming ambition to rule alone. Crassus, seeking to win renown through a campaign in Asia, managed to meet defeat and death in Mesopotamia

The first break in the Triumvirate helped to hasten a second. Such bonds as there were between the very dissimilar Pompey and Caesar, snapped at the time of the death of Pompey's wife, Julia, daughter of Caesar. When the Senate under pressure of Pompey voted to have Caesar removed from his army command, the break was complete. Following his celebrated remark, "The die is cast," Caesar crossed the Rubicon with his army and was in command of all Italy in only 60 days without shedding a drop of blood. In 40 days more, he had subdued Spain, Pompey's stronghold. Then shipping his legions to Greece, he defeated his adversary there at Pharsalus (48 B.C.). Badly-beaten Pompey fled to Egypt, where he was promptly assassinated by orders of the king of that land. Caesar was now ruler of Rome in all but name.

Sailing from Greece in pursuit of Pompey, Caesar landed at Alexandria in Egypt at the head of a relatively small force and blundered into one of the most critical moments of his brilliant military career. A large army, plus a mob of citizens, fell upon him, and he was in desperate circumstances by the time a somewhat motley army from the Syrian cities came to his rescue. Perhaps its most effective contingent was the 3000 troops commanded by the enterprising Antipater. He evidently saved the great Roman from serious embarrassment, if not from actual defeat, and did himself much good through his timely appearance.

This Idumaean Antipater had come into the spotlight prior to the arrival of the Romans in Palestine. He was the son of Antipas, who had been governor of Idumaea under Alexander Jannaeus, and had himself held this same office. In the struggle between Hyrcanus and Aristobulus he had aided Hyrcanus and actually had become the authority behind Hyrcanus' actions. Now he was about to exert his influence in a somewhat wider sphere. His penchant for being at the right place at the right time and giving assistance to the right people, continued to stand him in good stead.

As soon as resistance was at an end in Jerusalem, the deposed Aristobulus and his family were shipped off to Rome to take their place among the conquered in Pompey's triumphal procession in 61 B.C. Judaean affairs had been placed under the direction of the Roman governor in Syria. Although the Jews had been permitted a measure of freedom within their own domain, they were restrained from attempting to expand through conquest of neighboring lands.

When hostilities broke out between Caesar and Pompey, the results of this clash were promptly felt in Judaea. Aristobulus was quickly released from his confinement in Rome and hurried off to Syria, there to take command of two legions and employ them to the benefit of Caesar. His efforts, however, met with no success, for this unfortunate Maccabaean prince was soon poisoned. At about this same time, his son Alexander was beheaded by Scipio; while a younger son, hoping to revive the family fortunes, then hurried before Caesar with a plea for his favor.

But Antipater had the inside track there and encouraged a grateful Caesar to officially recognize Hyrcanus as hereditary high priest and confirm him as the ethnarch, or regent, of Judaea. Antipater received Roman citizenship and personal immunity from taxes. Also he was recognized as administrator of Judaea. Thus

while Hyrcanus, the dim-witted son of Alexander Jannaeus, continued as the nominal head of the little land, it was actually Antipater who wielded the power. He gave prompt evidence of this fact in 47 B.C. by appointing his eldest son, Phasael, governor of Judaea, while the younger one, twenty-five-year-old Herod, became governor of Galilee and almost at once started his march to fame.

Yet this Idumaean also managed to encourage Caesar to grant arrangements to the Jews more favorable, so it is claimed, than were enjoyed by any other vassal community. The little land was freed from tribute, Roman garrisons were withdrawn, religious liberty was assured; its people were able to live according to their own laws and subject only to their own tribunals. Also the walls of Jerusalem, thrown down by Pompey, could be restored, and Joppa was added to Judaea, giving it a port on the Mediterranean. The situation began to look more promising.

This turn of events seemed almost too good to be true. Antipater did his best to make the Jews content with their reasonably favorable position as a self-governing people within the vast empire of which Caesar had become the head. But the Jewish aristocrats in turn did their utmost to bring his efforts to naught. Typical of their strategy was the attempt to attack the father through his son. Herod had done an excellent job in ridding all of North Palestine of the robber bands which had long been a scourge of that section. In the hope of making this riddance more permanent, he had executed Hezekiah, the bandit chief, and a number of his outlaw band. Now it happened that employment of capital punishment was limited to the Jewish senate, the Sanhedrin, which suddenly became very jealous of its rights and privileges. So Herod was peremptorily summoned before this aristocratic body, determined to use this occasion to remove him from office and have him banished.

But Herod had an equal contempt for these "whited sepulchres," who made up this highest Jewish tribunal. Appearing in Jerusalem briefly, he was soon at Damascus, where he entered the Roman army and had himself appointed military governor of Lower Syria. In this important Roman office he was in a position to make real trouble for his erstwhile antagonists and to greatly strengthen his father's hands. The biggest news of this era, however, came from Rome itself. Caesar, before leaving Egypt, had established the beauteous Cleopatra upon the throne and bound that country to him. Next followed victories in Africa against Scipio and Cato. By then the master of Roman might was prepared to return to Rome to be received in well-deserved triumph. Yet the man was completely human, and in addition to exercising the powers of a king, he wished to bear the title as well. But the republican form of government long in use, while badly shaken, still appealed strongly to the old aristocratic families. Among them Caesar was far too dangerous a threat, so he must go. A plot promptly developed among the senators, and on the 15th of March, 44 B.C., he was slain in the Senate House. Once more the Roman world, soon to be an empire in name as well as in form, was thrown into turmoil.

XIX

IN THE DAYS OF HEROD THE GREAT

Along with the news of Caesar's assassination, a new proconsul appeared in Syria. Actually he was one of the murderers, and his name was Cassius. Quickly every political underling, from the mountains of Turkey to the mouth of the Nile, was making his way to him. Like most power-hungry Romans, he needed money badly, and to the eager Antipater was handed the onerous task of raising no less than 700 talents of silver, or the equivalent of nearly a million and a half dollars.

Very sagaciously he involved his enemies as well as his friends in the task of extracting this huge tribute from the reluctant people. Some of the former failed in their tasks and were either executed or sold into slavery by the greedy Cassius. One among these latter, whom Antipater helped to have pardoned, still became his benefactor's enemy. His name was Malichus, and their relations were not improved by the fact that young Herod had raised his allotment of 100 talents so promptly that he had materially improved his standing with the Romans.

Malichus now decided to do away with Antipater and started an undercover intrigue to this end with the Jews and Arabs in Trans-Jordan. But to the Idumaean's face he was all friendliness and seems to have completely deceived the normally shrewd man. Suddenly, a much easier means of achieving his purpose presented itself. The high priest's butler, it was discovered, could be bought, and, so it is alleged, he was suitably bribed; he disposed of Antipater with a lethal dose of poison administered during a feast at Hyrcanus' home.

Hardly was the administrator of Judaea dead, when Malichus marched the troops he had managed to raise into Jerusalem. This move was a serious threat to the murdered man's sons, Phasael and Herod. Their unsettled circumstances were further complicated by an upheaval at that moment in Roman affairs. Marc Antony, one of Caesar's lieutenants, was determined to avenge his late commander by doing away with Cassius and the other conspirators. So he and Octavian, a nephew and the heir of the mighty dictator, drew Cassius into battle on the plains of Philippi in Macedonia, where he was defeated and committed suicide. The Roman world now was at the disposal of these two brash young men.

Antigonus, younger son of the pretender Aristobulus, decided this would be a favorable time for another attempt at wresting Judaea from control by his uncle, the high priest Hyrcanus. To aid him in this enterprise, he called upon the Parthians, a warlike people from a land near the Caspian Sea. Many of the Jews who disliked Herod and Phasael joined with Antigonus as he made his way toward Jerusalem. There, through a ruse which hard-headed Herod avoided, Phasael and Hyrcanus were made prisoners. The former at length committed suicide, while the latter had his ears lopped off, which disqualified him for his priestly office, and he was then carried off to captivity in Babylon by the Parthians.

Herod, although having a substantial number of loyal followers, was still badly outnumbered and knew his best chance lay in flight. While as a very young man he had been married to a lady named Doris, member of a prominent Idumaean family, this, according to Jewish law of the time, was no deterrent to another marriage. Through his second choice, he strengthened his position materially, for the lady this time was Mariamne, granddaughter of Hyrcanus. Through his betrothal to her, he became a member of the Judaean royal house.

But flight was imminent. So under cover of night he took his first wife, his prospective second wife, her mother Alexandra, his own mother and younger brother, together with his household and troops, and set out for the south. His first objective was the impregnable fortress Masada, which stood on an isolated, flat-topped hill along the west coast of the Dead Sea. There he left both family and adherents under the

Ruins of Herod's Senate Hall at Sebaste

A   B   C   D   E   F

ABILENE
• Abila

Damascus

ITURAEA

PHOENICIA

Sidon

MT. HERMON

PANIAS
Panias •
*Ulatha and Panias were
placed under Herod's
control in 20 B.C.*

Tyre •

ULATHA

TRACHONITIS

Cadasa
(Kedesh)

GAULANITIS

BATANAEA

Ecdippa •
Gischala •
Semechonitis
*Herod's first territory
was Galilee, given to him
by his father, Antipater.*

Ptolemaïs •

GALILEE

Leontes R.

Raphana

The Great Sea (Mediterranean Sea)

MT. CARMEL

Taricheae (Magdala) •
Arbela •

Sepphoris •
Gaba •
Nazareth •

Sea of
Galilee

Hippos

Gamala •
Dion •

Kanatha

Philoteria •

AURANITIS

Dora •

Plain of
Esdraelon

Yarmuk R.
Abila •
Gadara •

Edrei •

Caesarea
(Strato's Tower)
*City and port were
rebuilt by Herod.*

Scythopolis •

*Hippos and Gadara were
cities of the Decapolis given
to Herod by Augustus.*

Bostra •

SAMARIA

Pella

DECAPOLIS

Plain of Sharon

*Herod rebuilt Samaria,
giving it the new name
of Sebaste.*

River Jordan

Amathus •

Gerasa •

*The Decapolis was a league of neigh-
boring city districts united for mutual
protection against marauding tribes.
It was not a compact geographical or
political unit with definite boundaries.*

Sebaste
(Samaria) •

Shechem •
Mt.
Gerizim

Apollonia •

NABATAEA

Antipatris •

Alexandrium •

Jabbok R.

Joppa •

Phasaelis •

PERAEA

Thamna •
Gophna •

Lydda •
Modin •
Jamnia •
Ekron •
Gazara •
Emmaus •

Bethel •
Beth-horon •

Jericho •

Beth-nimrah •

Philadelphia

AMMON

Jerusalem
Khirbet
Qumrân ×

Heshbon •

Azotus •
*Herod gained control of Jerusalem
in 37 B.C., defeating Antigonus, and
became King of Judaea.*

Mt.
of Olives
Hyrcanium •
Bethlehem •

Livias
(Beth-haram) •

Ascalon
*Birthplace
of Herod.*

JUDAEA
Beth-gubrin •
Marisa •

Herodium •

Anthedon
(Agrippium) •

Beth-zur •
Hebron •

Callirhoë •
Machaerus •

Gaza •

Salt Sea (Dead Sea)

En-gedi •

Dibon •

NABATAEANS

IDUMAEA

Masada •

Arnon R.

THE DOMINIONS OF
HEROD THE GREAT
37 to 4 B.C.

Copyright by C. S. HAMMOND & CO., N.Y.

Scale of Miles
0 5 10   20   30   40

Beersheba •

Kir-moab
(Kir-hareseth) •

Zered R.

Perennial Rivers ....
Seasonal Rivers & Streams ....

Capitals ....
Cities of the Decapolis □

Kingdom of Herod the Great–4 B.C.
Decapolis
Autonomous city state of Ascalon
Roman province of Syria
Kingdom of Lysanias

1 2 3 4 5 6 7

charge of his brother, Joseph, while he hurried on to Egypt and from there to Rome. The year was 40 B.C.

It was evidently a very astute move, for the thirty-two-year-old Herod was received with every mark of reliance and support. The two men of the hour, Octavian and Antony, promised their aid, and by a decree of the Senate Herod was named king of Judaea.

Back in Palestine during his absence, many things had been happening. Antigonus had risen to be both high priest and king in Jerusalem, but he had failed to make his position there very secure. Instead he had spent too much time and effort trying to capture distant Masada. This castle, which could be reached only by two crooked, hard-to-climb paths, had defied his best efforts, and he was still heavily involved there when Herod returned. Since the Parthians, whom Antigonus had brought into the land, had plundered people of all degrees, he had become most unpopular. Consequently, Herod was hardly ashore when the dissatisfied began joining his forces.

The siege of Masada was quickly relieved, whereupon the new king set out for Jerusalem. But his supporters were far too few in number at the moment to lay siege to its stout fortifications. So he was forced to bide his time and await assistance from the Romans. Finally, in 39 B.C., Antony came in person to Asia Minor to take supreme command of military affairs in the east. Caius Sosius was made legate of Syria and given the task of seeing that Antony's friend, Herod, was at once placed upon his throne. So as soon as spring arrived, Sosius, at the head of a considerable army, marched down through Phoenicia and fell upon Jerusalem. But so heroic was its defense that it was five long months before the city fell—and then on the most sacred day of the year, the Day of Atonement. Its defenders, it seems, stoutly refused to fight on holy days.

The Roman soldiery, maddened by this long resistance, cruelly slaughtered many of the inhabitants. This blood-bath was, in a manner, a fitting prelude to the forthcoming marriage of King Herod and the Princess Mariamne, a union which would one day come to a most bloody end. Antigonus, who fomented all the present trouble, was seized and hauled away to Antioch. There, after a plea on his part to Herod to end the brutality heaped upon him, he was beheaded.

The son of the late ambitious Antipater was in many ways as able a ruler as his father. But although surnamed "The Great," he had extreme weaknesses which brought him a notoriety of quite another sort. From the start it was clear that this man was dominated by but one consideration—to further his own ends at all cost. He was in this no exception in those times, not even in the ruthless ways in which he tried to preserve his power. However, he was possessed of an unusually suspicious and jealous nature, and many of his acts, especially in his later life, indicate the neurotic.

His flint-hard attitude became apparent when he ordered the slaughter of the 45 Sadducees who were members of the Sanhedrin which had opposed his entrance into the Holy City. His suspicions and jealousies very soon involved him in family troubles. After he made his brother-in-law, the 17-year-old brother of Mariamne, Aristobulus, high priest, the young man's growing popularity worried him so that

Ruins of Herod the Great's temple of Augustus in Samaria

he had him drowned during water games held at a feast in Jericho in 36 B.C. When the murdered Aristobulus' mother, not deceived about the true nature of her son's death, turned to Cleopatra of Egypt for help, Herod was ordered to appear before Antony, whom Cleopatra held firmly enmeshed in her wiles. Leaving his uncle Joseph—his sister Salome's husband—as regent, he hurried away to the north to meet the Triumvir at Laodicea.

The Jews wished fervently that he would never return, and their hopes were for a time fortified by rumors that things might take so fortunate a turn. In fact, upon a false report that he had been executed, the regent considered taking refuge with the royal family in the Roman garrison at Jerusalem.

But Antony had taken a bad drubbing at the hands of the Parthians and was so in need of Herod's unquestioned allegiance that he refused to even hear the case against the Judaean king. The accused thus set off for home scot-free; and to sweeten up that monarch's accuser, Antony gave Lower Syria to Cleopatra.

Herod's marriage to the exquisite Mariamne had been far more than one of convenience, for on Herod's part it had stemmed from a devouring love. But she appears to have been as cold and unresponsive as she was enticing. Upon his leaving for his trip, Herod had given explicit orders that, if he did not return, she was to be slain lest she come into the possession of some other man. A probable misunderstanding of what truly lay behind such an order, when she learned of it, could have made her even more frigid. Also, she most certainly sided with her mother in respect to the murder of her brother, Aristobulus. Fully realizing her subtle fascination for her husband, she on her part continued to resist him, slowly driving him crazy with jealousy by way of revenge.

However, she antagonized the king's sister, Salome, who was fully as unscrupulous as her brother. During the king's absence at Antony's headquarters, Mariamne had been forced because of circumstances to see much of Joseph, Herod's uncle and Salome's husband, who was left behind as regent. Salome spitefully and untruthfully hinted at an affair between her husband and the queen. The inevitable result was the ex-regent's execution; but Mariamne was forgiven.

About this same time, Cleopatra attempted to remove Idumaea from Herod's domains. But once again Marc Antony came to his rescue and upheld him. Yet there appears to have been a sop tossed by the Roman to his lady friend. The records are not too clear in the matter, but the cities of Gaza and Joppa were not, in 30 B.C., any longer parts of the Judaean kingdom.

The Egyptian queen's unfriendliness for him, however, managed to do Herod a good turn. When the break came between Antony and Octavian, the King of Judaea hastened to offer his support to the former, his patron. But Cleopatra, very likely jealous of the close relations between the two, refused his personal participation in the hostilities. As a consequence, he had no active part in the fatal battle of Actium, September 2, 31 B.C., which left Octavian—a few years later to be renamed Augustus Caesar—the complete master of the evolving Roman Empire.

Another incident which now took place showed again Herod's excessive suspicion. Old Hyrcanus in his dotage, whom his mutilation had debarred from his former sacred office, had been allowed to return to spend his remaining days in Jerusalem. However, as he was one of the last remaining male members of the Hasmonaean dynasty, Herod saw a possible rival in him and had him executed.

The time had now come when it was necessary for Herod to solidify his position with his new lord and master, Octavian. Putting Mariamne and her mother under guard in one fortress, and the other members of the family in another, a much troubled king set off to the island of Rhodes for his rendezvous. Here he readily proved he could be quite as useful to Octavian as he had formerly been to Antony. And having been reconfirmed in his kingdom, he hurried back home to make preparations for the entertainment of his newest patron, who was about to march into Egypt.

The reception was held at Ptolemaïs, the modern port of Acre, along the coast-front highway. There the Roman forces were provided with ample provisions, and a token consisting of 800 talents was presented the commander. To make his way safer and easier, Herod had organized a water supply all the way to Egypt.

After the death of Antony and Cleopatra there in 30 B.C., Herod hastened down for further congratulation to Octavian and was bountifully rewarded for his pains. Cleopatra's bodyguard of 400 picked Galatians was presented to him, and much territory that had been removed from his domains was restored. Once again he began to feel more secure.

But he was not long home again before Mariamne's treatment of him brought to full flower his torturing jealousy. How many times had he thought to put an end to it all! Now Salome reported that his lovely but distant wife was plotting against him. She bribed the king's cupbearer to report that Mariamne had offered him a very suspicious "love potion" to administer to his master, which he had withheld, certain it was but poison. The investigations, though inconclusive on this point, roused the king's jealousy still more, and he resolved that Mariamne must die. She was tried, and in 29 B.C. he signed her death warrant. Although there were countless other ghosts to haunt him, none filled him with remorse like the recollections of this proud, disdainful creature whose love and respect he had been totally unable to command.

While there would be other victims along Herod's bloody trail, still there were accomplishments which, in all fairness, deserve mention. Herod was a great builder. The fortress of Baris, standing hard by the Lord's House and so dominating Jerusalem, he had rebuilt and named Antonia for his former patron. For his own residence, he had constructed a combination home and fort—the Upper Palace —which was also capable of fully controlling the city. And following this, in 19 B.C., he started the rebuilding of the Temple. The Holy Place was completed in the second year of effort, the outer Temple at the end of six more years, while the work of restoration was still going on 40 years later at the time of the Crucifixion. What resulted was a far grander edifice than that which Zerubbabel had been able to erect.

On the coast, 20 miles south of Mount Carmel, he built the seaport of Caesarea, complete with a huge breakwater, and a temple with a colossal statue of Augustus, the name given Octavian when he had become the first Roman Emperor in 27 B.C. Herod did an admirable job, too, of the rebuilding of Samaria, renaming it Sebaste, the Greek equivalent of the name Augusta. Several of the other cities were greatly beautified and improved with gymnasia, temples, theaters and market places.

By the year 10 B.C. funds were running uncomfortably low, and once again David's tomb was opened and ransacked for treasure to carry such activities forward. Herod's sons by the beloved Mariamne, Alexander and Aristobulus, who had been educated in Rome, were now grown to manhood. So, too, were several more young men, the children of his other eight wives. Among them the firstborn was Antipater, son of Doris. His father does not seem to have been particularly partial to him, favoring instead his half-brothers Alexander and Aristobulus. They were handsome, polished youths, tremendously popular with the Jewish people, and Herod treated them for a time as his principal heirs. The elder had been married to Glaphyra, daughter of the king of Cappadocia, while Aristobulus, in an attempt to weld the family more closely together, had been wed to his own first cousin, Berenice, the daughter of Herod's sister, Salome. Naturally the greater attention paid these younger sons bred a lively jealousy on Antipater's part. He had apparently some of the persuasive powers of the grandfather for whom he was named, and so began to put it to work.

Roman ruins of the 2nd century A.D. at Jarash, ancient Gerasa, important Decapolis town

"Street of Columns," Gerasa

He seems to have had ready access to his father's ear, and into it he started to pour tales of the many defects in his two half-brothers. Antipater evidently had followers in the court circle, too, and with the help of this clique, he did an extraordinary job of poisoning the father's mind. A few missteps on the part of Alexander and Aristobulus, and Herod called for their heads. His one-time favored sons were put to death; Antipater was appointed his successor, with another son, Herod, second in line.

Very much emboldened by this success, Crown Prince Antipater was now ready for further double-dealing. This time his intended victim was none other than Salome, his father's sister, and thus his own aunt, plus two more of his half-brothers, Archelaus and Antipas, then in Rome being educated. This trio was accused of plotting to dispose of the king. But this time the accusation did not stick, for it was promptly turned upon Antipater himself, and also his uncle, Pheroras. The latter was done away with, while the once hopeful prince was tossed into prison.

Uneasy indeed lies the head that wears a crown, and this was particularly true in Herod's case. Whom could he trust? Surely not Antipater, so he was at last executed. For a time the son Antipas stood foremost in the aging king's mind. Then he was demoted in favor of the son Archelaus. As a consequence, Antipas

was made tetrarch of Galilee and Peraea, while still another son, Philip, was to rule over three other sections of the kingdom. This proved to be the final disposition of his affairs as confirmed at his death, except that the Emperor Augustus designated Archelaus as ethnarch, rather than as king, of Judaea.

One of the most sublime of all events, the birth of Jesus Christ, occurred very near the close of this active, bloody and in many respects revolting life. Herod was perhaps already in the grip of a terrible, fatal disease—some believe it to have been cancer—when, in 4 or 5 B.C., dismaying news was brought to him. A son, born to the line of David, would succeed to his throne ! That meant the dynasty he had founded was to be thrust aside. This must have been a bitter thought to the dying king, and the order for the legendary "Slaughter of the Innocents" is not outside the capabilities of this most ruthless man.

Even after his death, his opponents were not to live, if he could help it. So he asked his sister Salome and her husband Alexas to fulfill one final hideous duty. They were to have the principal Jews confined in the circus at Jericho. Then, at his death, all these unfortunates were to be slaughtered. This ogre was determined that there would be mourning at the time of his demise—even though that mourning would not be for him.

XX

UNTO US A CHILD IS BORN

There were two things in addition to sub-servience which the Roman Empire demanded of its subject peoples. One was taxes, and the other military service when necessary. The taxes were of two kinds. First there was an impost, levied upon goods or property, the collection of which was farmed out to publicans, or collectors whom the taxpayers looked upon with the utmost contempt (Luke 19:2, 7). There was also a head or poll tax assessed against each male. This latter, plus the need for draft records, required the frequent taking of the census. These proceedings were similar to those in use by the Hebrews as early as Moses' time (Ex. 30:12,13; Num. 1:18).

Such a numbering of the people was called for in the latter days of the reign of Herod the Great, which necessitated each family to make the journey to its "home town" to be properly registered. This demand had fallen also upon a carpenter, then living in Nazareth in Galilee. He had to make a three-day journey to Bethlehem of Judaea, far to the south; for this man, Joseph, belonged to the house and family of the great King David. It would be a most trying journey in his case, for his wife, Mary, was expecting a baby very shortly. But go he must, and she could not be left behind.

It was there in Bethlehem, in David's city, that the Child was born. The town was filled with people, there to register in many cases, as was Joseph, and the little family had to be content to make their home temporarily in a stable set in a cave in the hillside. There was perhaps a house standing before this grotto for animals, an arrangement such as may be found in Bethlehem even to this day.

But theirs was a very special Babe indeed, the promised King. The night was filled with a chorus of heavenly voices, and the shepherds from among their flocks of fat-tailed sheep on the neighboring hillsides came during the dark hours to pay Him humble homage. There was also another heavenly phenomenon of some sort in the night sky, popularly called today "The Star of Bethlehem," and reportedly it brought Wise Men from the far-off land of Media in search of the newborn Child which it heralded. Important persons these, so they stopped at Jerusalem to ask directions at Herod's court. St. Matthew relates that their inquiry aroused the king's suspicions, touching off the order for the slaying of the infants, and that Joseph, forewarned of impending danger, took Mary and the tiny Jesus away to Egypt. Where did they go in that land? While the Bible does not say, the traditions of the Coptic church offer a perplexing choice of localities. Chief among them is a little garden at the edge of ancient Heliopolis, six miles outside of modern Cairo. Here a very noble Egyptian sycamore, but without even one-quarter of the needed age, is pointed out as the *Virgin's Tree*. This location, though, has been venerated

Town of Bethlehem, looking toward the Dead Sea

Bethlehem

for centuries. But the stay in the land by the Nile could not have been for long, since Herod ended his days at Jericho in 4 B.C.

A brief explanation of that date is perhaps in order. The calendar which most of Christendom observes is known as the *Gregorian;* it was established by Pope Gregory XIII in 1582 and adopted in England and her American colonies in 1752. Its initial date, 1 A.D., was supposed to have been the year in which Jesus was born. This system of reckoning time originated with Dionysius Exiguus, a Roman abbot, who worked it out during the sixth Christian century. But the good abbot, using the fragmentary knowledge of his time, erred by somewhere between four and six years.

The first known attempt to pin-point the date of Jesus' birth had been recorded about two hundred years before. A fourth-century analyst had declared, "The Lord Jesus Christ was born on December 25th—a Friday—the fifteenth day of the New Moon." But neither the exact year, nor the month and date, have as yet been positively determined.

Herod, however, was made king by the Senate in the Roman year 714, and his death must have come in 750, or earlier, in 749—4 or 5 B.C., our reckoning. Thus it now seems that he died in 4 B.C., and, if Jesus actually was born in December, and on the final day of the depraved *Saturnalia* carnival, His natal year would have been at least 5 B.C., but very likely earlier both in date and time of year.

The leading Jews had been gathered from all over Palestine and herded together in the stadium at Jericho in keeping with the pain-crazed Herod's orders. But their mass slaughter was too revolting a procedure for even the callous Salome, and before news of the king's death was made public, she and her husband had dismissed this pitiful assembly. Then word of their ruler's passing was broadcast, but mourners were few indeed. Herod was buried at the fortress of Herodium, 3 miles to the southeast of town.

The will was opened and read; it disclosed that Archelaus was to accede to the throne. He was promptly acclaimed by the troops. In the division of the kingdom, the double portion of the first-born, or favored, son went to the eighteen-year-old Archelaus. But to him, the Emperor Augustus granted the title of ethnarch, rather than king. With the exception of some smaller cities bestowed on Salome, the balance of the realm was split between Herod Antipas and Philip, who each bore the title of tetrarch.

But Archelaus, whose reign was to end in disaster ten years later, began to have difficulty with the people almost from the start. Joseph, so some think, had planned to make his home in Bethlehem as he returned from asylum in Egypt. But the disturbances then going on in

PALESTINE IN THE TIME OF CHRIST

Copyright by C. S. HAMMOND & CO., N.Y.

Scale of Miles

0 5 10 20 30 40

Perennial Rivers _____
Seasonal Rivers & Streams
Capitals _____
Roads & Trade Routes _____

Tetrarchy of Lysanias
Tetrarchy of Philip
Tetrarchy of Herod Antipas
Territory under Roman procurator
Areas tributary to Salome
Decapolis *
Independent *
Roman province of Syria

Cities of the Decapolis........□

*The Decapolis and Ascalon retained their independence under the Roman governor of the province of Syria.

Archelaus, upon Herod's death, became ruler of Judaea, Samaria and Idumaea. His reign lasted until 6 A.D. when he was removed and exiled. His territory then was placed under a Roman procurator.

Salome, Herod's sister, was given Jamnia, Azotus and Phasaelis. They, in turn, passed to Livia, wife of Augustus and then to Emperor Tiberius.

The Dead Sea Scrolls were found in a cave here; also the ruins of an Essene monastery.

Here John the Baptist was imprisoned and beheaded by order of Herod Antipas.

Residence of Roman procurators.

The Great Sea

(Mediterranean Sea)

ABILENE
Abila
PHOENICIA
Sidon
Sarepta (Zarephath)
Tyre
MOUNT LEBANON
Damascus
ITURAEA
MT. HERMON
PANIAS
Dan Caesarea Philippi
ULATHA
Cadasa (Kedesh)
Lake Semechonitis
Gischala
GAULANITIS
BATANAEA
BASHAN
Raphana
TRACHONITIS
Ladder of Tyre
Seleucia
Ptolemais (Accho)
Jotapata
Cana
Sepphoris
Nazareth
GALILEE
Magdala (Dalmanutha)
Chorazin
Bethsaida (Julias)
Capernaum
Tabigha
Sea of Galilee
Gergesa
Gamala
Dion
AURANITIS
Tiberias
Hippos
Raphana
Philoteria
Abila
Edrei
Horns of Hattin (Kurūn Hattīn) is a possible site of the Sermon on the Mount.
Mt. Carmel
Horns of Hattin
Mt. Tabor
Plain of Esdraelon
Nain
Gadara
Capitolias
Dora
Bethabara
GILEAD
Caesarea
En-gannim (Ginaea)
Scythopolis (Beth-shan)
Pella
DECAPOLIS
Gerasa
SAMARIA
Samaria (Sebaste)
Mt. Ebal
Shechem Sychar
Mt. Gerizim Jacob's Well
Amathus
Apollonia
Antipatris
Arimathaea (Ramathaim)
Lydda (Diospolis)
Gophna
Phasaelis
Bethel
Archelais
Ephraim
PERAEA
Beth-nimrah
Philadelphia (Rabbath-ammon)
Joppa
Gezer (Gazara)
Ramah
Jericho
Jamnia
Ekron
Nicopolis (Emmaus)
Emmaus
Jerusalem
Bethany
Mt. of Olives
Khirbet Qumran
Julias (Livias, Beth-haram)
Heshbon
Azotus (Ashdod)
Bethlehem
Herodium
Wilderness of Judah
Ascalon
JUDAEA
Mareshah (Marisa)
Hebron
Ziph
En-gedi
Callirhoe
Machaerus
Dibon
Gaza
Juttah
Carmel
Salt or Dead Sea (L. Asphaltitis)
Gerar
Masada
Rabbath Moab (Areopolis, Rabba)
Raphia
Beersheba
IDUMAEA
Kir-moab (Kir-haresheth)
NABATAEANS
AMMONITAE
ARABIA
Jordan River
Jabbok R.
Yarmuk R.
Leontes R.
Kishon R.

This silver star in the Church of the Nativity indicates the traditional site of the birth of Christ

Jerusalem may have encouraged him to change his mind. Happily, heavenly direction was forthcoming, and he took his little family back to the former home in Nazareth.

At what time did Joseph, Mary and the Babe arrive there? One of the most violent outbursts in Jerusalem came as the Passover season was approaching, or in early April. If this clash had been the occasion for the change in plans, the Holy Family would have reached the northern hill country when it is at its loveliest. Even the journey home could have been a pleasant one. Being devout Jews, and so preferring to give the odious Samaritans a wide berth, they would probably have avoided the trail up along the highlands. Providing they had returned to Bethlehem, one choice would have taken them down the Joppa road as far as the great caravan route crossing at Lydda, their way leading home from there across the plains, first of Sharon, and then of Esdraelon, brilliant with spring flowers.

Beyond Sarid, the local trail would have begun to climb, for Nazareth lay in the hills. It was somewhat a place apart in this hellenized land, which was much more populous and bustling in those days than it is today and whose population was even then probably heavily Gentile. The village of twenty centuries ago presumably still lies buried beneath the much later structures which now blanket the hill above the never-failing spring known as the *Virgin's Fountain*. An hour's brisk walk to the north would have taken one to the provincial capital, Sepphoris, which stood on an important east-west road between the Sea of Galilee and the Mediterranean. This city was destroyed in 6 A.D., and the youthful Jesus may have witnessed its rebuilding which came almost at once.

It was about an equal distance to the south to the great channel of international commerce from which the returning travelers had just turned aside. Here was evidence that the home chosen for them lay in a quiet backwater of a surging sea of business and trade. By contrast with its surroundings, too, the town's population was almost completely Jewish and given to most orthodox customs and beliefs which were devoutly observed. So strict and conventional a place was it in fact that the apostle-to-be, Nathanael, quoted the slightly derisive question

often asked by its neighbors: "Can anything good come out of Nazareth?" (John 1:46). But while it was indeed Jewish to the core, it was surrounded by alien peoples, languages and practices, which most certainly spilled over to some extent upon this hillside community, so that as a place in which to grow up it did have merit in several respects.

By the time the later rains cease in early April, the grain fields would have painted the sear, lifeless winter hillsides a brilliant green. And Nature had other adornments there as well, for in those days, as now, there was a wealth of flowers. Perhaps the first among them to bloom in the spring were the crocuses. And they were followed promptly by cyclamens, anemones, the blooming flax, and other "lilies of the field" (Matt. 6:28-30).

The grain grows rapidly from then on, for both wheat and barley are ready for harvest in the highlands by late May. But along with the wild flowers, the fig tree—a leading Jewish symbol—hastily decks itself out in pale leaves and tiny fruit, while the pomegranate blossoms contribute flashes of vivid scarlet, and the apricot and other fruit trees add their own touches to this colorful array. Here is a rousing, annual promise that *all* may have life, and, out of God's great bounty, have it more abundantly (John 10:10).

Local hillsides are generally a little too steep for easy cultivation, but they do furnish pasture for many small flocks of sheep and goats. The herdsman usually has his creatures well trained (John 10:2-5) and may spend long hours watching over them from the pleasant shade of a tree or jutting rock. On such occasions one may sometimes hear the notes from his pipe rippling over the warming air. But it is far more probable, though, that he will be found with a tapering spindle, a baked-clay whorl, and a heap of combed wool, twisting and spinning the latter into yarn, from which his wife will weave the family's clothing. Life was then much changed, and perhaps far less severe than it had been when the Tribes fought their way into the land after bondage in Egypt. But among the common folk one still had to work hard, if he expected to eat.

What languages were spoken locally? At the time of the Babylonian Empire a Semitic tongue, known as *Aramaic,* came into general and widespread use. Laban had employed it in Haran, even in the early days (Gen. 31:47), and it eventually became the common tongue of Palestine as well as Syria after the return from the Babylonian captivity. Hebrew was still understood by the Jews there, for it continued to be their sacred language, yet it was this Aramaean speech which was spoken in the homes. In the streets and market places, despite the fact the Romans had been the overlords for many years, the conversations were generally carried on in Greek. This was not the classical Greek of the Golden Age in Athens, but a *Koinē,* or common, Greek, which had come to be the commercial tongue of Syria, Palestine and Egypt. This was the language, too, in which the great bulk of the New Testament was first written, yet the differences between it and classical Greek were not well known or appreciated until the 1890s. As soon as scholars had a better understanding of them, there was an expanding interest in new and revised translations of this later portion of our Bible.

Roman domination brought with it some use of Latin, while the trade routes which ran to the north and south of Nazareth resounded with numerous other dialects and lesser tongues. Thus one had need in those days to be quite a linguist.

And these trade routes were fairly alive with traffic. After the days of Solomon, international exchange, except perhaps for Phoenicia, seems to have tipped downward. Then it received a new impulse from those who returned from experience with the lively commercial affairs of Babylon. Freedom from local wars under the empires, especially that established by the Romans, was an encouragement to trade. It now appears that manufacturing increased by leaps and bounds in some sections of Italy, where finished goods were produced primarily to be traded for grain and other foodstuffs, of which Rome seemed always to be in need. Even today the remains of iron tools, utensils and horseshoes, bearing names of makers located in the Campania, south of Rome, are still unearthed, while a Roman manufacturer named Fortis seems to have fairly flooded Palestine with his oil-burning lamps molded from clay. Goods—and people—were then on the move, and the Jews were still dispersing to faraway places, even to Rome itself, from which they were later debarred. But the increased tempo of the times probably affected the staid little towns there like Nazareth least.

What were the homes there like? The bulk of them had but a single room. There were four limestone walls, pretty much devoid of windows, and covered over with a flat roof, made of poles as rafters, strewn with a thick coating of branches and then straw and weeds, and finally topped off with some eight inches of clay. This had to be tamped and then kept rolled, and ancient roof rollers still crop up quite frequently. The lower floor was customarily given over to the animals, while the family's living quarters were on a *rowyeh,* or raised platform across the rear, which was reached by a flight of very narrow stone steps. It was here, in the poorer homes, that a mat

Ruins of a synagogue (2nd or 3rd century A.D.) at site of Biblical Capernaum

was spread on the floor, and from it the family ate the evening meal. There, too, as the light began to fail, other reed pallets were laid out side by side, so that coverings could be shared, for the night's repose (Luke 11:7).

While home training long had been and still continued to be the principal "school" for most children, some group instruction seems to have been given in the synagogues. There the children sat on mats upon the stone or tile floors, and in unison recited quotations from the Law. Much time spent in expounding and explaining these Scripture passages helped to expand reasoning power. Also it is probable that individuals had to learn to read from the sacred rolls, and possibly to write as well. Some of the abler scholars, whose parents could afford to provide for them, were taken into the famous *beth ha-Talmud*, the great religious school in connection with the Temple at Jerusalem.

Jesus, however, seemed destined to spend His life on earth mostly among the common folk, and, as was the case with any and all Jewish boys, He was taught a trade. Since in His case it meant serving an apprenticeship with His own father, He must have gone to work when very young. While it is customary to think of the carpenter today primarily as a builder of houses and other structures, his tasks twenty centuries ago spread over quite a variety of objects. This was a farming and herding community, and many of the tools and utensils for carrying on such activities were wooden, made by the village carpenter. Since it was before the days of lumber yards, the craftsman's work began right in the woods, felling trees, or at least working their trunks and branches, yes, and even their roots, into timber and boards from which to shape and work out many needed objects.

When Jesus was 10 or 11 years old, Archelaus, who had become as great a tyrant as his father Herod, was summoned to Rome. Charges which had been brought against him were there proved to the Caesar's satisfaction, and the last king of Judaea was banished to Gaul, where he ultimately died. The ethnarchy he had held in his latter years was also abolished, and Judaea became a Roman province in A.D. 6. It was no doubt better that Jesus had grown up in Galilee under the milder rule of Antipas. But to the Jews generally, becoming merely another Roman province was quite a blow. The land which had been promised to their fathers, and for which their ancestors, and especially the Maccabees, had fought so heroically, was now clearly and finally in the hands of Gentiles. The pious Jews as a consequence were now most careful to visit their Holy City for as many of the sacred feasts as possible.

Since His parents regularly made the pilgrimage to Jerusalem for the celebration of the Passover, it is probable that their Son always accompanied them, even though but one such trip during His first 25 or more years is actually recorded. However, since a young Jew at the completion of his thirteenth year became a "son of the Law" and was subject to all its requirements, He would have had to make at least three trips annually after that milepost had been passed. As a tiny babe, Jesus had been in the Temple for the first time when He was but a little more than a month old (Luke 2:22), and it is to be presumed that He saw it on numerous other occasions between then and the time He was twelve years old.

It was then, as it was a dozen or more years later, still being either rebuilt, or at least repaired after the heavy damage it had received in the early days of Archelaus' reign. The sanctuary itself, which was very impressive, stood in a complex of courts, twice the size of those surrounding the Second Temple, and closed in by a wall 43 feet high. This was pierced by 9 huge gates, 4 on both the north and south side, and one to the east. Beyond the consecrated area, there was a ritual wall past which it was a capital offense for anyone not a Jew to go. Signs in Greek, hung at its various gateways, warned: "Let no Gentile pass through the barrier about the sanctuary. Anyone so trespassing will pay with his life."

This House of God was under the control of the high priest, who was also the presiding officer of the seventy-man Sanhedrin, or senate. This was the superior council for the whole province in temporal matters, and a supreme court in religious affairs. It could even pass a sentence of death, but any such had to be confirmed by the procurator before being carried out. It heard charges of blasphemy and the transgressing of the Law, and even Roman citizens accused of profaning the Temple were obliged to appear before this august body. It even maintained its own police force (Matt. 26:47), and in matters where Roman interests were not primarily involved, it had wide and

effective power. But where the affairs of the empire were at stake, the procurator was all-powerful; he could even remove the high priest and appoint another in his place. This Jewish council met in a building to the west of the Temple near the *xystus,* or market, and close by the innermost city wall.

Its members were men of prominence—priests, scribes and elders, some belonging to the Pharisees, while others were of the opposite religious party, the Sadducees. During Jesus' childhood, a third party was formed, the Zealots (Luke 6:15), who believed God to be the sole ruler of Israel, and that tribute was due to Him alone. Whether they were represented on the Sanhedrin is not quite certain.

However, they provided further evidence to convince the Romans that the Jews were not capable of governing themselves. After Judaea had been made into a province following the banishment of Archelaus, there began quite a procession of procurators. Nominally their duties were chiefly the collection of tribute and the sitting in judgement in tax matters. But in Judaea, since there was no legate as their superior officer in the province, their duties were much broader. They were responsible for general governmental matters and in direct charge of military and judicial concerns as well. As a rule, the incumbent lived at the Roman city of Caesarea on the coast and was usually in Jerusalem only at the time of the feasts, when, since the city was filled with visitors, he customarily brought with him a strong armed force.

The fifth among these procurators in Judaea was appointed in the year A.D. 26 and managed to last out a ten-year term. His name was Pontius Pilate; he was appointed by Tiberius, who had become emperor on the death of Augustus twelve years before. Almost at once he was at loggerheads with his Jewish subjects, the first occasion for trouble coming from his having marched troops into the Holy City bearing standards on which were "graven" images of the emperor. He also took money from the Temple treasury to build an aqueduct to conduct water from the highlands to the south into the city. In addition, there was a whole series of misunderstandings liberally mixed with what were downright tyrannical offenses. He made it very evident that his idea of justice was whatever worked to his particular benefit, and for his Jewish subjects he had nothing but the most thoroughgoing disdain.

It was at about the time Pilate was taking over duties in his new post that a young preacher was causing quite a stir and attracting extensive crowds down into the Jordan Valley. There, at Bethabara, or Bethany, on the east bank of the stream, and probably near where the trail into Peraea crossed, he was "making ready the way of the Lord," urging the need for immediate and sincere repentance. After the penitents confessed their sins, they were baptized by this preacher in the waters of the river as a token of their having been cleansed from sin. It was evidently a Sabbatical Year, when the fields were left to rest, so that many laborers had the leisure to attend his exhortations. In fact their numbers were sufficient to give concern to the Temple authorities in Jerusalem, who sent men to spy upon this person acting without their sanction, and who was announcing a new dispensation—the advent of the kingdom of God, and the baptism of the Holy Spirit (Matt. 3:2, 11).

It was either very late in this same year, or early in the year following, that this preacher, who was none other than John the Baptist, had a certain youngish Man, a relative actually, call upon him there by the Jordan. It was, of course, Jesus Christ, the Son of God and of man, and He asked to be baptized. When John hesitated, He persisted in His request, until He, too, had received this wondrous cleansing rite. At that moment He was at the very outset of His own glorious ministry, and on one of the earlier of the many journeys which He undertook, and which are described in the following section.

XXI

IN THE FOOTSTEPS OF JESUS

During the approximately 33 years which Jesus spent upon earth, the four Gospels record some 50 journeys of varying length made within that period. Certain of them were very short, while others ran into many, many miles and were perhaps of several weeks', or even months', duration. In a few cases His route is fairly well indicated, while in others there is no clear suggestion of either His path or the towns and cities passed through or visited. Unfortunately, too, there are instances where a town or place is mentioned by name, yet its location is impossible to determine today.

Of these latter, the spot where John the Baptist baptized Jesus is a case in point. It is spoken of in the Bible as Bethany beyond Jordan, and then, two centuries after the close of Bible times, a famous early Christian writer calls it Bethabara. Yet neither of these names helps in locating this site, briefly used, and for purposes which left no lasting traces. Much thus devolves upon assumption. In this instance it would seem to be but natural for the Baptist to have preached close by one of the leading travel routes, so that goodly audiences would be more certainly assured for his sermons and baptisms.

Some of Jesus' very earliest travels can hardly have resulted in "footsteps," since they were accomplished in the arms of His parents. Such was the short trip to Jerusalem and a return to Bethlehem upon His presentation in the Temple. Far longer was the flight into Egypt, which was presumably made over the caravan route along the sea coast, reached by the trail on down to Hebron, and which then swung across the Idumaean country to Raphia on the Mediterranean. There is an open question whether Bethlehem was visited on the return trip, or whether they made their way directly to Nazareth. In either event it would have been a long trip, tiring for Mary, for the Palestinian donkeys, one of which she apparently rode, have not a very smooth gait.

The other childhood journey recorded is Jesus' visit to Jerusalem when He was twelve. It came in April, the Passover month, by which time the rains were over and the trace down the west bank of the Jordan was again passable. It was then the preferred course for the pilgrims living about the Sea of Galilee and on to the north, and may have been used by the larger party with which Joseph and Mary and their Son chose to travel in the interest of greater safety. Or, from Nazareth they may have gone

Modern Nazareth

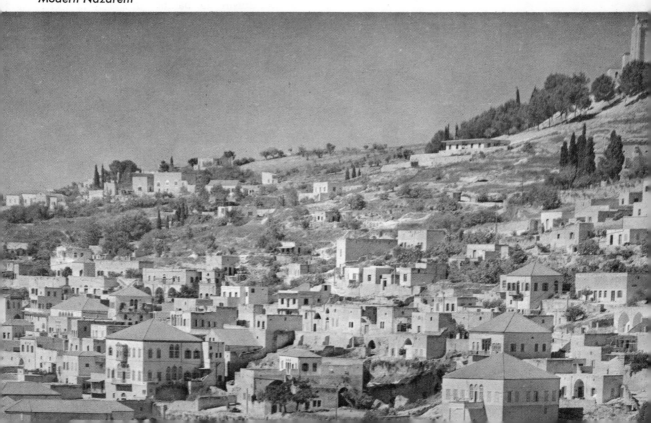

south to the Joppa road, and then on to Jerusalem.

At the very beginning of His ministry, Jesus probably used the Jordan Valley route down to receive His baptism. However, He could have forded the stream near Adamah and continued along the well-traveled road which paralleled the river on the eastern side. His Temptation came in the stark, forlorn wilderness which lies just to the west of the Dead Sea, and from it the Master returned to Bethabara, there enrolled five disciples, and then retraced His steps to Galilee.

He went first to Cana, the little city about two hours' walk north of Nazareth. Then, following the wedding feast, He took the path which presumably ran east through the hills to Magdala on the lake, and turned north along the shore road to Capernaum. This town, which lay upon the northwest curve of the Sea of Galilee, was to be the headquarters of His early ministry. Its remains have been uncovered at *Tell Hum,* which stands a little more than 2 miles from where the Jordan enters the lake.

From this bustling little city many recorded journeys, and quite likely others not mentioned, would originate. First among them was one to Jerusalem for the Passover of A.D. 27. This was undoubtedly made down the west side of the Jordan, and then up the long fifteen-mile climb from Jericho. Next came a swing through the Judaean countryside. It can have been quite an extensive one, for not too much else is recorded during the balance of that year. The places visited are completely unknown to us today. However, it probably terminated near the trail through the highlands, for the little party started north along it, and on this occasion traversed the customarily avoided Samaritan country. It was then that the celebrated meeting with the woman at the well took place, and a stop was made at neighboring Sychar. This particular journey extended as far as Cana, with a return to Nazareth about the time Jesus completed His 30th year.

After He was rejected by His home town early in A.D. 28, Jesus took the path which led over the shoulders of the mountain called the Horns of Hattin and dropped down to the lakeside at Tiberias. This latter town, built by Herod Antipas and named for the reigning Caesar, was strongly Gentile in population and spirit and so was carefully avoided by Jesus. It is very evident He applied His efforts almost with-

Via Dolorosa within the Old City of Jerusalem

out exception to centers of Jewish life and had little or nothing to do with areas which were chiefly Hellenistic, or Grecian, in population and outlook.

Turning north to Capernaum, He made a brief tour of the Galilean towns and then started on the yearly visit to keep the Passover. It was marked on this occasion by the healing Hill of Moreh, about 5 miles southeast of Nazareth. Following this third circuit of Galilee, there was an expedition over the lake into a rather uncertain area bearing a wide variety of names in the three Gospels: the country of the Gergesines, Gerasines or Gardarenes. Gergesa seems most probable as the original place, and its approximate location is now

The steep face of the traditional Mt. of Temptation, modern Jebel Quruntul

of the cripple at the pool of Bethesda. After the return to Capernaum, there was a retreat from the confusion of this combined trading center, manufacturing metropolis and fishing port, to the quiet of the hills. On the Mount of Beatitudes—traditionally the Horns of Hattin—twelve disciples were ordained and the magnificent Sermon on the Mount was preached.

Then there was a second, followed soon by a third, tour of Galilee. Few details have come down to us, except the dramatic raising of the widow's son at the gate of Nain. This was a small city on the hill known as *Jebel Dahi,* or placed near the Arab village of Kursi. As He returned from this phase of His ministry, Jesus was probably moving into His 32nd year.

This was about the time of His second rejection at Nazareth and the unaccompanied trial trip on which He had sent the twelve disciples. When they returned, the attempt was made to find a quiet respite in the desert area northeast of the Sea of Galilee, which resulted, instead, in the miraculous feeding of the 5000. There was a return from there to Capernaum and another wish to get away from the incessant crowds, where the instruction of the apostles

The Mount of Olives and Gethsemane seen from arcades in the Dome of the Rock compound in Jerusalem

would be less interrupted. This time the rural area along the border of Phoenicia was chosen, with a swing back through the section dominated by a number of Grecian cities and known as the Decapolis. This tour ended with a crossing from east to west of the northern portion of the lake, and a landing at the town Dalmanutha. Some scholars believe Magdala is meant, but the evidence is incomplete, and the location is still a mystery.

There was also a trip purportedly to the Jewish communities near the idolatrous city, enlarged and beautified by Philip the tetrarch and named Caesarea Philippi in honor of the Emperor Tiberius. Since it stood beside the main source of the Jordan at the foot of Mount Hermon, there has been a strong tendency to make this gigantic eminence the site of the Transfiguration. However, tradition has also shown strong partiality for Mount Tabor, far to the south near Nain and Nazareth. In fact, there have been three commemorative churches on this latter lofty hill; and still both sites are merely supposition. But from one or the other of them, or possibly from some unknown point, there was a return to Capernaum once again.

As the fall of A.D. 29 advanced, the Galilean ministry was at last completed, and Jesus started south, His purpose being to attend the

This small chapel stands on the traditional site of the Ascension on the Mount of Olives

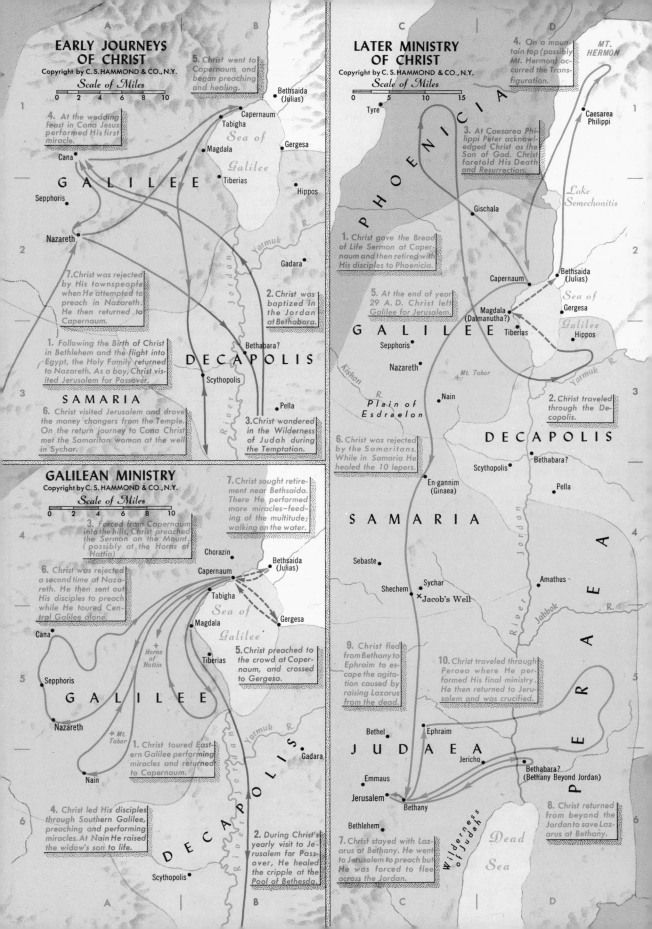

Feast of Tabernacles, which customarily fell in the latter part of October. The "former," or early, rains were then due and had perhaps begun and rendered the trail west of the Jordan impassable south of Scythopolis, which was the ancient Beth-shan. At least the Master this time passed again through the Samaritan country, where he was rejected.

For about two months He seems to have been in or about Jerusalem, staying much of the time at Bethany, which was located on the road from the city that swings first up over the Mount of Olives and then drops sharply down to Jericho. Toward the year-end, as He moved ahead into His 34th year, He took this very road down into the Jordan Valley and carried His ministry into the area just east of the river, then known as Peraea.

Here He spent the early months of A.D. 30, returning briefly to Bethany for the raising of Lazarus and possibly on another occasion. There were probably several days spent around Jerusalem, after which He headed back to Peraea again. This time His path may have taken a swing to the north, with a fording of the river quite a distance upstream from its mouth. The Ephraim mentioned in John 11:54 would surely have lain somewhere above Jerusalem and west of Jordan; but exactly where is still conjecture.

As He came back up the long grade from the valley in the closing days of March, A.D. 30, Jesus' extensive travels on this earth were virtually over, for He arrived at Bethany six days before the last Passover which He would celebrate. During each of these six days, He made the short trip back and forth to the city from this little town on the Mount of Olives. But on the Thursday evening following the "Last Supper," He was but part way along on His return to Bethany when He was seized by the Temple guard in the olive grove at Gethsemane. From then on His movements were highly restricted and, unfortunately, there is no absolute certainty of exactly where some of the stirring incidents of His last sad hours took place—even, in fact, where Calvary, that place called the Skull, actually was.

But although there are about fifteen localities mentioned in Bible text out of the many which He surely visited on His several trips through Galilee, there is little doubt of the meaning and import of what He taught there. And even though the precise spot on which the Crucifixion took place cannot be pointed out with certitude, there is little doubt in the minds of well over a half billion Christians concerning the full significance of all that lies behind that sublime death upon the Cross.

How many miles were involved in these journeys of Jesus? Not too many as distances are counted today. But what other travels in all history have so greatly benefited so many down the long corridor of the ages? What other journeys, since the world began, have had greater significance?

Bethphage, looking toward Dead Sea and mountains of Moab

XXII

THE FIRST CHRISTIAN MISSIONARIES

On that hazy spring morning when the risen Lord had met and breakfasted with His disciples by the lakeside in Galilee, He had given them very specific instructions. They were to return to Jerusalem and remain there until they had received power at the time the Holy Spirit was bestowed upon them. Then they were to be witnesses to their departed Master, not only in the Holy City itself, but throughout Judaea and Samaria and to the very ends of the earth (Luke 24:49 and Acts 1:8).

Almost immediately after Pentecost, which came apparently at the very beginning of June in the year A.D. 30, the primitive church began to take on visible form. Public worship was then quite evidently engrafted upon the synagogue service, and following the pattern which Jesus had so carefully set, the earliest efforts were spent in carrying the Gospel only to the Jewish people.

But Jerusalem was not a large city, neither was it nearly so important in Roman eyes as were numerous other places in Syria and Palestine. Thus there was a tendency within a short time to reach out into these communities and spread those religious beliefs rapidly taking form within the *ekklesia*—the assembly, or church—which the apostles had organized. And so it was that the missionary efforts, which have made the Church of Christ a most potent force in world affairs, began almost at the Church's inception. The report of these remarkable activities make the book, *The Acts of the Apostles,* one of the most fascinating in the Bible.

PHILIP Since events in this early church history are related in the order of their happening, the first Christian missionary seems to have been Philip, and not the Philip who was among the original followers of Jesus, but a newer convert, designated "the Evangelist." Having been chosen as a deacon to look after the welfare of the members in Jerusalem, his interests were quickly focused abroad after the converts had been scattered following Stephen's martyrdom (Acts 11:19).

He traveled up into Samaria, where he preached, did many miracles and made numerous converts, including the arch-sorcerer, Simon

the Great (Acts 8:4-25). On a second trip into ancient Philistia, he encountered and baptized the Ethiopian eunuch, whom many believe to have been the first Gentile convert to Christianity. He then carried his campaign to Azotus, and on as far as Caesarea, where he seems to have lived and worked for the remainder of his days (Acts 8:26-40; 21:8, 9).

PETER More effective were the efforts of the foremost among Jesus' early followers and the leading light of the first church at Jerusalem, Simon bar Jona, who had been given the surname Peter by his Master. His first ministry beyond the city and its environs took him north into Samaria, accompanied by John, the beloved disciple. There they brought word of the Holy Spirit and confirmed the believers in Him, preaching in many of the Samaritan communities.

It was probably in the following year that Peter, presumably alone this time, set out down the road toward Joppa, stopping in all the villages. At Lydda, an important trail junction, he healed a case of palsy and converted many there as well as throughout the Plain of Sharon. At Joppa he raised Tabitha, or Dorcas, to life and also experienced a most revealing vision.

In it God made it clear that His kingdom was to know no boundaries, and that the Church of Christ was to be taken to the Gentiles. Proceeding then to Caesarea, he there baptized Cornelius, the resident Roman centurion, together with his whole family, who were officially recognized by Peter as Christian believers. His act seems to have created a great stir among the hierarchy at Jerusalem, and it was evidently several years before this bold step, which had required Peter's abundant courage, became approved practice (Acts 9:32-11:2).

Meanwhile, this former gruff, impulsive fisherman, who had now acquired deep humility, seems to have made the journey up the coast to Syrian Antioch. This was the city where the followers of Christ were first known as *Christians,* and where the propriety of accepting Gentiles into the new faith became a moot question. Peter was now reconciled to their inclusion and soon defended his stand most resolutely and effectively at a council meeting in Jerusalem (Acts 15:1-14 and Gal. 2:11-15).

Later he seems to have been at Corinth (1 Cor. 1:12), and to have traveled rather widely, accompanied by his wife (1 Cor. 9:5). If he

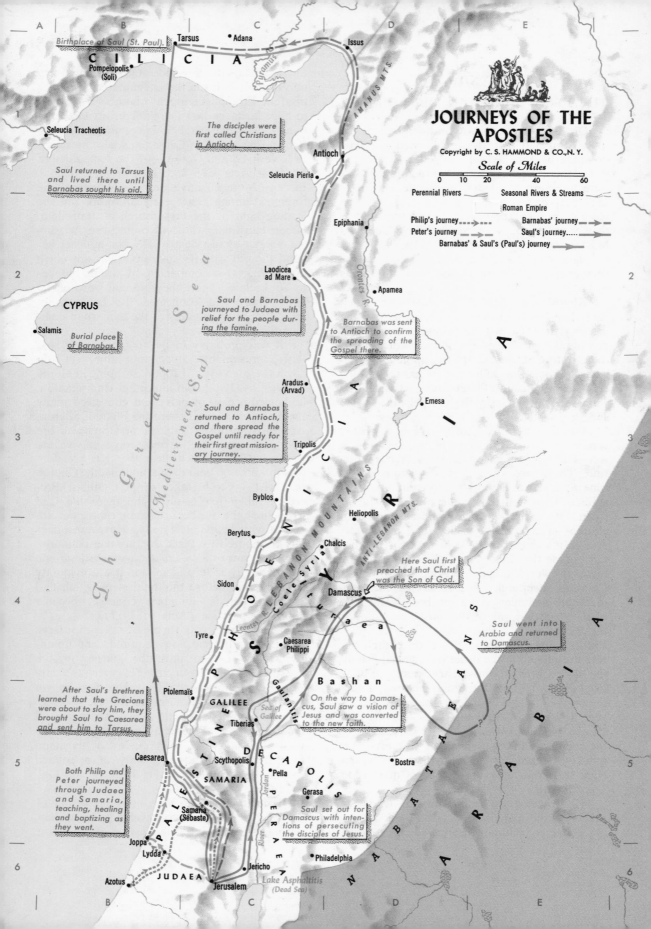

JOURNEYS OF THE APOSTLES

Copyright by C. S. HAMMOND & CO., N.Y.

Scale of Miles

0   10   20   40   60

Perennial Rivers .... Seasonal Rivers & Streams

Roman Empire

Philip's journey -------- Barnabas' journey ----▶

Peter's journey ----▶ Saul's journey ....

Barnabas' & Saul's (Paul's) journey ▶

A   B   C   D   E

Birthplace of Saul (St. Paul).

Tarsus   • Adana   Issus

Pompeiopolis
(Soli)

CILICIA

Seleucia Tracheotis

The disciples were
first called Christians
in Antioch.

Antioch

Saul returned to Tarsus
and lived there until
Barnabas sought his aid.

Seleucia Pieria

Epiphania

CYPRUS

Salamis

Burial place
of Barnabas.

Saul and Barnabas
journeyed to Judaea with
relief for the people during the famine.

Laodicea
ad Mare

Apamea

Barnabas was sent
to Antioch to confirm
the spreading of the
Gospel there.

Aradus
(Arvad)

Emesa

Saul and Barnabas
returned to Antioch,
and there spread the
Gospel until ready for
their first great missionary journey.

Tripolis

The Great Sea

(Mediterranean Sea)

Byblos

Heliopolis

PHOENICIA

LEBANON MOUNTAINS

Berytus

Chalcis

ANTI-LEBANON MTS.

Sidon

Coele Syria

Ituraea

Damascus

Here Saul first
preached that Christ
was the Son of God.

Tyre

Leontes R.

Caesarea
Philippi

Saul went into
Arabia and returned
to Damascus.

Bashan

After Saul's brethren
learned that the Grecians
were about to slay him, they
brought Saul to Caesarea
and sent him to Tarsus.

Ptolemaïs

GALILEE

Gaulanitis

Sea of
Galilee

Tiberias

On the way to Damas-
cus, Saul saw a vision of
Jesus and was converted
to the new faith.

NABATAEANS

ARABIA

Caesarea

Scythopolis

DECAPOLIS

Bostra

Both Philip and
Peter journeyed
through Judaea and
Samaria, teaching,
healing and baptizing as
they went.

SAMARIA

Pella

Gerasa

PALESTINE

PERAEA

Samaria
(Sébaste)

Jordan River

Saul set out for
Damascus with inten-
tions of persecuting
the disciples of Jesus.

Joppa

Lydda

Jericho

Philadelphia

Azotus

JUDAEA

Jerusalem

Lake Asphaltitis
(Dead Sea)

was not actually at Babylon (1 Pet. 5:13), then he was at the mystic Babylon which is Rome. And it was there most probably that he glorified God through a martyr's death (John 21:19). Beyond this, the Scriptures tell us nothing, yet tradition is rich with accounts of his other labors, fortunes and ministry.

BARNABAS Many feel that the Church began its material existence in the home of Mary, the mother of the John Mark to whom

tioch to aid in the work there among both Jews and Gentiles. Recalling Saul's ability to preach, Barnabas went north to Tarsus and persuaded this former persecutor of the Christians to return with him and aid in this missionary endeavor. There they worked as a team during a whole year (Acts 11:19-26).

At the end of that time, they set off together to bear a special offering to Jerusalem. Returning shortly with a third man, John Mark,

Roman theater in Amman, the Philadelphia of New Testament time

the writing of the second Gospel is attributed (Acts 12:12). She is reported to have had a nephew named Joses, or Joseph, who had come from the island of Cyprus and had served for a time as a Levite, probably at the Temple. An early convert, he had turned his wealth over to the apostles, who had given him the new surname of Barnabas (Acts 4: 36, 37).

The next mention of him in Scripture is his defense of Saul, then a new convert (Acts 9:27). Several years later he was sent to An-

they set out on what is generally considered to be the Apostle Paul's (Saul) first missionary journey, and which will be covered in the next section. Mark left them at Perga, and later, when another trip was being planned, Saul and Barnabas had a falling out over whether young Mark, the latter's cousin, should accompany them. As Saul headed into Asia Minor, Barnabas took Mark with him to Cyprus. This was perhaps the extent of Barnabas' journeys. At least no others are recorded, and tradition has it that he was ultimately buried there on the island which had been his early home.

SAUL (PAUL) This man, to be the great apostle to the Gentiles, was born in Tarsus, evidently of a pious Jewish family, and was sent to Jerusalem when fairly young to attend the famous school conducted by the celebrated rabbi, Gamaliel. Thus his journeys began some years before he started to employ his missionary efforts in behalf of the Church. One of the most remarkable of them was the trip to Damascus upon which his startling conversion took place. At once he preached his new faith with great energy and was forced to escape from the city in a basket (Acts 9:1-8, 25).

He then took refuge for a time somewhere in Arabia, possibly at Petra, the fabulous Nabataean capital, meditating upon the great changes which had encompassed him. He was once again, perhaps only briefly, at Damascus, finally returning after an absence of three years to Jerusalem. But the Christians there were still afraid of him because he had advocated their persecution before, and he was sent off home to Tarsus to see what he might accomplish in that area. It was here, after about six years of which there is no record, that Barnabas drew his tremendous abilities back into the main stream of Christian activities. He had been well prepared through his past travels for far greater ones yet to come.

JOHN, who was associated with Peter in and about the Holy City at the outset, and who made the trip up into Samaria with him in the early days, seems then to have remained at Jerusalem for some time. He was surely a pillar of strength there during the long series of persecutions that beset the infant Church. And he was definitely one of the apostles and elders who extended the warm handclasp of fellowship to Saul, now called Paul, as he came to headquarters to make his report following his first full-scale missionary undertaking (Acts 15:6 and Gal. 2:9).

Later in life, after the spade work had been done by Paul, and very likely after this latter's martyrdom, John appears to have taken charge of the churches of Asia. Tradition makes him a bishop, with his see centered at Ephesus. From here he is supposed to have been carried to exile on the island of Patmos in the Aegean Sea during the persecution under Domitian, where he wrote the Book of Revelation —the *Apocalypse*— in A.D. 95. Freed soon after the accession of the Emperor Nerva the following year, he is supposed to have returned to his diocese in Ephesus, dying there during the reign of Trajan (A.D. 98-117). He was perhaps the last of the twelve original followers of their Lord to die, and while not an extensive traveler, certainly a most faithful servant. Three of the more prominent of the apostolic fathers—Polycarp, Papias and Ignatius—were his pupils.

LUKE, probably a Greek of Antioch, is thought to have been first a convert to Judaism, and then, through Paul's ministrations, to Christianity. Though he has long been considered the author of both the Third Gospel and the Book of Acts, he himself is mentioned but three times in Bible text (Col. 4:14; Philem. 24; 2 Tim. 4:11). This might tend to give the impression that he had only a very minor part in the early missionary effort.

However, Paul in the above references indicates that Luke was with him in Rome, and in the second of them speaks of him as a fellow-worker. Consequently it has been assumed that at those points in the description of Paul's missionary journeys where the words "we" and "us" are used, Luke indicates he was with the apostle (Acts 16:10-17; 20:5-21:18; 27:1-28:16).

St. Stephen's Gate in the wall surrounding the Old City of Jerusalem

Eastern Gate at Damascus leading to the "Street called Straight"

Hence it seems that they were together on Paul's second journey from Troas as far as Philippi, where they may have parted, or perhaps Luke remained behind. They came together again at this same city on Paul's third trip; and Luke seems to have stood by in Jerusalem during the two years Paul was imprisoned at Caesarea. From there he accompanied his friend to Rome and probably was with him until his martyrdom. The time and manner of Luke's death, however, are not known.

JOHN MARK This man, who caused the disruption between Paul and Barnabas, is thought to have been a convert of Peter. Fortunately Paul's ill will toward him and his cousin was transient, and he evidently remained active in early Church affairs. It is possible he spent the next ten years in Jerusalem, or even in Cyprus with Barnabas. But at the end of that time he was in Rome, adding his salutations to those of Paul and Luke in the Epistles to the Colossians and to Philemon (Col. 4:10; Philem. 24).

From the former reference, it appears that he was soon to be in Asia Minor. It is even possible he met Peter in the east (1 Pet. 5:13), but it is presumed that it was at Rome where the Second Gospel was written. He certainly contributed his share of travel needed for the spread of the new faith and may have continued missionary activities after Peter was martyred, for the time of his death is uncertain.

TIMOTHY, TITUS, SILAS AND APOLLOS

The Book of Acts could have been as long as the New Testament itself and still not have answered half the questions which might readily be asked about the men who first carried Christianity into large sections of Asia and Europe during that first critical century. How many long miles did the beloved Timothy walk after setting forth from his home at Lystra in Lycaonia with Paul? Then, as the latter's apostolic deputy, he seems to have ranged back and forth between Rome and Ephesus, relieving the older man of much enervating travel.

Titus, too, appears to have covered much ground after he is first encountered while accompanying Paul and Barnabas to Jersualem from Antioch. He was also for a time Paul's deputy, and his appearances in such widely scattered places as Ephesus, Corinth, Macedonia, Crete and Dalmatia, indicate that he spent countless hours, making his way, staff in hand, over the Roman roads, or depending upon fitful winds to carry him from port to port.

There was also Silas, member of the Jerusalem church, sent first to Antioch, and later taken by Paul, in place of Mark, on that second memorable journey. They were in prison together in Philippi and also worked together in many cities. And at a later time, under his full name, Silvanus, he seems to have borne Peter's first epistle to its destination (1 Pet. 5:12).

There is still another traveler, whose activities are not too thoroughly detailed. He was the Alexandrian Jew, Apollos, eloquent and zealous, who in very early days passed through Asia Minor and Greece converting many. At Ephesus he met and worked with another energetic pair of wayfarers, the tent maker, Aquila, and his good wife, Priscilla. Paul had great confidence in Apollos, and some scholars have believed that he became the author of the stirring Epistle to the Hebrews.

It surely took much walking and dedicated preaching to introduce the new-born Christian faith to what constituted the civilized world in the years immediately following Christ's death on Calvary. But happily this admirable effort was not in vain, and to this day we owe a great debt of gratitude to these first true missionaries.

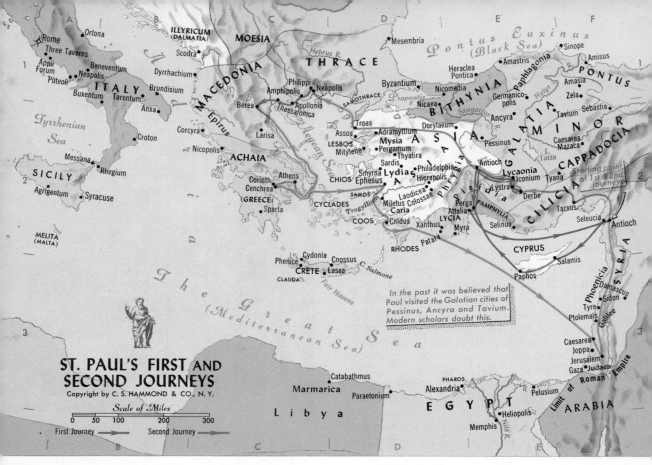

ST. PAUL'S FIRST AND SECOND JOURNEYS

Copyright by C. S. HAMMOND & CO., N. Y.

Scale of Miles

0   50   100   200   300

First Journey ⟶   Second Journey ⟶

In the past it was believed that
Paul visited the Galatian cities of
Pessinus, Ancyra and Tavium.
Modern scholars doubt this.

XXIII

PAUL'S FIRST AND SECOND
MISSIONARY JOURNEYS

Barnabas was a good and zealous disciple
of Jesus Christ and filled with the Holy Spirit.
Yet he was but one man in a bustling city
where the missionary church he was helping to
conduct was growing by leaps and bounds. He
needed help badly, and especially from one
who could expound, explain and argue the fine
points of this new faith to the full satisfaction of
the controversial minds—Jewish or Grecian—
which must be influenced. What should he do?

Less than 150 miles away—say, five vigorous days of walking—and around the end of an
arm of the Mediterranean in the very next province of Cilicia, was the man he needed. His
name was Saul, and he was full of fire and
thunderings since his startling conversion in a
noon-day vision on the Damascus road, but
he was still feared in Jerusalem because of his
former brutal persecution of Jesus' followers.
But here at Antioch he could be most helpful.
So Barnabas temporarily abandoned his flock
and started northward.

In what was then no doubt a lovely and
sightly city at the foot of the Taurus Mountains,
he found the brilliant Benjamite he sought,
probably living by his trade of tent maker and
presumably converting an occasional man or
woman in this university center much given to
Stoic philosophy. Whether Barnabas' persuasive powers were particularly compelling, or
Saul longed for more constructive work is
not certain, but in any event they were soon
both in Syrian Antioch, actively building the
House of the Lord.

A year of their combined efforts, and it
was a thriving church, where the followers of
Jesus were first known as *Christians* (Acts
11:22-26). And this new faith had now found
one of its truly dominant figures. The thirty-
six-year-old Jew, named for Israel's very first
king, was making plans and getting ready to set
off on a series of the most remarkable missionary
activities of which we have record. When the
time was right, the first of the trips, undertaken
in company with Barnabas, was carried out at
the direction of the Holy Spirit.

Leaving the handsomely located city in the
hills, they took the road which passed through

140

Antioch from the east, and followed it 16 miles to the port of Seleucia, which lay five miles north of the mouth of the Orontes River, away from the mud banks deposited by that stream as it entered the Mediterranean.

There they found passage on a ship headed for Cyprus, the eastern tip of which mountainous island lay about 80 miles to the southwest. Across this strip of open water their little ship would have crept cautiously, and then hugged the southern shore for another 50 miles to their destination at Salamis.

They preached for a time in the synagogue of this important town, assisted by young John Mark. Next they made their way to Paphos, the Roman capital of the island, which lay at the southwest corner of this very rugged, 3570 square mile block of land. They probably went overland, preaching as they went, taking one or the other of two possible routes, either of which would have been about 100 miles long.

At Paphos they were called upon to preach their message before the proconsul, Sergius Paulus. This official seems to have been almost on the point of conversion and baptism, when he was dissuaded by the court habitué, the sorcerer, Elymus. By way of rebuke, Saul called down temporary blindness upon this meddling deceiver, after which the Roman deputy "believed."

It was then decided to go next into the small Roman province of Pamphylia. The people among whom they would work from then on would be principally Gentiles. Thus it seemed prudent for this newer member of their little party, who was by now becoming its leader, to put away his given name of Saul and henceforth use the Gentile designation of Paul.

Taking ship at Paphos, the three headed northwest across the sea to the tiny country made up of a narrow strip between the towering Taurus Mountains and the Mediterranean. Presumably they landed at Attalia and then moved inland about 10 miles to Perga, famous for its nearby shrine to the goddess Artemis (Diana), who was known as the *Queen of Perga*.

Here, for some unexplained reason, John Mark parted with them and headed back to Jerusalem. Paul and Barnabas then set off north over the mountains through Phrygia to Pisidian Antioch, chief city of the Roman province

Syrian Antioch, modern Turkish Antakya, Orontes River in the foreground

of Galatia. There Paul preached the first sermon of which we have a record (Acts 13:16-41). It touched off such violent feeling, however, that the two missionaries were expelled from the town.

Moving east to Iconium, their many conversions there merely resulted in further persecution, and they then turned south through Lycaonia to Lystra and then to Derbe. At the first of these important cities the miraculous cure of the cripple made the heathen populace attempt to worship the two missionaries as if they were the Roman gods Jupiter and Mercury. And at Lystra, the very estimable Timothy was presumably converted (Acts 16:1-3). But feeling flared up here, too, and Paul was stoned and left by the mob for dead (Acts 14:19).

He recovered, however; and after working at Derbe, this brave pair retraced their steps through the very same cities where they had been so roughly used. They visited each town all the way back to Perga and strengthened the several churches they had founded. Then, sailing from Attalia, they returned to Antioch in Syria.

This meant that the first journeys of the great Apostle to the Gentiles had been completed. He and Barnabas had in no sense been wayfaring, for their steps had been under the direction of the Holy Spirit and so arranged that they might carry the Word to areas directly to the west of those lands in which the Gospel had previously been preached. Churches were

now being founded at the larger centers along the network of Roman roads, and from which points the influence would spread. A devout Jew, trained and steeped in Judaism, yet born, reared, and widely experienced in the Gentile world, and thus with a very broad outlook, was heading up this missionary activity. The future seemed promising indeed.

in Jerusalem seems to have been A.D. 49.

It was perhaps in this same year that Paul proposed a second tour to Barnabas, only to break with his staunch companion over whether or not to take John Mark with them. Choosing Silas, or Silvanus, instead, he set off overland to the north, visiting churches first in Syria, and then swinging west through Cilicia to Taurus,

The Taurus Mountains near Tarsus

But there came a threatened schism in this burgeoning faith. Certain converted Pharisees were demanding that the Gentiles accept circumcision, despite the Lord having revealed to Peter the fact that the non-Jewish converts were not to be bound by the full burden of the Mosaic Law. So great was the disturbance at Antioch, that the church there decided to send Paul, Barnabas and others to clear up this question with the apostles and elders in Jerusalem. It was truly a serious threat, but, fortunately, the crisis was safely passed. During it, Paul had won his point, having laid down the foundations of Salvation; and, while hatred and hostility would be directed against him from certain quarters, the way was now opened for carrying Christ to *all* peoples. The time of this important meeting of Paul and the other apostles

and then by way of the famous defile in the Taurus Mountains, the Cilician Gates, he went on to Derbe. The apostle was now once again in Lycaonia, where his life had been sought on the previous visit. But he and Silas soon moved on to Lystra, where they were joined by Timothy. They then seem to have gone as far as Iconium and Pisidian Antioch, but beyond this latter place the next leg of their journey is open to question.

It is reported that Paul was prohibited by the Spirit from preaching in the Roman province of Asia, and that he was also forbidden to enter Bithynia, which lay just below the Black Sea. Thus they seem to have made no stops in the next province to the west, Mysia, until they came to one of its chief seaports, Troas. It was here that the Spirit in a vision directed that their missionary efforts be carried over into Europe.

Here, too, Luke joined them, and by ship they crossed the upper end of the Aegean Sea to Neapolis in Macedonia. Then they moved inland by road 10 miles to the most important city in that district, Philippi. Here they planted the first church in Europe, and one which continued to be very dear to the apostle.

Luke remained behind, while the other three moved on west to Thessalonica, a seaport on the Thermaic Gulf. Paul labored valiantly there, but persecution finally forced him on to the southwest another 50 miles to Berea. There he met with considerable success, despite the fact his preaching was all done in the synagogue, and finally continued on his way to Athens.

He was, perhaps, disappointed by his indifferent success in the sophisticated city and soon moved along to Corinth. This was the great commercial port through which passed the traffic between the two major sections of Greece, and which also handled much of the booming trade between Asia and the West. It was one of the great crossroads in the Roman Empire, and here Paul lived for a year and a half plying his trade as a tent maker. He made his home with a fellow craftsman, Aquila, and his wife, Priscilla, both dedicated Jewish Christians.

There, too, he preached Christ regularly, first in the local synagogue, and then, after op-position arose, in the adjoining home of a Gentile, one Titus Justus. While in Corinth, he also wrote the two Epistles to the Thessalonians. But the local Jews at last stirred up much hostility and did their best to make trouble for Paul with the Roman authorities. Yet the new proconsul, Gallio, who arrived at his new post about midsummer of A.D. 51, refused to judge the dispute and permitted Paul to go on unhampered to one of his major accomplishments here at Corinth.

Realizing at length that there was much territory yet to be covered, the apostle finally decided to turn again to the east. Taking Aquila and Priscilla as his traveling companions, he boarded a ship sailing to Ephesus, some 250 miles directly east across the Aegean Sea. There they met the ardent Apollos, preaching fervently, but somewhat faultily, and hurriedly instructed him more perfectly in acceptable Christian doctrine.

Here Paul preached in the synagogue for a short time. But he had a report he was anxious to make to the elders at Jerusalem, and promising faithfully to return, he left the Ephesian church in charge of Aquila and Priscilla and set out by ship for Caesarea. From there he evidently made a fairly hasty trip to the Holy City and, having acquainted the authorities with his fine accomplishments in Europe, he returned once again to Syrian Antioch. His second great missionary undertaking had been completed.

Small craft in the harbor of Athens, Greece

XXIV
PAUL'S LATTER JOURNEY
AND TRIP TO ROME

Paul spent possibly a year at Antioch before entering upon his third missionary undertaking, which seems to have begun in the year A.D. 54. He was concerned for the churches that he had helped to found in Galatia and Phrygia, so he set out overland, presumably retracing his steps in the early part of his previous tour. Having completed his task of "strengthening all the disciples," he went on west from Pisidian Antioch to Ephesus.

Since this most influential city was the capital of Asia, and Paul now established himself there, it would appear that the Holy Spirit had completely removed the ban on preaching the Gospel within that province which had prevented working there five years before. For three years Ephesus would be the center of his ardent labors, and he must have come to know well this place of surpassing splendor, which had been built anew by the Emperor Tiberius following the devastating earthquake in A.D. 29. Besides a large stadium, a fine theater, baths

and an excellent public library, it was the site, too, of the magnificent temple of Diana which ranked as one of the seven wonders of the ancient world.

For three months Paul preached in the local synagogue, and for the next two years in a lecture hall belonging to one Tyrannus, also within the city. He made many converts and found friends among the leading people, but he also acquired his usual quota of fervid enemies. Probably it was at this time when trouble broke out in Galatia, and, to correct the situation, he penned and sent to the faithful there his Epistle to the Galatians. Questions were posed, too, by the church far away in the opposite direction at Corinth, and to it went one of his famous letters, but which has unfortunately not come down to us. Since more serious dissension continued to prevail there, he found it necessary to write the missile known to us as First Corinthians. There are even some scholars who believe he made a hurried trip to that city to bring harmony out of discord (2 Cor. 12:14; 13:1). But, more probably, the journey was made by Titus, for the latter did go there as Paul's deputy.

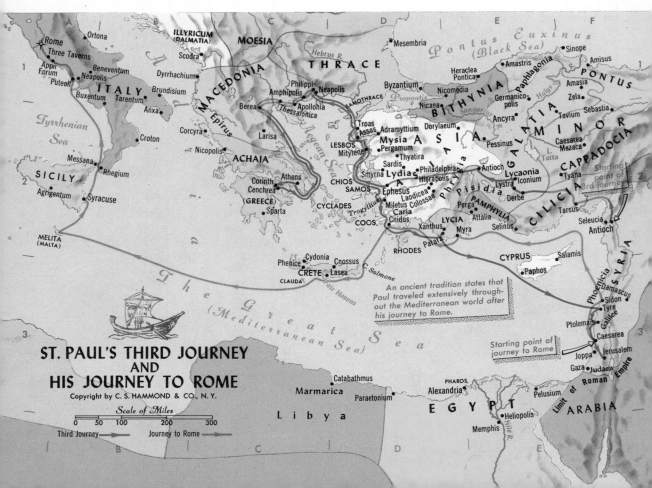

An ancient tradition states that Paul traveled extensively throughout the Mediterranean world after his journey to Rome.

Starting point of journey to Rome

ST. PAUL'S THIRD JOURNEY
AND
HIS JOURNEY TO ROME

Copyright by C. S. HAMMOND & CO., N.Y.

Scale of Miles

0   50   100   200   300

Third Journey ⟶   Journey to Rome ⟶

The Appian Way near Rome

Finally craftsmen, making tiny silver models of the temple of Diana for sale to pilgrims to the local shrine at Ephesus, found their business so endangered by the apostle's fiery preaching, that they rioted against him. This upsetting experience made Paul's position in the Asian capital most uncertain. So he sent Timothy and another disciple, Erastus, on into Macedonia ahead of him and moved up the coast to Troas, where he had arranged to meet Titus, who was supposed to bring word of how affairs stood at Corinth. But he was not there in the port-city, and so, after a reasonable wait, the apostle pushed on into Europe again, making his first call at the church at Philippi.

But somewhere along the way Titus did catch up with him, bringing cheering news—the situation at Corinth had finally adjusted itself. Paul then wrote Second Corinthians and sent this letter on ahead, following along through Thessalonica and Berea, at last arriving in the great trading city for a personal visit. There he seems to have passed a part of the winter of A.D. 57-58. Irrespective of what this second period in residence may have done for Corinthian affairs, it did produce a document of profound value to the Chrisitan Church—the important Epistle to the Romans. This, probably the greatest of his instructive messages, forcefully presents the doctrinal way of Salvation, and shows decisively the Gospel power of God for the saving of *all* who believe.

Since it has been indicated that many of the great apostle's activities had been carried out by the guidance of the Holy Spirit, it is quite probable that this Eternal Spirit had already shown Paul that his labors would culminate in Rome. The church previously founded there by his close friends and former associates was even then calling to him, and he had a great desire to visit it. But a most charitable duty first demanded his immediate attention.

He had induced the Gentile churches to make offerings for the relief of the poor Christians of Judaea, and he now proposed to take these funds to the Mother Church as a clear indication of the good intents of the congregations he had added to the fold. He was just about to set out for Jerusalem, sailing to Syria on the first leg of the journey, when a plot hatched by the local Jews forced him to change his plans and return to Macedonia.

Several had joined his party by the time he reached Philippi, and there he met Luke. Sending the remainder on ahead, he and the evangelist lingered with the Philippians until after the Passover. Then sailing across to Troas, they rejoined the others and stayed in the city for a week. It was here that Eutychus, often called the "church sleeper," fell from the third floor of a building during Paul's lengthy evening discourse, and was picked up dead, only to be miraculously restored to life by the apostle (Acts 20:9, 10).

The party now made its way down the island-studded coast, with stops at Assos, Mitylene and Samos, finally coming to Miletus, which was about 36 miles south of Ephesus. Since he still hesitated to visit that city in person, Paul asked the elders of the church to meet with him at this little seaport. There, in stirring words, he took most affectionate leave of them (Acts 20:18-35). Later, from captivity in Rome, he would send them his Epistle to the Ephesians.

He then set off again toward the south, the vessel making stops at the island of Coos, and next at Rhodes. It was at this latter place that the 105-foot statue of Helios, another of the seven wonders of the world, stood with its feet supposedly planted on the opposite shores at the entrance to the harbor. From there they swung east to Patara, on the coast of Lycia, where a change in ships was made. The Phoenician craft which he had now boarded sailed west of Cyprus and landed the party at Tyre. There they were well received, and the members of the church were loath to let Paul leave them.

But after a week's stay, the ship continued on down to Ptolemaïs, and then to Caesarea.

Air view of modern Rome with the Vatican City in the foreground

At this latter city Paul and his companions were entertained by Philip the Evangelist, and it was at his home that the prophet Agabus made a most distressing forecast. Binding his own hands and feet with the apostle's girdle, he foretold that the Jews would similarly bind this zealous missionary and hand him over to the Gentiles. He had been urged at Tyre not to go to Jerusalem, and here was a second unmistakable warning. But he could not be dissuaded. With his arrival there, he can be said to have completed his third missionary journey.

His reception by the Mother Church was most warm, and after having heard the report of his ministry among the Gentiles, the whole council praised God. But, since the Jewish Christians in many cases were still opposed to him, he was asked to demonstrate his own continuing fidelity to Judaic customs by taking part with certain others in a Nazarite vow at the Temple. During the ceremony various Jews from Asia raised a great tumult, accused him of bringing Gentiles into the sacred precincts, and would have slain him had he not most fortunately fallen into the hands of the Romans. Even then they plotted to kill him stealthily. So since he had shown himself to be a Roman citizen, the commander of the garrison at Jerusalem, Claudius Lysias, sent him under strong guard to Caesarea, along with a letter to the procurator, Felix, turning the whole matter over to the latter. Here he remained a prisoner for the next two years.

Despite violent allegations by the Jews, Felix refused to prefer any charges against him and gave him a reasonable amount of freedom in allowing friends to call upon him in Herod's castle, where he was detained. While the procurator seems to have trembled at the apostle's vehement preaching, he was very much in hopes Paul or his friends would produce a sizable bribe with which to purchase his liberty. But since it was not forthcoming, the apostle was still jailed when a new procurator, Porcius Festus, at last arrived in Judaea.

This man, hoping to please the Jews, sought to persuade Paul to go to Jerusalem to be tried by the Sanhedrin. But knowing it would certainly mean his death, the apostle asserted his rights as a Roman citizen and appealed his case to Caesar. But before he could start on his way to stand trial in Rome, he was forced to appear before a visiting dignitary, the former King of Chalcis, and now ruler of two tetrarchies, Herod Agrippa II, great-grandson of the founder of the Herodian dynasty. Although the original Greek text merely hints at it this king had a real contempt for all such disturbers of the peace. Still, Agrippa had to admit that the prisoner brought before him had committed no crime and could be set free had he not already appealed to Caesar.

It was apparently early in the fall of A.D. 60 that Paul was started on his historic trip to the city on the Tiber. Along with other prisoners, he was placed aboard a ship under the charge of the centurion, Julius, and started on that fateful voyage, Luke and a Thessalonian named Aristarchus being among his fellow-voyagers. This first vessel, a coasting ship of Adramyttium, took them only as far as Myra in Lycia, after having made a single stop at Sidon.

There they shifted over to an Alexandrian merchantman, bound for Italy. But the season was already well advanced, and the winds proved most unfavorable. Forced off at first to the northwest, they next had to run to the south, and with great difficulty rounded Cape Salmone at the eastern end of Crete. Working their way gingerly along that island's southern shore, they finally found anchorage in the sheltered bay called Fair Havens in the Bible, today known as Kali Limenes, near ancient Lasea. It was now mid-October, the end of the then safe-sailing season, and Paul counseled remaining where they were. But the ship's owner wished to push on to Phoenix (Phenice), furthur along the coast, where there was a safer harbor, and the centurion agreed to this move.

But they were hardly around the headland beyond Fair Havens when violent winds from the northeast struck them and sent them scudding to the westward. Fearing at first that they might run aground on the small island of Clauda, they did manage to swing below it. Then the tempest really seized hold of them, and the gale had them at its mercy for two full weeks, forcing them on and on to the westward. All aboard began to give up hope, that is, all save Paul, whom the Lord's angel had assured that not a single soul among them would suffer death. Eventually, on the fourteenth night, the sounding lead began to show shallower water— they were evidently approaching land. So they cast over all four of their anchors as darkness settled down, and with great patience and fear prepared to wait out the dark hours.

When at last daylight came, they could make out a small bay with a strip of beach not far ahead of them. So the anchors were quickly cut away, the foresail hoisted, and they drove in toward the strip of sand. The ship soon ran aground in the breakers, and under their crushing force began to fall apart. There was thus nothing left to do but leap overboard, which they all did, and, as Paul had forecast, reached the shore safely.

Where were they? It developed they had been shipwrecked upon the island of Melita, or Malta as it is known today, which lay just under 60 miles south of the far larger island of Sicily. There they were forced to stay for the next three months. Fortunately the people of the island, although spoken of as "barbarians" in the original Greek since they were neither Greeks nor Romans, proved to be most kindly and hospitable, and Paul, by his many remarkable deeds, gained special honor among them.

Finally, as the season became more favorable again, a ship of Alexandria, which had wintered in the harbor, took the castaways aboard and headed north for Italy. It made a stop at Syracuse on the island of Sicily, another at Rhegium at the toe of the Italian "boot," and then moved up across the Tyrrhenian Sea to Puteoli, a few miles west of the modern city of Naples. This was the chief port for vessels from North Africa, Egypt and the East. There Paul found a group of Christians, with whom he remained a week. But some of the ship's company had apparently moved on ahead, so word reached the Christian community in Rome that the great apostle was approaching. Consequently he had gone but part of the distance up the famous Appian Way to the city, when he met the first of two welcoming committees at the Appii Forum, or the Market of Appius, forty odd miles below his destination. Then, about ten miles further on at the Three Taverns was the second group anxiously awaiting him. There was no doubt but that Christ's followers were happy indeed to have him with them at the Roman capital.

With respect to what happened next, and just how Paul reached the city, and into whose custody he was delivered is a matter of speculation. This much, however, is certain. He was soon placed in some degree of military confinement, and chained to a soldier for safekeeping. Surely appeals were promptly made to the emperor in his behalf. Yet without friends in high places at court, or lacking payments to officials needed to expedite the matter, the hearing of one's case by the exalted ruler of the empire was a slow business indeed.

Since his "imprisonment" promised to last for a long time, the apostle seems to have hired a house in which to live. The last sentence of Luke's account tells that he continued in this manner for two whole years, and also emphasizes the fact that he pursued his missionary activities here in Rome unhampered. There is an ancient tradition that after two years Paul was released from prison, traveled extensively throughout the Mediterranean, was imprisoned again and finally executed in Rome at a later date. But in respect to these matters the Bible is silent. Even if Paul did make further journeys we are unable to trace them on the map.

XXV
HEROD, WHO PERSECUTED THE CHURCH

After accompanying the apostles, and especially Paul, on their arduous trips into a wider world to which they brought the Gospel, we now return to the Palestinian lands in order to follow the further history of the reigning house of the Herods.

Four men who had the designation of Herod are mentioned in the New Testament. The first among them is Herod the Great, the founder of the dynasty. The second is his son, Herod Antipas, who will be discussed below. Then there are his grandson, Herod Agrippa I, and his great-grandson, Herod Agrippa II. Both will have further attention.

Herod Antipas, better known to Bible readers as "Herod the tetrarch," is of course the badly henpecked ruler who permitted the cruel murder of John the Baptist. During his youthful student days in Rome, he had fallen madly in love with the wife of his own half brother. Having divorced a lawful previous wife, a Nabataean Arab princess, he now wed this Herodias, an unprincipled, designing woman, who had seen in this newer husband greater promise of riches and fame than the somewhat older Herod had offered.

She proved to be a masculine, headstrong creature, while her husband was a weak, peace-loving man. Thus she dominated him about as completely and as unfortunately as Jezebel had prevailed over Ahab. She it was who craftily brought about the death of the Baptist, who had questioned her morality and she would, a few years later, drive her husband to almost lose his own head because of her consuming jealousy, as will be disclosed.

Antipas had come to some wealth and prominence largely because another of his half brothers, Aristobulus, had been executed by their suspicious, irascible father. This departed Herodian prince had left five children behind him, the second of the three sons being known as Agrippa. His widowed mother, another strong-willed woman named Berenice, of whom he stood in some awe, managed to send him to Rome for an education and keep him amply supplied with spending money. He consequently became quite a wastrel, yet he craftily employed his funds—when he had them—in making himself highly popular with influential people.

Through his mother and his aunt, Salome, he became the companion of the emperor's sons, while the brilliant Antonia, daughter of Mark Antony and mother of the emperor Germanicus, was his patron and defender. He was especially friendly with Drusus, the ruling Tiberius' elder son, and also well acquainted with the younger Claudius, whose hesitancy in speech and whose retiring ways had earned for him the reputation of being a somewhat backward boy.

But with Drusus' death in A.D. 23, Rome lost much of its appeal for Agrippa. Then his own mother's passing stopped his income, and he soon headed for home, leaving behind him a host of angry creditors from whom he had borrowed heavily.

For a time he lived in Idumaea, found life excessively hard, and would, it is claimed, have attempted suicide had it not been for his resolute wife. He would also have been in most desperate straits had not his uncle, Herod the tetrarch, come to his aid. He appointed his nephew to a government post, provided him with a small income, and made life somewhat uncomfortable for the younger man by assuring all who would listen how big-hearted he really

The "Treasury" at Petra, built by the great Nabataean king, Aretas, father-in-law of Herod Antipas

A   B   C   D   E   F

P H O E N I C I A

The Great Sea
(Mediterranean Sea)

MOUNT LEBANON
Leontes R.

Sidon

Sarepta

Tyre

Ecdippa

Ptolemaïs

MT. CARMEL

Dora

Caesarea

Plain of Sharon

Apollonia

Joppa

Lydda

Jamnia
Gazara
Ekron
Azotus

Ascalon

Anthedon
Gaza

Gerar

Ziklag

Beersheba

IDUMAEA

JUDAEA

Beth-gubrin
Marisa
Beth-zur
Adora
Hebron

Emmaus
Beth-horon

Jerusalem

Bethlehem
Herodium

En-gedi

Masada

Lake Asphaltitis (Dead Sea)

MT. HERMON

ABILENE

Chalcis

Abila

Damascus

PANIAS
Dan • Caesarea Philippi

ITURAEA

TRACHONITIS

Agrippa received the tetrarchies of Philip and Lysanias in 37 A.D.

Cadasa (Kedesh)

Lake Semechonitis

Gischala

GALILEE
Capernaum
Bethsaida (Julias)

Seleucia

GAULANITIS

BATANAEA

Raphana

Jotapata
Taricheae (Magdala)
Gergesa
Sea of Galilee
Tiberias
Hippos
Gamala

Sepphoris
Philoteria
Dion
Kanatha

Nazareth

Plain of Esdraelon
Nahon R.

Yarmuk R.
Abila
AURANITIS
Gadara
Edrei

Scythopolis

En-gannim (Ginaea)

River Jordan

Pella

Agrippa received the tetrarchy of Antipas (Galilee and Peraea) in 39 A.D.

DECAPOLIS

Bostra

SAMARIA

Sebaste (Samaria)

Shechem
Mt. Gerizim

Gerasa

Antipatris

Thamna
Gophna

Phasaelis
Archelais

Bethel

Jericho

Jabbok R.

P E R A E A

Philadelphia

Julius (Livias, Beth-haram)

Heshbon

Machaerus

Agrippa died after a sudden and dramatic illness at Caesarea in 44 A.D.

Agrippa was given Judaea and Samaria by Claudius in 41 A.D.

Agrippa persecuted the disciples of Christ, as recorded in Acts 12:1-19.

Arnon R.

N A B A T A E A N S

Kir-moab (Kir-haresheth)

Zered R.

DOMINIONS OF HEROD AGRIPPA I
37 to 44 A.D.

Copyright by C. S. HAMMOND & CO., N.Y.

Scale of Miles
0   5   10   20   30   40

Perennial Rivers ....
Seasonal Rivers & Streams —
Capitals ....
Cities of the Decapolis ☐

Kingdom of Herod Agrippa I -41 A.D.
Decapolis
Autonomous city state of Ascalon
Roman province of Syria

was in so amply providing for this spendthrift.

Agrippa finally broke with his uncle, and in A.D. 36, about six years after Jesus' crucifixion, he set off to Rome, his purpose being to bring charges against the man who had befriended him. He cleverly worked his way back into the good graces of the Emperor Tiberius. Then a foolish remark, to the effect the old emperor had lived too long, landed him in prison, where he remained until Tiberius died. A very strange happening which according to legend took place at the prison camp perhaps deserves mention. One day as the unhappy Agrippa stood brooding beneath a tree, a large owl lighted on a branch directly above his head. A German prisoner quickly explained that this was a sign of good luck, for it meant the young man would soon be released and good fortune come to him. But, warned the prisoner, "Beware! The next time such an owl appears, it means you will be dead within five days." Happy over the first part of this prophecy, the rash man little realized in how few years the remainder of it would also come to pass.

Young Gaius, who now became the Roman ruler under the name of Caligula, was encouraged not only to set Agrippa free, but also to crown him king of a sizable tetrarchy in his native Palestine. Yet the new monarch appeared to be in no hurry to go back home, but instead remained in Rome for another year and a half, making friends of important people who might later be helpful to him. When he finally did return to take over his kingdom, he quickly found that his sister was bitterly jealous of the turn of events which had changed him from a penniless vagabond to an important ruler.

Almost at once she began persistently to nag her aging husband until, in the spring of A.D. 39, she had forced Antipas, better known as Herod the tetrarch, to go to Rome and to demand a kingdom superior to the one recently given his scapegrace nephew.

But when Agrippa found out what was happening, he sent one of his own freedmen hurrying off to Rome, too, bearing an accusation against the uncle, Antipas. This complaint reached the emperor first, and when Antipas appeared before his sovereign, he was quickly banished to faraway Gaul. Also Antipas' tetrarchy of Galilee was now added to the kingdom of Agrippa. This fine present called for a quick trip to Rome on Agrippa's part, so that Caligula might be properly thanked in person.

As he returned from it in the fall of A.D. 39, he stopped in Egypt, where the Alexandrian Jews, most unhappy about their treatment, asked his aid in obtaining concessions from the emperor with whom he seemed to be on such excellent terms. Their demands were but one of many indications of a tension that was then mounting. While Caligula gave them some help, still this Jewish question began to increase in importance from this time and managed to make the next 30 years of Palestinian history bloody ones indeed.

The trouble in Alexandria quickly came to a head when certain Greeks living in that city broke into a local synagogue and built in it an altar to the Emperor Caligula. When the Jews tore it out, the matter was referred to Rome as an evidence of gross disrespect to the divinity of the emperor. His imperial highness was highly incensed over this indignity. These subject people must be taught a lesson, one they would all understand no matter where they lived. And then what seemed a most brilliant countermeasure was suggested to him. So an order was hurried off to the newly appointed legate of Syria, requiring him to procure and erect a statue of Gaius Caesar Caligula in the likeness of Jupiter in the Holy of Holies of the Temple in Jerusalem.

One story has it that when the report came to him, Agrippa felt the sudden need to make a second hurried trip to Italy. Another version has it that he was en route there as this order was given and the statue being readied, and actually first heard of this project from the emperor's own lips. So great was the shock of this announcement that Agrippa promptly fainted dead away. But he evidently pulled himself together and with great courage and tact persuaded the monarch to put aside this profane enterprise which would have been an intolerable sacrilege to every Jew.

It was but a short time later that Caligula was set upon and assassinated. The date was January 24, 41, and Agrippa was still in Rome. Things were at once in turmoil over who should succeed the dead Caesar. It finally happened that certain soldiers hunting through the palace came upon the late emperor's uncle, Claudius. He was that son of Tiberius and brother of Drusus, whom Agrippa had known years before in their student days as the "backward" prince. Through the years he had been kept

The "Siq", only access to Petra, capital of the Arabic Nabataeans

in seclusion and away from the public, yet to a group in power at the moment he seemed the logical nominee for the vacant throne. One of the last things the Jewish monarch perhaps expected was to be cast as a king-maker, yet he soon found himself serving as the go-between in the case of Claudius versus the Roman Senate, and it was probably he more than anyone else who convinced the reluctant candidate that he should become the next emperor.

For this act, Agrippa received a prompt reward. Judaea and Samaria were added to his domain, along with the tetrarchy of Abilene, so that his holdings now equaled those of his grandparent, Herod the Great. At his request, his own brother Herod was made king of the tiny principality of Chalcis. The liberal treatment accorded him had in part been founded on the hope that, under a king of their own kind and religious beliefs, the freedom-loving Jews might be more tractable.

Agrippa hurried home to enjoy his increased power, but was soon to find that he was little more than a Roman puppet. He started to build a wall around one of the newer suburbs of Jerusalem so it, too, might be within the fortifications. But word came from Rome to stop such work. In Roman eyes the effort perhaps looked like no more than a distinct step toward Jewish independence.

Agrippa, too, may have given his backers a bit of concern in other directions. In his student days, and even later on, he had adopted many Roman ways. But on his return from his latest good fortune he had made many magnificent sacrifices at the Temple, and had even dedicated there the handsome golden chain his friend Gaius had given him after releasing him from the captivity under Tiberius. He was from now on determined to appear as a sincere pious Jew, even requiring that any and all Gentiles who married into the family of which he was the head be fully bound by every detail of the Law of Moses.

It was as the champion of strict Jewish practices that he took his strong stand against the heretical sect centering in Jerusalem—the Nazarenes, or followers of one Jesus of Nazareth, whom a former procurator, Pontius Pilate, had allowed to be put to death. To break up and stamp out this persistent sect, he had one of its leaders, James ben Zebedee, beheaded, and

another, known widely now as Peter, thrown into prison. After the Passover celebration was out of the way he intended to make a public example of this man, too, probably before a great audience. But to the amazement of all, Peter was mysteriously and miraculously freed from prison, and Agrippa himself left the city and hurried away to Caesarea (Acts 12:1-19). The king, however, managed to become very popular with his Jewish subjects, even though he allowed his own "graven" image to be stamped upon coins, had his statue set up in the Gentile sections of his realm, and took part there in pagan festivities.

But to his Roman overlords, he began to prove to be an ineffective and hence unsatisfactory ruler. Many of his acts seemed to the Romans to have at least a slightly treasonable air, and enough such instances were reported to Rome so that his patron, the emperor whom he had helped to set upon the imperial throne, sent Agrippa a sharp reprimand. He took an aggressive attitude, too, toward his neighbors, and made many moves without informing the Roman government. His ambitions, in fact, had he been able to continue to exercise them, might soon have made serious trouble for him. But instead his popular reign came to a sudden and rather dramatic end in the year A.D. 44.

He had gone to the capital city of Caesarea to attend the Roman games, where he might sit and dazzle the crowd in his new robes heavily ornamented with silver thread. They had indeed poured applause upon him, calling him a god, rather than a man, which was an act of blasphemy in the eyes of every reverent Jew.

Thus passed away another Herod, as ambitious as his grandfather had been, and far more amiable, yet without the older man's resolution and driving will. He had, for a time, restored Judaea and the other chief Jewish centers in Palestine to a kingdom, and had sought, so far as he dared, to foster Jewish hopes and abide by Jewish beliefs. There was unfeigned

Tiberias at the Sea of Galilee, founded by Herod Antipas, later an important Jewish center

Then came an appalling moment. The king suddenly looked up, and on an awning rope not too far above his head an ominous owl was perched. His heart seemed to stop within him as he recognized this desolating omen. Falling to the ground, he was stricken with pains and had to be carried away to the palace. There five days later he died, the victim of his pride, as the Bible assures us, which had kept him from giving honor at all times to God (Acts 12:20-23).

grief and lamentation throughout his realm at his departure.

He left behind him a son, due to become Herod Agrippa II, and two rather notorious daughters, Bernice (spelled Berenice in secular history) and Drusilla, all three of whom are found in Bible text. And the quarter century between his passing in A.D. 44, and the fall of Jerusalem in 70, was destined to be perhaps the most violent period of similar length in all of Jewish history.

XXVI

THE CLOSING DAYS OF BIBLE TIMES

Claudius wished to place Agrippa's seventeen-year-old son, then in Rome being brought up in the imperial household, upon the Judaean throne. But his advisers were in strong opposition, and once more the old method of control through procurators sent out from Rome was resorted to. This was perhaps a tactical error, which might have been avoided by placing a Jew, rather than a Roman, in direct charge of these proud people. Nonetheless, the seeds of discord were ready to sprout and take root, so that any provocative act might have been quite as effective as this withholding of the crown from the Herodian heir.

Trouble thus awaited Caspius Fadus, the first of a new series of procurators, when he appeared in Palestine in A.D. 44. The Zealots (Luke 6:15), long dedicated to opposing the Romans, were behind these disturbances. To counteract their efforts, Fadus did several things to win Jewish approval, including appointing Herod, prince of Chalcis and brother of the late king, to have charge over all religious matters, including the nominating of the high priest.

But while Fadus had prevented bloodshed and was beginning to get results in restoring better relations, he left the scene in his second year in office. He was succeeded by the carefully chosen Tiberius Alexander, nephew of the famous Jewish philosopher, Philo. But within a year this prodigy had proven to be a dismal failure. A Zealot revolt broke out, and by the time his replacement, Cumanus, arrived in A.D. 48, the situation was menacing indeed. I fact, when Herod of Chalcis died that same year, Claudius finally gave this little realm in the mountains of lower Syria to young Agrippa in an attempt to stop further trouble.

The newly-appointed king was still in Rome when Cumanus suddenly appeared there from Palestine to answer charges that he had been lax in permitting a savage outbreak between Jews and Samaritans. Agrippa was perhaps influential in having the procurator banished as a means of appeasing the Jews, while a Roman tribune who had offended them was sent back to Jerusalem to be executed there. Yet these harsh means did not mollify the angry people, and in the year A.D. 52 another procurator,

Marcus Antonius Felix (Acts 23:24), came to govern Judaea. The previous year the emperor had taken away the little kingdom of Chalcis and given Agrippa, in its place, a somewhat larger domain. It was also about this time that the king's too-constant companionship with his sister, Bernice, began to create a scandal.

The times were evil indeed, and the land started to fill with robbers, brigands and assassins who would commit murder for hire. Gangsterism had Palestine firmly in its malevolent grip. Then, in A.D. 54, Claudius was slain, and a new emperor, the unsavory Nero, came to the throne. He soon granted additional territory to Agrippa, and the little monarch delighted, as had his father before him, in styling himself "the Great King, the friend of Caesar, the pious, the friend of Rome." And he was decidedly Roman in his ways, considering himself a member of the Roman nobility, and using his full name of Marcus Julius Agrippa upon his coins and inscriptions. Yet he straddled the fence quite skillfully by appearing to be basically a Jew, and forcing those who entered the family by marriage to embrace the Jewish faith.

But in Judaea, where the early Christian Church and so much of the Bible story centered, Agrippa was an impassive observer of a now irresistible flow of events. When Felix was succeeded by Porcius Festus in A.D. 60, he came to Caesarea accompanied by Bernice to pay his respects. It was then, despite his need to court Jewish favor, that he was unable to convict the apostle Paul of any wrong-doing and would have set him free, except for the unalterable appeal to Caesar. He made it evident that he had no intention of becoming embroiled in any disputes where he had no primary interest, and he gave much of his time to his building operations, such as the enlargement of the palace in the Holy City, the extensive new structures at Caesarea Philippi and Berytus, the modern-day Beirut.

But Judaean conditions were worsening rapidly, despite a change in procurators every few years. The attitude of the Jews toward the Romans was exceedingly bitter, for the priests had turned the synagogues into virtual schools of sedition. Their own affairs were in sorry state, too, for the Jews were forming into factions, which extended through all levels to the temple aristocracy itself, so that even the ap-

"Inscription of Theodotus," the only trace of a synagogue in Jerusalem before 70 A.D.

pointments to the high priesthood were usually accompanied by bloodshed. From a distance of almost twenty centuries, it does not seem that this situation stemmed from the severity or unfairness of Roman rule so much as it did from the fact that these rulers were Gentiles and aliens. Diplomacy and concessions had been tried and had failed. Still the country was drifting rapidly into the throes of revolution, and the cure for that, in Roman eyes, was to garrison the land with sufficient legions to prostrate it at the first sign of mass lawlessness.

When Festus died in office in A.D. 62, supreme power in the province rested briefly in the hands of the newly-appointed high priest, Ananus. In a burst of misguided zeal, he called the Sanhedrin into session without proper authority, and summoned James the Just and other leading Christians before it. There they were condemned to death, and, without the sanction of a procurator, the whole group was dispatched by stoning. While Ananus was promptly deposed and replaced by Agrippa, his acts had turned Gentile sympathies away from the Jews and also showed the brutal attitude which prevailed even at the highest level among them.

It was at about this time that the restoration work on the Temple was finally completed, and some 18,000 men who had been on the payrolls were out of work, which was a serious threat in a time of general insecurity. An appeal was made to Agrippa to tear down some of the structure and rebuild it as a make-work project. While he refused to do this, he did approve of withdrawing Temple funds and repaving certain of Jerusalem's streets with marble. It so happened that a part of the Temple complex, faultily built, collapsed at about this time, and preparations to replace what had been destroyed were made although the work was destined never to be completed.

Albinus, who finally arrived as procurator in place of the deceased Festus, began his tour of duty with a show of vigor. But the extremists of the Zealots, termed the *Sicarii* because of the wicked curved knife which was their chief weapon, soon forced this Roman into a most unfavorable position. In A.D. 64, he was succeeded by Gessius Florus.

This newcomer's approach was openly agressive and soon became outright brutality. He was also unfortunate in that a decision made by Nero in Rome soon after Florus' arrival in Palestine set off serious riots in Caesarea. These were so severe that many Jews in that area fled from the land. In the following year, A.D. 66, he sought to raid the Temple treasury to make up the deficit of some 40 talents in the tribute. The forthcoming Jewish War might very well have begun then had not Agrippa, returning from a trip to Egypt, made a strong thought-provoking speech to the populace which had a sobering effect. He showed them conclusively that continued resistance might sound the death knell not only of the Jewish nation, but also of the Jewish religion as then practiced. He even persuaded the people to make up the deficit in the tribute, and personally led a cavalcade up to the Temple and began the work of rebuilding its damaged colonnades.

Then, feeling that he must continue on his way to his own kingdom where conditions demanded his attention, King Agrippa II left the Holy City which he was fated never to enter again.

Once he had left, the revolutionary elements began to foment trouble again. This time, under the leadership of one Eleazer, commander of the Temple, activities took on a decidedly treasonable form. He made a proposal that, from then on, no sacrifices be offered in the sanctuary in behalf of any Gentiles. Since the only such offering at that particular time was one in the interest of the Roman emperor, the intention behind this proposal was to roundly insult the volatile Nero.

The leading Jews realized what the results might be and tried valiantly to prevent this foolish move. The doctors of the law pleaded with the people at a mass meeting in the Temple courts, begging them not to call down destruction upon their heads—but to no avail. Tempers had been fanned to a white heat, and there were enough fanatics among the priests and Levites so that the sacrifice ceased. The great Jewish historian, Josephus, claims this to have marked the beginning of open revolt, which is probably true, since the Sanhedrin hurriedly sent requests to both Florus and Agrippa for military aid to put down the rebellion.

Their efforts, however, were entirely insufficient, and it was soon apparent effective help would have to come from the Roman legate in Syria, Cestius Gallus. It was late summer of the year A.D. 66 before he was able to set off to the south from Antioch with some 40,000 soldiers, and in September he appeared before the walls of Jerusalem. He was astounded when he met with resistance rather than capitulation and immediately attacked the well-fortified city.

But the siege was so valiantly withstood that Gallus was forced to abandon the assault. He had subdued Galilee, but not the neighborhood of Jerusalem, and as soon as he abandoned the attack upon the city he was in real trouble. His retreat rapidly turned into a rout, and then a headlong flight. By the time he reached Caesarea he had lost 6000 men, large quantities of war materials, and all hope of bringing Judaea into abject submission. Reveling in their easy triumph, all factions of the Jews now joined in promoting the cause of independence.

Word of Gallus' sorry failure was hurried to Rome, where its seriousness was fully understood, and Nero picked his greatest general, Titus Flavius Vespasian, to put Palestine back in its proper place. By the spring of A.D. 67, some 50,000 troops had been massed at Ptolemaïs on the coast 80 miles north of Jerusalem. Galilee was again subjugated, and then the Roman army went into winter quarters.

At that time anarchy took hold of the Holy City, and a violent civil war weakened its powers of resistance. Hoping this internal strife would continue to his benefit, Vespasian spent

The Wailing Wall in the Old City of Jerusalem showing masonry from the time of Herod the Great

The Great Sea

(Mediterranean Sea)

P H O E N I C I A

MOUNT LEBANON

Leontes R.

MT. HERMON

I T U R A E A

ABILENE

• Chalcis

• Abila

• Damascus

• Sidon

• Sarepta

• Tyre

S Y R I A

PANIAS

✛ Caesarea Philippi

T R A C H O N I T I S

Cadasa •

Ecdippa •

Lake Semechonitis

Gischala •

• Safad

GAULANITIS

BATANAEA

Ptolemaïs •

Seleucia •

• Raphana

Vespasian led the Roman armies in crushing the Jewish rebellion. Resistance in the north crumbled after the fall of Jotapata. Roman legions then swept south through Samaria, Peraea and Judaea.

GALILEE

Capernaum •

Bethsaida (Julias) •

MT. CARMEL

Jotapata •

Taricheae •

Sea of Galilee

• Gamala

Dion •

Sepphoris •

Tiberias •

Hippos □

AURANITIS

Kanatha □

Kishon R.

Nazareth •

Sennabris •
Philoteria •

Abila •

Dora •

Plain of Esdraelon

+Mt. Tabor

Yarmuk R.

Gadara □

N A B A T A E A

Caesarea ✛

Plain of Sharon

SAMARIA

Ginaea •

Scythopolis •

Pella □

D E C A P O L I S

Opposition to Roman rule and violence mounted until in 66 A.D. the Jews openly rebelled and gained control of their homeland.

Sebaste (Samaria) •

Gerasa □

River Jordan

Jabbok R.

Apollonia •

Neapolis •

Mt. Gerizim +

P E R A E A

Akrabatta •

Antipatris •

Coreae •

Joppa •

Thamna •

Lydda • Adida •

Gophna •
Ephraim •

Bethel •

Philadelphia □

Jamnia • Gazara •

Beth-horon •

Jericho •

Abila •

Ekron •

Gaba •

Julius (Livias, Beth-haram) •

Heshbon •

Emmaus •

Jerusalem •

Beth-jeshimoth •

Azotus •

Siege and destruction of Jerusalem by Titus in 70 A.D.

• Bether

Ascalon ✛

• Bethlehem

J U D A E A

• Herodium

Lake Asphaltitis (Dead Sea)

Marisa •

Anthedon •

Machaerus •

Gaza •

Hebron •

I D U M A E A

En-gedi •

Gerar •

Ziklag •

Masada •

Arnon R.

Beersheba •

The fall of Masada in 73 A.D. marked the end of the Jewish-Roman War.

Kir-hareseth (El Karak) •

A final effort to throw off Roman rule occurred in 132-135 A.D. when Bar Cochba led the Jews in a hopeless struggle against the might of Rome.

Zered R.

N A B A T A E A N S

PALESTINE AT THE TIME OF THE JEWISH-ROMAN WAR
66 to 73 A.D.

Copyright by C. S. HAMMOND & CO., N.Y.

Scale of Miles

0 5 10   20   30   40

Perennial Rivers............... Capitals...........✛
Seasonal Rivers & Streams..... Cities of the Decapolis □

Territory under Roman procurator
Kingdom of Herod Agrippa II
Decapolis
Autonomous city state of Ascalon
Roman province of Syria

his time the following spring in crushing such opposition as he could find in Samaria, Peraea and Idumaea. By summer he felt secure enough to lay siege to Jerusalem and was about to start such operations when word came of the death of the Emperor Nero (June, A.D. 68). This brought his activities to a halt until he could renew his orders from Rome itself.

Now for a time there was rebellion in the faraway Roman capital as well as in that of the Jews. First Galba, then Otho, and finally Vitellius, were elevated to the throne and each as promptly overthrown. Then the scene shifted to the east, where it appeared that the army attacking Palestine was probably the most formidable power block within the whole empire. It suddenly flexed its muscles, decided it wanted its own commander as emperor, and placed Vespasian very securely upon the throne. Consequently the Jewish War was forced to mark time for almost two years.

But it had not by any means been forgotten, and finally, in the spring of A.D. 70, another sizable army was put together, this time at Caesarea, and its command entrusted to the emperor's own son, Titus. And what of the Jews during this lull in hostilities? Rather than prepare for the inevitable, they had spent the intervening months in internal strife. The consequence was that by the time the Roman forces had swung down through Samaria and encamped before Jerusalem's walls, its defenders had to cease fighting within so they might withstand the pressure about to be applied from without. There were three stout rings of stone about the city and at least three massive towers guarding interior vantage points. And they would all now have to be defended with every bit of frenzied and fanatical valor that could be summoned.

Titus did give the people a chance to sur-render, but it was rather a foregone conclusion that it would be refused. And when it was, the siege began immediately. It took only a few short weeks to breach the two outer walls and gain full possession of the lower portion of the city. But the tower of Antonia and the interior fortifications were sufficiently difficult that Titus decided to throw up a defendable earthen wall and starve the remainder of the inhabitants into yielding. When this failed, an assault on the Antonia was carried out and brought it into Roman hands on the 5th of July. The attackers now concentrated upon the Temple and its surroundings, and it was August 10 before it fell. With their revered shrine destroyed, and starvation only days away, the defenders gave up, the Upper City finally was overrun, and by September 7, 70, the siege was completed. It is claimed that in this campaign alone over one million Jews had perished.

Titus ordered Jerusalem to be utterly destroyed, and the work of demolition soon began. A few choice objects and prominent personages were saved to adorn the commander's triumph. What was still left of the city was pretty much obliterated. Of its remaining people, 100,000 of them are said to have been led away to work as slaves in Egyptian mines, while great numbers were slain in various spectacles in the Roman ampitheaters. Fighting in Judaea dragged on for three years and terminated finally with the capture of the fortress Masada, in which years before Herod the Great had deposited his family when he went off to Rome in search of a kingdom.

And what of his great-grandson, Herod Agrippa II? He fought at the side of Vespasian and was wounded at the siege of Gamala. Following the fall of Jerusalem, he removed to Rome where he died about the year A.D. 100.

Masada, fortress of Herod the Great, fell to the Romans in 73 A.D.

XXVII

THE FINAL TRIUMPH OF ROME OVER THE JEWS

While the Zealots had started as a patriotic party, they had largely degenerated into a band of fanatical assassins, the Sicarii, and their violence had taught the Romans a lasting lesson. Titus, drawing upon the failure of those who had gone before him, fully realized that the basic scheme of governing Judaea must be changed. Following the plan in vogue quite generally throughout the empire, he decided that the Jews could not henceforth be allowed to administer their internal affairs themselves.

Actually it was hard for the secular-minded, matter-of-fact Roman to understand people who were so religiously dominated that their spiritual beliefs colored their whole lives, thoughts and actions. The Jew, taught from childhood to believe that he was indeed one of God's elect, and a member of a chosen people, could also be taught that government, except of his own choosing, was a burdensome and insufferable yoke. It had taken several generations of Roman overlords to realize fully just what unbridled Jewish "zeal" could do.

But now that the menace was understood, the Emperor Vespasian issued a decree to terminate it—and for all time if possible. His edict was thus a most harsh one. All outward marks and tokens of the Jews as a separate and distinct people were to be erased as completely as possible. Jerusalem—their Holy City—together with the Temple—the House of their invisible God — were laid in ruins. The high priesthood was abolished. So, too, was the once potent Sanhedrin. And, lest the religious center be moved to Egypt and revived there, a Jewish temple which had been in use for some time there was closed. The Temple tax of a half shekel imposed upon every Israelite twenty years of age or older, irrespective of where he lived (Matt. 17:24), was now to be paid for the upkeep of the principal shrine of the Roman Jupiter on the Capitoline Hill in Rome.

And in the manner in which Samaria had been treated by the Assyrians centuries before, a colony of Roman veterans was brought in and settled in the vicinity of the demolished Jerusalem. Other Jewish centers in Palestine were reorganized, and great efforts were expended in Romanizing the province. Yet the Jewish population continued to predominate, a large force had to police the land continually, and Roman control continued to be neither too certain nor too successful.

Soon after the fall of Jerusalem, Titus turned military affairs over to one of his lieutenants and gave his attention to other matters. One rather gory instance was the celebration, that fall, on the birthdays of his father, Vespasian, and his brother, Domitian. These were public spectacles at both Caesarea and at Berytus, and at them thousands of Jewish captives perished in the gladiatorial exhibits, or in the combats with lions and other wild beasts.

In quite another vein was Titus' love affair with the fascinating Bernice, daughter of Agrippa I. She was a woman of strong contrasts—exceeding beauty and charm, and very low morals. She had been married to her uncle, Herod, and left a widow by him. Her extreme and continued intimacy with her own brother, King Agrippa II, had led to a great scandal. To quiet it, she had been married briefly to Polemon, King of Cilicia, but she soon abandoned him to live again quite openly with Agrippa. Then for a time she had been the mistress of Vespasian and had now captivated his son.

Still she was faithful enough to her Jewish upbringing so that on one occasion at least she had shaved her head and abstained from wine for a month as part of the fulfillment of a vow. While it is possible her religious zeal may not have been wholly sincere, it is felt that she perhaps softened somewhat her powerful lover's attitude toward her people, particularly the Jews dispersed widely throughout the empire.

Titus, however, had his share of enemies, and they began to spread the rumor that he was planning to supplant his father on the throne. To scotch these stories, he now hastened home to Rome and joined with Vespasian in the combined triumph decreed them for their exploits in Palestine. In the procession certain utensils of the Temple, the golden seven-branched candlestick and the rolls of the Law, were exhibited. In it, too, marched 700 of the fairest and handsomest Jewish captives. As the huge parade made the traditional pause before the shrine of Jupiter Capitolinus, Simon bar Giora, a leader of the Zealots, and the equivalent of the enemy's commander-in-chief, was put to death.

Coins were struck to commemorate their victories, and a magnificent arch was later erected to give further testimony to the downfall of Jewish nationalism. It is said that the items from the shrine in Jerusalem were all deposited in the Roman *Temple of Peace*, excepting the Book of Law, which was carefully kept in the imperial palace.

Titus was appointed as a co-ruler with his father, but he withheld making Bernice his wife, since the Roman populace seems to have had particular hatred for women of the East. Yet she appeared in Rome again in A.D. 79 at the time Titus became emperor following his father's death. But this Herodian woman, one of the last of her family to play a conspicuous part in history, never became the emperor's wife.

Even if she had achieved her desires, her satisfaction would have been short-lived, for Titus' reign ended two years later, in A.D. 81. In this brief period he had become exceedingly popular, which fact tended to make the task of his brother Domitian, who succeeded him, somewhat more difficult. During the early part of the latter's 15 years upon the throne, he ruled astutely and well. Then, as he grew older, he seems to have become ferocious to the point of barbarity.

He made the lot of the Jews who had sought refuge in Rome completely unbearable. Some of them were reduced to begging for a livelihood. The more prosperous did their best to hide their origin so as to evade the special taxes heaped upon them. But Domitian was ever short of money in the latter part of his reign, and his tax collectors harried the Jews, not only in Rome but throughout the empire. Also he visited insult and the utmost penalties of the law upon those Gentiles who favored Judaism.

While there seems to have been no persecution of the Christians under either Vespasian or Titus, Domitian's hostile and cruel nature reached to this newer sect, and he made an attempt to crush this new belief. The Apostle John's exile to Patmos (Rev. [Apoc.] 1:9) is supposed to have come at this time, and some of Domitian's relatives with Christian leanings were either banished or executed.

But at last even the Emperor's wife could tolerate him no longer, and at her instigation he

The Triumphal Arch of Titus in the Roman Forum

was slain in his forty-fifth year. He was succeeded in A.D. 96 by the Emperor Nerva, whose reign was characterized by justice and clemency. The Jews appear to have found life less harsh, and it was then that John was permitted to return to Ephesus. He was one of the last of the apostles and is supposed to have survived for a year or more after Trajan took the throne in A.D. 98.

This new emperor had been the most famous general of his time, and during his nineteen-year reign the empire would reach its greatest extent in territory and also know unsurpassed prosperity. He had a whole complement of admirable qualities, and he was equally competent as a soldier, statesman and administrator. From him the Jews had little to fear, and it is believed they enjoyed some share in the general good times.

By contrast it was now the Christians who began openly to resist idolatrous worship of heathen gods or the emperor. Two highly interesting letters, still extant, by the famous Roman writer, Pliny the Younger, describe the situation as it presented itself in Asia Minor. Around A.D. 110, he was Roman governor of Bithynia and Pontus. For some years during his term of office, he was aware that more and more members of this sect were brought before him for judgment. Rather than take a completely arrogant stand, he did his best to learn

THE ROMAN EMPIRE
AT ITS GREATEST EXTENT
c. 117 A.D.

Copyright by C. S. HAMMOND & CO., N.Y.

Scale of Miles

0   100   200   300   400   600

Capital ....

Maximum extent of Roman control
in the time of Trajan, 98-117 A.D. ....

Roman walls ....

The Germanic tribes exerted
constant pressure on the Rhine-
Danube frontier, placing The
Empire on the defensive. The
western provinces and Italy
were overrun by Germanic
invaders in the 5th cent. A.D.

Trajan's conquests east
of the Euphrates were
abandoned by Hadrian
in 118 A.D.

In 395 A.D. the Roman
world was divided into separate eastern and western
empires.

PARTHIAN EMPIRE

ASSYRIA

MESOPOTAMIA

ARMENIA

Caspian Sea
(Mare Hyrcanium)

S a r m a t i a

Huns

Alans

Siraces

Amadoci

Bastarnae

Roxolani

Venedae

Aestii

Goths

Burgundians

Lombards

Vandals

Lugii

Quadi

Marcomanni

Germania

Iazyges

CARPATHIAN MTS.

DACIA

Sarmizegetusa

Potaissa

Carpi

Napoca

MOESIA
UPPER   LOWER

THRACE

Byzantium

BITHYNIA & PONTUS

GALATIA

CAPPADOCIA

CILICIA

SYRIA

PALESTINE

ARABIA

EGYPT

Black Sea
(Pontus Euxinus)

Bosporus Kingdom

Palus Maeotis

Tyras

Chersonesus

Panticapaeum

Sinope

Trapezus

Neocaesarea

Amisus

Ancyra

Nicomedia

Pergamum

ASIA

Sardis

Ephesus

LYCIA

PAMPHYLIA

Tyana

Caesarea

Tarsus

Antioch

Damascus

Tyre

Jerusalem

Gaza

Pelusium

Bostra

Petra

Salamis

CYPRUS

RHODES

CRETE

Athens

ACHAIA

Argos

Sparta

Thessalonica

MACEDONIA

EPIRUS

Aegean Sea

Red Sea
(Sinus Arabicus)

Thebes

Berenice

Ptolemais

Memphis

Naucratis

Alexandria

Nile R.

Cyrene

CYRENAICA

Marmarica

Berenice

Syrtis Major

Syrtis Minor

AFRICA

Leptis Magna

Sabratha

Hadrumetum

Carthage

Cirta

Hippo Regius

Caesarea

NUMIDIA

MAURETANIA CAESARIENSIS

TINGITANA

Gaetulia

SAHARA

ATLAS MTS.

Tingis

Gades

BAETICA

Corduba

Emerita Aug.

LUSITANIA

SPAIN

TARRACONENSIS

Caesaraugusta

Tarraco

Valentia

Carthago Nova

BALEARIC IS.

SARDINIA

CORSICA

SICILY

Syracuse

Agrigentum

Neapolis

Capua

ITALY

Rome

Ancona

Bononia

Genua

Mediolanum

Aquileia

DALMATIA

Salonae

ILLYRICUM

PANNONIA
UPPER   LOWER

NORICUM

RAETIA

Vindelicorum

Augusta

ALPINE PROVS.

Aquincum

Tarentum

Ionian Sea

Adriatic Sea

Tyrrhenian Sea

Mediterranean Sea
(Mare Internum)

Massilia

Narbo

NARBONENSIS

Tolosa

AQUITANIA

Burdigala

GAUL

LUGDUNENSIS

Lugdunum

Augustodunum

Lutetia

BELGICA

Durocortorum

GERMANIA
UPPER   LOWER

Colonia Agrippina

Augusta Treverorum

Vindobona

Chauci

Frisians

Batavi

Camulodunum

Londinium

BRITAIN

Deva

Eboracum

Isca

Wall of Hadrian

Hibernia

North Sea
(Oceanus Germanicus)

Atlantic Ocean

Baltic Sea

English Channel

PYRENEES MTS.

Bracara Augusta

Asturica

Salmantica

Bronze cast from Arch of Titus: Temple treasures from Jerusalem carried in triumphal procession

what he could about these followers of Christ and then reported his findings, along with suggestions concerning them, to Trajan.

The emperor sent word back to Pliny commending his conduct in this matter and ordering that the Christians were not to be hunted out by the police. Anonymous indictments were to be disregarded, and those willing henceforth to worship the gods of the Romans were to go free. However, those who persisted in this new faith were to suffer death.

But shortly after this Trajan had his own first extensive contact with Christianity. He conducted the war against the Parthians in the east in person and was for a time at Syrian Antioch. It was here of course that those converted to the faith had first been known as Christians. The church was still as active as it had been two generations before in Paul's time, and the number of communicants was large. Thus it nettled the emperor, fresh from his victories over his foes, when this considerable group, imbued with what he considered a reprobate spirit, refused to honor the Roman gods from whom he presumed his successes had come. When he indignantly threatened them with death, their bishop, Ignatius, begged the right to be heard.

Brought into the august presence, Trajan began to cross-examine this virile, fearless Christian leader. But Ignatius was not to be cowed, and as a result of his intrepid defense was condemned to be taken to Rome, there "to be devoured by the beasts for the gratification of the people." And so it was that Trajan turned against the Christians, and the venerable chief of the sect in Asia was brought into the Coliseum to make sport for the Roman mob.

The Parthian War, however, seemed to present an opportunity to that other religious group, and in A.D. 116 the Jews again sought to revolt. The uprising was fairly general and widespread but perhaps most determined in Mesopotamia. While the trouble there was being dealt with, other Jewish centers along the eastern Mediterranean shore blazed up in orgies of brutality. Their purpose seemed to be to exterminate if possible their Gentile fellow-citizens, and in the island of Cyprus alone it is claimed they slew the almost incredible number of 240,000. Almost as many Greeks and Romans were slaughtered in the province of Cyrenaica to the west of Egypt on the African coast. But when the Roman legate in the land of the Pharaohs was threatened, retaliation was swift and similarly brutal.

Death seized Trajan in A.D. 117 while he was en route home from his campaigns in the east. Although the Jewish disturbances had seriously interfered with the Parthian War, the empire to which Hadrian succeeded was at its greatest physical extent. It reached from Britain to the cataracts of the Nile, and from the Atlantic Ocean to the Tigris River, and embraced the widest possible sorts and types of people. Thus the new emperor would need every whit of his versatility and breadth of view to understand his various subjects and weld them together.

However, he was a staunch adherent of paganism and took direction from his patron, Trajan; thus the Christians came to suffer even more grievously at his hands. The sect, which had previously been loosely grouped with the Jews, was now separately recognized and expressly condemned. For a time the massacres which had formerly been visited upon the Jews were now turned upon the Christians. The situation finally got so far out of hand that even the proconsuls protested. As a consequence Hadrian was eventually forced to issue a decree forbidding the attacks upon Jesus' followers.

In the latter part of this emperor's reign, the Jews attempted another rebellion. They not only continued their unquenchable hatred of the Romans, but the early edict of Trajan prohibiting circumcision, the observance of the Sabbath, and the reading of the Law, had, for nearly fifteen years, festered in their fanatical spirits. Roman forces, too, had commenced to re-fortify Jerusalem as a Gentile city, debarring its use to its former inhabitants. This was indeed a time of trouble and very likely the one in which the promised Messiah (Jer. 23:5, 6) was to come and deliver his people and then execute judgment and justice on earth.

Suddenly, in A.D. 131, a pretender, one Bar Cochba, or Bar Kokba, appeared. He was a man of courage and military capabilities, but whether he was an outright impostor, or merely an excessive fanatic, is hard to judge. However, he had the endorsement of the famous doctor of the Law, Rabbi Akiba, and, taking command of the Jewish host, became the long-hoped-for deliverer of Israel. All the first moves in this desperate holy war were victories for Bar Cochba.

But the Romans soon brought in additional forces, and the revolt quickly turned to a war of extermination. It was then that the caves, in which Palestine abounded, filled with refugees from stern vengeance. The evident intent was to drive the children of Abraham from the Land of Promise, and the efforts exerted to this end left an indelible imprint upon that section of Palestine down into modern times. Even the term Judaea was discarded, and the area took the name of *Syria Palaestina*.

The Jews were prohibited by a death sentence from entering Jerusalem or coming to any point within sight of it. The city was rebuilt, but on a strictly Roman basis, and as one of the centers of Roman life in the east. The name Jerusalem was discarded, and it was called *Colonia Aelia Capitolina:* Colonia to denote its Roman colonial status, Aelia for the personal name of the emperor, and Capitolina since it was dedicated to Jupiter Capitolinus. Zion was no more, and this rebellion under Hadrian was the last heroic attempt of the Jews to regain national independence. The dispersion begun under Trajan had become well nigh complete under Hadrian. For almost 2000 years these people were deprived of a homeland.

Those Jews who continued in Palestine during the next two hundred years were still held together by their religion and the continual efforts of their rabbis. Some time about the year A.D. 200, a legal code, called the *Mishna* was produced there, and by the beginning of the 5th century, the work on the *Palestinian Talmud* was completed. But when Constantine closed the rabbinical schools in the Holy Land at about this same time, Jewish life and history centered elsewhere until modern times.

Those Jews who had chosen to remain in Babylonia following the captivity had prospered, and, after the destruction of the Holy City and the complete disruption of Jewish life there, Babylon had become the principal center of Jewish thought and religion. It was there that the compilation of the famous *Babylonian Talmud* was consummated in A.D. 550. That city's later Mohammedan rulers proved for generations to be far more congenial masters than the Romans.

Caesar had at last dispersed the Jews; but Christ and His followers would in due time conquer Caesar.

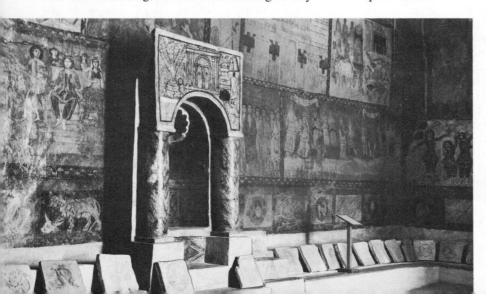

Wall painting from a synagogue at Dura Europos in Mesopotamia, 3rd century A.D.

XXVIII

THE GROWTH OF CHRISTIANITY

The term "church," from the Greek *ekklesia,* first appears in Bible text in the words of Jesus (Matt. 16:18). There it is intended to convey the idea of an assembly or society of men and women united under God, acknowledging Jesus Christ as Lord and Master, and which meets regularly for religious instruction and worship.

Such a community was coming into existence at that time, made up of the apostles, disciples, and other followers of this Man of Galilee. It was drawn together more firmly by the horrors of the Crucifixion, and then laid its foundations in the thrilling appearances to the believers of their risen Lord. The real welding together, however, came with the descent of the Holy Spirit in June of the year A.D. 30. From that moment the primitive Church began its march and started to add quantities of new members in and about Jerusalem.

At the outset, it was quite naturally considered an offshoot of Judaism, for it continued to be allied with the older faith for fully a generation after its founding. It was at Antioch, primarily a Gentile community, that the faith acquired its lasting designation. And it was here that the trouble welled up which brought on what might have been a disastrous schism. But the gap was bridged, and as this new faith, which seemed to arouse a special fervor in the Gentile breast, began to spread among them, it proved to have overwhelming significance in its own right, apart from Judaism or the Law of Moses.

Church history as recorded in the Bible terminates with the close of the Book of Acts. By then the followers of Christ were scattered from the Holy Land up through Asia, over into Greece and on to Rome. Paul expressed the wish to carry his missionary efforts to Spain, and tradition claims that he indeed "reached the bounds of the west." This rapid spread of the Gospel was due in large part to the ardor of that little group of dedicated men whose preaching carried the Word ever forward to new hearers. But their success might have been strongly limited were it not for *Pax Romana* and an empire that provided good roads, relative freedom from pirates and brigands who might have limited travel, and sufficient prosperity so that such missionary effort could find

Silver chalice, early Christian metalwork from Syrian Antioch

contributions for its support. The common culture widely spread by the Greeks and preserved by the Romans, was to prove fertile soil for the seeds of Christian teaching, while the maintenance of stable government over virtually the entire civilized world permitted the peaceful spreading of the Gospel.

One other prevailing condition worked to the distinct benefit of this new faith. Philosophy had for several centuries placed increasing emphasis upon personality, which brought about a new attitude of the human mind and heightened the value placed on individualism. Christianity, which was then but one among several *new* beliefs and religious systems, meshed more closely with this new manner of thinking and promised to produce far greater satisfactions.

The words of Jesus, "Come unto me, all you who are overburdened, and I will give you rest," may have registered first with the slaves and poor freedmen. But they were caught and acted upon by many whose lot in life seemed on the surface to be far more promising. A few at least of the names in the closing chapter of Paul's Epistle to the Romans are thought to have been persons of considerable consequence.

It is hard to say how great a distinction between Jew and Christian existed in Rome in the

THE SPREAD OF CHRISTIANITY

Copyright by C. S. HAMMOND & CO., N.Y.

Scale of Miles

0   100   200   300   400   500   600

INTRODUCTION OF CHRISTIANITY

Areas known to contain Christians at the time of Irenaeus, c. 185

185-325 (by the time of Constantine)

325-600 (by the time of Gregory I)

600-800 (by the time of Charlemagne)

800-1300

Northern limit of area permanently lost to Mohammedanism ....

During the 7th cent. the Christian Church introduced Nestorian Christianity into Central Asia.

The Christian Coptic Church was introduced on the Upper Nile and in Ethiopia in the 4th cent.

Christianity in Roman Britain was wiped out by the Anglo-Saxon invasion. The faith was reestablished in the 7th cent. by Irish missionaries.

Lithuanians (13th Cent.)

Prussians (13th Cent.)

Pomeranians (1122-1130)

Poles (962-1025)

Czechs (c. 1000)

Magyars (950-1050)

Russians (989-1015)

Saxons (785-805)

Thuringians (8th Cent.)

Alamanni (7th Cent.)

IRELAND

BRITAIN

GAUL

SPAIN

ITALY

SICILY

SARDINIA

CORSICA

EGYPT

ARMENIA

CYPRUS

CRETE

RHODES

BALEARIC IS.

North Sea

Baltic Sea

Atlantic Ocean

Mediterranean Sea

Black Sea

Caspian Sea

Red Sea

Sea of Azov

Volga R.

Don R.

Dnieper R.

Dniester R.

Danube

Tigris R.

Euphrates R.

Nile R.

Duero R.

Tagus R.

Clonard

York
Lincoln
London
Caerleon
Canterbury

Riga

Magdeburg
Bremen
Utrecht
Cologne
Fulda
Trier
Luxeuil
Mainz
Regensburg
Augsburg

Marienburg
Gnesen

Esztergom
Siscia
Sirmium
Singidunum
Sardica
Preslav

Kiev

Pityus

Chersonesus

Tomi

Anchialus
Develtum

Sinope
Amastris

Ityl

Vagarshapat

Arbela
Nisibis
Edessa
Melitene
Antioch

Ctesiphon
Seleucia

Palmyra
Damascus
Tyre
Jerusalem
Caesarea

Nantes
Tours
Bordeaux
Toulouse
Rouen
Paris
Reims
Bourges
Lyons
Vienne
Arles
Marseille
Narbonne

Astorga
Leon
Merida
Evora
Faro
Cadiz
Tingis
Seville
Cordova
Malaca
Valencia
Toledo
Saragossa
Tarragona

Milan
Genoa
Pisa
Florence
Verona
Aquileia
Ravenna
Ancona
Salona
Beneventum
Naples
Puteoli
Rome

Syracuse
Messina

Caesarea
Caesarea
Hippo Regius
Cirta
Madaura
Lambaesis
Carthage
Hadrumetum
Leptis Magna

Cyrene
Berenice

Alexandria
Memphis
Oxyrhynchus
Hermopolis
Thebes
Ptolemais

Philippi
Beroea
Thessalonica
Larissa
Nicopolis
Corinth
Athens
Sparta
Gortyna
Cnossus

Durazzo

Constantinople
Chalcedon
Nicomedia
Nicaea
Troas
Pergamum
Thyatira
Smyrna
Sardis
Ephesus
Laodicea
Peiga
Myra
Iconium
Tarsus
Antioch
Ancyra

Salamis
Paphos

years following Paul's residence and presumed martyrdom there. For another generation, or even longer, the two beliefs were often apparently confused. But it is probable that little attention was paid to either sect prior to one of the major decrees of Titus as emperor. During his two years on the throne he issued the historic edict claiming divinity for himself, his forebears, family and descendants, and their worship as gods.

Domitian built up this scheme of "emperor worship" to considerable heights, erecting a temple to the God-Emperors, and established a priestly college to foster such worship. He even required that he be addressed as "Our Lord and God." Such adulation was of course contrary to either Jewish or Christian tenets, and since members of both sects refused to bow down and worship these human deities, the two groups were marked for trouble. The persecutions in the latter years of Domitian's reign have already been mentioned.

Others beside the Christians suffered from his fury, but possibly that sect endured the brunt of his determination, at least in Rome. Many were put to death, including Flavius Clemens, the emperor's first cousin, while his wife, Domitilla, also a relative of the emperor, was banished since they would not renounce their faith. This early Christian woman has long been of much interest to scholars. It is believed to have been upon ground which had belonged to her that probably one of the first of the catacombs—the underground burial places in which Christianity maintained its existence at Rome for much of two centuries—was excavated.

While pressure was relaxed somewhat after Domitian's assassination, Trajan did apply it again in his closing years. Still the Church continued to spread, and was soon firmly established throughout the empire. There were growing Christian colonies in virtually all the more important commercial centers, with outstanding churches at Antioch in Syria, Smyrna, Ephesus, Alexandria and Carthage. The church at Rome, however, moved distinctly into the ascendancy. It had surely borne the brunt of persecution; it numbered among its martyrs Peter and Paul, and it had managed to find superior leadership. By the latter half of the second century Irenaeus, who became bishop of Lyons in Gaul in

177, thought it best to warn all believers that: "It is most necessary that each church should agree with this church (at Rome)." Some years later Cyprian, who died in 258, wrote, "Whoever separates himself from the Church is separated from the promises of the Church . . . If anyone could escape who was outside the Ark of Noah, so also may he escape who shall be outside the bounds of the Church." To this one universal Church all must belong who hoped to be saved.

But if there was to be effective leadership, there must needs be authority to deal constructively with all the other assemblies. As Irenaeus had pointed out, uniformity in the matter of doctrine was essential. But to assure such uniformity it was vital that the leading church have the power to demand uniformity, the alternate being excommunication. The threats of Gnostic heresy, rife at that time, called for a centralization of authority.

In several of his letters, for instance the first one to Timothy (I Tim. 3:2), Paul describes in detail what a type of man a bishop should be. Bishops were thus within the church structure from the very beginning, although at first they were mere overseers or superintendents. Gradually, their duties became more extensive, and by the year 160 the first synod of bishops was called. Such prelates became representatives of all the assemblies within their respective districts in the various councils of the Church. One of their basic purposes was preservation of this very uniformity which soon gave the whole body of believers the name of the *Catholic Church,* in that it was consistent throughout in all matters of belief, worship and government.

Back in this second Christian century, however, the Church faced a most severe threat. It came from a competitive belief, which had swept to the west from Persia and is now called Mithraism. Mithra, or Mithras, was the god of light, heat and fertility, and thus the giver of all good things. Since he was popularly represented as the sun-god and was in many respects like Apollo, he had a strong appeal for the pagan members of the Roman world. Worship of Mithra was especially strong in the army; and, since it did not conflict with emperor worship, it made many converts and be-

came the most formidable rival of Christianity.

There would be other competitive religions. Also there would be certain rebellious influences within the Church itself. But perhaps the chief oppositional influence continued to be emperor worship. It was but another expression of the same purpose which had encouraged the Seleucid kings to force the worship of Zeus upon the Jews, the hope of developing a truly "universal" faith. Such a compulsory cult also tended to keep all citizens completely subservient to the State.

The relations between the State and the Church, however, varied quite widely with the emperors who ruled from the year 180 on. There were periods of persecution, when the communicants at Rome had to conduct their worship underground. These were interspersed with peaceful periods of varying lengths, such as the one in the middle of the third century which lasted for 40 years, largely because it was a time of great uncertainty in empire af-

The Arch of Constantine in Rome

Profile view of the head of Constantine the Great

fairs. During it Christianity enjoyed rapid expansion, but the period ahead proved to be a most difficult one.

In A.D. 284, Diocletian took the throne. In order to cope with the dangerous situations that had developed on several of the borders and in some parts of the vast Empire, he set up a system of four rulers instead of one and succeeded in bringing order out of near chaos. At the same time, however, the last vestiges of a republican government disappeared under his reign and the monarchy assumed Oriental, autocratic traits. In his attempts to strengthen and unify the Empire, he began to encounter a threat from what had perhaps seemed a quite unlikely quarter. The challenger turned out to be Christianity; he began to regard it with suspicion, and then with dread, because this sect was increasing in numbers and growing unmistakably in influence.

By the year 303, he had determined to undertake the complete suppression of the Church, and in rapid succession published three edicts to that end, following along with a fourth the next year. Together they presented a far-reaching plan of complete extinction. All structures in which Christians held worship were to be torn down to their foundations, the land sold, and the proceeds turned over to the State. All Christian writings of any nature were to be delivered forthwith to the magistrates, who were to burn them in public. All known Christian persons were placed beyond the pale of the law. Complaints could be entered against them, but they were denied legal redress for any injuries they might suffer. And, to cap the climax, all were commanded to offer sacrifices to the four supreme associated rulers. Emperor-worship now had a pantheon of its own.

Diocletian made his own headquarters at the city of Nicomedia, the modern Izmit, at the eastern extremity of the Sea of Marmara in Turkey. It is said that the first Christian martyr under his decrees came from his own capital and won that distinction by tearing down the initial copy of the edict when it was posted for public viewing. But thousands more followed shortly, determined that preservation of their faith was worth the supreme sacrifice. These early Christians began to prove they could be as spirited as their Jewish brethren when their freedom of worship was tampered

with. Caesar began to realize that brutality could by no means overcome Christ.

Popular opinion, too, was definitely affected and turned so distinctly in favor of the persecuted that magistrates in many centers were forced to temper their handling of the matter. Could it be that Christ was actually about to overcome Caesar?

Diocletian retired from the throne after a twenty-year reign, and Maximian, one of his associates, abdicated. Thus the empire was thrown into civil war for several years. Galerius and Constantius, the other two members of the four-man commission, became *Augusti,* the new title of the two higher regents. Constantius, who had become the *Caesar* of Gaul and Britain in 293, died in the latter land in 306. Immediately his army seized the role which Diocletian had sought to deny it, and enthroned their late leader's son as Emperor of the West. His name was Constantine, and he was, in all probability, fully deserving of the designation finally given him of Constantine *the Great.*

However, he was but one of several contestants for the former imperial throne, and a number of years would intervene before he was firmly entrenched as ruler. What was needed was a unifying force, and by the year 311 it began to appear that the Christian Church might provide the medium. It was then, as one of three rivals contending for the throne, that

Constantine issued an edict promising toleration and clemency to the members of the faith, providing they did nothing "contrary to discipline." In the next year, 312, he published another decree making their freedom complete and giving Christianity an equal status with any and all other religions within the empire.

Constantine was not himself a Christian, and there is much probability that he knew but little about its beliefs and practices from personal experience. Most scholars assume that, as a thoroughgoing Roman, he was actuated principally by political motives. He needed the Church, and the Church in turn could do very well with his protection and patronage—and under his favor it surged ahead rapidly.

By the year 319, the clergy were exempted from public obligations, thus leaving them free for the primary purposes of their calling. But an even greater step was taken in that very same year, and one which would have strong appeal for the laity. All forms of heathen sacrifice were totally forbidden. Paganism was being stamped out, and Christ was coming definitely into the ascendancy.

Two years later, in 321, another significant law was enacted, by which all work was forbidden on the Christian Sunday. Also to better fortify the Church financially, it was permitted to inherit legacies, and it thus became the recipient of many fine gifts from the estates of departed members. To hasten the expansion of its physical plant, Constantine made extensive gifts to the clergy and otherwise aided in building fine church structures in the larger cities.

These attentions to the Church had been carried on while the question of who should finally rule as emperor was being settled. It was not until 323 that Constantine disposed of his last remaining rival, Licinius, and became undisputed master of the eastern world. It was perhaps fortunate that his victory came when it did, for the Church was just then wracked from within by the mighty controversy known

Syrio-Roman basilica near Aleppo commemorating St. Simeon the Stylite

Floor mosaic from a church at Jarash, 6th century A.D.

as the *Arian Heresy*. This debate over the nature of Christ was seriously threatening the stability and unity of the faith.

Constantine called it "an unprofitable question," and to adjust the matter convened a general council of the Church to meet in June, 325, at the small city of Nicaea, the present day Iznik, which lies about 50 miles southeast of Istanbul. Invitations went out to dioceses and churches throughout the empire, and transportation for leading prelates, along with their entertainment during the sessions, was provided at State expense.

There were some 320 bishops present, plus a numerous body of presbyters (priests), deacons and members of the laity. Yet the attendance was almost entirely from the east, since the schism precipitated by Arius had not yet agitated Europe and North Africa. Still the turbulence of its discussions pointed up one manifest need—a single declaration of faith that would be binding on all members of the universal Church. Before achieving it, there were stormy sessions, but out of the heat and heroics of the two months of deliberations was forged the celebrated Nicene Creed.

Christianity had indeed become the State religion, and Christ, in a measure, had conquered Caesar. And then, as though to make this welding of Church and State more certain, Constantine was baptized upon his deathbed in the year 337.

The Church for a time flourished as never before, but all was not as it should be, for the problem of the intimate association of civil and ecclesiastical affairs, which had similarly bothered and hampered the Hebrews centuries before, now reappeared. The Church of Christ, which had struggled, survived and grown, despite many hardships in its earliest days, was now at a point where its efforts must be turned to preserving the purity of its primitive beginnings. There were still some uncertain days ahead.

The records from the Council of Nicaea as well as those from an earlier meeting of bishops held in 314 at Arles in southeastern France or Gaul, give an indication of the extent the Christian Church had attained in the fourth century. In each case a list of the bishops in attendance has been preserved, and it is interesting to find that the conclave at Arles drew at least three prelates from faraway Britain—Eborius of York, Restitutus of London, and Adelfius, presumably from Lincoln. It is thus probable that Christianity had been carried to this northwestern extremity of the empire as early as the second century.

Beyond these factual records, there is also a wealth of tradition which would indicate that the Church moved out well beyond the limits of the Roman Empire. Such additional expansion would of necessity have had to be principally to the east, and it is very probable that bodies of believers were established as far away as Bactria and India. Closer at hand, it seems clear that churches existed from a very early time in Mesopotamia and Babylonia. The country of Armenia in the mountains of eastern Turkey has the distinction of being the first land to adopt Christianity as its "official" religion—in A.D. 303, years before the efforts of Constantine.

In the Great Commission which closes the Gospel of Mark, our Lord had ordained a mighty missionary effort, saying, "Go into *all* the world, and preach the good news of the Gospel to *everyone*." And during the three hundred years following His death on the Cross His instructions had been carried forward with fine spirit and purpose, and often in the face of great obstacles and merciless persecution. Happily that wondrous work was due to continue unabated down through all the centuries, as He had ordained.

XXIX

ANCIENT JERUSALEM

So much of the Bible story centers in Jerusalem that it is most natural that it should have long been the focal point of Christian interest in Palestine. It was, of course, the very center of the Hebrew nation during its "Golden Age" under David and Solomon, and the capital of the Kingdom of Judah before and after the Babylonian captivity, and of the Judaean Kingdom under the Maccabees. Thus it has been the object of veneration by fully a hundred generations of Jews. In addition, it is a holy place in the estimate of the Mohammedans, next in importance to their Mecca and Medina.

Since it is indeed the *Holy City,* it is quite natural that it has stimulated the desire down the ages to know it in the form in which it existed at various periods in Bible times. What was the "city of David" like, that is the Jebusite town which he captured and finally turned over to Solomon to enlarge and beautify? What was it like after Solomon had poured great wealth out upon it? How beautiful was the city Herod built and that Jesus knew? And what sort of

place was it that Titus ordered razed in the unfulfilled hope of erasing Judaism permanently from the earth?

Strangely enough this most interesting city of the ancient world has been by far the most difficult to unearth and reconstruct. Jericho, Megiddo, Beth-shan and other Bible towns yielded up their secrets with astounding clarity, while Jerusalem's are in many respects totally obliterated. Unlike the others, this ancient site has developed no *tell,* no pile of debris, heaped tier upon tier and filled with artifacts and telltale ruins of former buildings. Jerusalem from very early times has been built of stone, rather than of clay bricks. Whenever it was destroyed, the remains of its walls and its houses were not leveled off for a new start and thus left to be unearthed at a later time, carefully examined and reconstructed at least in words and drawings. Instead, the stone was reused, and for the most part all traces of older buildings disappeared in the new.

It is true that some parts of old walls and structures remained in place. Also debris like potsherds accumulated at certain points, particularly where it could be dumped conveniently down a hillside into a valley, and where some

The Old City of Jerusalem seen from the air

King David Tower, Jerusalem

of it still lies today up to 50 or more feet deep. Yet the story it tells is general and confused, and not at all specific as in other ancient city sites.

Archaeological excavations in the Holy Land began first at Jerusalem, and just over a century ago. Several things, however, tended to defeat these earlier efforts. Chief among them was the almost complete lack at that time of anything approaching effective archaeological methods. There was also a human equation somewhat annoying and difficult to solve. This revolved about the Turkish overlords, from whom permission to dig was often hard to come by. And allied with this phase was the Arab population, whose land had to be leased at enormous rentals, or whose indifferent labor had to be bought and employed. Some latter day archaeologists claim that even the Bible itself proved something of a handicap to unbiased findings, since it was thought that every second spade full of dirt should uncover some object related to Bible text, or that every conclusion drawn must be confirmed and verified by an appropriate Biblical reference.

It is only in fairly recent years, particularly the period between the two World Wars, that truly dependable progress has been made in the Jerusalem area. But even now the opinions of the more able archaeologists and the popular guide books to the city are strongly at variance in many respects. Of the evidence thus far unearthed there are conservatively far more "probabilities" than there are "certainties." Far more is reliably known about Ur of the Chaldees, dead for twenty-two centuries, than about Jerusalem, still alive today.

Even the length of time during which the site has been inhabited cannot be positively determined. Certain relics have come to light which seem to go back as far as 3000 B.C. In fact there are burial remains which "might" possibly antedate the oldest found at Damascus. If this is true, this latter place may yet have to release to Jerusalem its present distinction of being the oldest continually inhabited city site in the world.

To date evidences from the original Jebusite stronghold, other than a short stretch of wall and one good-sized gate, have been disappointingly few. However, it is possible now to determine with fair accuracy the limits of the city which David captured, owned as his personal property, and made the capital of the combined kingdom. While its walls were stout and had to be carried by stealth, its size may seem to many to have been disappointingly small. It has been likened in shape to a foot print and was not above 1250 feet long and 400 feet wide in its greatest dimensions. Its walls thus embraced no more than 8 acres, which would have made it about equal to Jericho, but much less than one-third the size of important Megiddo on the international caravan route to the north. Little that David may have done to his city, beyond repair of the walls, has yet come to light.

This Davidic city, however, must have seemed like cramped quarters indeed for Solomon's soaring ambitions. Since the threshing floor purchased for the site of the altar and then the Temple lay to the north, and the nature of the land favored such a move, Solomon expanded up along the west side of the Kidron

Jerusalem, Mount Zion

Valley and about the upper end of the vale, *el Wad,* which separates the two ridgelike hills over which the city ultimately spread. There, in the section known today as *Haran,* he built the Temple and its neighboring complex of structures, his own palace, and the related government buildings.

Presumably the city increased rather rapidly in population between the time of its capture by David and the middle years of Solomon's reign. While the spring at Gihon, to which there had been an enclosed passageway in early times, had been sufficient at first, the demands of the Temple seem to have made it inadequate. The Talmud records that water was brought by aqueduct a distance of 7 miles from pools at Etam, a favorite rendezvous of Solomon just beyond Bethlehem. It is possible that he first built this conduit, which is thought to have been employed as part of a similar project which made great trouble for Pontius Pilate. But like the city of David, little but fragments of walls seem to have been preserved of all of Solomon's extensive building activities.

The geography of Jerusalem in the long period between the death of Solomon and the return of Nehemiah is subject to much debate. According to one theory, the city even in Solomon's time had probably spread to include most of the southwest ridge as shown on the map of Old Testament Jerusalem. A further expansion into the Mishneh or "New Quarter" northwest of the temple area took place at the time of Manasseh and Josiah in the 7th century. Some scholars dispute the inclusion of the southwest hill and visualize a more modest expansion prior to 400 B.C. According to this second theory, the western limit of Nehemiah's city would be that shown by the dashed line on the

map. Still, if the gates and ramparts mentioned in the second and third chapters of the Book of Nehemiah were then located at the same points where they were later known to be, the physical growth of Jerusalem had been substantial in the centuries between the building of the first and second Temples. From Bible text it would appear that even before the close of the Persian period the walls encircled most of the top of the hill to the west of the site of the Jebusite town.

During the Hellenistic and Maccabaean periods, the city presumably spread to the north but seems to have remained more or less stationary along its other boundaries. As has already been pointed out, it was not by any means the largest or most important city in Palestine in Roman times. This is evidenced in part by the fact the procurators and the bulk of the Roman troops left it for Caesarea rather promptly after the crowds which had assembled for the three annual festivals had set off for their homes. Herod the Great had started to rebuild some of the walls destroyed by Pompey, and the characteristic masonry employed during his reign is still in evidence in the remains of the ancient fortifications still standing today.

This monarch had a passion for building, very much like Solomon, and not uncommon among eastern rulers in the long ago. While he expended much effort at other points, he spent rather lavish sums on the improvement and beautification of Jerusalem itself. Beyond its walls, other items of fortification included three strong towers close by his own combination fortress and palace at the far edge of the western hill.

This seems to have been both a handsome and a formidable group of buildings, set in

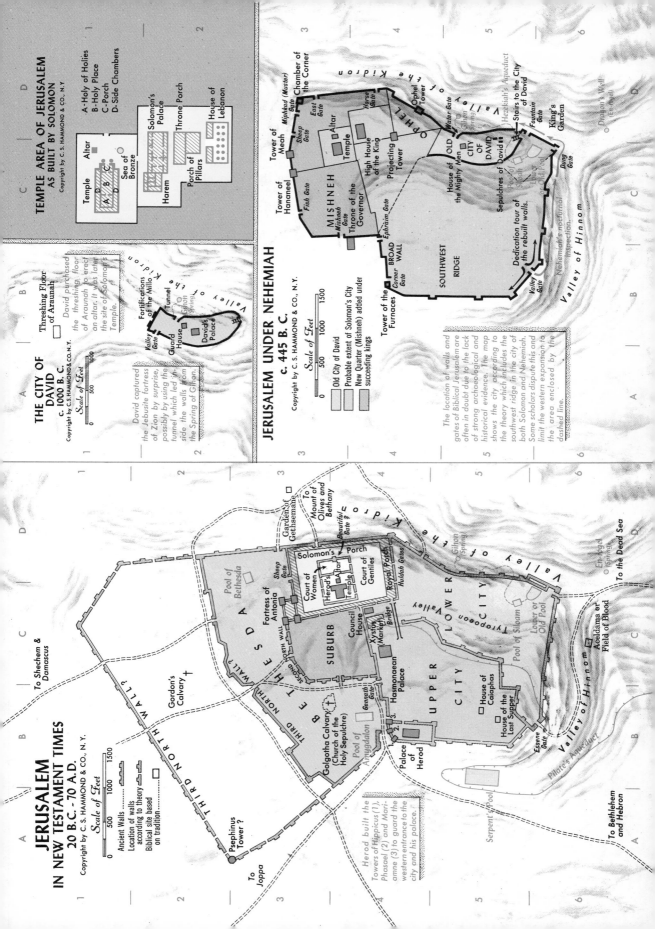

TEMPLE AREA OF JERUSALEM
AS BUILT BY SOLOMON
Copyright by C. S. HAMMOND & CO. N.Y.

A - Holy of Holies
B - Holy Place
C - Porch
D - Side Chambers

Temple   Altar

Sea of Bronze

Solomon's Palace

Harem

Throne Porch

House of Lebanon

Porch of Pillars

THE CITY OF DAVID
c. 1000 B.C.
Copyright by C.S.HAMMOND & CO. N.Y.

Threshing Floor of Araunah

David purchased the threshing floor of Araunah to erect an altar. It was later the site of Solomon's Temple.

Scale of Feet
0   500   1000

Valley of the Kidron

Fortifications of the Millo

Tunnel

Gihon Spring

Valley Gate

Guard House

David's Palace

David captured the Jebusite fortress of Zion by surprise, possibly by using the tunnel which led inside the walls from the Spring of Gihon.

JERUSALEM UNDER NEHEMIAH
c. 445 B.C.
Copyright by C. S. HAMMOND & CO. N.Y.

Scale of Feet
0   500   1000   1500

Old City of David

Probable extent of Solomon's City

New Quarter (Mishneh) added under succeeding kings

The location of walls and gates of Biblical Jerusalem are often in doubt due to the lack of strong archaeological and historical evidence. The map shows the city according to the theory which includes the southwest ridge in the city of both Solomon and Nehemiah. Some scholars dispute this and limit the western expansion to the area enclosed by the dashed line.

Valley of the Kidron

Chamber of the Corner

Miphkad (Muster)

East Gate

Tower of Meah

Sheep Gate

Altar

Temple

Horse Gate

Ophel Tower

Water Gate

OPHEL

Gihon Spring

Hezekiah's Aqueduct

Stairs to the City of David

Fountain Gate

King's Garden

Dragon's Well (En-Rogel)

Tower of Hananeel

Fish Gate

MISHNEH
Mishneh

Throne of the Governor

High House of the King

Projecting Tower

House of the Mighty Men

Sepulchres of David

OLD CITY OF DAVID

Old Pool

Dung Gate

Tower of the Furnaces

Ephraim Gate

Dedication tour of the rebuilt walls.

BROAD WALL

Corner Gate

SOUTHWEST RIDGE

Nehemiah's nocturnal inspection.

Valley Gate

Valley of Hinnom

JERUSALEM
IN NEW TESTAMENT TIMES
20 B.C. - 70 A.D.
Copyright by C. S. HAMMOND & CO. N.Y.

Scale of Feet
0   500   1000   1500

Ancient Walls
Location of walls according to theory based on tradition
Biblical site based on tradition

To Shechem & Damascus

THIRD NORTH WALL

Psephinus Tower ?

To Joppa

Gordon's Calvary

Golgotha Calvary (Church of the Holy Sepulchre)

Pool of Amygdalon

Gennath Gate

Palace of Herod

Serpent's Pool

To Bethlehem and Hebron

Herod built the Towers of Hippicus (1), Phasael (2) and Mariamne (3) to guard the western entrance to the city and his palace.

Garden of Gethsemane

To Mount of Olives and Bethany

Beautiful Gate ?

Pool of Bethesda

Sheep Gate

Fortress of Antonia

SECOND NORTH WALL

BETHESDA

SUBURB

Court of Women

Herod's Altar Temple

Solomon's Porch

Court of Gentiles

Royal Porch

Huldah Gates

Council House

Xystus Market

Bridge

Hasmonaean Palace

Tyropoeon Valley

LOWER

CITY

Gihon Spring

Valley of the Kidron

Pool of Siloam

Lower or Old Pool

UPPER

CITY

House of Caiaphas

House of the Last Supper

Essene Gate

Pilate's Aqueduct

Aceldama or Field of Blood

En-Rogel (Spring)

To the Dead Sea

Valley of Hinnom

gardens adorned with pools and porticoes. He also rebuilt the castle of Birah, or Baris, which had formed a strong point at the northwest corner of the wall from quite early times, and renamed it for his patron, Marc Antony. Grecian influences had begun to enter the land nearly three centuries before, and many of them were continued in their Roman form by the later conquerors. To cater to these interests, Herod built a theater, an ampitheater and a hippodrome in Jerusalem despite continuing opposition by many of the leading Jews to such Gentile structures and their purposes.

The more fanatical of Herod's subjects never forgot that he was an Idumaean, and thus of the line of Esau rather than that of Jacob. In the hope of filling this awkward chasm, he included in his pretentious building efforts the rebuilding of the five-hundred-year-old Temple started by Zerubbabel. It is conceivable that there may have been opposition to the enterprise when first proposed, for when the work finally got under way about 19 B.C., it was carried on at the outset by specially trained priests. This gave assurance that sacred areas would not be violated, and also that there might be no interruption in its daily use. While the sanctuary proper was entirely reconstructed in a year and a half, work of one sort or another was in progress within the Temple complex up to the time of its final destruction in the

summer of A.D. 70 by Titus' Roman legions.

The city which Jesus knew, which He visited during the festivals and where he labored briefly in the early part and again toward the end of his ministry, was in decided contrast to the city David had wrested from the Jebusites. Similarly, the modern city is quite unlike that through which the Master walked, for Hadrian, years later, did his best to clear away all traces of it. Yet the flow of the land is little changed, and some at least of its permanent features remain to this day. Such could be the Pool of Siloam, quite certainly located at the edge of the Tyropoeon (Cheese Makers') Valley, near the lower tip of the original city. Different locations have been given to the Pool of Bethesda, but the only acceptable site is that on the property of the Church of St. Anne where the sites of two pools have been unearthed which fit the ancient description.

The sites of certain of the buildings with which He had some association have been fairly well established, such as the Temple, the Hasmonaean Palace and the Palace of Herod. Certain gates through which He entered and left the city are fairly well-known, and the location of the Garden of Gethsemane just off the Jericho road as it rises out of the Kidron Valley, is pretty certainly marked by the Church of Gethsemane. The problem of the location of Pilate's Praetorium has not been completely settled, but most authorities accept the Tower of Antonia as the most likely location. The alternative site is the Palace of Herod near Jaffa Gate. The point where the Crucifixion took place is still contested due to the difficulty of locating the exact line of the second north wall. Yet the traditional site recognized by the Church of the Holy Sepulchre seems far more probable than such assumptions as the distant hillock outside the walls now known as "Gordon's Calvary."

What archaeologists most hopefully sought through the years in Jerusalem have been the Tomb of the Savior and the Tombs of the Kings. Great has been the religious desire to locate that miraculous spot where the Resurrection took place, but as yet no sepulcher which bears conclusive evidence of being it has been uncovered. A thirst to dig up buried treasure has stimulated many attempts to locate the series of crypts in which the Bible infers that David and

The Church of the Holy Sepulchre, Jerusalem

The Temple Terrace with the Dome of the Rock, probable site of the Jewish altar, in the foreground

some of his successors were buried. Two recorded instances during which Judaean rulers rifled these tombs have already been noted, yet the belief has long persisted that great wealth still lay hidden away at some point beneath the city. In fact, in the early part of the present century a European syndicate spent two years and thousands of dollars to no avail in such hopeful excavation, the work being carried on in accord with instructions cabled by a clairvoyant from Europe. Up to the present time, the last resting places of both Jesus and the Kings of Israel have not been established with certainty.

The primitive Church received its start and gathered strength in Jerusalem, and it would be nice to know the location of the home of Mary, mother of John Mark, where it is presumed the believers gathered for worship. This, like the site of the Last Supper, has so far eluded all attempts at determination. There evidently was a great deal of building and rebuilding during that first century. Mention has been made of the wall started by Herod Agrippa I, but stopped by the Romans, and also of the 18,000 men which his son had on the Temple payrolls at one time, in what appears to have been, to some extent, a make-work program. The city's fortifications were extensively rebuilt and relocated during these years, and their courses are now a matter of great speculation.

And then to end the animosity and rancor which many years of Jewish fanaticism had built up, Titus razed Jerusalem after its capture in A.D. 70. Sixty odd years later, following the last serious Jewish revolt, Hadrian crushed and expunged this Holy City and built Roman, and completely Gentile, Aelia Capitolina in its stead. Two centuries later Constantine, espousing the Christian cause, made Jerusalem and neighboring Bethlehem Christian centers. He ruled from Byzantium, which he had renamed Constantinople and made the capital of the eastern part of the Roman Empire. Several of Jerusalem's commemorative churches were first built under his direction, and the city's older portion began to take on some of the characteristics it still has today. Then, about the year 400, when the separation of the Roman Empire into an eastern and a western part became final, Jerusalem came under the control of the Byzantine Empire.

In the early seventh century, the land passed under control of the Arabs and would know Mohammedan rulers for the next twelve centuries, with the exception of a period during the Crusades. At that time, Jerusalem fell to the Europeans after a two-month siege in the spring of 1099. Following a shockingly barbarous massacre of its inhabitants, Godfrey of Bouillon became its ruler with the title of "Defender of the Holy Sepulchre." After somewhat uneasy possession by the Crusaders, the city was retaken in 1187 by Saladin, Sultan of Egypt and Syria, and finally lost by the Christians in 1244. It then returned to Moslem control, where it remained until the time of the first World War.

XXX

THE BIBLE LANDS TODAY

During most of the Christian Era, the Holy Land has drawn its quota of pilgrims and visitors and has held the attention of large numbers from among the three great living religions which worship but one God. In more recent times, as man's interest in precise historical knowledge grew, this land has also attracted more and more scholars and researchers.

Through the centuries, churchmen and others, like the renowned traveler Pietro della Valle, made records of Bible sites. In the late 1830s, the American theologian Robinson for the first time carefully mapped Arabic place names and identified many Biblical towns. And the study of old Semitic languages was greatly stimulated, when in 1868 a young Frenchman, Clermont-Ganneau, discovered the famous Moabite Stone with one of the oldest known Semitic inscriptions.

Archaeological research, begun in the middle of the last century, steadily improved its methods. Its discoveries became especially numerous in the time between the two World Wars, when conditions in Palestine were comparatively unhampered and allowed very extensive excavations. During those years several of the old city sites in Palestine, such as Jericho and Megiddo, were carefully studied, and our knowledge of early civilization was greatly advanced. Yet, up to the present, archaeology has made only a beginning in this historically so immensely interesting land. Many more finds will come to light, and some of them may be as unexpected as the recent dramatic discovery of the Dead Sea Scrolls.

Today the governments of the countries in the Middle East take an interest in this research and have their own departments of antiquities. But the political climate of the years between the two World Wars, so helpful to archaeological research, unfortunately did not last, and Palestine has recently become again the scene of tension and even strife.

Under treaties hopefully made, and some of which antedate World War I, Palestine was to become a "homeland" for Jewish people. To aid resettlement, the World Zionist Organizations began to pour funds into that land, intending to improve economic conditions there and pave the way for the reception of immi-

View of Haifa and the bay from Mt. Carmel

THE HOLY LAND TODAY

Copyright by C. S. Hammond & Co., N.Y.

Scale of Miles

0 10 20 30 40 50

Perennial Rivers ....
Capitals ....
Armistice Demarcation Lines ....
Railroads ....
Seasonal Rivers & Streams
International Boundaries ....
Demilitarized Zone Boundaries ....
Ancient Sites ....

Map labels

Mediterranean Sea

LEBANON

UNITED ARAB REPUBLIC

SYRIA

JEBEL ED DRUZ

SYRIAN DESERT

ISRAEL

NEGEV

JORDAN

UNITED ARAB REPUBLIC

EGYPT

SINAI PENINSULA

Gulf of Aqaba

Saida (Sidon)
Jezzin
Rasheiya
Damascus
Sarafand (Zarephath)
Qatana
Kiswe
Buraq
Litani R.
Merj 'Uyun
Sur (Tyre)
Qir. Shemona
Baniyas (Caesarea Philippi)
Es Sanamein
Tibnin
Dan
El Quneitra
En Naqura
Kedesh
Hulata
L. Hula
Nawa
Sheikh Miskin
Nahariya
Safad
Abu Sinan
Yirka
Acre
Qiryat Yam
Kefar Ata
Ginneisar
Tiberias
Fiq
El Qanawat (Kanatha)
Es Suweida
Haifa
Nazareth
Capernaum Tabigha
Sea of Galilee (Lake Tiberias)
Tirat Karmel
Mt. Tabor
'Afula
'Afiqim
Yarmuk R.
Samar
Der'a
Busra (Bostra)
Salkhad
Dor
Megiddo
Beit Shean (Beth-shan)
Irbid
Ramtha
Zikhron Ya'aqov
Taanach
Husn
Caesarea
Pardes Hanna
Jenin
Tabaqat Fahl (Pella)
Mafraq
Hadera
Tubas
'Ajlun
Jarash (Gerasa)
Natanya
Tulkarm
Taiyiba
Sabastiya (Samaria)
Nablus
Er Rumman
Kefar Sava
Shechem
Zarqa R. (Jabbok)
Herzliya
Mt. Gerizim
Petah Tiqva
Salfit
Shiloh
Es Salt
Safut
Zarqa
Tel Aviv-Jaffa
Ramat Gan
Jifna
Shunat Nimrin (Beth-nimrah)
Amman (Rabbath-ammon, Philadelphia)
Holon
Lydda (Lod)
Bira
Modin
Ramallah
Jericho
Hisban (Heshbon)
Ramle
Gezer
Rehovot
Kefar 'Eqron (Ekron)
Eizariya (Bethany)
Jericho
Ashdod
Beit Shemesh
Jerusalem
Mt. Nebo
Madaba
Jiza
Migdal Ashqelon
Ascalon
Bethlehem
Khirbet Qumrân
Lakhish
Beth-zur
Negba
'Uzza
Mareshah
Hebron
'Ein Gedi
Machaerus W. el Heidan
Dhiban (Dibon)
Khan ez Zabib
GAZA STRIP
Gaza
Lachish
Dead Sea
W. el Mujib (Arnon)
Sa'ad
Dura
Dhahiriya
Masada
Rabba (Rabbath-moab)
Qatrana
Khan Yunis
Gerar
Ziklag
Beit Qama
W. el Hafira
Rafiah
Sharuhen
Habesor
Beersheba
Omer
Arad
Mazra
El Karak
Nir Yits-haq
Nevatim
Sedom
Mazar
Manzil
El 'Arish
Revivim
Safi
W. el Hasa
Muhai
Kefar Yeroham
Tenr
'Aina
Abu Aweigila
Hasa
W. el Aqaba
Sede Boqer
Tafila
'Abur
El Qusaima
Kadesh-barnea
'Ein Hatseva
Dana
River of Egypt
Nitsana
Shaubak
'Uneiza
Paran
'Ein Yahav
Petra
Wadi Musa
Hijon
Taiyiba
Ma'an
Gharandal
El Kuntilla
Nakhl
Yotvata
Ras en Naqb
Giraffa
W. el Aqaba
El Quweira
El Thamad
Beer Ora
W. Abu Tarefiya
'Ein Netafim
Eilat (Elath)
Etzion-geber (Elath)
'Aqaba

Inset map

THE INHERITANCE OF THE TWELVE TRIBES

Scale of Miles

0 20 40 60 80

Mediterranean Sea
Tyre
Damascus
Dan
Sea of Galilee
R. Jordan
Jerusalem
Dead Sea
AMMON
Beer-sheba
MOAB
EDOM

cludes most of the hill country above Jerusalem. Running southward, the border curves back sharply so that only a portion of the Holy City, that is, most of the Old City, is within the domain of this Arab country; all of the New City of Jerusalem lies in Israel. Then the border swings west again, taking in most of the Judaean highlands.

Israel retained only a long, irregular sliver of land, ranging from the foothills of Mount Hermon in the northeast down along the Mediterranean coast from Achzib to just below the ruins of ancient Ashkelon. From there its border swings southeast to the upper end of the Gulf of Aqaba, where it holds a few miles of valuable seacoast, and then turns north up the Wadi 'Arabah to take in about half the western shore of the Dead Sea.

This, then, is the state of Israel, the new country of the Jews, where they have established a modern republic and are building an independent nation, after their people lived under foreign governments and in other lands for almost 2000 years.

Along Israel's borders are four Arab lands. The frontage with Lebanon to the north, being in rugged mountain country, has posed few serious problems. By contrast, the forty-mile common boundary with Syria to the northeast has occasioned a continuing series of unfortunate incidents, some of the bloodiest of which have taken place in the 33-foot-wide shore strip on the eastern edge of the Sea of Galilee held by Israel. To the southeast, the Egyptian-held "Gaza-Strip" has bred clash after clash, some of them with international repercussions.

To the east, Israel and Jordan face each other across a common boundary which is approximately 350 miles long. It is an unfriendly frontier, as shown by the sobering statement in contemporary travel literature—"The *only* land connection between Israel and the neighboring Arab countries is at Jerusalem, where the border between Israel and Jordan can be crossed at a special post known as the Mandelbaum Gate." And as if this was not enough to emphasize the precarious situation, the following warning has to be added: "Travelers can cross this border in one direction only. No recrossing will ordinarily be permitted."

In spite of these difficulties, there is today a need and a desire of ever greater numbers to

grants. At first these endeavors were calculated to increase the living standard of all residents, the Arabs quite as much as the Jews.

However, economic and social conditions in combination forced the Jewish people in certain European countries to migrate in very great numbers in the 1920s and 1930s. Since many of them chose Palestine, the influx was very heavy, and tension with the Arab population there and in neighboring lands began to mount. Such tension outlived World War II and in fact became sufficiently aggravated so that the matter was eventually laid in the lap of the United Nations General Assembly.

Finally, in November 1947, it was deemed necessary that Palestine be partitioned. But before the plan approved by the United Nations could become reality, the situation got out of hand and war ensued. When a settlement finally was reached in 1949, the new boundaries, shown on the accompanying map, largely followed those established by the troop action.

Jordan, which for some years had been ruled by Britain under a mandate, received its independence in March 1946 as the Hashemite Kingdom of Jordan. From a point about 20 miles south of the Sea of Galilee, its territory extends west of the River Jordan and in-

know the wonders of the Bible Lands at first hand. While the great bulk of the Bible Story took place in Palestine, or what is at present both Israel and Jordan, other Asian lands such as Syria, Lebanon, Iraq, Iran and Turkey as well as Egypt in Africa, have had significance for happenings in the Bible. And across the sea, Greece and Italy, and also the islands of Cyprus and Malta, played a part in the Bible Story, mainly in the journeys of the Apostle Paul and others. But while the European countries and the Mediterranean islands need not concern us here, it might be well to consider briefly what the other lands have to offer the modern visitor.

ISRAEL

Even a casual examination of the map will indicate what a relatively small portion of all the better known Bible scenes took place within the area that constitutes present-day Israel. But in spite of its small size, this is typical Bible country, where the great past is vividly felt.

Galilee, where Jesus spent much of his life, lies in Israel. At Mary's Well in Nazareth people fetch the water today as they did in Gospel times. In Capernaum at the shore of the Sea of Galilee, the ruins of a beautifully built synagogue of the third century A.D. have been found and partly restored, while most synagogues of ancient times have been lost. Between the hills of Galilee and Mount Carmel extends the plain of Esdraelon, famous Biblical battlefield. To the south of Mount Carmel headland stretches the plain of Sharon, in Bible times known for its flowers, today a land of farms, fields and citrus groves. Further along the shore is the plain once inhabited by ancient Israel's formidable foes and neighbors, the Philistines. East of this plain lie the foothills of Shephelah, where stood the important stronghold of Lachish. Its tell has yielded priceless letters in ancient Hebrew from the time of the Prophet Jeremiah (6th century B.C.). From the Shephelah there is a corridor stretching up into the highlands to embrace the new section of Jerusalem.

To the south, Israel's holdings include Idumaea, or ancient Edom where copper was mined in very early times by the Egyptians and then by the enslaved Edomites in Solomon's

Suliman Mosque at Damascus

time. Further south, in the point running down to the Gulf of Aqaba, an arm of the Red Sea, is the Negev. Here is a wilderness that was dotted with Nabataean towns in the time of Christ, and which the people of Israel today are striving to again make habitable and productive.

While ancient sites are carefully preserved and exhibited, Israel has gone a long way toward becoming a very modern country, where one may witness the efforts of an active people to build a modern state with Western conceptions on the basis of Old-Testament faith in an ancient Asian land.

JORDAN

When it is recalled that such well-known places as Samaria, Shechem, Shiloh, Bethel, Bethany, Bethlehem, Hebron, and all of the Old City of Jerusalem itself, lie within the modern Kingdom of Jordan, it is readily evident that it now encompasses an appreciable portion of the Holy Land. Thus any who are stimulated even in part by the Bible in making a journey to the lands east of the Mediterranean, will wish to visit the Hashemite State.

In the Judaean highlands south of Jerusalem is Hebron, where over the cave of Mach-

pelah, burial place of the Patriarchs, and above fine ancient walls and Byzantine ruins, a Moslem mosque has been erected. About six miles north of Jerusalem is ancient Gibeon, and the capital city of Amman lies on the "King's Highway", old in Moses' time, in the hills east of the Jordan. This is ancient Rabbah, outside whose walls Bath-sheba's husband, Uriah, was slain through David's connivance. The Church of the Nativity in Bethlehem, begun by Constantine, rises above the traditional site of the manger. And in the Old City of Jerusalem, besides ancient walls, like the Wailing Wall, parts of which date back to Solomon's time, there are magnificent Moslem mosques, like the Dome of the Rock built in the 7th century A.D., at the site of Solomon's temple and some of them, like the Church of the Holy Sepulcher, of great antiquity. In sacred memory and veneration, it is indeed Jerusalem the Golden.

The land, which reaches to within nine miles of the Mediterranean at Qalqilye, west of Nablus (Shechem), extends far to the east into the Syrian desert, where it touches the western reaches of Iraq. Burdened by nearly a half million Arab refugees, once residents of Israel, and without either the enterprise or the outside capital assistance by which its neighbor to the west has profited, Jordan's progress and modernization have been far more limited. The land suffers greatly from lack of natural resources. Although life there in many respects has remained quite unchanged since the times of the Bible, this colorful country is making a definite attempt to become a modern nation.

EGYPT

This large Arab country lies at the southwestern point of the "Fertile Crescent" which swings up through Palestine and Syria and then curves south through Mesopotamia to find its other end at the joint mouth of the Tigris and Euphrates rivers. Egypt's civilization was established when the Hebrew people were still wandering herdsmen. This great country to the south offered a refuge to the Hebrews on several occasions. Abraham came there, and Jacob and his descendants lived under the Pharaohs for an extended time. Egypt exerted influence upon both the Kingdom of Judah and of Israel, and it received the infant Jesus and His parents in the hazardous days following His birth. Later, Alexandria, at the delta of the Nile, became a center of learning for the western world including Palestine, and it was one of the great strongholds of early Christianity.

In this land along the Nile, amidst a hopeful but somewhat turbulent atmosphere of an emerging modern statehood stand the great monuments of a fabulous past. Signs of a valiant attempt to come abreast of our technical age often lie near the sites of Biblical happenings. And out in the desert and in the small villages along the irrigation canals, the people live very much as they did at the time of the Pharaohs.

SYRIA

Egypt has today united with Syria to form the United Arab Republic, a land which lies both on the African and the Asian continent. Syria's boundary reaches the shores of the Mediterranean above Lebanon, skirts the southern frontier of Turkey far to the east to a point above ancient Nineveh. It then swings to the southwest along the Iraq border, eventually reaching down to the Sea of Galilee.

In this area, which includes the upper valley of the Euphrates River, many of the pages of the Bible Story have taken place. Crossed by caravan routes, it was a country where goods from Africa, Asia and Europe were exchanged and where great civilizations met and fused. In this land, where roads and roadways always mattered, can be seen one of the best-preserved Roman roads between Aleppo and Antioch (Haleb and Antakya today). Beautifully located Damascus is the oldest continously occupied city site known today. About 140 miles to the north lies Hama, the Hamath of the Bible. From there, the caravan route led to Aleppo, which is a great trading center today as it was in ancient times. These are but a few of the many Syrian points of interest worthy of attention.

LEBANON

This little land, stretching for about 120 miles along the Mediterranean and averaging about 40 miles in width, includes such great attractions as ancient Tyre (Sur), Sidon (Saida) and Byblos (Gebal). It was from Byblos that the famous "Cedars of Lebanon" were shipped to build David's and Solomon's palaces as well as the "House of the Lord" erected by the latter. Its name, from which the Greek term for the papyrus scroll was developed, eventually gave us our word "Bible."

Also along the coast is the lovely capital city of Beirut. About 40 miles to the northeast, in the interior at the headwaters of the Litani and Orontes rivers, stands one of the most famous of the many ruins of the Roman world, the "Temple of the Sun," at Ba'albek, the ancient Heliopolis.

IRAQ AND IRAN

Iraq lies at the northeastern end of the "Fertile Crescent," in the valley of the Euphrates and Tigris rivers. This was Mesopotamia, the other great center of ancient civilization. Abraham and his tribesmen had been under its influence before they left for the "Promised Land." Indeed, as modern excavations penetrate deeper into the ancient layers of *tells* and towns and our interpretations of inscriptions and sherds reach farther into the past, old and most interesting connections between Mesopotamian and Hebrew traditions appear.

Northwestern shore of Dead Sea, where Dead Sea Scrolls were found

This land is fairly saturated with ancient history. Within its borders are the ruins of such fabled cities as Nineveh, Babylon and Ur of the Chaldees. Here the Ten Tribes marched away into bondage and were swallowed up and passed into oblivion. In Babylon and its vicinity the people of Judah were in captivity. Many of their number remained there and centuries later made that city a more important Jewish center than Jerusalem itself.

then was called. Here that great missionary of the Gospel, Paul, traveled, preached and founded churches on his first two journeys, and part of his third journey led through this land. Even on his final trip, when he was en route from Sidon to Rome, his ship touched at the Asian port of Myra, which also has another interesting association. In the 4th century A.D. the city had a bishop who was famous for his gifts and who later was canonized as St. Nich-

A typical shepherd of the Holy Lands with his flock

Iran, too, has its place among the lands of the Bible. From here, which then was Persia, came the mighty Cyrus, who became God's instrument, terminating by his decree the Babylonian captivity. It was also in this land that the Jewish maiden, Esther, became the queen, and helped to give modern Jerusalem its most popular festival, Purim. This spring carnival still celebrates the deliverance of the exiles in Persia of Esther's day from wholesale massacre.

TURKEY

Many Bible scenes in the New Testament take us farther afield than the Holy Land, into "Asia," as a large area of present-day Turkey

olas; he became the prototype for our Santa Claus.

Besides Paul's birthplace, Tarsus, and the many towns which he and his companions visited, there are other points of great historical interest within this land. In its eastern mountains is Ararat, traditional place where Noah's Ark came to rest. At the Hellespont, Xerxes built two tremendous bridges of boats as he marched into Europe and defeat. And when Alexander set out to avenge this campaign— but actually planning to conquer the Persian empire—he won his first decisive battle against the Persians on the banks of the Granicus River (Kocabas River today) not far from Ilium of Homeric fame. His great contemporary, lantern-carrying Diogenes, was born in the little Black Sea port of Sinope. During the development of the young Christian Church from a sect toward an official religion, a little town in Turkey rose to importance. It is Iznik, ancient Nicaea, about 50 miles southwest of Istanbul, where the Nicene Creed was formulated.

Some 100 miles further to the south and west is the modern city of Bursa, important town and famous spa in Ottoman times. Its magnificent monuments recall the Ottoman rule during the Middle Ages, when this country was at the heart of a vast empire, presenting for some 200 years a serious threat to Europe and Christianity. Against this backdrop of a varied history appears present-day Turkey, a republic since the end of World War I, with its very remarkable record of modernization.

* * * *

With the constantly improving facilities for travel, it is to be hoped that the world may build far greater and more lasting peace and security so that more and more people will be able to visit this remarkable meeting ground of three continents. This is a land where important discoveries in archaeology are certain to be made, where so much history, sacred and profane, has been enacted, and where some of the most important political problems of our day are taking new form. To know it well is rewarding from whatever angle we approach it. Here we can follow the roots of our civilization farther into the past than anywhere else in the world, and the promise that has gone out from this land is our best hope for the future.

Boy with bushel of wheat

THE NAMES OF THE BOOKS OF THE BIBLE

OLD TESTAMENT

Names *	Abbreviations	Names *	Abbreviations
Genesis	Gen.	Ezekiel (Ezechiel)	Eze.
Exodus	Ex.	Daniel	Dan.
Leviticus	Lev.	Hosea (Osee)	Hos. (Os)
Numbers	Num.	Joel	Joel
Deuteronomy	Deut.	Amos	Amos
Joshua (Josue)	Josh. (Jos)	Obadiah (Abdias)	Ob. (Abd)
Judges	Judg.	Jonah (Jonas)	Jonah (Jon)
Ruth	Ruth	Micah (Micheas)	Mic. (Mi)
1 Samuel (1 Samuel or 1 Kings)	1 Sam. (1 Kings)	Nahum	Nah.
2 Samuel (2 Samuel or 2 Kings)	2 Sam. (2 Kings)	Habakkuk (Habacuc)	Hab.
1 Kings (3 Kings)	1 Kings (3 Kings)	Zephaniah (Sophonias)	Zeph. (So)
2 Kings (4 Kings)	2 Kings (4 Kings)	Haggai (Aggeus)	Hag. (Ag)
1 Chronicles (1 Paralipomenon)	1 Chron. (1 Par)	Zechariah (Zacharias)	Zec. (Za)
2 Chronicles (2 Paralipomenon)	2 Chron. (2 Par)	Malachi (Malachias)	Mal.
Ezra (Esdras)	Ezra (Esd)		
Nehemiah (Nehemias or 2 Esdras)	Neh. (Neh or 2 Esd)	APOCRYPHA	
Esther	Esth.	Tobit (Tobias)	To. (Tb)
Job	Job	Judith	Jth
Psalms	Ps.	Wisdom	Wis.
Proverbs	Prov.	Ecclesiasticus	
Ecclesiastes	Eccl.	(also Sirach)	Eccl. (Sir)
The Song of Solomon		Baruch	Bar.
(Canticle of Canticles)	Sol. (Ct)	1 Maccabees	
Isaiah (Isaias)	Is.	(1 Machabees)	1 Mac. (1 Mc)
Jeremiah (Jeremias)	Jer.	2 Maccabees	
Lamentations	Lam.	(2 Machabees)	2 Mac. (2 Mc)

NEW TESTAMENT

Matthew	Matt.	1 Timothy	1 Tim.
Mark	Mark	2 Timothy	2 Tim.
Luke	Luke	Titus	Titus
John	John	Philemon	Philem.
The Acts	Acts	To the Hebrews	Heb.
Epistle to the Romans	Rom.	Epistle of James	Jas.
1 Corinthians	1 Cor.	1 Peter	1 Pet.
2 Corinthians	2 Cor.	2 Peter	2 Pet.
Galatians	Gal.	1 John	1 John
Ephesians	Eph.	2 John	2 John
Philippians	Phil.	3 John	3 John
Colossians	Col.	Jude	Jude
1 Thessalonians	1 Thes.	Revelation (Apocalypse)	Rev. (Ap)
2 Thessalonians	2 Thes.		

* Where Protestant and Catholic names differ, the
Catholic version appears in parenthesis.

NOTE

The spelling of Biblical names used in this book is that of the Authorized Version, better known as the King James Version. Cross references to most of the variant forms found in Confraternity of Christian Doctrine Text and the Douay and Knox versions of the Catholic Bible have been included in the index, therefore making it possible to use this book with either Protestant or Catholic Bibles.

GEOGRAPHIC INDEX

This index gives the location of all sites and geographical features found on the maps. Each entry gives the key reference, always a letter and number in combination, followed by the page numbers of the maps on which the name appears at that particular key reference. For example Abel-meholah appears at key reference D4 on the map on page 44. It also appears at key reference C4 on the maps on pages 61 and 68.

Abana River E1-16, 61, 68
Abdon C2-44
Abela-Bethmaachah,
  see Abel-beth-maachah (Abel)
Abel-beth-maachah (Abel)
  D2-44, 48, 61, 68, 84; B3-53, 72
Abel-maim,
  see Abel-beth-Maachah
Abel-meholah D4-44;C4-61, 68
Abel-Mehula, see Abel-meholah
Abel-Sattim, see Abel-shittim
Abel-shittim D5-44
Abila (in Abilene).........E1-117,
  124, 149, 156
Abila (in Batanaea).......D3-109,
  117, 124, 149, 156
Abila (in Peraea).........D5-156
Abilene E1-117, 124, 149, 156
Abydos (in Asia Minor)....B1-77
Abydos (in Egypt)............C5-77
Accaron, see Ekron
Acchad, see Akkad
Accho (Ptolemaïs) ...C3-16, 32,
  44, 48, 61, 68, 84, 96, 109, 124;
  C1-40; B3-53, 72
Aceldama or Field of Blood
  C6-173
Achad, see Akkad
Achaia (Greece)......D3-113, 160;
  C2-140, 144
Achazib, see Achzib
Achmetha (Ecbatana) D2-89
Achsaph, see Achshaph
Achshaph C3-32, 44
Achzib (Ecdippa).......C2-32, 44,
  48, 84
Acrabathane C6-109
Acrabbim, see Akrabbim
Acre, see also Accho........C2-177
Acron, see Ekron
Actium D3-113
Adad, see Hadid
Adada(h), see Aroer in Judah
Adam D4-32, 44
Adamah D4-48
Adana C1-136
Adarsa, see Adasa
Adasa C5-109
Adida (Hadid)....B4-109; B5-156
Adora B5-109, 149
Adoraim B5-61, 68, 84
Adramyttium D2-140, 144
Adria, Sea B1-140, 144
Adriatic Sea C2-113, 160
Adrumythium, see Adramyttium
Adullam C5-32, 44, 48, 61, 68,
  96, 109; B5-84
Aegean Sea A2-25; B2-77,
  89, 101; C2-140, 144; D3-160
Aestii D1-113, 160
Africa C3-20; B3-113, 160
Africa Nova B3-113
Agrigentum ..A2-140, 144;C3-160
Agrippium (Anthedon)....A5-177
Ai C5-32, 44, 84, 96; C1-40
Aialon, Aijalon, see Ajalon
Aila, see Elath
Ailath, see Elath
Aion, see Ijon
Ajalon B5-61, 68, 84
Ajalon, Valley of B5-16, 44
'Ajlun C2-177
Akhetaton (Tell el Amarna)
  C5-77
Akkad F3-25; G3-77
Akkrabattine, see Acrabathane
Akrabatta C4-156
Akrabbim, Ascent of........C7-16,
  32, 44
Alalakh D2-25
Alamanni B2-164
Alans F2-113, 160
Albania F2-113, 160

Albis River (Elbe)............C1-113
Aleppo, see Khalab
Alesia B2-113
Alexandria (in Egypt)....B2-101;
  D3-113,140, 144, 160, 164
Alexandria (in India) G3-101
Alexandria Arachosiorum..F2-101
Alexandria Arion
  (Herat)....F2-101
Alexandria Eschate G1-101
Alexandrium C4-109, 117
Alisar Huyuk (Kushshar)...C2-25
Alpine Provinces............B2-160
Alps B2-113, 160
Alus, see Alush
Alush B3-40
Amadoci D1-113, 160
Amalecites, see Amalekites
Amalekites B6-32, 48; B4-53
Amanus Mts. D1-136
Amardi H2-77; E2-89
Amardos River G2-25
Amarna, Tell el (Akhetaton)
  C5-77
Amasia F1-140, 144
Amastris E1-140, 144; E2-164
Amathus D4-109, 117,124, 133
Amisus F1-140, 144
Amman (Rabbath-ammon,
  Philadelphia)....C3-177
Ammaus, see Emmaus
Ammon E5-16, 32,124;
  D2-40; E4-44, 48, 61, 68, 84;
  C4-53; E3-77; D5-96, 101
Ammonium B4-77; B3-89, 101
Amorites D3-25; D5-32; C2-40
Amorrhites, Amorrites
  see Amorites
Amphipolis C1-140, 144
Amygdalon, Pool of........B4-173
Anab B6-44
Ananla(h), see Bethany
Anas River A3-113, 160
Anatho F3-77
Anathoth C5-84, 96
Anchialus D2-164
Ancona C2-113, 160, 164
Ancyra D2-77; C2-89, 101;
  E3-113; E2-140, 144, 160, 168
Anthedon, (Agrippium)...A5-109,
  117, 149, 156
Anti-Lebanon Mts. D4-136
Antioch (in Phrygia) E2-140, 144;
  E3-160, 164
Antioch (in Syria).........C2-101;
  E3-113, 164; D1-136; E2-140, 144
Antipatris (Aphek)........B4-117,
  124,149, 156
Anti-Taurus Mts. D2-25, 77
Antonia, Fortress of C3-173
Anxa B1-140, 144
Aorsi F2-160
Apamea D2-136
Aphec(a), see Aphek
Aphek (in Asher)............C3-44
Aphek (in Ephraim).......B4-32,
  44, 48, 61, 68, 84; C1-40
Aphek (in Geshur)......D3-44, 61,
  68, 84; B3-72
Apherema, see Ephraim, city
Aphik, see Aphek (in Asher)
Apollonia (in Macedonia)
  D2-113; C1-140, 144
Apollonia (in Palestine)..B4-109,
  117, 124, 149, 156
Appollonia (in Thrace)....B1-89;
  D2-113
Appii Forum A1-140, 144
'Aqaba C5-177
Aqaba, Gulf of C3-40, 177
Aquileia C2-113, 160, 164
Aquincum (Budapest)......C2-160
Aquitania B2-113, 160

Ar D6-32, 44, 48, 53, 68, 84;
  C2-40; B4-53, 72
'Araba, Wadi C4-177
Arabah C7-16, 32; C2-40;
  B4-53, 72
Arabella, see Arbela
Arabia F3-20; C2-72; D7-84;
  F4-113, 160; E5-136; E3-140, 144
Arabia (province)............E4-160
Arabian Desert E3-20
Arabian Sea F3-89, 101
Arabs F1-77; E6-84; C7-96
Arach, see Erech
Arachosia F2-89, 101
Arad C6-32, 44, 109; C3-177
Aradus (Arvad).............D3-136
Aral Sea E1-89, 101
Aram E2-20; D2-61; E3-77
Arama, see Hormah
Aramaeans (Syrians).D2-48, 77;
  C3-53
Aram-maachah, see Maachah
Aram-zobah, see Zobah
Ararat, Mt. C3-77
Ararat (region) see Armenia
  and Urartu
Araunah, Threshing Floor of
  B1-173
Araxes River F2-25; G2-77;
  D1-89; F2-113
Arbela (in Media)..........F2-25;
  G2-77; D2-89, 101; F3-164
Arbela (in Palestine).C3-109, 117
Arbella, see Arbela
Archelais C5-124
Arepolis (Rabbath Moab).D6-124
Areuna, see Araunah
Argob E3-44
Argos D3-160
Aria F2-89, 101
Arib (Arabs) F4-77
Arimathaea (Ramathaim)C4-124
Arimathea, see Arimathaea
'Arish, Wadi el (River of
  Egypt)........A7-16; A4-177
Arles B2-164
Armenia D2-89, 101; F3-113,
  160, 164
Armorica A2-113
Arnon River (Wadi el Mujib)
  D6-16, 32, 44, 48, 61, 68, 96,
  109, 117, 124, 149, 156; C2-40;
  C3-177
Aroer (in Judah).........C6-44, 48
Aroer (in Moab)....D6-32, 44, 48,
  61, 68, 84; B4-53
Arpad E2-77
Arphaxad, see Arphaxad
Arphad, see Arpad
Arphaxad F2-20
Arrapakha E2-77
Artaxata F3-113, 160
Arvad C3-25, 136; B2-53, 72;
  D3-77; C2-89
Arzawa B2-25
Asasonthamas,
  see Hazezon-tamar
Ascalon (Ashkelon)........B5-109,
  117, 124; A5-149, 156; B3-177
Aschenez, see Ashkenaz
Aser, see Asher
Ashdod (Azotus)....B5-32, 44, 48,
  68, 84, 96, 109, 124; C2-40;
  B4-53, 72; B3-113
Ashdod (district)............B5-96
Asher, Allotment of.........C2-44
Ashkelon (Ascalon)....A5-32, 44,
  48, 61, 68, 84, 96, 109; C2-40;
  B4-53, 72; D4-77
Ashkenaz ..D1, F1, E2-20; G1-77
Ashtaroth ..D3-32, 44, 48, 61, 68,
  84; D1-40; C3-53
Ashur E3-25; F3-77

Asia F2-20; D3-113, 160;
  D2-140, 144
Asia Minor E2-140, 144
Asiongaber, see Ezion-geber
Askelon, see Ashkelon
Asophon D4-109
Asor, see Hazor
Aspadana E2-89
Asphaltitis, Lake (Dead Sea)
  C6-124, 136, 149, 156
Asshur (Assyria)..............F2-20
Assos D2-140, 144
Assur, see Asshur, Assyria
Assuwa A2-25
Assyria F2-20, 77; E2-25;
  C2-89; F3-160
Assyrian Empire F3-77
Astacus C1-77
Astharoth, see Ashtaroth
Astorga A2-164
Astures A2-113
Asturica A2-160
Asur, Tell..................C5-16
Ataroth (in Ephraim).......C4-44
Ataroth (in Moab) ...D5-44, 61
Athens A2-77; B2-89, 101;
  D3-113, 160, 164; C2-140, 144
Atlantic Ocean A2-113, 160
Atlas Mts. A3-113, 160
Attalia E2-140, 144
Augsburg C2-164
Augusta Treverorum (Treves)
  B2-160
Augusta Vindelicorum
  (Augsburg)........C2-160
Augustodunum (Autun)..B2-160
Auran, see Hauran
Auranitis E3-117, 124, 149, 156
Avaricum B2-113
Avaris, see Rameses or Tanis
Aven, see On
Azeca, Azecha, see Azekah
Azekah B5-44, 48, 61, 96
Azotus (Ashdod)......B5-109, 117,
  124, 149, 156; B6-136
Azotus, Mt. B5-109
Azov, Sea of E2-164
Azzah, see Gaza
Baal-maon, see Baal-meon
Baal-meon D5-44, 61
Baal-Saphon, see Baal-zephon
Baal-zephon B2-40
Babel, see Babylon
Babylon F3-25, 77; D2-89,
  101; F3-113, 160
Babylonia F3-25;
  G3-77; D2-101
Babylonian Empire, New...D2-89
Babylonian Empire, Old.....F3-25
Bactra F2-89, 101
Bactria F2-89, 101
Baetica A3-160
Bagae F2-89, 101
Balearic Islands.........B3-113,
  160, 164
Balikh River D2-25
Ballah, Lake..................B2-40
Baltic Sea C1-160, 164
Baniyas (Caesarea Philippi)
  C1-177
Barasa, see Bostra
Barca B2-89; D3-113
Basan, see Bashan
Bashan D3-16; D2-32, 44;
  D1-40;E3-48, 61, 68, 96, 124;
  C3-53, 72; D4-136
Bastarnae D2-113, 160
Batanaea ..D3-117, 124, 149, 156
Batavi B1-113
Beautiful Gate D4-173
Beelmeon, see Baal-meon
Beelsephon, see Baal-zephon
Beer Ora B5-177

Beeroth C5-32, 109
Beer-sheba B6-16, 32, 44, 48, 61, 68, 84, 96, 117, 124, 149, 156; C4-25; C2-40; B4-53, 72; B3-177
Beeshterah, see Ashtaroth
Behistun D2-89
Beit Shean (Beth-shan)...C2-177
Beit Shemesh B3-177
Bela, see Zoar
Bene-Barac, see Bene-berak
Bene-berak B4-44
Benenennom, see Hinnom
Beneventum B1-140, 144; C2-164
Beni Hasan B4-25
Benjamin, Allotment of....C5-44
Berea C1-140, 144
Berenice (in Cyrenaica) C3-160, 164
Berenice (in Egypt) E4-113, 160
Beroea, see also Berea....D2-164
Beroth, see Beeroth
Berotha, see Berothai
Berothai C3-53, 72
Bersabee, see Beer-sheba
Berytus B3-72; C4-136
Besor, Brook A6-16, 32, 48
Bethabara D3-124; B3, D3, D6-133
Bethania, see Bethany
Bethany C5-124; C6-133; C3-177
Bethany Beyond Jordan...D6-133
Beth-aram, Betharan, see Beth-haram
Beth-dagon B5-109
Bethel C4-25; C5-32, 44,48, 61, 68, 96, 109, 117, 124, 133, 149, 156; B4-72
Beth-Emec, see Beth-emek
Beth-emek C3-44
Bether C5-156
Bethesda, Pool of C3-173
Beth-gubrim B5-117, 149
Beth-haccherem C5-96
Beth-Hagla, see Beth-hoglah
Beth-haram (Livias) D5-117, 124, 149
Beth-hoglah C5-44
Beth-horon C5-44, 48, 61, 84, 96, 109, 117, 149, 156
Bethiesimoth, see Beth-jeshimoth
Beth-jeshimoth D5-44
Beth-jesimoth, see Beth-jeshimoth
Bethlehem C5-16, 32, 44, 48, 61, 68, 96, 109, 117, 149, 156; C6-133; C3-177
Beth-maachah, see Abel-beth-maachah
Beth-Nemra, see Beth-nimrah
Beth-nimrah D5-44, 117, 124; C3-177
Bethoron, see Beth-horon
Beth-palet, or Beth-phelet B6-44, 96
Beth-Phaleth, see Beth-palet
Bethsaida (Julias) D3-124; B1, D2-133; D3-149, 156
Beth-Sames, see Beth-shemesh
Beth-San, see Beth-shan
Beth-shan (Scythopolis).D4-16, 20; C1-40: C4-44, 48, 61, 68, 96, 109, 124; B3-53; C2-177
Beth-shean, see Beth-shan
Beth-shemesh B5-32, 48, 84; C5-44, 61, 68; B4-53
Bethsimoth, see Beth-jeshimoth
Beth-sur(a), see Beth-zur
Bethzacharam, see Beth-zacharias
Beth-zacharias C5-109
Beth-zatha, see Bethesda
Beth-zur ..C5-44, 61, 68, 96, 109, 117, 149; C3-177
Betonim D5-44
Beycesultan B2-25
Bezec, see Bezek
Bezek C4-44, 48
Bibracte B2-113
Bileam, see Ibleam
Bira C3-177
Bithynia C1-89, 101; E2-113, 160; E1-140, 144

Bitter Lakes B2-40
Black Sea (Pontus Euxinus) E1-20, 77, 140, 144; D1-25; C1-89, 101; E2-113, 160, 164
Bogaskoy (Hattushash)....C1-25
Bononia (Bologna)..........C2-160
Bordeaux A2-164
Borsippa F3-77
Borysthenes River (Dnieper) C1-101; E1-113, 160
Bosor E3-109
Bosora, see Bostra
Bosporus Kingdom ...E2-113, 160
Bosra, see Bozrah
Bostra (Bursa)......F3-117, 149, 156; D5-136; E3-160; D2-177
Bourges B2-164
Bozrah ..D7-32; C2-40; B4-53, 72
Bracara Augusta A2-160
Breman B1-164
Brick Walls, City of, see Kir-haresheth
Brigantium A2-113
Britain A1-113, 160, 164
Brundisium .C2-113; B1-140, 144
Bubastis (Pi-beseth)........A2-40; C4-77
Bubastus, see Bubastis
Bucephala G2-101
Burdigala (Bordeaux)A2-113,160
Burgundians C1-160
Busra (Bostra)...............F3-117
Buxentum A1-140, 144
Byblos (Gebal).........C3-25, 136; B2-53; D3-77; C2-89, 101
Byzantium (Istanbul)......C1-77; B1-89, 101; D2-113, 160; D1-140, 144
Cabul C3-44, 48, 61, 68; B3-53
Cadasa (Kedesh)......C2-117, 124, 149, 156
Cades (Kedesh)...............D2-109
Cadesbarne, see Kadesh-barnea
Cadiz A3-164
Cadusii H2-77; D2-89
Caerleon A1-164
Caersaraugusta (Saragossa) B2-160
Caesarea (in Mauretania) B3-160, 164
Caesarea (in Palestine)..B3-16, 117, 144, 149; B4-124; B5-136: E3-140, 164; F3-144; B2-177
Caesarea Mazaca.....E2-140, 144; E3-160
Caesarea Philippi (Baniyas) D2-124, 149, 156; D1-133; C4-136; C1-177
Caesariensis A3-160
Caesar's Bridge B1-113
Caiaphas, House of B5-173
Caiphas, see Caiaphas
Calah E2-25; F3-77
Caleb C6-44
Callirhoe D5-117, 124
Calvary or Golgotha........B3-173
Camon D3-44, 48
Camulodunum (Colchester) B1-160
Cana ...C3-124; A1, A5-133
Canaan E2-20; C3-25; C1-40
Canaanites B5, C3-32, 48
Cantabri A2-113
Canterbury B1-164
Capernaum .D3-124; B1, D2-133; C3-149, 156; C2-177
Capharnaum, see Capernaum
Capharsaba B4-109
Capharsalama C5-109
Caphthor(im), see Caphtorim
Caphtorim D2-20
Capitolias D3-124
Cappadocia D2-77; C2-89, 101; E3-113, 160; F2-140, 144
Capua C2-113, 160
Carchemish D2-25; E2-77; C2-89
Caria B2-101; D3-113; D2-140, 144
Cariathaim, see Kiriathaim
Cariath-Arbe, see Kirjath-arba
Cariathiarim, see Kiriath-jearim
Cariath-jarim, see Kirjath-jearim
Cariath-sepher, see Kijath-sepher

Carmania E3-89, 101
Carmel C6-44, 48, 124
Carmel, Mt. C3-16, 32, 44, 48, 61, 68, 84, 96, 109, 117, 124, 149, 156; C1-40; C2-177
Carnaim, see also Karnaim E3-109
Carnion, see Carnaim
Carpathian Mts. D2-113, 160
Carpi D2-113, 160
Carrhae E3-113
Cartagena A3-164
Carthage C3-113, 160, 164
Carthago Nova (Cartagena) A3-113, 160
Casaloth, see Chesulloth
Caspian Gates E2-101
Caspian Sea, (Mare Hyrcanium) F1-20; G1-25; H2-77; D1-89, 101; F2-113, 160, 170
Catabathmus D3-140, 144
Caucasus Mts. D1-89, 101; F2-113, 160
Cauda, see Clauda
Cedes, see Kedesh
Cedron (torrent), see Kidron
Cedron B5-109
Ceila, see Keilah
Celaenae C2-77
Celesyria see Coele Syria
Celtiberi A2-113
Celtic Gaul B2-113
Cenabum B2-113
Cenchrae, see Cenchrea
Cenchrea C2-140, 144
Cenereth, Ceneroth, see Chinnereth
Cerethi, Cerethites, see Cherethites
Cethim, Cetthim, see Kittim
Chalcedon .C1-77: B1-89; D2-164
Chalcis ...D4-136: D1-149, 156
Chaldea F3-20; G4-77
Chaldean Empire, see New Babylonian Empire
Chale, see Calah
Chanaan, see Canaan
Charcamis, see Carchemish
Chaseleth, see Chesulloth
Chatti B1-113
Chauci B1-113, 160
Chenereth, see Chinnereth
Chephirah C5-32, 96
Cherethites A6-44, 48
Cherith, Brook C5-61
Chersonesus C1-89; E2-113, 160, 164
Chesalon C5-44
Cheslon, see Chesalon
Chesulloth C3-44
Chetthim, see Kittim
Chinnereth C3-32, 48, 61, 84; D3-44, 68
Chinnereth, Sea of (Sea of Galilee)......D3-16, 32, 44, 48, 61, 68; C3-53, 72
Chinneroth, see Chinnereth
Chios B2-77; D2-140, 144
Chisloth-tabor, see Chesulloth
Chittim, (Cyprus)...A2-53, 72
Choaspes River F3-25
Chorasmia F1-89
Chorasmii E1-101
Chorazin D3-124; B4-133
Chus, see Cush
Cibroth-Hatthaava, see Kibroth-hattaavah
Cilicia ...E2-20, 140, 144; D2-77; C2-89, 101; E3-113, 160; B1-136
Cilician Gates.......D2-77; C2-101
Cimmerians, see also Gomer.......D1-77
Cirta B3-113, 160, 164
Cisalpine Gaul B2-113
Cison, see Kishon
Clauda C3-140, 144
Clonard A1-164
Cnidus D2-140, 144
Cnossus D2-140, 144; D3-164
Coele Syria D1-109; C4-136
Colchis D1-89, 101; F2-113, 160
Cologne B1-164
Colonia Agrippina (Cologne) B1-160
Colossae D2-140, 144

Commagene F3-113, 160
Constantinople D2-164
Coos D2-140, 144
Cophen River (Kabul) G2-89, 101
Corcyra B2-140, 144
Cordova A3-164
Corduba A3-113, 160
Corduene F3-113
Coreae C4-156
Corfinium C2-113
Corinth A2-77; C2-140, 144; D3-28
Corner Gate B4-173
Corsica B2-113, 160, 164
Cos, see Coos
Council House C4-173
Crete D2-20: A3-25; B3-77; B2-89, 101; D3-113, 160, 164; C2-140, 144
Croton C3-113; B2-140, 144
Ctesiphon F3-113, 160, 164
Cush (Ethiopia)......E4-20; C3-89
Cutha, see Cuthah
Cuthah G3-77
Cyclades D2-140, 144
Cydonia C2-140, 144
Cyprus E2-20, 140, 144; C3-25; A2-53, 72; D3-77; C2-89, 101; E3-113, 160, 164; B2-136
Cyrenaica B2-101; D3-113, 160
Cyrene A3-77; B2-89, 101; D3-113, 160, 164
Cyrus River F1-25; G1-77; D1-89, 101; F2-113, 160
Cyzicus C1-77
Czechs C2-164
Dabir, see Debir
Dacia D2-113, 160
Dadan, see Dedan
Dahae E1-89, 101
Dalmanutha (Magdala?) C2-124; D2-133
Dalmatia (Illyricum)B1-140, 144; C2-160
Damascus E2-16, 32, 124; D3-25; D1-40, 177: E1-44, 48, 61, 68, 84, 96, 109, 117, 124, 149, 156; C3-53, 72; E3-77, 113, 160, 164; D4-136; F3-140, 144
Damascus (Aramaean Kingdom) C3-53; E2-68, 84
Dan ...D2-16, 32, 44, 48, 61, 68, 84, 96, 124, 149; C1-40, 177; B3-53, 72
Dan, Allotment of D2, B5-44
Danube River (Ister)........B1-89, 101; C2-113, 160; D2-164
Daphca, see Dophkah
Dead Sea (Salt Sea)........C5-16; C4-25; C6-32, 44, 48, 61, 68, 84, 96, 109, 117, 124, 136, 149, 156; C2-40; B4-72: D4-77; C3-177
Debir B6-32, 44, 61, 68, 84; C2-40
Deblatha, see Riblah
Decapolis D4-117, 124, 149, 156; C5-136
Dedan (descendent of Ham) F3-20
Dedan (descendent of Shem) E2-20
Dephca, see Dophkah
Der'a (Edrei) D2-177
Derbe E2-140, 144
Deva (Chester) A1-160
Develtum D2-164
Dhiban (Dibon) C3-177
Diala River F3-25; D2-89
Dibon (Dhiban)...D5-32, 44, 48, 61, 68, 84, 109, 117, 124; C2-40; D6-96; C3-177
Dictones A2-113
Dion E3-109, 117, 149, 156
Diospolis (Lydda).........B4-124
Diyala River, see Diala River
Dniester River D2-164
Doch, see Dok
Dok C5-109
Don River D1-101; F2-113, 160
Dophkah B3-40
Dor (Dora).......B3-16, 32, 44, 48, 53, 61, 68, 72, 84,96,109; C1-40; B2-177

Dor (district) B4-96
Dora (Dor).......B3-109, 117, 124
149, 156
Dorylaeum D2-140, 144
Dothain, see Dothan
Dothan C3-25;
C4-32, 44, 61, 68, 84
Drangiana F2-89, 101
Druz, Jebel ed D2-177
Duero River A2-164
Dumah (in Arabia).........E4-77
Dumah (in Judah)...........B6-84
Dung Gate C6-173
Dura B3-177
Dura-Europus E3-160
Durazzo C2-164
Durius River A2-113, 160
Durocortorum (Rheims)..B2-160
Dur Sharrukin F2-77
Du'ru B4-84
Dyrrhachium D2-113;
B1-140, 144
Eastern Sea, see Dead Sea
East Gate D3-173
Ebal, Mt. C4-16, 32, 44, 48,
61, 68, 84, 124; C1-40
Eboracum (York).......A1-160
Ebro River A2-113, 160
Ecbatana (Achmetha)....H3-77;
D2-89, 101
Ecdippa (Achzib)..........C2-117;
149, 156
Edessa E3-113, 164
Edom ...D7-16, 32, 44, 48, 61, 68
84; C2-40; B4-53, 72; D4-77
Edomites B6-96
Edrai, see Edrei
Edrei (Der'a)...E3-32, 44, 48, 61,
68, 84, 109, 117, 124, 149;
D1-40; C3-53, 72
Eglon B5-32, 44, 48; C2-40
Egypt E2-20; B4-25, 177;
A3-40; C4-77; B3-89, 101;
E4-113, 160, 164; D3-140, 144
Egypt, River of (Wadi el 'Arish)
A7-16, 32; B2-40; A4-53, 72;
B4-177
Egyptian Copper Mines....C4-25
Eilat (Elath)...................B5-177
'Ein Gedi C3-177
Eizariya (Bethany).........C3-177
Ekron B5-32, 44, 48, 61, 68, 84,
109, 117, 124, 149, 156; B4-53,
72; B3-177
Ela, see Elah
Elah, Valley of............B5-16, 48
Elam (Susiana)....F2-20; G4-25;
H3-77; D2-89
Elasa C5-109
Elath ...C3-40, 89; B5-72; C5-177
El 'Auja B4-177
Elbe River C1-113
Elbruz Mts. G2-25; H2-77
Eleale, see Elealeh
Elealeh D5-44, 61, 84
Elephantine Island..D5-77; C3-89
El Ghor D4-16
Elim B3-40
Elisa, see Elishah
Elishah C2-20
El Karak (Kir-moab)......C3-177
El Kuntilla B4-177
Ellip G3-77
El Qanawat (Kanatha)...D2-177
El Quneitra C1-177
El Qusaima B4-177
Eltekeh B5-44, 68, 84;
D4-77
Elthece, Eltheco, see Eltekeh
Emath, see Hamath
Emath (Tower of), see Meah
(Tower of)
Emerita Augusta (Merida)
A3-160
Emesa D3-136
Emmaus C5-124; C6-133
Emmaus (Nicopolis)........B5-96,
109, 117, 124, 149, 156
Enan, see Hazar-enan
En-dor C3-44, 48
En-gaddi, see En-gedi
En-gannim (Ginaea)
C4-124, 133, 149
En-gedi C6-32, 44, 48, 61, 68,
84, 96, 109, 117, 124, 149, 156;
B4-53; C3-177

English Channel A1-113, 160
En-Harad, see Harod
En-Hasor, see En-hazor
En-hazor C2-44
En-mishpat, (Kadesh-barnea)
A7-32
Ennom, see Hinnom
En-rimmon B6-96
En-rogel (Dragon's Well).D6-173
Ephesus B2-89, 101; D3-113,
160, 164; D2-140, 144
Ephra, see Ophrah
Ephraim (city in Judaea)
C5-109, 124, 133, 156
Ephraim (district)..........C4-16
Ephraim, Allotment of.......C4-44
Ephraim Gate C4-173
Ephron, see also Ephraim (city)
D3-109
Epiphania D2-136
Epirus B2-89, 101; D3-113,
160; C2-140, 144
Erech F4-25; G4-77; D2-89
Eridu F4-25
Er Rumman C2-177
Esdraelon, Plain of, see also
Plain of Jezreel...C3-16, 109,
117, 124, 149, 156
Esdrelon, see Esdraelon
Eshnunna F3-25
Esthemo, see Eshtemoa
Eshtemoa, Eshtemoh C6-44
Essene Gate B6-173
Esztergom C2-164
Etam C5-44, 61
Etham B2-40
Etham, Wilderness of.......B3-40
Ethiopia (Cush)......E4-20; C3-89
Etruria C2-113
Euboea A2-77
Euloeus River (Ulai)
G4-25
Euphrates River F2-20;
E3-25; D2-53, 72, 89, 101;
G4-77; F3-113, 160, 164
Europe B1-20
Evora A3-164
Ezion-geber C3-40;
B5-53; C5-177

Fair Havens D3-140, 144
Faro A3-164
Farther Spain A3-113
Fish Gate D3-173
Florence C2-164
Fountain Gate D5-173
Frisians B1-113, 160
Fulda B1-164

Gaba (Geba).....C3-117; C5-156
Gabaa, see Geba,
Gibeah, Gibeon
Gabaath, see Gibeah
Gabae, see Geba
Gabaon, see Gibeon
Gabee, see Geba
Gad, Allotment of D4-44
Gadara D3-109, 117, 124, 149,
156; B2, B6-133
Gaderoth, see Gederoth
Gades (Cadiz)...........A3-113, 160
Gaetulia B3-113, 160
Galaad, see Gilead
Galatia E3-113, 160;
E2-140, 144
Galgal(a), see Gilgal
Galilee C3-16, 84, 96, 109,
117, 124, 149, 156; C5-136;
F3-140, 144
Galilee, Sea of (Sea of
Chinnereth) D3-16, 84, 96,
109, 117, 149, 156; C5-136;
C2-177
Gallaecia A2-113
Gamala D3-109, 117, 149, 156
Gandara G2-89
Garizim, see Gerizim
Gasgas D1-25
Gath B5-32, 44, 48, 68, 84;
C2-40; B4-53, 72
Gath-hepher C3-44, 68; B3-72
Gath-rimmon B4-44
Gaugamela D2-101
Gaul B2-113, 160, 164
Gaulanitis D3-117, 124, 149,
156; C5-136
Gaulon, see Golan
Gaver, see Gur

Gaza A5-16, 32, 44, 48, 61, 68,
84, 96, 109, 117, 124, 149, 156;
C2-40, 89; B4-53, 72, 101;
E3-113, 160; F3-140, 144; B3-177
Gazara (Gezer)......B5-109, 117,
124, 149, 156
Gaza Strip B3-177
Gazer, Gazera, see Gezer
Geba C5-44, 48, 61, 84, 96
Gebal (Byblos) B2-53, 72
Gebbethon, see Gibbethon
Gederoth B5-84
Gedrosia (Maka)...F3-89, 101
Geennom, see Hinnom
Gehenna, see Hinnom
Gelboe, see Gilboa
Genesar, Water of
(Sea of Galilee)........D3-109
Genesareth, Lake of,
see Sea of Galilee
Gennath Gate..............B4-173
Genoa B2-164
Genua (Genoa)........B2-113, 160
Gerar C4-25; B6-32, 44, 48,
61, 68, 84, 96, 109, 124, 149, 156;
B4-53, 72; B3-177
Gerar, Valley of...........B6-16, 32
Gerara, see Gerar
Gerasa, (Jarash)......D4-109, 117,
124, 149, 156; C5-136; C2-177
Gergesa D3-44, 124, 149; B1,
D2-133
Gergovia B2-113
Gerizim, Mt. C4-16, 32, 44, 48,
61, 68, 84, 96, 109, 117, 124, 149
156; C1-40; C2-177
Germania C1-113, 160
Germanicopolis E1-140, 144
Germany, Lower.............B1-160
Germany, Upper.............B2-160
Gesen, see Goshen
Geshur D3-44, 48, 61; B3-53
Gessen, see Goshen
Gessur, see Geshur
Getae B1-101
Geth, see Gath
Geth-hepher, see Gath-hepher
Geth-Remmon, see Gath-rimmon
Gethsemane, Garden of...D3-173
Gethsemani, see Gethsemane
Gezer (Gazara)....B5-32, 44, 48,
61, 68, 84, 96, 109, 124;
C1-40; B4-53; C3-177
Gharandal C4-177
Ghesen C1-164
Ghor, El D4-16
Gibbethon B5-44, 84
Gibeah C5-48; B4-53; B5-68
Gibeon C5-32, 44, 48, 84, 96;
C2-40
Gideroth, see Gederoth
Gihon (spring)...........B2, D5-173
Gilboa, Mt. C4-16, 44, 48;
B3-53
Gilead D4-16, 44, 48, 61, 68,
84, 96, 124; C1-40; B3-53, 72;
D3-109
Gilgal C5-20, 48, 68, 84, 96;
C2-40; D5-44, 61; B4-72
Ginaea (En-gannim) C4-124,
149, 156
Ginneisar C2-177
Gischala C2-117, 124, 149, 156;
D2-133
Gittah-hepher, see Gath-hepher
Golan D3-44
Golgotha (Calvary)........B3-173
Gomer E1-20; F1-77
Gomorrah D6-4
Gomorrha, see Gomorrah
Gophna .C5-84, 109, 117, 149, 156
Gordium D2-77
Gordon's Calvary B2-173
Cortyna D3-164
Goshen A2-40
Goths C1-113, 160
Gozam, see Gozan
Gozan F2-77
Great Sea, The,
see Mediterranean Sea
Great Zab River E2-25; F2-77
Greece D2-20; A2-77; B2-89;
C2-140, 144
Gur (Ibleam)..................C4-72
Habesor (river).............B3-177

Haceldama, see Aceldama
Hadid (Adida)........B5-96, 109
Hadrumetum C3-113, 160, 164
Hai, see Ai
Haifa B2-177
Halys River C1-25; D2-77;
C2-89; E1-140, 144
Ham D3-32
Hamath .D3-25; C2-53, 72; E3-77
Hamath (Aramaean Kingdom)
C2-53, 72
Hamath-zobah, see Zobah
Hammath D3-44; C3-48, 53,
68, 84
Hammon C2-44
Hamon, see Hammon
Hannathon C3-44
Harad, see Harod
Haran D2-25; E2-77; C2-89
Harbor River E3-25; F2-77
Harmozia E3-101
Harod C3-44
Harodi, see Harod
Haroseth, Haroseth-Goim,
see Harosheth
Harosheth C3-44
Harun, Jebel (Mt. Hor)...C2-40
Hasa C4-177
Hasa, Wadi el (Zered River)
D7-16; C3-177
Hasarmoth, see Hazarmaveth
Haseroth, see Hazeroth
Hasor, see Hazor
Hatra F3-160
Hattin, Horns of..C3-124; A5-133
Hattushash (Bogazkoy).....C1-25
Hauran E2-16; E3-84
Havilah F3, F4-20
Havoth-jair D3-44, 48, 61, 68
Hazar-enan C2-53, 72
Hazarmaveth F4-20
Hazezon-tamar (En-geddi?)
C6-32
Hazeroth C6-32
Hazor C3-25; D2-32, 44, 48,
68, 84, 96, 109; C1-40;
B3-53, 72
Hebron C5-16, 32, 44, 48, 61,
68, 84, 96, 109, 117, 124, 149,
156; C2-40; B4-53, 72; C3-177
Hebrus River C1-140, 144
Hecatompylus E2-101
Heliopolis (Baalbek)......D3-136
Heliopolis (On)....A2-40; E3-113,
140, 144
Hellal, Jebel..........A7-16; B2-40
Hellas (Greece)........B2-101
Hellespont B2-101
Helvetii B2-113
Hemath, see Hamath
Hennom, see Hinnom
Heraclea C1-101
Heraclea Pontica E1-140, 144
Heracleopolis A3-40; C4-77
Herat F2-101
Herma, see Hormah
Hermon, Mt. ...D2-16, 32, 44, 48,
61, 68, 84, 96, 109, 117, 124,
149, 156, 177; B3-53, 72;
DI-133
Hermopolis D4-164
Hermunduri C1-113
Hermus River A2-25; B2-77
Herodium C5-117, 124, 149, 156
Hesebon, see Heshbon
Heshbon D5-32, 44, 48, 61, 68,
84, 96, 109, 117, 124, 149, 156;
C2-40; B4-53, 72; C3-177
Heth E2-20
Hethite, see Hittite
Hevila, see Havilah
Hibernia A1-113, 160
Hierapolis D2-140, 144
Hindu Kush G2-89, 101
Hinnom, Valley of........C6-173
Hippo Regius B3-113, 160, 164
Hippos D3-109, 117, 124, 149,
156; B2, D3-133
Hisban (Heshbon).........C3-177
Hither Spain A2-113
Hittites, Hittite Kingdom.C2-25;
C6, E1-32; C1-53
Hivites C5-32
Holy Sepulchre, Church of the
B4-173
Hor, Mt. (Jebel Harun)....C2-40

Horeb, Mt. (Mt. Sinai).....B3-40
Horma, see Hormah
Hormah C6-32, 44, 48; C2-40
Horns of Hattin C3-124
Horrites, see Horites
Horse Gate D4-173
Hucoc, see Hukkok
Hukkok C3-44
Hula, Lake......D2-16; C1-177
Huldah Gates D4-173
Huleh, Lake, see Lake Hula
Huns F2-160
Hurrians (Horites)..........F2-25
Hydaspes River................G2-101
Hyphasis River (Beas).....G2-101
Hyrcania E2-89, 101
Hyrcanium C5-117
Iazyges C2-160
Iberia F2-113, 160
Ibleam ..C4-32, 44, 61, 68; B3-72
Iconium E3-113, 164; E2-140, 144
Icosium B3-113
Idumaea B6-16, 96; C6-109,
117, 124, 149, 156
Idumea, see Idumaea
Iim, see Ije-abarim
Ije-abarim C2-40
Ijon D2-48, 61, 68, 84,
B3-53, 72
Ilerda B2-113
Ilium (Troy)...................B2-101
Illyria A1-89, 101
Illyricum (Dalmatia)......C2-113,
160; B1-140, 144
India G3-89, 101
Indo-Iranians (Ayrans)......G3-25
Indus River G2-89, 101
Ionian Sea C3-160
Ipsus C2-101
Irbid C2-177
Ireland A1-164
Iris River C1-25
Iron C2-44
Ir-shemesh, see Beth-shemesh
Isca (Caerleon) A1-160
Israel B3-53, 72, 177; C4-61
Issachar, Allotment of C3-44
Issin F4-25
Issus C2-101; D1-136
Ister River (Danube).......B1-89,
101; D2-113, 160
Italy C2-113, 160, 164;
B1-140, 144
Itil F2-164
Ituraea E2-109, 117, 124, 149,
156; D4-136
Iturea, see Ituraea
Jaazer, see Jazer
Jabbok River (Zarga)......D4-16,
32, 44, 48, 61, 68, 84, 96, 109,
117, 124, 149, 156; C1-40; C2-177
Jabes-Galaad, see Jabesh-gilead
Jabesh-gilead D4-32, 44, 48,
61, 68
Jabneel (in Naphtali) D3-44
Jabneel (Jamnia).......B5-44, 48,
61, 68, 84
Jabneh (Jabneel).....B5-68, 109;
B4-72
Jabnia, see Jabneh
Jaboc, see Jabbok
Jacob's Well C4-32, 124, 133
Jaffa, see Tel Aviv-Jaffa
Jahas, see Jahaz
Jahaz ...D5-32, 44, 61, 84; C2-40
Jahaza, Jahazah, Jahzah,
see Jahaz
Jamnia (Jabneel)...B5-109, 117,
124, 149, 156
Janoe, see Janohah
Janohah C4-44, 61
Japho (Joppa)................B4-44
Jarash (Gerasa)..............C2-177
Jarmo F3-25
Jarmuth C5-32, 44; C2-25
Jassa, see Jazer
Jattir C6-44, 48
Javan D2-20
Jaxartes River F1-89, 101
Jazer D5-32, 44, 109;
C2-25
Jeabarim, see Ije-abarim
Jeb (Elephantine Island) ..D5-77
Jeblaam, see Ibleam
Jebneel, see Jabneel
Jeboc, see Jabbok

Jebus (Jerusalem) C5-32, 44,
48; C2-25
Jecmaam, Jecnam, Jeconam,
see Jokneam
Jecnaam, see Jokneam
Jectan, see Joktan
Jegbaa, see Jogbehah
Jericho C5-16, 32, 44, 61, 68,
84, 96, 109, 117, 149, 156;
C2-25; B4-53; C6-133, 136;
C3-177
Jerimoth, see Jarmuth
Jeron, see Iron
Jerusalem ..C5-16, 32, 44, 48, 61,
68, 84, 96, 109, 117, 124, 149, 156;
C4-25; C2-40, 101; B4-53, 72;
D4-77; F3-113, 144, 149, 160,
164; C6-133, 136; C3-177
Jeshanah C4-61
Jeshua B6-96
Jesrael, see Jezreel
Jeta, see Juttah
Jether, see Jattir
Jetta, see Juttah
Jezrael, Jezrahel, see Jezreel
Jezreel ..C3-44, 48, 61, 68, 84, 96
Jezreel, Plain of, see also
Plain of Esdraelon...C3-16, 44,
48, 61, 68, 84
Jogbehah D4-44
Jokneam C3-32, 44, 84
Joktan F4-20
Joppa B4-16, 32, 44, 48, 68,
84, 96, 109, 117, 124, 149, 156;
C1-40; B3-53, 72; B5-136;
E3-140, 144
Joppe, see Joppa
Jordan C4-177
Jordan, River...D4-16, 32, 44, 48,
61, 68, 84, 96, 109, 117, 124, 149,
156; C3-25; C1-40; B3-53, 72;
D3-77; C5-136; C2-177
Jotapata, (Jotbah)........C3-124,
149, 156
Jotbah (Jotapata)...........C3-84
Juda, see Judah
Judaea C5-16, 109, 117, 124,
149, 156; C2-101; E3-113, 140
144; C6-136
Judah ...C6-48, 61, 84; B4-53, 72;
C5-68, 96; D4-77; C2-89
Judah, Allotment of.........B5-44
Judah, Wilderness of..C6-16, 48,
61, 68, 124, 133
Judea, see Judaea
Judgment Gate,
see Miphkad Gate
Julias (Bethsaida)..........D3-124,
149, 156
Julias (Livias, Beth-haram)
D5-124, 149, 156
Juttah C6-44, 124
Kabul River (Cophen).G2-89, 101
Kadesh (in Syria).........C2-53, 72
Kadesh-barnea A7-16, 32;
C2-40; B4-53, 72; 177
Kanah C2-32, 44, 48
Kanah River B4-16, 44
Kanatha (El Qanawat)...F3-117,
149, 156; D2-177
Kanish C2-25; D2-77
Karkar E3-61; C2-72
Karnaim D3-32, 44, 61, 84, 96;
C3-72
Karnaim (district)............D3-96
Kassites F3-25
Kazallu F4-25
Kedar E3-77
Kedesh (in Naphtali)..C2-32, 48,
53, 61, 68, 96, 124; C1-40, 177
D2-44, 84, 109; B3-53, 72; C1-177
Kedesh (in Negeb),
see Kadesh-barnea
Kefar 'Eqron (Ekron)......B3-177
Keilah C5-44, 48, 96
Kenites C6-32, 44, 48
Khalab D2-25; C1-53, 72
Khirbet Qumrân, see Qumrân
Kibroth-hattaavah C3-40
Kidron, Valley of the..B2, D4-173
Kiev E1-164
Kir-hareseth, (Kir-moab).D6-32,
44, 48, 61, 68, 96, 109, 117, 124,
149, 156; B4-72
Kiriathaim D5-32, 44
Kirjathaim, see Kiriathaim

Kirjath-arba (Hebron).......C5-32
Kirjath-jearim ..C5-32, 44, 48, 96
Kirjath-sepher (Debir) B6-32
Kir-moab (Kir-haresheth)..D6-16,
32, 44, 48, 61, 84, 96, 109, 124,
149, 156; C2-40; B4-53, 72
Kish F3-25; G3-77
Kishon River.....C3-16, 32, 44, 48,
61, 84, 96, 124, 149, 156; C2-177
Kition A2-72
Kittim (Cyprus)................E2-20
Kizzuwadna D2-25
Kurûn Hattin, see
Horns of Hattin
Kushshar (Alisar Huyuk)...C2-25
Laabim, see Lehabim
Labana, see Libnah
Labyrinth B4-25
Lachis, see Lachish
Lachish B5-32, 44, 48, 61, 68,
96; C2-40; B4-53, 72; B3-177
Ladder of Tyre C2-124
Lagash F4-25
Lais, see Laish
Laisa, see Elasa
Laish (Dan)....D2-32, 44; C1-40
Lakhish (river)................B3-177
Lambaesis B3-164
Laodicea D3-113, 164;
D2-140, 144
Laodicea ad Mare C2-136
Larisa C2-140, 144; D3-164
Larsa F4-25
Lasea D2-140, 144
Last Supper, House of the
B5-173
Lebanon C2-44
Lebanon, Mt. ..D1-16, 32, 44, 48,
61, 68, 84, 96, 101, 117, 124,
149, 156; C1-40, 177; B3-53, 72;
C4-136
Lebna, see Libnah
Lebona, see Lebonah
Lebonah C4-44
Lehabim D2-20
Lemovii C1-113
Leon A2-164
Leontes River (Litani)..D2-16,
32, 44, 48, 61, 68, 84, 96, 109,
117, 124, 149, 156; C2-96;
C4-136; C1-177
Leptis Magna....C3-113, 160, 164
Lesbos B2-77; D2-140, 144
Lesem, see Leshem
Leshem (Dan)..................D2-44
Libnah B5-32, 44, 61, 68, 84;
C2-40
Libya D3-20; B2-101; D3-113;
C3-140, 144
Libyan Desert A4-25; B5-77;
B3-101
Libyans B4-77; B2-89
Liger River (Loire)...A2-113, 160
Lincoln B1-164
Lisht B4-25
Litani River (Leontes)
D1-16; C1-177
Lithuanians D1-164
Livias (Julias)...D5-117, 124,
149, 156
Lixus A4-113
Lod (Lydda)....B5-32, 44, 48, 61,
96, 109
Loire River B2-113, 160
Lombards C1-113, 160
Londinium (London)........A1-160
London B1-164
Lower or Old Pool......C6-173
Lubim D3-20
Luca B2-113
Lud D2-20
Lugdunensis B2-160
Lugdunum (Lyon)...B2-113, 160
Lugii C1-113, 160
Lulu F2-25
Lusitani A3-113
Lusitania A3-180
Lutetia (Paris) B2-113, 160
Luxeuil B2-164
Lycaonia E3-113; E2-140, 144
Lycia ..B2-89, 101; E3-113, 160
D2-140, 144
Lycopolis A4-40
Lydda (Lod).....B5-109, 117, 124,
149, 156; B6-136; B3-177
Lydia D2-20, 140, 144

Lydian Kingdom C2-77, 89
Lyons B2-164
Lystra E2-140, 144
Maacha, see Maachah
Maachah D2-48; B3-53
Ma'an C4-177
Maceda, see Makkedah
Macedonia ...B1-89, 101; D2-113,
160; C1-140, 144
Macedonians A1-77
Machaerus D5-109, 117, 124,
149, 156; C3-177
Machmas, see Michmash
Madaba (Medeba).........C3-177
Madai (Medes)................F2-20
Madaura B3-164
Madian, see Midian
Madmannah B6-44
Madon C3-32, 44; C1-40
Maeander River B2-25, 77
Magadan, see Magdala
Magdala (Dalmanutha) ..C3-109,
117, 124, 149; B1, D2-133
Magdeburg C1-164
Mageddo, see Megiddo
Mageth E3-109
Magog C1-20
Magyars D2-164
Mahanaim D4-32, 44, 48, 61,
68, 84; B3-53
Mainz B2-164
Maka (Gedrosia) F3-89
Makkedah B5-32, 44; C2-40
Malaca A3-113, 164
Malta (Melita)........A2-140, 144
Mamre C4-25; C5-32
Manasse(s), see Manasseh
Manasseh, Allotment of
C4, D3-44
Maon C6-44, 48
Mara, see Marah
Maracanda (Samarkand)
F2-89, 101
Marah B3-40
Marathon B2-89
Marcomanni C2-113, 160
Mare Hyrcanium (Caspian Sea)
D1-89, 101; F2-113, 160
Mare Internum,
(Mediterranean Sea)
C3-113, 160
Maresa, see Marisa
Mareshah (Marisa).....B5-44, 61,
68, 84, 109, 124; B3-177
Margiana E2-89
Mari E3-25
Mari, Kingdom of E3-25
Marienburg D1-164
Marisa (Mareshah)........B5-109,
117, 124, 149, 156
Market of Appius,
see Appii Forum
Marmarica D3-113, 160;
C3-140 ,144
Marqash E2-77
Marseille B2-164
Masada C6-109, 117, 149, 156;
C3-177
Masepha, see Mizpeh
Mash F2-20
Maspha, see Mizpeh
Masrephoth-maim,
see Misrephoth-maim
Massagetae F1-89
Massilia (Marseille)..B2-113, 160
Mauretania A3-113, 160
Mazaca C2-101; E3-113
Meah, Tower of C3-173
Medeba D5-32, 44, 48, 61, 84,
96, 109; B4-53, 72
Medemena, see Madmannah
Medes H3-77
Media F2-20; D2-101
Median Empire D2-89
Mediolanum (Milan) C2-160
Mediterranean Sea (Great Sea)
A3-16, 32, 61, 84; D2-20;
B3-25, 44, 61, 72, 136; B1-40;
A4-44, 48,96,109, 124; B2-53,
89, 101, 117, 149, 156, 177;
C3-113, 140, 144, 160, 164
Megiddo C3-32, 44, 61, 68, 84,
96; C1-40; B3-53, 72;
C2-89, 177
Megiddo (district)........C3-84, 96
Melita (Malta)........A2-140, 144

Melitene E3-164
Mello, see Millo
Memphis (Noph)..B4-25; A3-40;
　C4-77; C3-89, 101; E4-113, 164;
　E3-140, 144
Mephaath D5-44
Merida A3-164
Merom C3-32; C1-40
Mes, see Mash
Mesembria D1-140, 144
Meshech F1-20
Mesopotamia F2-20; D2-101;
　F3-113, 160
Mesraim, see Mizraim
Messana (Messina)..C3-113, 164;
　A2-140, 144
Michmash C5-48, 84, 96, 109
Midian, Land of C3-40
Migdal Ashqelon B3-177
Milan B2-164
Miletus B2-77, 89; D2-140, 144
Minoan Dominions A3-25
Miphkad (Muster) Gate..D3-173
Mishneh Gate C3-173
Misphat, see En-Mishpat
Misrephoth-maim C2-32, 44;
　C1-40
Mitylene D2-140, 144
Mizpeh or Mizpah
　(in Benjamin)......C5-44, 48, 61,
　68, 84, 96, 109
Mizpeh (in Gilead)..........D4-44
Mizraim (Egypt)....E3-20; A3-40
M'lefaat E2-25
Moab D6-16, 32, 44, 48, 61, 68,
　84, 96; C2-40; B4-53, 72; E4-77
Moab, Plains of D5-16, 32
Modin C5-109, 117; C3-177;
　C4-77
Moëris, Lake B4-25; C4-77
Moesi D2-113
Moesia C1-140, 144; D2-160
Molada, see Moladah
Moladah B6-44, 96
Moreh, Hill of C3-16
Moresheth-gath B5-84
Mosoch, see Meshech
Mujib, Wadi el (Arnon R.)
　D6-16; C3-177
Munda A3-113
Musasir G2-77
Myra E2-140, 144; E3-164
Mysia B2-101; D3-113;
　D2-140, 144

Naara, see Naarath
Naarath(a)..........C5-44
Naasson, see Hazor
Nabataeans C3-101; D6-109;
　E3-113; B7, E5-117, 124, 149,
　156; D5-136
Nablus C2-177
Nabo, see Nebo
Nabutheans, see Nabataeans
Naim, see Nain
Nain C3-124; A6, C3-133
Naissus D2-160
Nantes A2-164
Naphtali, Allotment of.....C3-44
Naples C2-164
Narbo (Narbonne)....B2-113, 160
Narbonensis B2-113, 160
Narbonne B2-164
Narona C2-113
Naucratis B2-89; D3-113, 160
Navari D2-160
Nawa C2-177
Nazareth C3-16, 117, 124, 149,
　156; A2, C3-133; C2-177
Neapolis (in Italy)..C2-113, 160;
　A1-140, 144
Neapolis (in Macedonia)
　C1-140, 144
Neapolis (in Palestine)....C4-156
Neballat B5-96
Nebo, Mt. D5-16, 32, 44, 48,
　61, 68, 84; C2-40; C3-177
Negba B3-177
Negeb or Negev....A7-16; B4-177
Nemrod, see Nimrod
Neocaesarea E2-160
Nephthali, see Naphtali
Nervii B1-113
Nicaea G2-101; D1-140, 144;
　D2-164
Nicephorium E3-113
Nicomedia E2-113, 160, 164;
　D1-140, 144

Nicopolis (in Asia Minor).E3-113
Nicopolis (in Greece)
　C2-140, 144; D3-164
Nicopolis (in Palestine)
　B5-109, 124
Nile River E3-20, 140, 144;
　B4-25; A3-40; C5-77; C3-89,
　101; E4-113, 160, 164
Nimrod F2-20
Nineve, see Nineveh
Nineveh E2-25; F2-77
Ninus D2-101
Nippur F3-25; G3-77, D2-89
Nisibis F2-77; F3-160, 164
Nisir, Mt. F3-25
No (Thebes)..........C3-89
Nob C5-48, 84, 96
Nobah C3-53
Nobe, see Nob
Noph (Memphis)..............C3-89
Noreia C2-113
Noricum C2-113, 160
North Sea B1-160, 164
Numidia B3-113, 160
Nuzi F3-25
Oboth C7-32; C2-40
Oceanus Germanicus
　(North Sea)....B1-160
Odollam, see Adullam
Og, Kingdom of D3-32; D1-40
Olbia C1-89, 101; E2-113
Olives, Mt. of C5-16, 117, 124
Olivet, Mt., see Olives, Mt. of
'Omer B3-177
On (Heliopolis)..........B4-25
　A2-40; C4-77; C2-89
Ono B4-32, 44, 96
Ophel D4-173
Ophera, see Ophrah
Ophir F4, G4-20
Ophrah (in Benjamin)......C5-48
Ophrah (in Issachar)..........C3-44
Opis G3-77; D2-89, 101
Ornan, see Araunah
Orontes River D3-25; C2-53,
　72; E3-77; D2-136
Ortona A1-140, 144
Oxus River F2-89, 101
Oxyrrhynchus D4-164
Pactyans F2-89
Padan-aram D2-25
Palestine E2-20; C5-136; E3-160
Palmyra (Tadmor).........D3-25;
　D2-72; E3-109, 160, 164
Palus Maeotis E2-113, 160
Pamphylia E3-113, 160;
　E2-140, 144
Paneas, see Panias
Panias D2-109, 117, 124,
　149, 156
Pannonia C2-160
Panticapaeum C1-89, 101;
　E2-113, 160
Paphlagonia ..C1-89, 101; E2-113;
　E1-140, 144
Paphos ..D3-77; E3-140, 164, 164
Paraetonium D3-140, 144
Paran (river)..........C4-177
Paran, Wilderness of C3-40
Parathon C4-109
Pardes Hanna C2-177
Paricanians F3-89
Paris B2-164
Parthia G2-20; E2-89, 101
Parthian Empire.......F3-113, 160
Pasargadae E2-89
Patara D2-140, 144
Pathros E3-20; C3-89
Pathrusim E3-20
Pattala F3-89, 101
Pella (in Gilead)....D4-32, 44, 84,
　96, 109, 117, 124, 149, 156;
　C4-133; C5-136; C2-177
Pella (in Macedonia)
　B1-101; D2-113
Pelusium (Sin)....B2-40; D4-77;
　C2-89, 101; E3-113, 140,
　144, 160
Peniel (Penuel)....D4-32, 44, 48,
　61, 68
Peraea D4-117, 124, 149, 156;
　C5-136
Perea, see Peraea
Perga E2-140, 144; E3-164
Pergamum D3-113, 160, 164;
　D2-140, 144

Perge, see Perga
Persepolis E2-89, 101
Persian Gulf G3-20; G4-25;
　H4-77; E3-89, 101; F4-160
Persis G3-20; E3-89, 101
Pessinus E2-140, 144
Petra (Sela)......B4-53; C2-101;
　E3-113, 160; C4-177
Phaddan-Aram,
　see Padan-aram
Phanuel, see Penuel
Phara, Pharathon, see Pirathon
Pharos D3-140, 144
Pharpar River D2-68
Pharsalus D3-113
Phasaelis C4-117, 124, 149
Phaselis C2-77
Phasga, see Pisgah
Phasis D1-89; F2-160
Phatures, see Pathros
Phenice C2-140, 144
Phethrusim, see Pathrusim
Philadelphia (Rabbath-amman)
　D5-109, 117, 124, 149, 156;
　C6-136; D3-177
Philadelphia (in Asia Minor)
　D2-140, 144
Philippi D2-113, 164; C1-140, 144
Philippopolis D2-160
Philistia B4-53, 72;
　B5-48, 61, 68, 84, 109
Philistia, Plain of B5-16
Philistim E2-20
Philistines B5-44, 96
Philoteria D3-109; C3-117,
　124, 149, 156
Phinon, see Punon
Phithom, see Pithom
Phoenicia ..C2-16, 61, 68, 84, 101
　109, 117, 124, 149, 156;
　B3-53, 72; D3-77;
　C4-136; E3-140, 144
Phoenicians C2-32, 44, 48, 96
Phoenis, see Phenice
Phrygia C2-101; D2-140, 144
Phrygian Kingdom C2-77
Phunon, see Punon
Phut C3-20
Pi-beseth (Bubastis).........A2-40
Pirathon C4-44
Pisa B2-164
Pisgah, Mt. D5-32; C2-40
Pisidia C2-89, 101; E3-113;
　E2-140, 144
Pithom A2-40
Pityus E2-164
Plain, Sea of the, see Dead Sea
Po River B2-160
Poles C1-164
Pomeranians C1-164
Pompeiopolis (Soli)......B1-136
Pontus C1-101; E2-113, 160;
　F1-140, 144
Pontus Euxinus (Black Sea)
　C1-89; E1-140, 144; E2-160
Potaissa D2-160
Preslav D2-164
Prophthasia F2-101
Propontis B1-25; C1-77;
　D1-140, 144
Prussians D1-164
Pteria C1-89
Ptolemaïs (in Egypt).E4-160, 164
Ptolemaïs (Accho)..C3-101, 109,
　117, 124, 149, 156; B5-136;
　E3-140, 144
Punon ...D7-32; C2-40; B4-53, 72
Pura F3-101
Puteoli (Pozzuoli)..A1-140, 144;
　C2-164
Pyramus River D2-25; C1-136
Pyrenees A2-113, 160
Qarnini D2-84
Qatna D4-25
Quadi C2-160
Qumrân, Khirbet C5-109, 117,
　124; C3-177
Raamah G3-20
Rabba (in Ammon),
　see Rabbath-ammon
Rabba (Rabbath-moab)..D6-124;
　C3-177
Rabbath-ammon (Philadelphia,
　Amman)......D5-16, 32, 44, 48,
　61, 68, 84, 96, 109, 124; D2-40;
　C4-53, 72, 89; D3-113

Rabbath Moab (Areopolis,
　Rabba)....D6-124; C3-177
Raetia B2-160
Raetii C2-113
Rafiah (Raphia)..........B3-177
Ragaba D4-109
Rama, see Ramah
Ramah (in Benjamin)......C5-48,
　61, 96, 124
Ramah (in Naphtali)...C3-44, 84
Ramallah C3-177
Ramat Gan B2-177
Ramatha, see Ramah,
　Ramathaim
Ramathaim (Arimathaea).C4-48,
　124; B4-109
Rameses (Tanis, Zoan)....A2-40
Ramle B3-177
Ramoth-Galaad, see
　Ramoth-gilead
Ramoth-gilead E3-32, 44, 48,
　61, 68, 84, 96; C3-53, 72
Raphana E3-117, 124, 149, 156
Raphia (Rafiah)....A6-16, 32, 44,
　48, 84, 96, 109, 124; B4-53, 72;
　D4-77
Raphidim, see Rephidim
Raphon E3-109
Ravenna C2-113, 164
Rebla, Reblatha, see Riblah
Red Sea (Arabian Gulf)
　E3-20; C4-40; D5-77; C3-89,
　101; E4-113, 160, 164
Regensburg C2-164
Regma, see Raamah
Rehoboth B6-32, 44
Reims B2-164
Remi B2-113
Remmon, see Rimmon,
　En-rimmon
Rephidim B3-40
Reuben, Allotment of......D5-44
Rha River (Volga)....F2-113, 160
Rhagae E2-89, 101
Rhandeia E3-160
Rhegium B2-140, 144
Rhine River B2-113, 160, 164
Rhodes B2-25, 89, 101;
　C2-77; D3-113, 160, 164;
　D2-140, 144
Riblah C2-53
Riga D1-164
Rimmon C3-44, 48
Riphath E1-20
Rock, The, see Sela
Rohoboth, see Rehoboth
Rome C2-113, 160, 164;
　A1-140, 144
Rouen B2-164
Roxolani E2-113; D2-160
Ruben, see Reuben
Rubicon C2-113
Rugians C1-113
Russians E1-164
Saba, see Sheba
Sabastiya, see also
　Samaria and Sebaste....C2-177
Sabratha C3-113, 160
Safad D3-156; D2-177
Sagartians E2-89
Sahara C4-113, 160
Saida, see also Sidon....C1-177
Sais C4-77; C2-89
Sakas G1-89, 101
Salamina, see Salamis
Salamis ...A2-53, 72, 136; D3-77;
　B2-89; E3-113, 160, 164;
　A1-136; E2-140, 144
Salcah, (Salkhad)..........C3-53
Salecha, see Salcah
Salem (Jerusalem)..........C5-32
Salkhad (Salcah) D2-177
Salmantica
　(Salmanca)........A2-160
Salmone, Cape D2-140, 144
Salona(e) C2-160, 164
Salt Sea, see Dead Sea
Salt, Valley of........C6-53, 61, 68
Samaga D5-109
Samal E2-77
Samaria (Sebaste)......C4-16, 61,
　68, 84, 96, 109, 117, 124, 149,
　156; B3-72; D3-77; B3-113;
　C5-136; C2-177
Samaria (district).......C4-16, 84,
　96, 109, 124; C5-136

Samarkand (Maracanda) F2-89, 101
Samos B2-77; D2-140, 144
Samothrace D1-140, 144
Sangarius River B1-25; C1-77; E1-140, 144
Sanhedrin, see Council House
Saphir B5-84
Saphon, see Zaphon
Saraa, see Zorah
Sarafand (Zarephath, Sarepta)—C1-177
Saragossa A2-164
Sarangians F2-89
Sarath-sahar, see Zareth-shahar
Sardica D2-164
Sardinia B2-113, 160, 164
Sardis C2-77; B2-89, 101; D2-140, 144; D3-160, 164
Sarea, see Zorah
Sarepta (Zarephath)......C2-124, 149, 156
Sarid C3-44
Sarmatia E1-113, 160
Sarmizegetusa D2-160
Sarohen, see Sharuhen
Saron, see Sharon
Sarus River C2-25
Saxons B1-164
Scandia C2-113; C1-160
Scodra C2-77; B1-140, 144
Scorpion Pass, see Akrabbim, Ascent of
Scythians ..G1-77; C1, G1-89, 101
Scythopolis (Beth-shan).C4-109, 117, 124, 149, 156; B3, D4-133; C5-136
Sea of the Plain ....see Dead Sea
Sebaste (Samaria).........C4-117, 124, 133, 149, 156; C5-136
Sebastia F2-140, 144
Sedada, see Zedad
Segor, see Zoar
Sehon, see Sihon
Seir or Mt. Seir (Edom) D7-16, 32; C2-40
Sela (Petra)...B4-53, 72; D4-77
Selcha, see Salcah
Seleucia (Opis)....D2-101; F3-113
Seleucia (in Gaulanitis) D3-124, 149, 156
Seleucia (in Syria).F2-140, 144; F3-160, 164
Seleucia Pieria C1-136
Seleucia Tracheotis B1-136
Seleucid Empire.............
Selinus E2-140, 144; E3-160
Semechonitis, Lake (Lake Hula) D2-16, 32; C2-117, 149, 156
Semeron, see Shimron
Semnones C1-113, 160
Semron, see Shimron
Sennabris C3-156
Sepphoris .C3-117, 124, 149, 156; A2, C3-133
Sequani B2-113
Serbal, Jebel B3-40
Serpent's Pool A5-173
Sevan, Lake..........F1-25; G1-77
Seville A3-164
Sharon, Plain of...B4-16, 32, 44, 48, 61, 68, 84, 96, 109, 117, 124, 149, 156
Sharuhen A6-32, 44; B3-177
Sheba (descendent of Ham) F3-20
Sheba (desendent of Shem) F4-20
Shechem C4-16, 32, 44, 48, 61, 68, 84, 96, 109, 117, 124, 133, 149; C3-25; C1-40; B3-53, 72; C2-177
Sheep Gate D3-173
Shephelah B5-16
Shihor-libnath River...B3-16, 44
Shiloh C4-44, 48, 61, 68, 84; C1-40; C2-177
Shimron C3-32, 44, 48;C1-40
Shinar F2-20
Shoco, Shocho, Shochoh, Socoh (in Judah)...B5-61
Shunem C3-44, 48, 61, 68, 84
Shunat Nimrin (Beth-nimrah) C3-177

Shur, Wilderness of B2-40
Shuruppak F4-25
Shushan (Susa)......G3-77; D2-89
Siceleg, see Ziklag
Sichem, see Shechem
Sicily C3-113, 160, 164; A2-140, 144
Siddim, Vale of..................D6-32
Sidon (Saida)........C1-16, 32, 40, 44, 61, 68, 84, 96, 109, 113, 117, 124, 149, 177; C3-25; B3-53, 72; D3-77; C4-136; F3-140, 144
Sidonians (Phoenicians) C2-32, 44
Sihon, Kingdom of............D5-32
Sihor-Labanath, see Shihor-libnath
Silo, see Shiloh
Siloam, Pool of, (Pool of Siloam)....C5-173
Siloe, Pool of, see Siloah
Simeon, Allotment of.........B6-44
Sin (Pelusium)..................B2-40
Sin, Wilderness of B3-40
Sinai, Mt. (Mt. Horeb) C4-25; B3-40; C3-89, 101
Sinai Peninsula C4-25; B3-40; D4-77; B5-177
Singidunum D2-164
Sinope D1-77; C1-89, 101; E2-113, 160, 164; F1-140, 144
Sinus Arabicus (Red Sea) E4-113, 160
Sippar E3-25; F3-77; D2-89
Siraces F2-113, 160
Sirmium C2-164
Siscia C2-164
Siut C5-77
Smyrna D2-140, 144; D3-164
Soan, see Zoan
Soba, see Zobah
Socchoth, see Succoth
Sochoh (in Sharon)......C4-32, 61
Socoh (in Judah)..............C5-48
Sodom D6-32
Sogdiana F2-89, 101
Soli (Pompeiopolis).........B1-136
Sophene E3-113
Sorec, see Sorek
Sorek, Valley of B5-16, 44
Spain A2-160, 164
Sparta A2-77; B2-89, 101; D3-113, 160, 164; C2-140, 144
Strato's Tower (Caesarea) B4-109, 117
Subartu F3-25
Succoth (in Egypt)............B2-40
Succoth (in Gad)...D4-32, 44, 48
Suez, Gulf of B3-40
Sumer F4-25; G4-77
Sunem, see Shunem
Sur (Tyre).......................C1-177
Sur, Desert of, see Shur, Wilderness of
Susa (Shushan)......G3-25, 77; D2-89, 101
Susan, see Susa
Susiana (Elam) D2-89, 101
Sychar C4-124, 133
Syene (Elephantine Island) C3-89, 101
Syracuse C3-113, 160, 164; B2-140, 144
Syria E2-20, 48; C2-72, 101, 117, 124, 149, 156; E3-77, 113, 160; D2-109; D3-136; F3-140, 144
Syrian Desert D3-177
Syrians (Aramaeans)........C3-53; D2-61
Syrtis Major C3-113, 160
Syrtis Minor C3-113, 160
Taanach ...C3-32, 44, 48, 61, 68, 84; B3-53, 72; C2-177
Taanath-shiloh C4-44
Tabaqat Fahl (Pella)......C2-177
Taberah C3-40
Tabigha ..D3-124; B1, B4-133; C2-177
Tabor, Mt. C3-16, 32, 44, 48, 61, 68, 84, 96, 109, 124, 156; C2-177
Tadmor (Palmyra)........D3-25; D2-53, 72; E3-77; C2-89
Tagus River A3-113, 160, 164
Tahpanhes C2-89

Tamar B4-53
Tanais River (Don)........D1-101; F2-113, 160
Tanis (Rameses, Zoan) B4-25; A2-40; C4-77
Taphnes, Taphnis, see Tahpanhes
Tappuah C4-32, 44
Tarentum C2-113, 160; B1-140, 144
Taricheae ...C3-117, 149, 156
Tarraco (Tarragona) B2-113, 160
Tarraconensis A2-160
Tarragona B2-164
Tarshish A2, E2-20
Tarsus D2-77; C2-89, 101; E3-113, 160, 164; B1-136; E2-140, 144
Tatta, Lake E2-140, 144
Taurus Mts. C2-25, 77, 101
Tavium E2-140, 144
Taxila G2-89, 101
Tekoa ...C5-44, 48, 61, 84, 96, 109; B4-72
Tel Aviv-Jaffa B2-177
Tell Asur C5-16
Tell el Amarna (Akhetaton) C5-77
Tepe Gawra E2-25
Tepe Giyan G3-25
Tepe Siyalk G3-25
Thaanach, see Taanach
Thaanath-Silo, see Taanath-shiloh
Thabera, see Taberah
Thabor, see Tabor
Thalassa, see Lasea
Thamna C4-117, 149, 156
Thamnata, see Timnah
Thamnath-Sare, see Timnath-serah
Thaphsa, see Tiphsah
Thapphua, see Tappuah
Thapsacus (Tiphsah) D2-53; C2-89, 101
Thapsus C3-113
Tharsis, see Tarshish
Thasos B1-77
Thebes (No)...D5-77; C3-89, 101; E4-113, 160, 164
Thebez C4-44, 48
Thecua, Thecue, see Tekoa
Thermopylae B2-89
Thersa, see Tirzah
Thessalonica (Salonika).B1-101; D2-113, 160, 164; C1-140, 144
Thiras, see Tiras
Thogorma, see Togarmah
Thrace D1-20, 140, 144; B1-89, 101; D2-113, 160
Thracians B1-77
Three Taverns A1-140, 144
Thubal, see Tubal
Thuringians C1-164
Thyatira D2-140, 144; D3-164
Tiberias D3-124, 149, 156; B2, D3-133; C5-136; C2-177
Tiberias, Lake (Sea of Galilee) C2-177
Tieum D1-77
Tigranocerta F3-113, 160
Tigris River F2-20; E2-25; F3-77, 113, 160, 164; D2-89, 101
Til Barsip E2-77
Timnah B5-44, 48, 61, 68, 84, 109
Timnath-serah C5-44
Timsah, Lake................B2-40
Tingis A3-113, 160, 164
Tingitana A3-160
Tiphsah (Thapsacus)......D2-53
Tiras D1-20
Tirzah C4-32, 44, 61, 68
Tishbe D4-61
Tob D3-48; B3-53
Togarmah E2-20
Toledo A3-164
Toletum A3-113
Tolosa (Toulouse)....B2-113, 160
Tomi D2-113, 164
Toulouse B2-164
Tours A2-164
Trachonitis .E2-117, 124, 149, 156
Trapezus E1-77; C1-89, 101; E2-113, 160

Treveri B2-113
Trier (Treves).................B2-164
Tripolis C3-136
Troas (Troy)..........D2-140, 144; D3-164
Troy A2-25
Tubal E1-20; E2-77
Turdetani A3-113
Turushpa (Tushpa)..........F2-77
Tuz, Lake C2-25; D2-77
Tyana E2-140, 144; E3-160
Tyras D2-113; E2-160
Tyras River D2-113, 160
Tyre (Sur) ...C2-16, 32, 44, 48, 61, 68, 84, 89, 96, 101, 109, 124, 149, 156; C1-40, 177; B3-53, 72; D3-77; E3-113, 160; C4-136; F3-140, 144
Tyre, Ladder of........C2-109, 124
Tyropoeon Valley C5-173
Tyrrhenian Sea........C3-113, 160; A2-140, 144
Ubi E1-32; D1-40
Ugarit C3-25
Ulai River (Euloeus) G4-25; D2-89
Ulatha D2-117, 124
Umma F4-25
United Arab Republic.......A4, D1-177
Ur F4-25; G4-77
Urartu, Kingdom of F2-77
Urmia, Lake..........F2-25; G2-77; D2-89
Utians E3-89
Utica B3-113
Utrecht B1-164
Uxellodunum B2-113
Uzal F4-20
Vaccaei A2-113
Vagarshapat F2-164
Valencia A3-164
Valentia (Valencia)..A3-113, 160
Valley Gate B2, B6-173
Van, Lake ..E2-25; F2-77; D2-89
Vandals C1-160
Venedae D1-160
Veneti A2-113
Verona C2-164
Verulamium B1-113
Vesontio B2-113
Vienne B2-164
Vistula River D1-113, 160
Volga River ..F2-113, 160, 164
Wadi Musa C4-177
Wall of Hadrian A1-160
Water Gate D5-173
Xanthus D2-140, 144
Xois B4-25
Xystus (Market)............C4-173
Yarmuk River D3-16, 32, 44, 48, 61, 68, 96, 109, 117, 124, 149, 156; C2-177
York A1-164
Yusha', Jebel D4-16
Zabulon, see Zebulun
Zagros Mts. F3-25; G3-77
Zanoah B5-96
Zaphon D4-44
Zareah B5-96
Zared River, see Zered River
Zarephath (Sarafand)......C2-32, 44 ,48, 68, 84, 124; C1-177
Zareth-shahar D5-44
Zarqa River (Jabbok) E4-16; C2-177
Zebulun, Allotment of........C3-44
Zedad C2-53, 72
Zela E2-113; F1-140, 144
Zelea B1-101
Zemaraim C5-61
Zered River (Wadi el Hasa) D7-16, 32, 44, 48, 61, 68, 84, 96, 109, 117, 124, 149, 156; C2-40; C4-177
Ziklag B6-44, 48, 61, 68, 96, 149, 156; B4-53; B3-177
Zin, Wilderness of B7-16, 32, 44; C2-40
Zion, see Jerusalem
Ziph C6-44, 48, 61, 124
Zoan (Rameses, Tanis)....A2-40
Zoar C6-32, 84; C2-40
Zobah D1-48; C3-53
Zorah B5-44; C5-61

Aaron 39, 63
Abana River 24
Abel-beth-maachah 56
Abishag (Abisag) 56
Abner 54
Abraham (Abram).........19ff., 29
Absalom 55
Accaron, see Ekron
Achab, see Ahab
Achish (Achis)..............50
Actium 119
Adam 19
Adasa 106
Adonijah (Adonias).............56
Adoram 62
Adullam, Cave of 15, 50
Aegean Islands 21
Aegean Sea 21
Aggeus, see Haggai
Ahab ....65 ff.
Ahasuerus (Xerxes) 95
Ahaz 79
Ahmose 30
Ai 26, 42
Ajalon (Aialon), Vale of...15, 43
Albinus 154
Alcimus 106
Alexander Jannaeus 110
Alexander the Great 99
Alexandria 100, 102, 150
Amalekites (Amalec).............49
Amaziah 70
Ammon 39
Ammonites 46, 55
Amos 73
Amri, see Omri
Ananus 154
Ansan (Anshan)................91
Antigonus
  (son of Aristobulus II).116, 118
Antigonus Cyclops 100
Antioch (in Pisidia)..........141
Antioch (in Syria).......135, 137
          140, 141, 144
Antiochus III...........103-105
Antiochus IV Epiphanes.........103
Antiochus V Eupator............105
Antiochus VII 107
Antipas (son of Herod)......121,
          127, 130
Antipater (father of Herod)
          110, 114-116
Antipater (son of Herod)..120 ff.
Antonia, Fortress of.......120, 174
Antony, Marc......116, 118, 119
Aod, see Ehud
Apollonius 104
Apollos 139, 143
Aqaba, Gulf of 18, 30, 38
Aquila 139, 143
Arabah 18, 39
Arabian Peninsula 22, 30, 55
Arabs, Southern 22
Aram, Plain of 24
Aramaeans, see also Syrians
          22, 28, 64
Ararat, Mt. 19
Archelaus (son of Herod)
          121, 123, 127
Aristobulus II (son of Salome
  Alexandra)............110, 114
Aristobulus III (brother of
  Mariamne)................118
Arles, Council of 169
Arnon River 39
Arphaxad (Arphachsad),
          see also Chaldea..22
Artaxerxes Longimanus...95, 97
Asa 63, 65
Asher (Aser), Tribe of.........43
Ashkenaz (Aschchenaz).........21
Ashur, town 75
Ashurbanipal 86
Ashurdaninapal 78
Ashurnasirpal II 75, 76
Asia Minor 21
Asiongaber, see Ezion-geber
Asshur (Assur), see also
          Assyria..22, 75
Assuerus, see Ahasuerus
Assyria 75
Astarte 34, 65
Athaliah (Athalia).............70

Athens 143
Attalia 141
Baal 65
Baalhasor, see Tell Asur
Baal-zephon (Baal-Saphon)...38
Baasha (Baasa)................63
Babylon 75, 78, 90, 92, 93
Babylonia 29
Babylonians 86
Balaam 39
Balak (Balac), Moabite King..39
Balikh River 24
Barak (Barac) 46
Bar Cochba (Bar Kokba)......162
Barnabas ..137, 139, 140, 141, 142
Bashan (Basan).....18, 28, 39, 43
Bath-sheba 56
Beatitudes, Mount of..........131
Beer-sheba 14, 18, 26
Belshazzar 93
Ben-hadad I (Benadad)....64, 65
Ben-hadad II (Benadad).........64
Beni-Hassan 35
Benjamin 28, 45
Benjamin, tribe 45, 46
Berenice (mother of Herod
  Agrippa I)..........120, 148
Bernice (sister of Herod
  Agrippa II).....52, 153, 158
Bethabara 128, 129, 130
Bethany 134
Bethany beyond Jordan..128, 129
Bethel 26, 27, 42
Bethesda, Pool of 131
Bethlehem 18, 122, 129
Bethsabee, see Bath-sheba
Bethsaida, see Bethesda
Beth-shan (Bethsan)...26, 34, 51
Beth-shemesh
          (Beth-Sames)...34, 71
Beth-zur (Beth-Sur)...........43
Black Sea 21
Botta, Paul Emile..............81
Byblos 35
Caesar, Julius........114, 115
Caesarea ..120, 128, 135, 143, 152
Caesarea Philippi 132
Calah 76
Caleb of Judah................41
Cambyses 91
Cana 130
Canaan 21, 22, 24, 27, 28
          conquest 42 ff.
Canaanite Federation..........46
Canaanites 26
Capernaum (Capharnaum)
          130, 131, 132
Carchemish 67, 86
Carmel, Mt. 14, 17, 66
Carthage 71, 114
Caspian Sea 21
Cassius 116
Chanaan, see Canaan
Charcamis, see Carchemish
Chetthim, see Kittim
Chus, see Cush
Cimmerians 21
Cison River, see Kishon River
Claudius 150, 153
Claudius Lysias 146
Cleopatra 115, 119
Colonia Aelia Capitolina..162, 175
Constantine ....167 ff., 175
Copper 59
Corinth 135, 143, 145
Cornelius 135
Crete 47
Crimean Peninsula 21
Croesus 91
Cush 21
Cyprus 137, 141
Cyrus ....91 ff.
Dabir, see Debir
Dalmanutha 132
Damascus ...24, 28, 30, 39, 69, 71,
          79, 99, 138, 139
Dan 14, 45
Daniel 90
Darius I 95
Darius III 99
David ....15, 49 ff.
Dead Sea 18
Dead Sea Scrolls 111

Debir 43
Deborah (Debora) 46
Decapolis 132
Demetrius I Soter 106
Demetrius II 107
Demetrius III 110
Derbe 141, 142
Diadochi 100
Diala (Diyala) 93
Diocletian 167
Dispersion of the Jews 95
Dodanim 21
Domitian 158, 159, 165
Domitilla 165
Dothan 28
Drusilla 152
Drusus 148
Ebal, Mt. 17
Eber 22
Ecbatana (Achmetha)...91, 95
Edom 30, 39, 55
Edomites 28, 39
Eglon, King 46
Egypt 14, 21, 26, 28, 29,
          30, 37, 180
Ehud 46
Ekron 85
Elah, King 63
Elah, Vale of 15
Elam 22
Elamites 22
Elasa 106
Elath 59
Elias, see Elijah
Eliezer 24
Elijah (Elias) ....66 ff.
Elim 38
Elisha (Eliseus) 69
Elishah (Elisa) 21
Eltekah 85
Elymus 141
Emath, see Hamath
Emmaus 105
En-dor 51
Ephesus 138, 139, 143, 144
Ephraim (Ephrem), tribe..41, 45
Ephraim (Ephrem), town.......134
Erastus 145
Esau 28
Esarhaddon 86
Esdraelon, Plain of 17
Esdras, see Ezra
Essenes 111
Esther 95
Etam 57
Etham 38
Ethiopia 21
et-Tell (Ai)..................42
Euphrates River 14, 19, 22,
          23, 24, 75
Eupolemos 106
Exodus, Time of the............36
Ezekiel (Ezechiel).........90, 91
Ezion-geber 30, 38, 59
Ezra 97-98
Fadus, Caspius 153
Fair Havens 147
Felix 146
Festus, Porcius 146, 153, 154
Florus, Gessius 154
Gabaa, see Gibeah
Gabaon, see Gibeon
Gabaonites, see Gibeonites
Gad, tribe 41, 42
Gaius (Caligula)..............150
Galaad, see Gilead
Galgal, see Gilgal
Galilee 15, 17, 26
Galilee, Sea of.......17, 18, 24, 27
Gallio 143
Gallus, Cestius 155
Garizim, see Gerizim
Gath 50, 55
Gath-hepher 73
Gaza 34, 99
Gazer, see Gezer
Gedeon, see Gideon
Gelboe, see Gilboa
Gerar (Gerara)................34
Gergesa 131
Gerizim, Mt. 17, 108
Gesen, see Goshen

Geth, see Gath
Geth-Opher, see Gath-hepher
Gethsemane (Gethsemani)....134
Gezer 41
Ghazzeh, Wadi...............49
Gibeah 46, 49
Gibeon 43
Gibeonites 42
Gideon 46
Gilboa, Mt. 51
Gilead 17, 18, 28, 39, 43
Gilgal 42, 43, 49
Goliath 15, 50
Gomer, see also Cimmerians...21
Gomorrah 27
Goshen 29, 37
Gracchus, Gaius..............114
Gracchus, Tiberius..............114
Granicus 99
Habiru, see also Hebrew....22
Hadramaut 22
Haggai 95
Hai, see Ai
Ham 19, 21
Hamath 56
Hanging Gardens, Babylon...92
Haran 23, 26
Harod River 34
Harum, Jebel (Mt. Hor)........39
Hazor 43
Hebrew 22
Hebron ..27, 28, 30, 38, 43, 52, 54
Helcias, see Hilkiah
Heliopolis 27
Hermon, Mt. 14, 18, 24, 132
Herod Agrippa I.......148-152
Herod Agrippa II 146, 152-157
Herod Antipas (Herod the
          Tetrarch)..130, 148, 150
Herod of Chalcis......151, 153
Herod the Great ....115 ff.
Herodias 148, 150
Herodotus 92
Heshbon (Hesebon)........30, 41
Heth, see also Hittites.......22
Hezekiah 82
Hilkiah 85
Hiram of Tyre 15, 54, 56
Hittites 22, 67
Hor, Mt. 39
Horns of Hattin 131
Hosea 73
Hoshea 80
Hula, Lake 18, 43
Hyksos 29, 30, 35
Hyrcanus II 110, 116, 118, 119
Ignatius 138, 161
Ionian 104
Iran 182
Iraq ....181 ff.
Irenaeus 165
Iron 49, 55
Isaac 24, 27
Isaiah 73
Ish-bosheth (Isboseth).........54
Israel 30
Israel, Children of 28
Israel (Kingdom)
  greatest extent 71
  end of 81
Israel (modern)...............179
Issachar 45
Issus 99
Jabbok River 28
Jabesh-gilead (Jabes Galaad)..51
Jabin, King 43
Jacob 28-30
James 151
Japheth 19
Jason 106
Javan, see also Ionian 21
Jebus 26, 54
Jebusites 22
Jectan, see Joktan
Jehoash 70
Jehoiachin 87
Jehoiakim 87
Jehoram 70
Jehoshaphat 67
Jehu, prophet 63
Jephthah (Jephte).............46
Jeremiah 86, 90
Jericho 27, 33-35, 41-42

Jeroboam II 60-63
Jeroboam II 71
Jerusalem: Capture by David, 54,
  171; Solomonic building, 57,
  172; siege of Nebuchadnezzar,
  87; falls to Pompey, 111, 118;
  building of Herod, 120, 174;
  visits of Jesus, 127, 129, 134;
  projects of Herod Agrippa I,
  154; general description, 170-
  175.
Jeshua 94
Jesus Christ 122-134
Jezebel (Jezabel)..............65, 67
Jezreel, Plain of 15, 17, 26, 51
Joab 56
Jaokim, see Jehoiakim
Joash (Joas)..............................69-70
John Hyrcanus 107
John 138
John the Baptist 128, 129
Joktan 22
Jonah (Jonas)..............................73
Jonathan 49
Jonathan Maccabaeus 106
Joppa (Joppe)...................14, 135
Joram, see Jehoram
Jordan ....179 ff.
Jordan , River....18, 24, 26, 28, 42
Jordan, Valley of the.........18, 27
Josaphat, see Jehoshaphat
Joseph (husband of Mary)
  122, 123, 129
Joseph (son of Jacob)........28-30
Joseph (uncle to Herod)........119
Josephus 29
Joshua ....41 ff.
Josue, see Joshua
Josiah (Josias).................85, 86
Judaea 17, 18, 26, 28
Judah, tribe..................................45
Judah, Kingdom of 62
  end of 87
Judas Aristobulus 108
Judas Maccabaeus 105
Kadesh-barnea 38
Kamose ....
Karkar 67, 78
Khorsabad 81
King's Highway....26, 30, 39, 59
Kirjath-jearim 45
Kishon River 17
Kittim, see also Cyprus 21
Laban 28
Lachish (Lachis)..............43, 83
Laish (Leshem)..........................45
Layard, A.H. 76
Lazarus 134
Lebanon 181
Lesem, see Laish
Levites, tribe 45
Libya 21
Litani River 15
Lot 26, 27, 42
Lud, see also Lydians 22
Luke 138-139, 143, 145
Lydda 135
Lydia 92
Lydians 22
Lysias 105
Lysimachus 100
Maccabees (Machabees).105-111
Macedonia 99
Machabees, see Maccabees
Machpelah (Machphela)...30, 53
Madai, see also Medes 21
Madian, see Midian
Magdala 132
Magnesia 103
Magog 21
Mahanaim 30, 54
Malichus 116
Manasseh, King (Manasse)....85
Manasseh, tribe......41, 42, 43, 45
Manetho 29
Marah 38
Mari 22, 24
Mariamne ....116 ff.
Marius 114
Mark, John 137, 139, 141
Mary 122, 124, 129
Mary (mother of Mark).........137
Masada 116, 118
Maspha, see Mizpeh
Mattathias (Mathathias).....105
Medes 21, 86

Median Wall 92
Mediterranean Sea 14
Megiddo 34, 58, 86
Melita 147
Mello, see Millo
Memphis 27, 29, 30, 86
Menahem 74, 79
Merodach-baladan 83
Merom, Waters of 43
Mesha 67
Meshech 21
Mesopotamia 19
Mesraim, see Mizraim
Micah (Micheas).......................73
Micaiah 67
Midian 37, 39
Midianites 39, 46
Millo of Solomon 58
Mishna 163
Mithraism 166
Mithridates (also Mithradates)
  114
Mizpeh (Mizpah)......................47
Mizraim 21, 22
Moab 17, 18, 39, 55
Moab, Plains of 41
Moabites 39, 46, 64, 67
Moabite Stone 67
Modin 105
Moreh, Hill of 131
Moses ....29, 37 ff.
Mosoch, see Meshech
Naaman 69
Nabonidus 92
Nabuchodonosor,
  see Nebuchadnezzar
Nabopolassar 86
Nadab 63
Nahor 24
Nain 131
Naphtali, tribe 43
Nathan 56
Nazareth 125, 129, 131
Nebo, Mt. 39
Nebuchadnezzar 86
Necho (Nechao)........................86
Negeb 45
Nehemiah (Nehemias).....97-98
Nephthali, see Naphtali
Nero 153, 157
Nerva 159
Nicaea, Council of 169
Nile River 21, 26, 29
Nimrod 22, 76
Noah (Noe).........................19, 21
  descendants of,..................19 ff.
Odollam, see Adullam
Olives, Mount of......................134
Omri 64
On, see also Heliopolis 27
Ophir 22, 59
Osee, see Hosea
Padan-Aram 24, 28
Palestine .....14 ff., 26, 27, 33, 35
Palmyra 24
Pamphylia 141
Panias 103
Paphos 141
Papias 138
Parthians 116
Patmos 138
Paul (Saul).....................137, 147
Pekah 79
Peleg 22
Penuel 62
Peraea 134
Perga 137, 141
Persian Gulf 21, 23
Peter 135-137, 139, 151
Petra 138
Phacee, see Pekah
Phaddan-Aram, see Padan-Aram
Phaleg, see Peleg
Pharisees 128, 142
Pharos, island 102
Pharsalus 115
Phasael 115, 116
Philip of Macedon 99
Philip, regent 105
Philip the Evangelist 135
Philip (son of Herod)....121, 132
Philippi 116
Philistia 15
Philistia, Plain of 15
Philistines ....15, 47 ff.
Phoenicia 14, 132

Phoenicians 59
Phul, see Tiglath-pileser III
Phut 21
Pisgah, Mt. 41
Pithom 37
Pliny the Younger 159
Polycarp 138
Pompey 110, 111, 114
Pontius Pilate 128
Pottery 33
Princes' Wall, Egypt 26, 37
Priscilla 139, 143
Procurators 128
Pteria 91
Ptolemaïs 107
Ptolemy I 102
Ptolemy II (Philadelphus)....102
Ptolemy IV (Philopator) 103
Pul, see Tiglath-pileser III
Punon 39
Puteoli 147
Rachel 28, 33
Ramah (Rama)..........................63
Rameses II 37
Rameses III 47
Rameses, city 37, 38
Ramoth-gilead 67
Raphia 103
Rebekah (Rebecca).........24, 27
Red Sea 21
Rehoboam 60-62
Rephraim, valley 55
Reuben, tribe 41, 42, 46
Rezin, King 79
Rhodes 145
Rimmon 65
Riphath 21
Robinson 176
Rodanim, see Dodanim
Rome 79, 112, 147
Romulus and Remus 79
Ruben, see Reuben
Saba, see Sheba
Salamis 99, 141
Salatis 29
Salem 30
Salmanasar, see Shalmaneser
Salome Alexandra 110
Salome (sister of Herod).......119
Samaria, city 17, 64, 69, 81
Samaria, region 17, 28, 108
Samaritans 81
Samson 15, 46
Samuel ....47 ff.
Sarah (Sarai)......................26, 27
Sardis 92
Sargon II 81
Sassabasar, see Sheshbazzar
Saul ....47 ff.
Scaurus 110
Scythians 21
Sebaste (Samaria) 120
Sehon, see Sihon
Sekenenre 30
Sela 70
Seleucia 141
Seleucid Era 102
Seleucus I Nicator 100
Sem, see Shem
Sennacherib 82, 90
Septuagint 38, 102
Sergius Paulus 141
Shabaka 82
Shallum 74
Shalmaneser III 67, 78
Shalmaneser V 80, 81
Shamshi-Adad V 78
Sharon, Plain of 14, 17
Sheba (Yemen).................22, 59
Sheba the Benjamite 56
Shechem 17, 26, 28, 62
Shem 19, 21, 22
Shephelah 15, 17, 43
Sheshbazzar 94
Sheshonk (Shishak)................60
Shiloh (Silo)......................45, 63
Shur, Wilderness of................26
Siceleg, see Ziklag
Sichar, see Sychar
Sidon (Zidon).............................22
Sihon the Amorite 39
Silas (Silvanus)............139, 142
Simeon, tribe 45
Simon bar Giora 158
Simon Maccabaeus 107
Simon the Great 135

Sinai, Mt. 38
Sinai Peninsula 15, 30
Sisera 46
So (Sewe)...................................80
Socchoth, see Succoth
Sodom 27
Solomon ....15, 56 ff.
Sorek (Sorec), Vale of 15, 45
Sosius, Caius 118
Stables, Solomon's 58
Stephen 135
Succoth 37, 38
Suez, Gulf of 30
Sulla 114
Sychar 130
Syria 14, 180
Syrian Desert 24
Syrians ....55, 64 ff.
Taanach 34
Tabor, Mt. 132
Tadmor (Palmyra)...................24
Talmud 163
Tanis 37
Tarshish 21, 59
Tarsus 137, 138, 139
Tekoa (Techua)........................73
Tell Asur 17
Tell Beit Mirsim (Debir)........43
Tell ed-Duweir...........................43
Tell el-Ful 49
Temple, Jerusalem: building
  fund, 55; building by Solomon,
  57; ceremonial objects, 59; de-
  stroyed by Babylonians, 87;
  rebuilding by Zerubbabel, 94;
  Herod's Temple, 120; visited
  by Jesus, 127; reconstruction
  completed, 154; destruction by
  Titus, 157
Terah 23
Thaanach, see Taanach
Thabor, see Tabor
Thamnath-Sare,
  see Timnath-serah
Tharsis, see Tarshish
Thebes 86
Theglathphalasar,
  see Tiglath-pileser
Thermopylae 99
Thessalonica 143
Thiras, see Tiras
Thogorma, see Togarmah
Thubal, see Tubal
Thutmosis III 30
Tiberias 130
Tiglath-pileser I 75
Tiglath-pileser III (Pul) 74, 78 ff.
Tigris River 14, 19, 22, 75
Timaus 29
Timnath-serah 45
Timothy 139, 141, 142, 145
Timsah, Lake..............................37
Tiras (Thracians)......................21
Titus, apostle.........139, 144, 145
Titus, emperor........157, 158, 159
Togarmah 21
Tower of Babel 22
Trajan 161, 165
Triumvirate 114
Troas 142
Trypho 107
Tubal 21
Tumilat, Wadi 37
Turkey 19, 182
Tyre 54, 99
Ugarit 35
Ur 19, 23, 24, 29
Ussher of Armagh,
  Archbishop.........36
Uzziah 71
Vespasian 155, 158
Woolley, Sir Leonard 23
Xenophon 92
Xerxes 95, 99
Zab River 75
Zacharias 74
Zealots 128, 153, 154, 158
Zered, Brook 39
Zebulon (Zabulon), tribe 45
Zedekiah 87
Zelea 99
Zerubbabel (Zorobabel).........94
Ziggurat of Babylon 92
Ziggurat of Ur 23
Ziklag 50
Zimri 64